Democracy, Equality, and Justice

In addressing democracy, equality, and justice together, the book stimulates discussions that go beyond the sometimes increasingly technical and increasingly discrete literatures that now dominate the study of each concept. The chapters fall into four categories: on justice and democracy; justice and equality; justice and community; and justice and the future. Concerns of justice unite all the chapters in this volume. However, these concerns now manifest themselves in interesting and new directions. Politically, the book confronts urgent problems of democracy, equality, community, and of how to respond to potentially catastrophic climate change. The response to these problems cannot only be pragmatic and piecemeal. What emerges are a number of interlinking questions and themes that together constitute the central core of contemporary political philosophy.

This book was previously published as a special issue of the *Critical Review of International Social and Political Philosophy.*

Matt Matravers is Professor of Political Philosophy at the University of York. He is the author of *Justice and Punishment* (Oxford University Press, 2000) and *Responsibility and Justice* (Polity Press, 2007) as well as of numerous articles and chapters on political and legal philosophy.

Lukas H. Meyer is Professor of Practical Philosophy at the University of Graz, Austria. He is the author of *Historische Gerechtigkeit* (de Gruyter, 2005). He is also the editor of *Legitimacy, Justice and Public International Law* (Cambridge University Press, 2010) and *Justice in Time* (Nomos, 2004); and the co-editor of *Intergenerational Justice* (Oxford University Press, 2009) *Rights, Culture and the Law* (Oxford University Press, 2003) and *Neukantianismus und Rechtsphilosophie* (Nomos, 2002). He is the author of numerous articles on political and moral philosophy, especially intergenerational justice.

Democracy, Equality, and Justice

Edited by
Matt Matravers and Lukas H. Meyer

Routledge
Taylor & Francis Group
LONDON AND NEW YORK

First published 2011
by Routledge
4 Park Square, Milton Park, Abingdon, Oxon OX14 4RN
605 Third Avenue, New York, NY 10017

Routledge is an imprint of the Taylor & Francis Group, an informa business

This book is a reproduction of the *Critical Review of International Social and Political Philosophy*, vol.13, issue 1. The Publisher requests to those authors who may be citing this book to state, also, the bibliographical details of the special issue on which the book was based.

Typeset in Times New Roman by Taylor & Francis Books

British Library Cataloguing in Publication Data
A catalogue record for this book is available from the British Library

Disclaimer
The publisher would like to make readers aware that the chapters in this book are referred to as articles as they had been in the special issue. The publisher accepts responsibility for any inconsistencies that may have arisen in the course of preparing this volume for print.

ISBN13: 978-0-415-59292-5 (hbk)

Contents

Notes on Contributors vii

1. Introduction: democracy, equality, and justice
Matt Matravers and *Lukas H. Meyer* 1

Justice and democracy

2. Representing future generations: political presentism and democratic trusteeship
Dennis F. Thompson 17

3. Justice, legitimacy, and constitutional rights
Wilfried Hinsch 39

Justice and equality

4. Why equality? On justifying liberal egalitarianism
Paul Kelly 55

5. Luck, equality and responsibility
Keith Dowding 71

6. Coercive redistribution and public agreement: re-evaluating the libertarian challenge of charity
Clare Chambers and *Philip Parvin* 93

Justice and community

7. Human rights and moral cosmopolitanism
Charles Jones 115

8. On the interrelations between domestic and global (in)justice
Peter Koller 137

9. Cultural diversity and biodiversity: a tempting analogy
David Heyd 159

10. Linguistic justice and the territorial imperative
Philippe Van Parijs 181

Justice and the future

11. Climate change and the duties of the advantaged
Simon Caney 203

12. Climate justice and historical emissions
Lukas H. Meyer and *Dominic Roser* 229

13. Brian Barry: 1936–2009 255

Index 258

Notes on Contributors

Simon Caney is Professor of Political Theory and Fellow and Tutor in Politics at Magdalen College, University of Oxford. He is the author of *Justice Beyond Borders: A Global Political Theory* (Oxford University Press, 2005). He is currently working on two books – 'Global justice and climate change' (with Derek Bell – under contract to Oxford University Press) and 'On cosmopolitanism' (under contract to Oxford University Press). From 2008 to 2011 he will hold an ESRC Climate Change Leadership Fellowship.

Clare Chambers is University Senior Lecturer in Philosophy and Fellow of Jesus College, University of Cambridge. Her recent publications include *Sex, Culture, and Justice: The Limits of Choice* (Penn State University Press, 2008); "Each outcome is another opportunity: problems with the moment of equal opportunity" in *Politics, Philosophy and Economics* (PPE) Vol. 8 No. 4 (2009); 'Inclusivity and the constitution of the family' in the *Canadian Journal of Law and Jurisprudence* (2009); and 'Gender' in Catriona McKinnon (ed.) *Issues in Political Theory* (Oxford University Press, 2008). She is currently writing a book on marriage and the state.

Keith Dowding is Professor of Political Science in the School of Politics and International Relations, Research School of Social Sciences, and Director of Research, College of Arts and Social Sciences at the Australian National University, Canberra, Australia. He is the author of *Rational Choice and Political Power* (Elgar, 1991) and many articles in political philosophy, comparative and urban politics, anima politici lacunae and rational choice theory.

David Heyd is Chaim Perelman Professor of Philosophy at the Hebrew University of Jerusalem. He is the author of *Supererogation* (Cambridge University Press, 1982) and *Genethics* (University of California Press, 1992), editor of *Toleration* (Princeton University Press, 1996) and the author of many articles on ethics, political philosophy and bioethics.

Wilfried Hinsch is Professor of Practical Philosophy at the RWTH Aachen University. He is the author of *Gerechtfertigte Ungleichheiten. Grundsätze sozialer Gerechtigkeit* (Walter de Gruyter Verlag, 2002) and *Menschenrechte militärisch schützen. Ein Plädoyer für humanitäre Interventionen* (C. H. Beck Verlag, 2006).

Charles Jones is Associate Professor and Chair of the Department of Political Science at the University of Western Ontario, Canada. He is the author of *Global justice* (Oxford, 1999) and *The Rights of Nations* (Palgrave, 2000, with Desmond Clarke). He is currently writing a book entitled 'A world of equals: on distributive justice, equality, and human rights'.

Paul Kelly is Professor of Political Theory at the London School of Economics. He is editor of the journal *Utilitas* and was previously joint editor of *Political Studies*. His research interests include British political theory from the seventeenth century and contemporary political philosophy. His most recent books include *Multiculturalism reconsidered* (Polity Press, 2002); *Liberalism* (Polity Press 2004) and *Locke's Second Treatise of Government* (Continuum, 2007).

Peter Koller is Professor of Law at the Karl-Franzens-University of Graz. His recent publications include: 'The concept of law and its conceptions', *Ratio Juris*, 19 (2006); *Die globale Frage* (Passagen, 2006); 'Ökonomische Verteilungsgerechtigkeit', in: C. Langbehn (ed.), *Recht, Gerechtigkeit und Freiheit* (mentis, 2006); 'Law, morality and virtue', in: R.L. Walker and P.J. Ivanhoe (eds), *Working Virtues* (Clarendon Press, 2007); and editor of *Politisches Denken. Jahrbuch 2006/2007: Politik und Ökonomie* (Duncker & Humblot, 2007).

Matt Matravers is Professor of Political Philosophy at the University of York. He is the author of *Justice and Punishment* (Oxford University Press, 2000) and *Responsibility and Justice* (Polity Press, 2007) as well as of numerous articles and chapters on political and legal philosophy.

Lukas H. Meyer is Professor of Practical Philosophy at the University of Graz, Austria. He is the author of *Historische Gerechtigkeit* (de Gruyter, 2005). He is also the editor of *Legitimacy, Justice and Public International Law* (Cambridge University Press, 2010) and *Justice in Time* (Nomos, 2004); and the co-editor of *Intergenerational Justice* (Oxford University Press, 2009) *Rights, Culture and the Law* (Oxford University Press, 2003) and *Neukantianismus und Rechtsphilosophie* (Nomos, 2002). He is the author of numerous articles on political and moral philosophy, especially intergenerational justice.

Philip Parvin is a Lecturer in Politics at Loughborough University. He is author of numerous articles on issues at the intersection of political theory and practice, including 'Against localism: does devolving power to communities fail minorities?' *The Political Quarterly* 80(3) (2009); 'Identity and integration in an international context: problems and ambiguities in the new politics of multiculturalism", *Political Studies Review* 7/3 (2009); *Friend or foe? Lobbying in British democracy* (Hansard Society, 2007); and *Neglecting Democracy: Participation and Representation in 21st-Century Britain*, 2nd ed. (Hansard Society, 2006, with Declan McHugh). His first book, on the social and political thought of Karl Popper, was published by Continuum in 2010.

Dominic Roser studied economics, philosophy, and politics at the Universities of Berne, Geneva, and Oxford, and has been a doctoral student at the University of Zurich in a programme on interdisciplinary ethics. His research interests are in political philosophy; more particularly, in climate justice and ethical issues pertaining to economics and the economy. He publishes articles on intergenerational justice, global justice and risk in climate policy as well as the normative standing of climate economics.

Dennis F. Thompson is Alfred North Whitehead Professor of Political Philosophy at Harvard University. His books include: *Restoring Responsibility: Ethics in Government, Business, and Healthcare* (Cambridge, 2004); *Just Elections: Creating a Fair Electoral Process in the United States* (Chicago, 2002); *Why Deliberative Democracy?* (Princeton, 2004, with Amy Gutmann); and *Democracy and Disagreement* (Harvard, 1998, with Amy Gutmann).

Philippe Van Parijs holds the Chaire Hoover d'éthique économique et sociale at the Université catholique de Louvain and is a regular Visiting Professor of Philosophy at Harvard University. His recent publications include *L'Allocation universelle* (2005, with Yannick Vanderborght) and *Redesigning Distribution* (2006, with Bruce Ackerman and Anne Alstott).

Introduction: democracy, equality, and justice

Matt Matravers[a] and Lukas Meyer[b]

[a]*Department of Politics, University of York, York, United Kingdom;* [b]*University of Graz, Graz, Austria*

In this chapter, we consider the relationships between democracy, equality, and justice and the ways in which those relationships define the territory of contemporary political philosophy.

Many of the papers collected here emerged from a symposium generously hosted by the British Academy. The topic of the symposium, and of this volume, was 'Democracy, Equality, and Justice'. This theme, or themes, in turn was inspired by the lifelong work of the political philosopher Brian Barry to whom this volume is dedicated.

In addressing democracy, equality, and justice together, we hoped to stimulate discussions that went beyond the sometimes increasingly technical and increasingly discrete literatures that now dominate the study of each concept. The papers fall, rather roughly, into four categories: on justice and democracy; justice and equality; justice and community; and justice and the future. 'Rather roughly' because some – for example, Dennis Thompson's – could easily fit into two more of the subsections, and others focus rather more on one of the two in each pair of concepts. Nevertheless, what emerges are a number of interlinking questions and themes that together constitute the central core of contemporary political philosophy.

Justice and democracy

In his paper, Dennis Thompson considers the fate of future generations in democracies. His argument is that democratic decision-making results in the neglect of future citizens. From the political response to the consequences of global warming to the use of current taxation to fund retirement, policies that are unfair to future citizens emerge from current democratic practices. That they do so is the result of first, people – including politicians and those who vote for them – 'prefer the immediate to the distant'. Second, quite properly, representatives respond to their constituents and their constituents do not include citizens who are yet to exist. Third, politicians try to pass laws and policies that produce results during the period in which they are in office (or shortly thereafter). Finally, there is a tendency in most modern, established democracies, with ageing populations who are prepared to invoke 'ageism' as analogous to 'sexism' and 'racism', for politics to favour older age groups.

Thompson's four reasons seem both plausible and difficult to avoid. Moreover, the results are both morally and pragmatically undesirable; it is surely both wrong and imprudent for us to be continuing to create the conditions for catastrophic climate change. Thus, if democratic decision-making has these results, one might expect Thompson to argue that either democracy is a bad idea and we should find some other way to make policy, or that democracy's reach should not extend so far. One variation of this theme would be to say that democratic decisions should not be allowed to violate the fundamental requirements of justice; that destroying the planet constitutes such a violation with reference to future citizens; and so that future citizens should be protected by being included in the account of justice.

Interestingly, Thompson does *not* go down this route. Instead, he argues for an idea of 'democratic trusteeship' that 'allows citizens and their representatives today … to see clearly not only their own democratic needs but also those of future citizens' (p. 524). The kinds of institutions that might achieve this are the subject of much of his paper. Yet, as Thompson acknowledges, given existing arrangements such institutions are difficult to establish at all let alone with sufficient teeth to make the necessary difference. Why, then, not pursue the argument from justice where – for all that the leaders of the modern world seem as blind to the requirements of justice as they would be to Thompson's institutional inventiveness – the case seems both more clear and more familiar? After all, we are used to fighting injustice and there is a well-used rhetorical toolkit at the disposal of activists who wish to do so.

Thompson's argument is that future citizens – particularly those many generations hence – cannot be included within the principles of justice. In the case of contractualist accounts of justice, 'the principles that are chosen will determine who will exist' and 'it is not coherent to include as parties to the agreement individuals who will not exist if the agreement is concluded' (p. 513). This basic problem means that contractualist thinkers have to try to accommodate future citizens in some other way. The twists and turns involved in their doing so is evidence of the fundamental flaw in the approach when it comes to the future. Thompson illustrates his argument by tracking Rawls's arguments over the just savings principle from their original presentation in *A theory of justice* to the later formulations given in *Political liberalism* and *Justice as fairness: a restatement* (Rawls 2001, 2005).

Utilitarian accounts of justice fare little better according to Thompson. Whilst they avoid 'the identity problem' that hinders contractualism, they do so at a motivational cost: we are concerned (insofar as we are) about future citizens – individuals who will be worse off – not about future states of affairs. Moreover, and more damagingly, utilitarians may be committed to the 'repugnant conclusion' (Parfit 1984, p. 430) that we should promote a vast population of miserable people so long as the welfare of any given person is positive (albeit very low).

Thompson's concludes from this that 'the problem of representation of future generations cannot be adequately addressed … by appeals to theories of justice or utility applied in the present'. Thus, 'to respect the rights and goods of future generations, we need more than a temporal extension of principles of justice and utility. We need a revised conception of representation that enables democracies to represent future citizens who are not now present. We need a conception of democratic representation for citizens-to-be' (p. 516).

Thompson's view is not that we must choose between justice and democracy, rather we must recognize that neither is sufficient. However, combining these values is potentially complex, and this complexity is the subject of the next paper by Wilfried Hinsch. Hinsch recognizes that there is a tension between the ideal of popular sovereignty and the idea that there are certain constitutional liberties and rights that have a normative authority irrespective of popular sovereignty. On the one hand, there is the claim that the content of political justice, at least as far as basic liberties are concerned, is to be fixed solely by substantive political argument, while on the other there is the claim that it is the people who determine the specific scheme of basic liberties under which they live.

Hinsch argues that this apparent tension between the two claims can be resolved by introducing a distinction between *proto-rights* and *constitutional rights*. Proto-rights are less specific than constitutional rights, and one set of proto-rights can allow various schemes of constitutional rights. Thus, proto-rights are part of the principles of justice and can be established only by substantive argument while constitutional rights are established by the procedures of democratic legitimization, and are therefore a result of the exercise of popular sovereignty. This distinction allows us to specify the scope of each claim and therefore consistently affirm both simultaneously. Using the example of the protection of freedom of speech in the constitutions of the USA and Germany, Hinsch argues for 'political justice and democratic legitimacy' as 'two equally necessary and mutually dependent components of a well-ordered society that is effectively regulated by publicly justified principles and norms' (p. 541). How best to conceive of justice and, in particular, how the notion of justice reflects a commitment to equality is the focus of the contributions in the next section.

Justice and equality

Paul Kelly and Keith Dowding both focus on the idea of equality and its place in contemporary liberal egalitarian writing. The very term 'liberal egalitarian' is indicative of what has happened in contemporary political philosophy at least since the publication of *A theory of justice*. That is to say, liberal theory now starts from a commitment to the fundamental moral equality of persons and considers what follows from that commitment (for example, do we treat people as equals by equalising resources or welfare?). But, Kelly asks, what grounds the basic idea of equality?

One possibility is to argue that equality is an axiom, and that there is nothing more to be said about it. However, Kelly argues that there are good reasons to reject that possibility. For a start, egalitarians have to be able to respond to the claims of non-egalitarians; not just those who believe that there are morally significant inequalities between cultures, races, genders, and so on, but also Nietzscheans, and those who think that the claim that all persons have equal moral status is false. Moreover, even amongst egalitarians there is debate about the scope of justice that seems to overlap with the question of basic equality. If *all* persons are of equal moral value, then it might be thought that this speaks in favour of a cosmopolitan scope for the principles of justice. Yet, some liberal egalitarians are prepared to give significance to membership of a shared scheme of social co-operation and thus to restrict the scope of justice in various ways. Whilst not reducible to the question of basic equality, Kelly argues, it is hard to see how we can make much progress in this debate without saying something about 'the basis and character of fundamental equality' (p. 551).

Kelly proceeds by examining Jeremy Waldron's recent critique of liberal political philosophy's failure to provide a defence of basic equality (Waldron 2002). Waldron argues that Rawls's (and by extension other) accounts of justice fail because of the lack of an account of the meaning and significance of the capacities by virtue of which people are morally equal. Kelly takes issue with this interpretation of Rawls arguing that, for Rawls, 'the meaning and significance of the two basic features of moral personality' – these being 'the capacity to form and pursue a conception of the good and the capacity for a sense of justice' in terms of which Rawls frames his account of basic equality – 'is provided by the role they play in making sense of a just social order' (p. 556).

In explicating and defending Rawls's approach, what Kelly reveals is that we need not confront the unpalatable choice between saying nothing about basic equality or giving an account of it as 'a basic natural property in virtue of which people become moral equals'. Rather, the appeal to basic equality is part of the overall egalitarian project: the strategy is to see 'part of the task of theory construction as specifying the nature of basic equality whilst the appeal to basic equality places constraints on the character of that theory construction' (p. 556).

As Kelly makes clear, the implication of this defence of basic equality is that debates about what follows from the idea of equality matter not just in terms of, for example, getting the right set of egalitarian criteria for distribution, but also because they contribute to the articulation and defence of the very idea of basic equality. Egalitarian thinking, then, casts light on the idea of equality and the social relationships on which it depends. This is clearly demonstrated in the next paper, in which Keith Dowding takes issue with the recent 'luck egalitarian' move that locates inequalities as justified only to the extent that they result from choices made in conditions that allow responsibility attribution.

Dowding argues that the luck egalitarian position is problematic not least because 'we cannot distinguish luck and responsibility in either theory or practice to the degree theorists have assumed' (p. 562). The concept of luck, in fact, is difficult to unpack. Dowding argues that it is best understood in relation to the value of outcomes. These outcomes depend on what he calls the 'reward structure' (p. 566). What this means is that the entire focus of egalitarian thinking needs to change. Luck egalitarians start with the idea that we can distinguish brute luck and responsibility. That done, we then ask which outcomes belong to which, and then engage in (re)distribution to compensate for the operations of brute luck. Dowding's argument is that both what is down to luck and what to responsibility are determined by the reward structure. Thus, the focus of egalitarian thought ought to be the reward structure, which is to say that we should be asking directly about the extent of individual responsibility and inequality we are prepared to accept.

Dowding invites us to consider a pair of tennis players who meet in two big finals. Through the operation of luck, one wins both. Through a combination of luck and skill, this sequence continues. The result is that one player gains a 'big match temperament' and the other develops into someone who finds it hard to win big games (a 'choker'). What this shows is not only that distinguishing luck and responsibility is difficult, but that there are aspects of the interaction of luck and responsibility that are more complex than is usually assumed. We may, for example, think that 'fate and fortune' are important aspects of human life; fighting back after misfortune (whether successfully or not) to develop from a choker to a big match player being something that shows 'character'. However, on the one hand, egalitarians should not want the difference made by luck to be too great; the advantage (inequality) gained by the winning tennis player should not be vast. On the other hand, the inequality needs to be sufficient to motivate the players, and in particular to motivate the losing player to try to rectify the situation (and thus display character). As Dowding remarks, if this example is applicable to life more generally, then it points to the problem for the luck egalitarian 'that we need incentives that will not exacerbate the effects of contingent brute luck without unduly affecting the incentives for people to make choices and take on responsibilities' (p. 573).

Thus, for Dowding, luck and responsibility are not merely intertwined, but when it comes to the requirements of egalitarianism, both are epiphenomenal. They rest on 'the incentives that people have to choose from the opportunity sets available' (p. 578). What is needed then is not so much abstract theorising about responsibility, free will and determinism, and so on, but empirical investigation into the link between rewards and behaviour. The focus of government, Dowding concludes, should be to 'reduce inequality and … utilize the results of social research that demonstrates systematic effects creating inequities' (p. 579).

As Dowding notes, one attraction of the luck egalitarian position (although, as we have seen, an attraction that Dowding thinks false) is that it incorporates individual responsibility (long a clarion call of the right) into left-of-centre theorising. The challenge from the right is also the concern of Clare Chambers and Phil Parvin. Chambers and Parvin argue that the attempt by liberal theorists to defend liberalism without invoking arguments that depend on some or other comprehensive conception of the good – an attempt that can find formulation in either political liberalism (Rawls 2005) or justice as impartiality (Barry 1995) – may make liberalism more hospitable to multicultural or communitarian concerns, but it does so at the price of making it vulnerable to the libertarian critique. The particular challenge Chambers and Parvin consider is Nozick's (1974) argument that insofar as there are redistributive requirements, they are duties of charity owed to individuals and not duties of justice owed to the state. In short, 'why should principles of redistributive justice be coercive?' (p. 585).

Chambers and Parvin offer three general justifications for the use of coercive state power to enforce principles of justice. First, reasonable people may disagree about the demands of justice, and a proportion of them may deny that redistribution is required by justice. In these circumstances, Chambers and Parvin argue, it will be necessary to enforce the principles of justice coercively. Second, society may contain unreasonable people who are unwilling to engage with others co-operatively as part of a well-ordered society. They, too, will have to be coerced. Third, even reasonable people who agree that justice demands redistribution from them to others may fail to act justly in the absence of coercion for reasons of selfishness or weakness of will.

Chambers and Parvin's strategy is to consider whether these general justifications are available to political liberals. In the case of the argument from disagreement, their conclusion is that, whilst this move can easily be made by comprehensive liberals, it is not available to political liberals for whom reasonable disagreement is a mark of illegitimacy (a problem that is even more acute for those political liberals who have included elements of deliberative democracy in their theories). In the case of the second argument – the argument from unreasonableness – Chambers and Parvin claim that political liberals will find themselves in a dilemma: in order to respond to the libertarian challenge, political liberals need to be able to categorise and define 'the unreasonable'. However, to do so, they will need to give an account of the foundations of liberalism and this will draw them closer to the comprehensive liberal position. In order to avoid this, the political liberal can try to sustain the project of defending liberalism without recourse to some or other comprehensive conception of the good, but in doing so they preclude themselves from using the argument from unreasonableness to respond to the libertarian.

If political liberals are unable to appeal to the argument from disagreement, and the argument from unreasonableness collapses into the argument from disagreement, then success in replying to the libertarian challenge rests on the argument from motivation. However, G.A. Cohen has argued that political liberals cannot use the argument from motivation since political liberalism requires an 'egalitarian ethos' such that 'coercive enforcement of redistribution is at least unnecessary and at most unjust'. Chambers and Parvin point out that to the degree that Cohen's pushes for an 'egalitarian ethos' that is both necessary and sufficient for justice, he cedes the libertarian challenge. To the degree that he resists the libertarian challenge, he must give up several of his most important claims about the need for an 'egalitarian ethos'.

In short, Chambers and Parvin conclude that the attempt by liberals to accommodate multiculturalists, and the turn away from comprehensive liberalism, have left liberalism vulnerable to established libertarian criticisms that may have been marginalised in the recent literature, but that are no less important for that.

Justice and community

Debates over culture and the scope of justice are picked up in the papers in the third section. For Jones and Koller, the demands of justice are so important and so urgent that they trump arguments that would allow injustice in the name of cultural or national diversity.

Having considered a range of conceptions of human rights, Charles Jones describes and defends a view he calls 'human rights cosmopolitanism' that 'emphasizes the dignity of individual human beings, the fundamental importance and urgency of the basic claims these individuals may make on one another, and the universality of the correlative duties to which these claims give rise' (p. 610). What, though, is the status of these rights, and in particular, how do they relate to debates about social justice and political legitimacy?

Like Chambers and Parvin, Jones identifies a trend in contemporary political philosophy towards trying to separate contested and controversial matters of social justice arising out of persons' comprehensive conceptions of the good, and matters of right (in this case, of human rights) on which all persons can agree. This trend gives rise to the 'restricted view' of human rights that, quoting Beitz, maintains that 'human rights represent the common element in a range of views about social justice or political legitimacy found amongst the world's cultures' (p. 613). The restricted view is to be contrasted with the 'liberal or full view', in which human rights 'provide standards by which to judge the justice or legitimacy of any society's social, political and economic institutions, even where the standards conflict with those prevailing in a given society' (p. 614). To take the liberal or full view, then, is not merely to give content to human rights, but also to give them a status in abstraction from what happens to be believed in the world about the demands of justice and the conditions of legitimacy.

Much of the central part of Jones's paper is taken up in evaluating the arguments for a restricted view of human rights. Jones identifies four, although each is finally rejected. First, the argument from toleration – that is, the argument that it should be the conventional morality of a given society that is used to evaluate that society's structures and political norms – is criticized on the grounds that it is implausible to hold that social acceptance is a right-making property and because it trades on a tendency to overlook the internal complexity of cultures themselves. Second, one might defend the restricted view by interpreting imposing human rights on those who reject them as paternalistic because imposed for the good of those who nevertheless reject them. If one combines this with a general anti-paternalism, then one arrives at the restricted view. However, Jones claims, this argument fails because it depends on a tendency to think of states as akin to individual persons and as a consequence fails to recognise that persons are separate moral agents. Third, advocates of the restricted view could appeal to the need to avoid parochialism; we should not impose an extensive set of rights on others when some of those rights merely reflect our 'liberal democratic' norms. Of course, the core rights (such as freedom from slavery) will be shared by all decent societies, but we should not mistake that for agreement on all rights. Jones, although happy to encourage discursive pluralism, doubts that this can be sustained. Specifically, he finds no compelling argument to limit rights such as equal rights to political participation only to those liberal democratic countries that happen to believe in them. Finally, fourth, Jones considers the argument from pluralism; that is the argument that appeals to the value of 'diversity as such' (a theme also considered in David Heyd's paper). This is also rejected, because once it is granted that that diversity as such is not defensible (because it would condone a range of morally objectionable practices), and only diversity constrained by a universal framework – such as one provided by human rights – can be defended, the value of pluralism can no longer be used to reject the liberal full view in favour of the restricted view. This comparative critical evaluation leads to the conclusion that the liberal full view is more faithful to the fundamental normative commitments of moral cosmopolitanism.

The relationship between the demands of global justice, and those of justice within states, as well as the institutional implications of this relationship, is also the theme of Peter Koller's contribution. Koller argues that domestic and global justice are conceptually interrelated because global justice both frames domestic justice and is dependent on it. They are also contingently interrelated in ways that flow both from the domestic to the international and *vice-versa*. For example, there are the ways in which indefensible domestic orders are stabilised by provoking external conflict; internal conflicts are pacified by exploiting other nations; and the privileges of ruling elites in different societies are preserved through their international co-operation. In the direction from international to domestic injustices, there are, for example, domestic injustices that may result from hegemonic power structures in international relations; the absence or failure of international governance; and distorted decision-making in international institutions.

Koller examines the ways in which these relationships can be seen in effect in several contemporary cases of domestic and global injustice. Moreover, he argues, it is clear that the negative consequences of the relationship between domestic and global injustice are diffused faster and wider in the context of contemporary globalisation. In particular, he focuses on three examples: political repression, world poverty, and the erosion of politics and democracy.

In the case of politically repressive regimes, these depend for their survival in part by their being tolerated under international law; promoted by other nations; and by the ways in which international institutions allow them access to resources and borrowing privileges. In the case of world poverty, the system of international financial institutions, and their domination by rich countries, has contributed to a deepening marginalisation of many regions of the world whose populations suffer from extreme poverty. Finally, globalisation has created problems that escape political control, because those problems occur in areas over which neither nation states nor international institutions have any effective power.

Having analysed the problems, Koller argues that in order to deal with these negative effects of the relationship between global and domestic injustices, the world requires sufficiently strong and independent global institutions, capable of appropriately sanctioning human rights violations and of regulating the dynamics of the global economy in favour of the global poor. Further, in addition to greater power, these institutions will also, when compared to the ones that presently exist, require more transparent decision-making procedures, better representation of the nations concerned, and more executive impartiality, if they are to help in eradicating the enormous injustices of our globalised world. In short, we need a new type of global politics.

Both Jones and Koller are concerned with the connections and possible conflicts between an overarching account of global justice and domestic practices and understandings. Moreover, as Chambers and Parvin note, contemporary political philosophy in general often takes issues in this area to be central to the discipline. Much work has been done to try to accommodate difference and diversity, but why should be value diversity, and, when it is of value, what should we do about it? This is the theme of the next two papers, by David Heyd and Philippe Van Parijs.

David Heyd's project is to interrogate the idea of diversity, and in particular to question whether it is plausible to think diversity of intrinsic value. His strategy is to compare biodiversity with cultural diversity. As he notes, the analogy between the two is common, and occurs in both The Universal Declaration on Cultural Diversity and The Convention on Biological Diversity. Yet, the idea of 'diversity' is complex and, according to Heyd, necessarily normative. It is complex because it may, for example, apply at the inter-species or intra-species level, just as it may apply to the internal diversity within a particular culture or nation or the total number of cultures in the world. It is normative because we need, therefore, always to invoke a principle of individuation before trying to measure, or say anything about, diversity. It is also normative in the sense that it is usually used to commend rather than describe. In calling a student body, or a work force, 'diverse', the speaker often intends not merely to describe, but to praise. And this, of course, is part of what drives the analogy: we worry about the extinction of species, so we should worry about the extinction of cultures (and *vice-versa*).

Heyd, though, asks directly why we should so worry. Citing scientific speculation, he points out that 99.9% of the species that have existed on the Earth are extinct, and, similarly, many cultures must have come and gone without leaving much trace. How then can we defend our concern for protecting and promoting diversity? One answer may be that diversity has extrinsic value. This seems clear in biodiversity, where the existence of other species is useful for human beings. However, it is, as Heyd points out, far less clear in the cultural case.

In any event, Heyd is interested in the question of intrinsic value. The first argument he considers he calls the 'person-affecting' argument. This is that diversity may have intrinsic value because of the way it affects human interests. However, given that the ways in which those interests are affected depends on the persons involved – and their cultural backgrounds – this would mean that the value of diversity is culturally relative. Second, we might think that both nature and past human beings have created things – species and cultures – that we should respect. Gazing out into the world, we feel a sense of awe at nature's achievement in creation, just as we do looking at the products of different civilizations. Of course, this may be true, but it still does not seem like much of an argument. In addition, the language of achievement and creation is inappropriate when it comes to nature and evolution, which depend on chance and from which intention is missing. Finally, whilst gazing at some aspects of the natural world, and the products of some cultures, may stir in us these feelings of awe and respect, it is by no means true of all. In the end, perhaps, what we are left with is a feeling that we ought to protect the beautiful or the interesting, but these cannot be arguments for the intrinsic value of diversity.

Perhaps the most familiar arguments (at least for cultural diversity) appeal to the need for a broad context in which human beings can flourish by making choices between meaningful options and/or to the need for a certain degree of openness and toleration towards other ways of doing things. However, these are not arguments for diversity as such. In the end, Heyd concludes, whilst the analogy between cultural and biological diversity is sometimes interesting – as, for example, when we can see that we probably worry more about species that we think we have harmed directly just as we worry more about cultures that have been the victims of past injustice – it is unsustainable. 'The analogy between cultural and biological diversity holds', Heyd writes, 'only if we either regard the two spheres as guided by teleological principles or if we view them both as driven by causal-mechanical forces'. We should do neither, though, since 'natural evolution is a blind causal process while human development is at least partly driven by choice and purpose' (p. 666).

As Heyd makes clear, being sceptical about the analogy of cultural and biological diversity, and even about the value of diversity, does not mean being sceptical about the political significance of membership of some groups, or about the importance to persons of their communal and other identities. Some identities, and memberships, do matter. Philippe Van Parijs argues forcefully that linguistic communities are important, and that the spread and dominance of English is a matter of justice not only because it affects the opportunities available to non-Anglophone speakers, but because the domination of English violates the demand of equal dignity. Much of his paper, then, considers how best to respond to this injustice.

Given how English spreads and other languages die, Van Parijs argues that the injustice would be best addressed through the institution of linguistic territorial regimes (LTRs), which are a set of legal rules that constrain the choice of the languages used for purposes of education and communication. LTRs are to be preferred to other means of securing the survival of the weaker language since these other means fail. For example, voluntarism fails because of the standard collective action problem and because of the difficulties associated for individuals with unilaterally insisting on using the weaker language even though the dominant language is the maximin language. Similarly, the linguistic personality principle has been tried but without much success because in places where the linguistic divide correlates with economic inequality, it would be unfair that different people have access to services of differing quality simply because of a feature they cannot control, and because it creates a deep political problem, insofar as it creates a structure where distinct political communities elaborate their political project separately and then need to negotiate with each other on countless issues because they share the same territory.

That said, Van Parijs admits that LTRs suffer from problems of their own. The first is the issue of deciding which languages should have priority within which borders; no neat solutions are available, but the answer can be guided by the suggestion that there must be a sufficiently large and geographically concentrated population who regard themselves as sharing the same language and are willing to pay the costs of implementing an LTR. This raises the second problem, that the costs – such as and caused by the asymmetric flow of human capital towards those areas where English is the official language – of adopting LTRs might outweigh the benefits. However, these costs can be mitigated by remittances sent back home by migrant workers, the transfer of knowledge by those returning to their home country, and free-riding on Anglophone knowledge production. Moreover, the creation of 'linguistically free zones' within an LTR would also have positive effects. For these reasons, Van Parijs argues, the problems associated with LTRs are not insurmountable.

Justice and the future

In the first paper, Dennis Thompson considered the problem of democracy accounting for the views of future generations, and it is to the theme of the future that the last two chapters turn. Both concern the effects of climate change and the demands of justice. Climate change, and its consequences, give rise to two types of burdens: first, the burdens of changing existing behaviour to reduce the future extent and effects of climate change; second, the burden of protecting people from the ill effects of climate change. Following the literature, Simon Caney refers to these as the burdens associated with duties of 'mitigation' and 'adaptation' respectively. His question is, who should bear these burdens? One answer – perhaps the most common – is that they should be borne by those who caused the problem: the so-called Polluter Pays Principle (PP Principle). Caney argues that this principle is insufficient and needs to be complemented by a principle that says that the burden should be borne by those who have the greatest ability to pay: the Ability to Pay Principle (ATP Principle).

As Caney says, the PP Principle is intuitively attractive. It seems right and just that the moral obligation to deal with the costs of a given problem lie with those who created the problem in the first place. However, Caney expresses two concerns about the principle. First, estimating the causal contribution of human-caused climate change for any given action, *and* estimating the costs of the ill effects of that climate change are both extremely difficult. Second, it is clear that some of the people whose actions contributed to climate change were excusably ignorant at the time at which they acted. In such conditions, it is unjust to impose the full costs of their actions on them.

In response to the first concern, Caney points out both that such empirical difficulties do not affect the moral force of the PP Principle. Moreover, as technology and climate science improve, we can expect these problems to be reduced. Finally, whilst the PP Principle requires both that one can identify the polluter and the effect of his pollution in order to be realisable, that knowledge is required by any principle that might be used to distribute the burdens resulting from climate change. Under the ATP Principle, for example, we still need to know 'the extent of the harms caused by dangerous climate change and what causes those harms' (p. 698) in order to know what those who are able to pay ought to do.

In response to the second, Caney considers a number of possible counterarguments before settling on a 'modified strict liability principle' that holds that 'if people engage in activities which jeopardize other people's fundamental interests by emitting excessive amounts of greenhouse gases then (i) they should bear the costs of their actions even if they were excusably ignorant of the effects of their actions if *they have benefited from those harmful activities* and (ii) *their costs should be proportionate to the benefits they have derived.*

Thus, Caney thinks that the PP Principle can survive these two concerns. However, it cannot be sufficient for three reasons. First, it cannot accommodate emissions from earlier generations (polluters who no longer exist). Thus, it needs to be supplemented by a principle that tells us how to distribute the burdens caused by the pollution of those who are dead. Second, it cannot tell us how to distribute the burdens associated with non-anthropogenic climate change. A purist might insist that such burdens are just bad luck (or some such) and should not be borne by anyone, but as Caney says, that is implausible. We care about the effects of climate change because they affect people's vital interests. Something needs to be done about all the effects, and that means that we need an additional principle to dictate who ought to do what needs to be done. Finally, Caney argues that the emissions of some currently, and historically, disadvantaged people are legitimate and should not bring with them liability for burdens.

The PP Principle, then, needs to be supplemented and Caney's argument is that the right additional principle is the ATP. The ATP Principle is, as Caney says, 'indifferent to who caused a harm: its emphasis is on who can rectify that harm' (p. 703). Much of the rest of his paper is dedicated to rebutting criticisms of the ATP Principle, whilst also refining that principle. The criticisms include the claim that it is unjust to pay for something that is not one's fault; that it is unjust to ignore the historic causes of the harm (a criticism that leads Caney to try to accommodate a distinction between those who have the ability to pay and whose wealth came from climate-changing activities and those whose wealth came in other ways); and finally that it is unjust to give more of the burden only to those who wealth came about in climate-endangering ways rather than to those whose wealth came about in unjust ways (which again leads Caney to revise his ATP Principle). The result is what Caney calls a hybrid model consisting of a revised PP Principle and a revised ATP Principle, and in the final parts of his chapter, Caney explores some of the policy implications of this model.

In the final chapter, Lukas Meyer and Dominic Roser take on the same issues as Caney, although their approach is to separate the costs of mitigation and adaptation. They thus distinguish the question of the distribution of (some assumed just) global quota of emissions from the question of who should pay for the damages caused by emissions.

Meyer and Roser favour a prioritarian account of justice; an account that holds that benefiting people matters independent of what other people have, but that greater weight should be given to benefiting those who are worse off. What is to be distributed are emission rights, but of course the point of these rights – the good to be distributed – is the opportunity to use those rights in activities such as travel, economic growth, and so on.

As Meyer and Roser note, it is problematic to deal with the issue of emission rights in abstraction from the distribution of all other goods. In overall terms, poor underdeveloped countries are so badly off (not least as a result of injustice) that one might be inclined to think they should get all of whatever good is now going. However, such a procedure would be odd as well. Of course, we should respond to global injustice and deprivation, but not by perversely reallocating only one good.

Meyer and Roser assume that if we were to ignore the issue of past emissions the priority view would demand at least equal per capita emission rights for the South (they use North and South as tokens for individuals in certain areas who benefit in certain ways from carbon emissions). They argue that 'the historical inequality in emissions gives us reason to tilt the present allocation of emission rights in favour of the South in the sense that its per capita emission rights should be higher than in the North'. (p. 723). Once one includes reference to the past, Meyer and Roser argue, the allocation of emission rights should be adjusted in favour of the South.

Interestingly, Meyer and Roser confront some of the same issues as Caney; issues over the fairness of paying for harms one did not cause, or did not knowingly cause. However, their response is slightly different from his in part because they distinguish between the burdens of mitigation and those of adaptation. Caney, as we have seen, is sympathetic to taking past injustice into account in his revised ATP Principle. Those whose present wealth was acquired unjustly should bear more of the burden. As far as mitigation is concerned, Meyer and Roser think this irrelevant to what they argue is a pure distributive question about emission rights. The prioritarian account they favour does not rely on 'the idea of compensation for past wrongs' (p. 734) in distributing emission rights.

Past wrongs, though, are surely relevant to compensatory (or corrective) justice; that is to questions of adaptation? Meyer and Roser, though, point to many difficulties of this view and prefer a broadly distributive justice response to questions of adaption. In short, 'a prioritarian redistributive scheme concerned with climate damages' requires 'that those who are lucky in terms of not being affected much by climate change should assist those who are unlucky in terms of being affected heavily'. The critical point is that 'they owe this assistance *independently* of who caused climate change' (p. 737).

Concluding remarks

It is sometimes said that John Rawls's *A theory of justice* revitalised political philosophy. It should be no surprise, then, that concerns of justice unite all the chapters in this volume. However, what is clear is that those concerns now manifest themselves in interesting and new directions (or, sometimes, in forgotten old ones). Politically, we confront urgent problems of democracy, equality, community, and of how to respond to potentially catastrophic climate change. However, the response to these problems cannot only be pragmatic and piecemeal. It needs to be coherent, and most of all just.

Acknowledgements

The editors would like to thank Alfonson Donoso for editorial help. Our sincere thanks are also owed to the British Academy who funded the conference where many of these ideas came together.

References

Barry, B.M., 1995. *Justice as impartiality. A treatise on social justice, Vol. II.* Oxford: Clarendon Press.

Nozick, R., 1974. *Anarchy, state and utopia.* New York: Basic Books.

Parfit, D., 1984. *Reasons and persons.* Oxford: Oxford University Press.

Rawls, J., 2001. *Justice as fairness: a restatement.* Cambridge, MA: Harvard University Press.

Rawls, J., 2005. *Political liberalism: expanded edition.* New York: Columbia University Press.

Waldron, J., 2002. *God, Locke, and equality: Christian foundations of John Locke's political thought.* Cambridge: Cambridge University Press.

Representing future generations: political presentism and democratic trusteeship

Dennis F. Thompson

Department of Government, Harvard University, USA

Democracy is prone to what may be called presentism – a bias in the laws in favor of present over future generations. I identify the characteristics of democracies that lead to presentism, and examine the reasons that make it a serious problem. Then I consider why conventional theories are not adequate to deal with it, and develop a more satisfactory alternative approach, which I call democratic trusteeship. Present generations can represent future generations by acting as trustees of the democratic process. The general principle is that present generations should act to protect the democratic process itself over time. They should try to make sure that future citizens continue to have competent control over their collective decision-making.

Democracy is partial toward the present. Most citizens tend to discount the future, and to the extent that the democratic process responds to their demands, the laws it produces tend to neglect future generations. The democratic process itself amplifies this natural human tendency. These characteristics of democracy lead to what I call its presentism – a bias in the laws in favor of present over future generations.

Democracy's presentism is not entirely unwelcome. Compared to other forms of government, democracy is not disposed to sacrifice citizens or a whole generation for some distant future goal. It is less vulnerable to the claims of utopian idealists, religious zealots, or radical revolutionaries who call for great sacrifices from the present generation to bring about even greater good for the future of mankind. It is a virtue of democracy that it pays attention to actual citizens and seeks to hold actual rulers accountable for the actions they take on behalf of citizens.

Nevertheless, this virtue of democracy becomes a vice when the good of future citizens are at stake. Presentism manifests itself in laws that neglect of long-term environmental risks, the consequences of genetic engineering, problems of population growth, and development of the democratic process itself. It also is evident in effects in the nearer term in laws that favor the elderly at the expense of children. Examples include the disproportionate allocation of resources for health care of the elderly and the financing of social security out of current taxes. In these and other similar instances, the persons who are most adversely affected are not yet citizens (and therefore have no voice). The policies are not sustainable at a level that would enable the young to enjoy similar benefits when they grow old.

Democracy itself affirms that the citizens bound by laws should have a voice in making them. Yet future citizens who will be bound by the laws cannot have such a voice. Democracy's conventional way of addressing the problem of those who do not have a voice is to grant greater opportunities for participation and to institute more extensive representation. But making democracy more inclusive – expanding citizenship and enhancing representation – would not help future citizens. They do not have a voice because they cannot be citizens now. Yet they have to live with the consequences of the laws made by the citizens of an earlier generation. They may try to change the laws when their time comes, but that may be difficult or futile. The effects of many laws are irreversible. The damage may have been done. Critical resources may have been depleted, and environmental treasures spoiled. The political institutions needed to cope with the damage may have been corrupted or weakened.

If future citizens cannot be present now, how should they be represented? This question has not traditionally been a concern of political theorists or public officials. Governments did not expect most of their laws and policies to affect distant generations. Even when they did, they often could not foresee what the effects would be. The effects of laws now reach further into the future than ever before, and knowledge about those effects is greater than ever before. The problem of representing the unrepresentable – those who are bound by laws but cannot have a voice in making them – is therefore increasingly urgent. It poses a practical challenge, but it also raises some neglected and distinctive theoretical issues.

To explore the question of the representation of future generations, I identify the characteristics of democracies that lead to presentism, and examine the reasons that make it a serious problem. Then I consider why conventional theories are not adequate to deal with it, and try to develop a more satisfactory alternative approach, which I call democratic trusteeship.

Democratic myopia: why democracies neglect the future

Democracy's neglect of future citizens has at least four sources. First, there is the natural human tendency to prefer the immediate to the distant, both in what one fears and what one desires. The tendency shows itself in politics as in ordinary life.[1] Political leaders, like ordinary people, are not naturally inclined to defer gratification. Democratic government is supposed to be responsive. To the extent that it transfers these psychological tendencies to the political process, it produces laws and policies that reflect this bias toward the present. (Notice: this bias is not the same as self-interested motivation. Even if one treats the future as an extension of one's self, one tends to be biased in favor of the present self.)

The second reason for neglecting future generations appeals to the oldest and still one of the most influential justifications for the principle that representatives should be responsive to their constituents. The justification holds that the individuals who will be affected by the laws are the best judges of the laws. As John Stuart Mill wrote: 'each is the only safe guardian of his own rights and interests' (Mill 1977, p. 404).[2] Adopting this justification for citizen participation, citizens and their representatives should judge a law according to how they experience, or expect to experience, its effects. This rationale does not assume that citizens are self-interested or that representatives are only delegates, but it does imply that representatives should give great weight to citizens' views about the effects of the laws on them and people like them living in circumstances like theirs. Some other conceptions of democracy are even more closely tied to the views of the present citizens. Any conception – such as interest group pluralism, in which the preferences of citizens are aggregated to produce the collective result – is inevitably present-oriented by virtue of its reliance on the demands of existing citizens.

The third source of the neglect of the future stems from the fact that democracy is government pro tempore. The rulers exercise power for a limited period of time, after which they stand for reelection and reappointment, or retire from office. Although one can imagine a democratic government (with majority rule) that is absolute (as in Hobbes's 'democracy') (Hobbes 1991, Bk. II, ch. XIX), political power in nearly all actual democracies is subject to temporal limits. Even an absolute majority can be eventually overruled by a subsequent majority. Consequently, even (or especially) well-intentioned rulers and representatives try to make a difference sooner rather than later. They try to pass laws and policies that produce results within the limit of their time in office. The supporting institutions of democracy, such as the press, also reflect (and because of their own dynamics, reinforce) this appetite for the immediate.

Finally, there is a tendency in most modern democracies today to favor the older age group. Because this group are more numerous, and also able to exercise greater political influence than younger groups, they are privileged in law and public policy. At first one might think that the bias for the elderly is just the opposite of presentism. The policies in question provide more for the needs of citizens in the later than earlier stages of life and in this sense provide for the future. But that description applies only when we look at the time horizon from the perspective of an individual. From the perspective of the democratic majority at any particular time, the decision to favor the older generation is actually a form of presentism. Social Security in the US is a telling example: it creates tax obligations for not only younger citizens but children yet to become citizens in order to provide for the older age group at any particular time. This might be a fair distribution over time, were it not for the fact that the younger age group cannot expect to receive proportionate return for the benefits it is providing for the current elderly generation. Laws against mandatory retirement are another case of discrimination in favor of the old (at least where the number of highly desirable positions is limited and unlikely to expand over time).

Presentism – in both the form that neglects citizens not yet born, and those who are too young to be citizens – should be distinguished from the short-sightedness that afflicts the same individuals over time. Some of the same pressures toward presentism also tilt laws and policies against the long-term interests of current citizens. But this is a different problem; it is more a failure of prudence than morality. It can be addressed by showing that sacrificing now for a future benefit is in the self-interest of some individual or group. The individual or group of identifiable individuals can usually recognize that they will benefit from the sacrifice later. Younger citizens may vote for policies that benefit older citizens because they will themselves be older citizens someday. The problem of future citizens cannot be addressed in this way because the individuals who sacrifice are not the same as those who benefit.

Democratic evasions: why presentism is a serious problem

Many theorists assume that the claims of future citizens can be addressed within the framework of conventional democratic theory and practice.[3] The theorists offer several reasons for assuming that the claims of future citizens do not require any special attention, and in most cases should be discounted. One common approach starts with these observations. The composition of the demos changes gradually.[4] Citizens and their representatives do not leave the democratic stage all at the same time. They continue to have some connections to those who follow. Citizens care about their children and grand-children, and both citizens and their representatives care about sustaining democratic institutions. But this argument from generational connections is not sufficient. The further we look to the future, the weaker and more indeterminate the connections. Many policies now have their most significant effects a century or more in the future, when the connections between present and future perspectives are tenuous.

Another set of arguments for discounting future generations suggest, not that it is unnecessary to give any special attention to future generations, but rather that such attention is unjustified. One reason it is thought to be unjustified is that future generations in all democracies are likely to be much better off than any present generation, because they will benefit from the accumulated knowledge and technological capital of previous generations. They should be able to take of themselves because we have given them more than we had.

This view fails to take into account the large and often irreversible harms that current generations can inflict on future generations. The destruction of the earth's atmosphere as a result of global warming is only one of many such environmental harms that almost certainly cannot be reversed. We can assume that technological progress will provide future generations better ways of coping with the harm than those we now have, but we should not assume that they should regard the accumulated knowledge they receive reasonable compensation for the massive damage we have done.

Even damage to political institutions is not so easily repaired as is often assumed. The health of democracies depends not only on explicit practices and formal laws but also as much on implicit customs and informal norms that are developed fitfully over time and often with difficulty. Some of the traditions may constrain future generations too much, and some too little. Achieving the right balance is a long and difficult project that requires that citizens continue to believe in the goals of democracy even while their own governments fall short. Once the confidence of citizens in their form of government begins to erode, it may be impossible to restore it.

Giving special attention to future generations is said to be unjustified for another reason – one that seems more morally attractive because it refers not to everyone in a current generation but only the most disadvantaged. The argument is that it would not be fair to transfer resources from the relatively disadvantaged in the present to the relatively disadvantaged in the future. If justice requires that we concentrate on the least advantaged, then the claims of the present generation in the less developed nations would seem to be more compelling.

This argument rests on a mistake that is all too common and distorts the analysis of problems of global justice as well as future generations. The mistake is to separate too sharply the claims of foreign and future citizens. Their identities and therefore their moral status is not so distinct as many theorists assume. The further we look into the future, the less plausible it is to keep the question of foreign and future citizens separate. The citizens of our future democracy are just as likely to be descendants of some other present democracy or some present non-democracy. Even if the states remain the same (which is unlikely in the further future), the citizens of any particular future state are not any more connected to any current democracy than the citizens of some other future state. Even if we tried, we could not completely limit our efforts to help future citizens to only those who will be living in our own state in the future. Even from the perspective of the present, boundaries between states begin to dissolve the further into the future we look.

Because present boundaries matter less in the future, they should also matter less in any decision about how the claims of future citizens should be weighed in the present. This may mean that developed nations should provide more aid than they do now to developing nations before worrying about the debt their own citizens will carry in the next several generations. But it does not mean that the claims of more distant generations should be radically discounted. It does not provide any warrant for ignoring the problem of future generations, or discounting their moral claims.

Perhaps the most common reason for neglecting or discounting future generations is uncertainty. Those who put forward this reason may concede that it would be necessary and desirable to give more respect to their claims if we had any rational basis for predicting what they will be, or what weight we should give to them. But it is difficult if not impossible to trace the causes the harms that present states visit upon future states, and no less difficult to make reliable predictions about the policies intended to remedy those harms. Uncertainty about the needs of future citizens is therefore great. We cannot be confident now that they will, for example, want national parks and green spaces, or even (if we look far enough ahead) whether they will need renewable fuels. Under conditions of such uncertainty, any plausible discount rate will give the claims of distant future generations no weight at all.

The argument from uncertainty has considerable force, and militates against any theory or principle that would try to specify a wide range of the needs and wants of future generations, and instruct representatives to pursue policies to satisfy them. But in the radical form in which it is often stated, it is not plausible. We can be fairly confident about some of the harms we are causing or to which we are contributing. Even in the remote future, we can reasonably assume that citizens will not want to live with toxic chemicals, foul air, and chronic disease.[5] More importantly for the conception of representation I suggest below, we can assume that future generations will need a way of deciding collectively how they want to cope with these harms, and what rights and goods they want to pursue or forgo under these conditions.

The argument from uncertainty, then, may cast doubt on any approach that would promote the welfare or the rights of future generations across the whole range of welfare or rights, but it does not justify ignoring all of their potential claims. More positively, it provides a reason to protect their capacity for making their own collective decisions. The very uncertainty that warrants doubts about what their needs will be supports an obligation to try to make sure that they have a process for deciding together what their needs are and how they should be met.

Democratic justice: why conventional theories fail

Most democratic theorists and most democratic politicians would agree that the citizens of a particular democracy should act justly toward future citizens.

For if future citizens cannot be present in the current democratic process, and if we cannot know much about what their views will be, it would seem that the best we can do now is to act on our own principles of justice, and treat them fairly from our own perspective. Justice is indeed an important consideration in deciding how future citizens should be represented, and the philosophical literature on this subject is clearly relevant to this project.

Unfortunately, conceptions of justice do not work well when extended to future generations. They do not work well or at all when they are applied to the distribution of benefits and burdens over many generations.[6] The basic problem is that future citizens cannot be parties to the actual or hypothetical agreement that is typically assumed to be necessary to generate the principles of justice. The principles that are chosen will determine who will exist (they will affect the distribution of population over time, for example). It is not coherent to include as parties to the agreement individuals who will not exist if the agreement is concluded.

The most systematic search for a place for future generations in a theory of justice – exemplified in the work of John Rawls – shows how difficult the task is. In the initial full-length version of his theory, Rawls had trouble formulating within the 'original position' a justification for a just savings principle, which requires earlier generations to save for later generations (Rawls 1971, pp. 284–293).[7] In the original position, individuals are to reason, on the basis of our self-interest, behind a 'veil of ignorance' that prevents them from knowing who in particular they are, or in what generation they happen to live. Under these conditions, the reasons any individual gives would not be biased in his favor, but they would not appeal to any moral considerations.

What role could future generations play in reasoning under these conditions? As part of their self-interest, individuals could take into account the interests of their immediate descendents but they would have no reason to consider the interests of more remote generations. The veil of ignorance leads people to maximize their interests (and those of their immediate descendants). As one critic points out, 'since nothing can be done to change the past, there is no advantage to the people in the original position in choosing a principle that requires any net savings (or indeed, one might add, prevents them from running things down) unless they actually care about the welfare of the next generation' (Barry 1989b, p. 200). Even if we assume that people in the original position care about the well-being of their children and their children's children, their concern for future generations must diminish rapidly as they contemplate each passing generation. From a moral point of view the concern diminishes too rapidly. But there is no way to prevent its premature expiration without introducing into the original position the very moral considerations it is designed to do without.

In a later version of his theory, Rawls puts some of these moral considerations back into the original position. To choose a just savings principle for future generations, we are now to apply a kind of golden rule to savings: do unto future generations as you would have past generations do unto you (Rawls 1993, p. 274; 2001, pp. 159–160).[8] We can justify a just savings principle 'because society is a system of cooperation between generations over time' (Rawls 1993, p. 274). The parties in the original position 'can be required to agree to a savings principle subject to the further condition that they must want all previous generations to have followed it' (Rawls 1993, p. 274). This argument, and the kind of reasons it tells representatives to give, moves quite a distance from the self-interested reasoning of the original position. It begins to look like a trustee conception of representation applied to the original position.

The course of Rawls's journey – from constrained self-interest to generational reciprocity – carries a lesson for any democrat who would seek to protect future generations. They are not adequately represented if representatives are held accountable only for pursuing the interests of current constituents and their near progeny. To be sure, if these interests are defined to include 'moral interests', and constituents are said to have a moral interest in the well-being of future generations, then accountability to the interests of constituents will ensure that representatives care about future generations. But this move either smuggles in a moral argument under the guise of self-interest, or treats the concern for future generations as purely contingent on the interest the current generation takes in them. We need a principle that holds representatives accountable not only for satisfying the interests of their constituents but also for acting in a way that can be justified to future generations.

'Do unto future generations as you would have past generations do unto you' could provide a good starting point for representatives who seek to protect the future. But the principle would have to be interpreted in a way that does not refer to specific individuals, and such an interpretation would be difficult to fit within the perspective of a representative as an agent (trustee or delegate) acting on behalf on constituents (present or future). The reason that the principle should avoid reference to individuals is so that it can escape the dreaded non-identity problem (Parfit 1983, pp. 166–179; Parfit 1986, pp. 351–379).[9] Decisions that representatives make now cannot be said to harm any particular individuals in the future because those individuals would not exist at all but for these decisions. For example: risky or depletive energy policies are not against the interests of people in the further future. No matter how depletive our present policy, it does not make anyone in the further future worse off because without those policies they would not have been born. To oppose depletive energy policies, then, we need an argument that does not appeal only to the interests of future persons. What needs to be represented are not the claims of future individuals but something like the value of human flourishing in the future. But the ordinary conception of political representation – which assumes a relationship between a representative and identifiable constituents – does not fit well with such an abstract value. Of course actual constituents could themselves value human flourishing in the distant future, and demand that their representatives pursue this value now. But neither the constituents nor the representatives would then be acting on principles found in conventional theories of justice.

It might be thought that utilitarian conceptions could do better. After all, utilitarians are criticized for not respecting individuals enough. They are charged with sacrificing the utility of some individuals to achieve a greater social utility, in which the individuals whose welfare is promoted are fungible. Their identity is irrelevant, and hence their non-identity creates less of a problem. Furthermore, utilitarianism does not rely on agreements among individuals, or prohibitions against wronging individuals. It does not have to assume that any wrong is done to particular individuals in the future. It seeks to determine only whether some future state of affairs is preferable (produces greater utility) to another state of affairs (produces lesser utility).

However, to the extent that utilitarian goals are detached from identifiable individuals, they provide less motivation for citizens (and therefore their representatives) to pursue them. Utilitarianism undermines the reasons that most citizens find most persuasive for respecting future generations – making individuals in the future worse off. In practice, utilitarianism could even undermine itself by causing citizens to give future generations less than what the correct utilitarian calculation would require. This possibility has led some utilitarians to suggest that the non-identity problem should not be widely publicized (Parfit 1983, pp. 175–176; Parfit 1986, pp. 451–452).

Another problem with utilitarianism at least in some forms also partly stems from its focus on social welfare rather than the welfare of each individual. A principle that would maximize total welfare over time implies that population should be maximized (Ryberg *et al.* 2006). As long as the welfare of any particular individual is positive however low the level, the principle calls for increasing the number of individuals in the world. We should continue to not only allow but encourage population growth, even at the cost of great reductions in the level of welfare of future citizens.

The problem of representation of future generations cannot be adequately addressed, then, by appeals to theories of justice or utility applied in the present. Even if principles of justice or utility can provide some guidance for thinking about future citizens, they need to be supplemented by principles specifying how the anticipated views of those citizens should be taken into account when the principles of justice run out or the principles of utility are contested. The problem of representation for future citizens is not entirely coincident with the problem of justice or utility. Democratic representation poses a prior (independent) question: who should have a voice in deciding whether laws are just or policies promote utility? Democrats believe that actual citizens should have a voice and should be represented in the making of laws whether or not they hold the correct principles of justice or the right concept of utility. They should have a voice because disputes about some policies do not depend entirely on questions of basic justice or social utility, because there may be reasonable disagreement about what is just or utile, and because sometimes even when what justice or utility demands is clear the values of democratic autonomy and legitimacy should prevail.

To respect the rights and goods of future generations, we need more than a temporal extension of principles of justice and utility. We need a revised conception of representation that enables democracies to represent future citizens who are not now present. We need a conception of democratic representation for citizens-to-be.

Democratic trusteeship: how the future can be represented in the present

If future generations cannot be present now, how can they be represented? Present generations, I suggest, can represent future generations by acting as *trustees of the democratic process.* The general principle of the trustee conception that we need to develop is that present generations should act to protect the democratic process itself over time. They should try to make sure that citizens continue to have competent control over their collective decision-making. The principle does not seek to maximize popular control as such. That is not a plausible aim over time. It would imply that earlier majorities could place no constraints on later majorities at all, even those that later majorities wish they had. It is also not a desirable aim. Popular control is ultimately valuable only insofar as expresses a genuine will, not transient impulses or uninformed preferences. The principle should permit only constraints that are necessary to make a majority at any particular time *competent* in the sense of having the capacity to express a sufficiently settled and an adequately informed judgment. The capacity depends on the continuing existence of robust social and political institutions sufficient to support at least a minimal form of democratic government

The principle can take at least two different forms – one less demanding than the other. The first (less demanding) version holds that citizens or their representatives in democratic states at any present time should seek to preserve a democratic process that gives future citizens at least as much capacity for collective decision-making as present citizens have. This can be seen as a political adaptation of the Lockean principle regarding property, which grants a right to appropriate land 'where there is enough, and as good left in common for others' (Locke 1965, section 27). Present democratic sovereigns should leave their successors 'enough and as good' democratic sovereignty as they themselves enjoy.

If we believe that the control that citizens now enjoy is inadequate, we may wish to adopt a more demanding version of the principle. It would stipulate that any current political generation should seek, up to the point that control over their own decision-making begins to decrease, to maximize the control that future generations will enjoy. Although this version would more reliably overcome the dead hand of past generations, it may also place excessive and unrealistic demands on earlier generations.

It is not necessary to decide between the two versions in order to develop the essential ideas of the trustee conception I am proposing. On either version of the principle, representatives (and their constituents) in the present should protect the democratic capacity of future representatives (and their constituents). The idea underlying both is that on whatever grounds any present democracy bases its authority, it should protect the democratic capacities of future democracies.

This trustee conception does not say simply – as a traditional trustee theory would – that representatives (or citizens) should use their best judgment and act in the interest of future citizens (Pitkin 1967; Thompson 2004, ch. 5). The future-oriented representatives are trustees of the democratic process, not the whole range of interests or welfare of future citizens. Representatives may not know the preferences, needs or life plans of future citizens, or even the best form of democracy for a future society. But they can know enough to try to preserve the conditions that would empower future citizens to make collective choices democratically.

Compared to theories of justice, this conception of representation has the advantage of requiring no reference to specific individuals, and little knowledge of the preferences or life plans of individuals or societies in other cultures or in the future. Present citizens would not be in the position of trying to imagine what future citizens might need while making policies that would determine whether future citizens exist. Compared to theories of utility, this conception does require complex predictions about the wide range of needs and desires that future citizens might have and the consequences of policies that future representatives might adopt. The principle (in either form) assumes that there will be a democratic state to which future citizens will belong, but not that it will have the same character as any present state. The principle assumes only that future citizens should have a voice in the making of the laws by which they are bound, and should be able to hold accountable officials who carry out those laws. To have an effective voice and to exercise effective accountability, they will need a democratic process that preserves their competence to control their government. But this is a less substantive – and less constraining – assumption than those required by most other theories that seek to protect future generations, including general theories of justice and utility.

It may be objected that we do not know what kind of democratic process future citizens will want – any more than we can know what kind of justice or utility they will seek. They may reasonably prefer an electoral system based on proportional representation rather than a winner-take-all majoritarian system. They may favor more direct forms of democracy (greater use of initiatives, recall, referenda). They may want to modify a presidential type of government in the direction of a parliamentary type. These and many other forms of government are quite compatible with the trustee conception I am suggesting. Except for the constraints necessary to promote competent control, the conception does not prescribe a particular form of democracy. Indeed, it implies that as far as possible a current democratic majority should leave open the possibility of changes to other forms, including those, such as the adoption of a different electoral system, that would alter the definition of the majority itself.

Some people who are prepared to accept the principle of democratic trusteeship may doubt whether it can be of any use in practice. One doubt is quite general: it expresses skepticism about the relevance of theory for practical questions of institutional design. All theory can do is to present and justify principles: it has nothing to contribute to the hard practical work of designing institutions to realize those principles. To be sure, theory does not usually offer much specific guidance to institutional designers, even those who make constitutions. But it can identify values that are likely to be neglected and prescribe priorities that should be adopted in creating and reforming institutions. As in the preceding analysis, which was mostly theoretical, it can show why some arguments standing in the way of institutional change should be rejected, why some theories claiming to provide sufficient guidance are mistaken or incomplete, and why widely recognized institutional biases (what I called democratic presentism) should be resisted.

Still, some may still doubt whether the theoretical aims can be realized at all, whether there any institutional forms that could distinctively promote the values and priorities to which it calls attention. The practical problems is that all representative institutions suffer from two kinds of risks – that representatives will have too little power to serve their constituents, or they will have too much power to serve only themselves. The trustees of the democratic process that I favor may not have sufficient power to ensure that future citizens receive the respect they should; or if the trustees have enough power, they will use it for their own political purposes (or for ends other than the democratic capacities of future citizens). In designing the institutions of trusteeship, we need to be concerned about both possibilities, but the first is the more probable. In most current and foreseeable democracies, trustees of the future are not likely exercise great power.

No single representative institution can guarantee that future citizens will receive the attention they should. Certainly the constituents who are supposed to be represented cannot actually hold anyone accountable. By the time some of them come into existence, their representatives will have passed from the scene. Nevertheless, it may be possible to create a role whose occupant is dedicated to looking out for future generations. The representatives would be accountable to the requirements of the role, which would express the perspective of future citizens. The role requirements would in effect stand as a surrogate for future citizens. As we know from experience and from studies of role behavior in a variety of institutions, a role can change its occupant's attitudes and actions, sometimes for the better (see Biddle 1986, pp. 84–85; Ilgen and Hollenbeck 1991; Strijbos *et al.* 2003; Gehlbach 2004). Roles can be designed so that their occupants have incentives to give special attention to, and to advocate with special zeal, the interests of the persons or purposes that they are charged with representing. The general idea of a division of labor and special roles is familiar in constitutional design, and could be applied more generally to any claim of future generations, but for reasons indicated earlier, the idea is more appropriately limited to claims related to their democratic capacities.

To protect future democratic capacities, we should therefore establish some institutions that create roles that give special attention to democratic potential of individuals or groups who are otherwise not represented, or not adequately represented. Even when the incentives operate more through conventional habit and social approval than in response to any explicit expectation of rewards or punishments, they can be nonetheless effective in an institutional context.

What kind of institutional roles could encourage representatives in the present to give more attention to the democratic fate of citizens in the future? The most natural place to start is with the paradigmatic representative institution – the legislature. The chief advantages of situating the role in the legislature are that the representatives would participate directly in the process of making laws and would be accountable to an electorate. But the role of a representative dedicated to future constituents does not fit comfortably into an assembly of representatives accountable to actual constituents. The conflict between what each role requires can be seen in the difficulties raised by proposals to create special representatives of the future.[10] How many representatives should the future have? Because the numbers obviously cannot be proportional to the potential constituents, the proposals usually set an arbitrary quota, typically two. But apart from the objection that in such small numbers these representatives are not likely to have much influence, the arbitrary quota would undermine the principle of equal representation – which is part of the idea of democracy that the proposal purports to uphold. Although current systems do not consistently observe strict principles of equality, the deviations (such as racial redistricting) are justified on democratic principles (such as equal opportunity), and do not set a fixed number of seats in the legislature without regard to changes in the electorate.

An even more fundamental difficulty with these proposals is evident when we ask: what is the electorate to whom these representatives are accountable? One proposal would create a 'proxy electorate' consisting of members of groups committed to 'environmental sustainability' (Dobson 1996, pp. 132–135). But as a critic points out, the goals of such groups do not encompass all or even the most important interests of future generations

(Ekeli 2005, pp. 148–149). In any case, environmental groups differ among themselves. Also, the proposal does not respect the right to equal votes: it would give members of the proxy electorate two votes each and other citizens only one each. On an alternative proposal (presented by the critic) each citizen would have two votes, one to cast for ordinary representatives and another to cast for special representatives dedicated to future citizens (so called F-representatives). Any group or party that legitimately is devoted to the interests of future generations could put forward candidates for the reserved positions in the legislatures. These 'F-representatives' would have a suspensive veto. To make sure that political groups and parties would not abuse the two-vote system (for example, by strategically running candidates in both campaigns), the government would strictly regulate which groups and candidates could qualify as legitimate representatives of the future.

The basic problem with these proposals – and any similar efforts to combine in one body a representational role that has constituents with one that does not – is that they assume that to be legitimate the representatives of the future must be as much like ordinary representatives. But the attempt to make the role of the future representatives replicate as far as possible the role of the ordinary representative is bound to fall short, and consequently destined to undermine the legitimacy of the future representatives. In trying to restore one democratic element to the role (accountability), the proposals inevitably sacrifice another (equal votes or free association). Instead of trying to square the representational circle by putting future representatives in the legislature, we should face up to the fact that they cannot have constituents in any normal sense. We should consider alternatives that model their roles more on those of trustees who are able to act independently, capable of influencing ordinary politics but free of the constraints that produce its presentism.

Democratic futures: what duties trustees should have

We may take some guidance from an ancient institution, the Tribune of the Plebs (tribunus plebis) in the Roman Republic (Cornell 1995, pp. 259–261; Staveley 1953, pp. 30–60; Homo 1996). Standing apart from ordinary politics but ready to intervene to defend the interests of a class otherwise unrepresented in politics, the Tribune in several key respects exemplifies the kind of institution that could provide representation for future generations. At the height of its power, it could intercede in judicial proceedings, veto legislative acts, and force the legislative consideration of its own proposals. Its only mission was to protect the rights and interests of plebs. Although elected (in the plebeian assembly) for fixed and usually non-renewable terms, the tribunes were accountable to no one but themselves while in office. The role of the tribune does not of course provide an exact model. The constituents whom the tribunes represented did actually exist, even though for the purposes of legislation they were an abstract class. Some of the tribunes' powers – to impose capital punishment on anyone who interfered with their duties – may be somewhat excessive for our purposes. But several elements of the role are worth retrieving: a specialized duty toward the unrepresented, independence from other political authorities, and specific powers over the legislative agenda. The tribunes themselves should be public figures who have no political ambitions, except those that can confer (in Hobbes' terms) 'fame after death' (Hobbes 1991, I, xi).

The closet modern analogues are independent commissions and citizens' assemblies. The advantage of a commission is that it makes possible the appointment of experts, persons with experience in promoting the interests of future generations. To realize this advantage, the appointment procedures would have to be designed to prevent the commission's capture by partisans of presentism. But even so, the commission's advantage is also its disadvantage: the special qualifications would set the members apart from ordinary citizens (not only present but also future). The members would be doubly deprived of democratic legitimacy: not only would they be unaccountable but they would be unlike the constituents they represent.

Although the lack of accountability cannot be avoided, the lack of resemblance can be diminished by the institution of a citizens' assembly. The members are ordinary citizens, and therefore more plausibility seen as surrogates for the ordinary citizens of the future (though of course no one can be sure what ordinary citizens will be like in the distant future). This institution too has ancient antecedents, but in modern times is relatively rare and only recently used at the level of national politics. The most promising examples are the assemblies created to consider reforms of the electoral systems in several Canadian provinces. In British Columbia in 2004, some 60 citizens, chosen more or less randomly, met weekly for nine months to decide whether to recommend a change in the provincial electoral system, and if so what new system to recommend (Thompson 2008). The recommendation in this case went to a popular referendum, but in some other cases the recommendation could go to a legislature. By all accounts, nearly all the members became remarkably competent in the technical and broader political aspects of electoral systems, and more importantly managed to rise above parochial concerns and concentrate on the long-term public good of the province. When it works well as it did in this case, a citizens' assembly provides a greater degree of legitimacy than a commission, and with little sacrifice of expertise.

In either of its forms – commission or assembly – an office of trusteeship could be established not only at the national but also at the international level. Because, as I emphasized earlier, national boundaries are less significant the further we look into the future, an international trustee would be eventually necessary, even if currently difficult to implement. Some of the proposals to establish a 'guardian' for future generations under the auspices of the United

Nations would create an office that could in effect serve as a trustee (see for example Bruce 1998) – although when formally proposed at the UN, they are always blocked by member nations (Malhotra 1998, pp. 48–49). But none of the objections the opponents raise undermine the principled reasons for institutionalizing in an international body a greater concern for future generations. Some of the objections, however, point to legitimate questions about the responsibilities such a body should have. Proponents of a UN guardian differ among themselves about whether there should be one office or several offices each for different issues, and about what issues the office or offices should address (Stone 1998, pp. 65–79).[11] Some of these disagreements and even some of the opposition could be ameliorated if the guardian is conceived as a trustee for the democratic process.

Whether at the national or international level and whether in the form of a commission or an assembly, these trustees should have some specific powers beyond the important duty of speaking for the interest of future generations in sustaining a robust democratic process. To indicate the range of possibilities, I mention some examples of such powers. (These are intended as merely speculative gestures, not concrete proposals.)

Suspensive interventions: The Trustees would have the authority to stop temporarily actions by the legislature or executive that could be shown seriously impair the capacities of the democratic process in the future. Their authority could be limited to challenges to political procedures – for example, claims that the current legislature or executive unduly limited the discretion of future majorities. The Trustees would not have the authority on their its own to overrule the legislature or the executive. Their challenge would have to be reviewed by an independent judiciary. The power to overrule would be less important than the power to challenge. The Trustees could create an official and prominent forum for deliberating about the effects of current constraints on the democratic capacities of future sovereigns.

Posterity impact statements: The Trustees would require governments to issue statements justifying any adverse effects their actions might have on the democratic capacities of future citizens. These statements are analogous to the environmental impact assessments, now required in the US and European Union countries, which have been shown to be effective if properly administered (Glasson *et al.* 2005, pp. 211–239; Tzoumis and Finegold 2000, pp. 557–578; Dayton 2002, pp. 355–405). Governments would have to show that their actions were necessary to implement the will of current citizens, and that no other actions less restrictive of future citizens could achieve this end at reasonable cost. The statement would have to be defended before an independent authority, perhaps the trustees themselves. The main advantage would be the effect on representatives and other officials, who in making decisions and enacting laws would know that they would have to defend them before other representatives (the Trustees) who care more about the future than the present. The subsequent deliberation – and therefore, in anticipation, the prior action – would be more likely to be more favorable to future citizens than it would have otherwise been.

Democratic balance sheets: Extending the idea of the impact statements, the Trustees could require governments at all levels to report annually the gains and losses in democratic control experienced by their agencies. The reports would be combined to publicize a 'democratic deficit' (or, probably more rarely, a 'democratic surplus'). The aim, as with the impact statements, would be to focus public attention on the question of whether the government is improving the capacity of the people in the future to control their own destiny. Like the budget deficit, the democratic deficit would reflect not only the current condition of the process, but also its future capacity. It would display the state of health of the democratic process that the current citizens leave for future citizens.

Age-differentiated political rights: The Trustees could seek legislation to enhance the political rights of future citizens. Several schemes for changing the distribution of electoral power to give future citizens more power have already been proposed. Limiting the voting age at the top (instead of only at the bottom) and giving parents extra votes may shift the balance of power, and therefore the perspectives of representatives (see, for example, Van Parijs 1998). These schemes do not directly address the problem of distant future generations. They are intended chiefly to ameliorate the tendency toward presentism in the relations between generations that live at the same time. But they could nevertheless serve an important expressive purpose for future generations. They convey the institutional message that representatives should look beyond the present; they would help develop a culture of more forward-looking representation. Even though representatives would still be responding to actual constituents, they would begin to attend more often to the interests of future constituents, and in particular their political rights.

Contingency trust fund: When governmental officials fail to protect the political interests of future generations (whether through negligence or necessity), the Trustees could require the government to provide compensation for the damage done to the democratic process. The compensation would go not to individuals but rather to a trust fund administered by the Trustees. Generally, the grants would be dedicated to improving the democratic process – correcting defects in voting systems, for example. For major problems, the fund would probably be too small to provide adequate compensation. Additional revenues would have to be sought from the legislature. But even if the amounts were small, the symbolic value would be significant. Present democratic representatives would be held retrospectively responsible for the effects of their actions on future democratic representatives.

Constitutional conventions: One important way the democratic capacities of future citizens can be diluted is by entrenched political constraints (such as constitutional prohibitions) that make it difficult for representatives to respond to social and technological changes. The Trustees could from time to time recommend the calling of a constitutional convention in order to keep the government and its constitution in sync with the changing circumstances and needs of its citizens. Such a power could enable a current generation to overcome the dead hand of the past, and reclaim its capacity for competent control. To be sure, many observers are thankful that the convention route to amending the US constitution has never been used.[12] The fear of a runaway convention is strong among both liberals and conservatives. But any constitutional convention the Trustees would recommend should be strictly limited so as to ensure that delegates could deal only with provisions that affect the democratic process (such as voting). Other limitations would include strict qualifications for the delegates, who should be respected citizens with no special attachments to the special interests or the partisan loyalties of a current generation. They too would care only about ‘fame after death’.

International collaboration: The Trustees of each nation would have the power (subject to approval by domestic legislatures) to enter into agreements with their counterparts in other nations to promote the democratic capacities for future citizens without regard to national boundaries. Because national governments may understandably have more concern for their own present (and immediate future) citizens, the Trustees may find more helpful allies in extra-governmental organizations. Strengthening international associations would help respond to the diminishing significance that national boundaries should have the further one looks into the future. A more robust international civil society, especially if populated by groups with long term aims such as preserving the environment and strengthening democratic institutions, would be more likely than most governments to give future sovereigns their due.[13] International NGOs do not assume, as most representatives of governments tend to assume, that the most important consideration is the welfare of citizens in some particular state. This is partly because they are often more cosmopolitan in their outlook with respect to present generations. But the deeper reason they must be more cosmopolitan – not always appreciated by the NGOs themselves – is that the future generations they seek to benefit cannot be located now in any particular state. The distribution of neither future harms and benefits, nor future citizens themselves, will track the contours of present national boundaries.

Conclusion

Hobbes wrote that man is endowed with ‘notable multiplying glasses’, which enlarge his own desires and accomplishments compared to those of others (Hobbes 1991, Book II, chapter xviii). The same may be true of generations: the desires and accomplishments of our own generation loom larger in our field of vision than do those of the generations that will come later. Democratic trusteeship prescribes the institutional equivalent of bifocals: citizens and their representatives today should be able to see clearly not only their own democratic needs but also those of future citizens. We need new institutions, or new devices within old institutions, to provide the clearer perspective that would extend our democratic vision.

Notes

1. One of the most influential surveys of time preferences found that 'people attach less importance to saving lives in the future than to saving lives today'. See Cropper *et al.* (1992, 1994). Subsequent studies have shown that at least some of the heavy discounting of future lives is due to framing effects and other variations in the questions asked in the surveys. See Johannesson (1997) and Frederick (2003).
2. The earliest version of this rationale was presented by Aristotle in what is sometimes called the 'shoes-pinching argument' (Aristotle 1967, Bk. III, 128.b24).
3. For a sample of various philosophical approaches to the problem of future generations, see Sikora and Barry (1979); Barry (1989a); Laslett and Fishkin (1992); De-Shalit (1995); and Beckerman and Pasek (2001).
4. See for example Laslett (1992).
5. 'It is true that we do not know what the precise tastes of our remote descendants will be, but they are unlikely to include a desire for skin cancer, soil erosion, or the inundation of all low-lying areas as a result of the melting of the ice-caps' (Barry 1989a, p. 500).
6. The most trenchant discussion of this general problem is in Barry (1989a, pp. 496–510). On the problem of the identity of future persons, see Parfit (1983, 1986, pp. 351–453).
7. Choosing a just savings rate or even a discount rate for the distant future is notoriously difficult. See for example Broome (1992) and Barry (1989a, pp. 502–506).
8. This argument for a just savings principle was already present in certain passages in the statement of Rawls's initial theory: the principle, Rawls writes, is partly based on 'an estimate that seems fair from both sides, with due allowance made for the improvement in their circumstances' (1971, p. 289).
9. For a proposed escape from the problem, see Kumar (2003).
10. Two of the most specific proposals for legislative representation are: Dobson (1996) and Ekeli (2005). Ekeli presents his more developed proposal partly in critical response to Dobson's.
11. Stone provides the most systematic set of questions that any proposed reform of this type would have to address.
12. On the risks and benefits of constitutional conventions (or constituent assemblies), see Fafard and Reid (1991), Weber and Perry (1989), and Caplan (1988).
13. For recent views of the prospects for international civil society, see Keane (2003), Chandler (2004), and Slaughter (2004, esp. pp. 131–165). Specifically on NGOs (with a useful bibliography) is Simmons (1998).

References

Aristotle, 1967. *Politics,* trans. H. Rackham. Cambridge MA: Harvard University Press.

Barry, B.M., 1989a. Justice between generations. *In*: B.M. Barry. *Democracy, power and justice.* Oxford: Clarendon Press, 494–510.

Barry, B.M., 1989b. *Theories of justice.* Berkeley, CA: University of California Press.

Beckerman, W. and Pasek, J., 2001. *Justice, posterity, and the environment.* Oxford: Oxford University Press.

Biddle, B.J., 1986. Recent developments in role theory. *Annual review of sociology,* 12, 67–92.

Broome, J., 1992. *Counting the cost of global warming.* Cambridge: White Horse Press.

Bruce, M., 1998. A draft instrument establishing the role of a guardian. *In:* E. Agius and S. Busuttil, eds. *Future generations and international law.* London: Earthscan, 163–165.

Caplan, R., 1988. *Constitutional brinksmanship: amending the constitution by national convention.* New York: Oxford University Press.

Chandler, D., 2004. *Constructing global civil society: morality and power in international relations.* London: Palgrave Macmillan.

Cornell, T.J., 1995. *The beginnings of Rome.* London: Routledge.

Cropper, M., Aydede, S. and Portney, P., 1992. Rates of time preference for saving lives. *American economic review,* 82 (2), 469–472.

Cropper, M., Aydede, S. and Portney, P., 1994. Preferences for life saving programs: how the public discounts time and age. *Journal of risk and uncertainty,* 8 (3), 243–65.

Dayton, D., 2002. Evaluating environmental impact statements as communicative action. *Journal of business and technical communication,* 16 (4), 355–405.

De-Shalit, A., 1995. *Why posterity matters: environmental policies and future generations.* London: Routledge.

Dobson, A., 1996. Representative democracy and the environment. *In:* W.M. Lafferty and J. Meadowcroft, eds. *Democracy and the environment.* Cheltenham: Edward Elgar, 124–139.

Ekeli, K.S., 2005. Representative democracy and future generations. *In:* F. Tersman, ed. *Democracy unbound: basic explorations*, *Stockholm studies in democratic theory,* Vol. 1, Stockholm: Stockholm University, 141–165.

Fafard, P. and Reid, D.R., 1991. *Constituent assemblies: a comparative survey.* Kingston, Ontario: Institute of Intergovernmental Relations, Queen's University.

Frederick, S., 2003. Measuring intergenerational time preference: *are* future lives valued less? *Journal of risk and uncertainty,* 26 (1), 39–53.

Gehlbach, H., 2004. A new perspective on perspective taking. *Educational psychology review,* 16 (3), 207–234.

Glasson, J., Therivel, R. and Chadwick, A., 2005. *Introduction to environmental impact assessment,* 3rd ed. Abingdon: Routledge.

Hobbes, T., 1991. *Leviathan,* ed. R. Tuck. Cambridge: Cambridge University Press.

Homo, L., 1996. *Roman political institutions.* London: Routledge.

Ilgen, D.R. and Hollenbeck, J.R., 1991. The structure of work: job design and roles. *In:* M.D. Dunette and L.M. Hough, eds. *Handbook of industrial and organizational psychology,* vol. 2. Palo Alto, CA: Consulting Psychologists Press, 165–207.

Johannesson, M., 1997. Saving lives in the present versus saving lives in the future – is there a framing effect? *Journal of risk and uncertainty,* 15 (2), 167–176.

Keane, J., 2003. *Global civil society?* Cambridge: Cambridge University Press.

Kumar, R., 2003. Who can be wronged? *Philosophy & public affairs,* 31 (2), 99–118.
Laslett, P., 1992. Is there a generational contract? *In:* P. Laslett and J. Fishkin, eds. *Justice between age groups and generations.* New Haven: Yale University Press, 25–47.
Laslett, P. and Fishkin, J., eds., 1992. *Justice between age groups and generations.* New Haven: Yale University Press.
Locke, J., 1965. *Two treatises of government,* ed. P. Laslett. New York: New American Library.
Malhotra, A., 1998. A commentary on the status of future generations as a subject of international law. *In:* E. Agius and S. Busuttil, eds. *Future generations and international law.* London: Earthscan.
Mill, J.S., 1977. *Considerations on representative government. In:* J.M. Robson, ed., *Essays on politics and society, collected works.* Toronto: University of Toronto Press.
Parfit, D., 1983. The further future: the identity problem. *In*: D. MacLean and P.G. Brown, eds., *Energy and the future.* Totowa, NJ: Rowman and Littlefield, 166–179.
Parfit, D., 1986. *Reasons and persons.* Oxford: Oxford University Press.
Pitkin, H., 1967. *Concept of representation.* Berkeley: University of California Press.
Rawls, J., 1971. *A theory of justice.* Cambridge, MA: Harvard University Press.
Rawls, J., 1993. *Political liberalism.* New York: Columbia University Press.
Rawls, J., 2001. *Justice as fairness: a restatement,* ed. E. Kelly. Cambridge, MA: Harvard University Press.
Ryberg, J., *et al.*, 2006. The repugnant conclusion. *The Stanford encyclopedia of philosophy,* ed., Edward N. Zalta, at http://plato.stanford.edu/archives/spr2006/entries/repugnant-conclusion/.
Sikora, R.I. and Barry, B.M., eds. 1979. *Obligations to future generations.* Philadelphia: Temple University Press.
Simmons, P.J., 1998. Learning to live with NGOs. *Foreign policy,* 112, 82–96.
Slaughter, A.M., 2004. *A new world order.* Princeton, NJ: Princeton University Press.
Staveley, E.S., 1953. The significance of the consular tribunate. *Journal of Roman studies,* 43, 30–36.
Stone, C., 1998. Safeguarding future generations. *In*: E. Agius and S. Busuttil, eds. *Future generations and international law.* London: Earthscan.
Strijbos, J.W., *et al.* 2003. The effect of roles on group efficiency. *In*: B. Wasson, *et al.*, eds. *International conference on computer support for collaborative learning.* Bergen: Intermedia.
Thompson, D., 2004. *Restoring responsibility.* Cambridge: Cambridge University Press.
Thompson, D., 2008. Who should govern who governs? The role of citizens in reforming the electoral system. *In*: M. Warren and H. Pearse, eds. *Designing deliberative democracy: the British Columbia citizens' assembly.* Cambridge: Cambridge University Press, 20–49.
Tzoumis, K. and Finegold, L., 2000. Looking at the quality of draft environmental impact statements over time in the United Sates: have ratings improved?. *Environmental impact assessment review,* 20 (5), 557–578.
Van Parijs, P., 1998. The disfranchisement of the elderly, and other attempts to secure intergenerational justice. *Philosophy & public affairs,* 27 (3), 292–333.
Weber, P. and Perry, B., 1989. *Unfounded fears: myths and realities of a constitutional convention.* New York: Greenwood Press.

Justice, legitimacy, and constitutional rights

Wilfried Hinsch

RWTH Aachen University, Germany

There is a tension between the idea of popular sovereignty and our understanding that basic constitutional rights and liberties have a normative authority which is independent from the results of democratic decision-making procedures. On the one hand there is the claim that the content of political justice, at least as far as the basic liberties are concerned, is to be fixed solely by substantive moral and political argument, while on the other there is the claim that it is the people who determine the specific scheme of basic liberties that they live under. The apparent tension between the two claims can be resolved by introducing, firstly, a distinction between the concept of justice and the concept of legitimacy and, secondly, between proto-rights and constitutional rights. Unlike constitutional rights, proto-rights are moral, not legal, rights, and they are less specific than constitutional rights: one set of proto-rights allows for various schemes of legal constitutional rights. Proto-rights are part of the principles of justice and can be established only by substantive argument while constitutional rights have to be established by the procedures of democratic legitimization, and, therefore, they are a result of the exercise of popular sovereignty. The correlated distinctions between justice and legitimacy, and between proto-rights and constitutional rights, allow us to specify the scope of the two claims and, hence, to affirm both simultaneously. The philosophical and legal relevance of the distinctions made is elucidated by a brief discussion of the constitutional rights of freedom of speech in the US and Germany.

Two concepts of legitimacy

It is helpful to distinguish between concepts of legitimacy and conceptions of legitimacy.[1] A concept of legitimacy gives us the basic meaning of the term 'legitimate' and tells us what we say about, e.g., a social rule or a political decision, when we call it legitimate. It also specifies the role of 'legitimacy' in social theory and practical political deliberation. Conceptions of legitimacy, on the other hand, specify the criteria that have to be met by a rule or decision in order to actually be legitimate in the relevant sense.

Moreover, it is important to distinguish clearly between two different concepts of legitimacy: the empirical concept of the social sciences and the normative concept of political philosophy. It seems that the empirical and the normative concept of legitimacy are easily confused. Political commentators are prone to vacillate between them. There are two reasons for this. First, the empirical and the normative concepts have in common that both take 'legitimacy', 'legitimate', and their cognates to be terms that indicate normative status. In one way or other, legitimate rules and decisions are characterized by the fact that they have (or that they are believed to have) *normative authority* (cf. Flathman 1993, p. 527). They are conceived of as 'mandatory' or 'binding' by those who ascribe legitimacy to them.[2] Second, in line with both concepts, 'legitimacy' applies primarily in the domain of the political and relates to the exercise of coercive state power. Assuming that legitimate rules and decisions are mandatory, we think it appropriate that they be *enforced* by state action should that prove necessary. In any case, legitimacy is taken to be a necessary condition of any justifiable use of state power.

We ascribe legitimacy to monarchs, national and international regimes, laws, or parliamentary decisions. I shall confine myself mainly to discussing the legitimacy of norms. This helps to keep things manageable. Moreover, norms seem to have a certain priority. Whatever we may wish to call legitimate in the domain of the political is either itself a norm – or something made up of norms like institutional arrangements – or it is legitimate in virtue of being in conformity with certain norms. Hence, to understand the legitimacy of norms is basic to understanding political legitimacy in general.[3]

The empirical concept of legitimacy goes back to Max Weber, whose understanding of it is still looming large in the social sciences and also enjoys some prominence among political analysts and commentators. There are, however, alternative empirical conceptions; for instance, Niklas Luhmann's account of procedural legitimacy or Beetham's conception of 'legitimacy in context'. Both are explicitly critical of Weber but share the latter's concern with empirical meaning and explanation (cf. Luhmann 1969, chap. 1, section 2; Beetham 1991, ch. 1). For the purpose of conceptual clarification, a basic understanding of Weber's conception of legitimacy should suffice.[4] Roughly speaking, Weber's view is that a norm or an institutional arrangement is legitimate if, *as a matter of fact*, it finds the approval of those who are supposed to live in this group. 'Approval' in this context is to be understood as 'sincere recognition' of a norm as providing an appropriate standard of conduct that must be complied with because it is the correct or right standard and not only because of the threat of social sanctions. Sincere approval of norms constitutive for a social order by the participants turns an order into what Weber called *geltende Ordnung*, i.e., into an order that has normative authority for those involved. To call an institutional arrangement legitimate thus implies that there are people who sincerely believe that these arrangements should regulate their conduct irrespective of external sanctions. Legitimate arrangements are, therefore, arrangements that receive voluntary support. Since no political regime or social order could persist without a fairly high level of unenforced compliance with its rules, the empirical understanding of legitimacy naturally occupies a central place in explanatory theories of social order.

Notwithstanding the air of higher moral ambition that goes with the term 'legitimacy', the empirical concept does not imply any evaluative or normative commitment on the side of those who, as external observers, use it to describe a social order. One may maintain that a particular institutional arrangement is legitimate in the empirical sense – that it finds the approval of those who have to abide by it – and still believe that it is highly unjust or unacceptable for other reasons. 'X is legitimate' taken in the empirical sense implies that there are people who approve of x, but the person making the statement (say, a social scientist) need not be one of them. Given Weber's empirical understanding, to say that an institutional arrangement is a legitimate one is to make a factual claim about the subjective state of mind of particular individuals that belong to one political society. This is how Weber uses the term 'Legitimitäts-Glaube', to refer to the subjective basis which makes the crucial difference between mere social regularity and expediency, on the one side, and social order based on recognized rules, on the other (cf. Weber 1922, §6).[5] Let us now turn to what I have called the normative concept of legitimacy. This is central for the understanding of legitimacy, e.g., in the work of Jürgen Habermas (1988) and John Rawls (1993).

In comparison with Weber's empirical concept the normative concept of legitimacy has two distinctive features. *First*, it involves 'objective' criteria of legitimacy that are alien to Weber's empirical concept. To say that an institutional arrangement is legitimate in the normative sense is not simply to say something about the subjective state of mind of particular individuals. It is to say that the arrangement meets certain substantive requirements – say, standards of justice and rationality expressed in a normative conception of legitimacy – irrespective of whether people believe that they are met or not. Mere factual approval of social rules and institutions, therefore, does not suffice to lend normative legitimacy to them, though in case the approval is sufficiently widespread and stable, the empirical conception of legitimacy may apply. Objectivity here is to be understood in a weak sense. I do not mean to say that the normative concept of legitimacy involves uniquely correct or true criteria of legitimacy. On the contrary, I assume that there are various incompatible, normative *conceptions* of legitimacy specifying different criteria for legitimate norms. In order to employ a normative concept of legitimacy, we are not tied to any particular conception of legitimacy. We do not even need to assume that all but one of these conceptions are wrong. What we do have to presuppose, however, is that legitimacy is not simply a matter of subjective belief but one of actually meeting substantive requirements and, in particular, requirements of basic justice and rationality.

Second, the normative concept of legitimacy involves moral approval on the side of those who apply it to a rule or a system of rules. To say that an institutional arrangement is legitimate in the normative sense is to publicly recognize that it has moral standing, and not simply to report that there are people who believe that the arrangement has moral standing. The difference between normative and empirical legitimacy is that between (1) *expressing* a normative belief that one actually holds and thus *committing* oneself to the normative and inferential consequences of holding that belief and (2) *stating that* there are people who hold that belief without committing oneself to the truth (or validity) of this belief and its inferential consequences, on the other. Normatively speaking, legitimate institutional arrangements are not simply schemes of social rules we (or others) approve of, but arrangements that have normative authority in actually imposing obligations or liabilities on participants. Any particular normative conception of legitimacy, therefore, has to expound its substantive criteria of legitimacy in a way that explains why meeting these criteria actually confers normative authority on norms, institutions, or persons. Thus, a normative conception of democratic legitimacy, for instance, has to be laid out in a way that makes intelligible the normative capacity of democratic procedures to generate morally (as opposed to merely legally) binding rules.

Contractualism

I shall now turn to a particular normative conception of legitimacy, the contractualist conception, and then discuss the relationship between the concepts of justice and legitimacy in the next section. The contractualist ideal of a just and legitimate social order is well expressed by Rawls's conception of a well-ordered society. A well-ordered society is a fair system of social and political cooperation which is effectively regulated by a public conception of justice. More specifically, the following conditions must be fulfilled: (1) all political and social institutions conform to principles of justice which are, after due consideration and for good reasons, recognized by all citizens; (2) everyone acts in conformity with the public conception of justice; (3) everyone knows that conditions (1) and (2) are satisfied, and this is itself common knowledge; and (4) a consensus exists as to the justification of the first principles of justice (Rawls 1993, pp. 35ff, 66f).

Two features of a well-ordered society are worthy of special attention. *First*, all citizens willingly comply with its laws and with fair settlements in general. In a well-ordered society, what game theorists call 'the compliance problem' has been solved. It is a stable and, moreover, highly efficient system of social cooperation. *Second*, the institutions and rules governing such a society are recognized by all citizens as being just and legitimate, not only *de facto* but for 'good reasons'. An easily recognizable causal relationship obtains between the two features since the rational beliefs held by the citizens of a well-ordered society as to the justice and legitimacy of its institutions provide the empirical basis for its stability. Unlike stability-oriented considerations, however, the 'good reasons', which are presumed to justify the citizens' beliefs, raise a genuine philosophical question: the problem of justifying political principles and institutions.

Contractualist conceptions of justice and legitimacy are based on a notion of *public justification.*[6] Presupposing the idea of free and equal democratic citizenship, it is assumed that all members of a society have an equal claim to live in a society the norms and institutions of which they can freely endorse in the light of their well-considered beliefs and interests. To expect a person to comply with rules that must seem arbitrary from her point of view is normally inconsistent with recognizing her as a free and equal person with a firm intention to cooperate fairly, and it is unreasonable to expect a person to recognize (as opposed to merely comply with) rules that have been established against her will and which are arbitrary or partial from her point of view. The rules of fair social cooperation are ideally rules that can be rationally accepted by all citizens who are supposed to comply with them.

The requirement of publicity incorporated in the idea of a well-ordered society may seem important for several reasons, one of which is stability. Stable political and social cooperation presupposes that the parties involved not only recognize and obey certain rules but that they also be aware of the fact that each of them is doing so. Moreover, in recognizing fair principles of cooperation, citizens make manifest to one another that they respect each other as partners with equal rights, which again contributes to stability. More importantly, publicity and public justification matter because of the difficulties in realizing the value of autonomy in pluralistic societies. From the standpoint of a contractualist understanding of justice, what is of primary importance is not that only publicly recognized norms are capable of establishing a stable scheme of cooperation. What matters primarily is that citizens as autonomous moral agents have a claim that the norms regulating their mutual affairs be norms they can reasonably accept in the light of their well-considered beliefs and interests. Given the fact of pluralism, the requirement of public justification means that basic norms of a well-ordered society must secure the consent of citizens whose moral, philosophical, and religious views are at least partially incompatible. It is thus not inconceivable that no publicly justified political principles can be found.

If the contractualist ideal of a just and legitimate political order is to amount to more than an elusive utopia, two things must be shown: *First*, that principles of political justice can be formulated upon which citizens who hold incompatible moral and religious views might reasonably be expected to agree, and, *second*, that the content of these principles can be specified through the processes of democratic decision-making in such a way that the resulting laws and institutions may also be expected to find reasonable approval. The first problem concerns the most basic normative foundations of a well-ordered society. It is resolved when a conception of political justice is found which can be publicly justified. The second problem concerns the legitimization of particular political decisions regarding the concrete institutional set-up of a well-ordered society. From a contractualist point of view, the latter problem is solved once a conception of political decision-making is found that is capable of lending normative authority to specific norms that go well beyond basic moral principles and address concrete questions of social organization.

Justice vs. legitimacy

'Justice' and 'legitimacy', when applied to political institutions, are often treated as interchangeable concepts. This seems reasonable insofar as legitimate political decisions are first and foremost decisions that meet the most basic requirements of political justice. We should be aware of the fact, however, that we are dealing with two normatively distinct, if related, concepts. Principles of political justice are identified by means of *rational argumentation* which, in accordance with the contractualist approach, takes the form of a public justification of norms. If, after due consideration of all the relevant facts, values, and principles, a reasonable disagreement concerning first principles of justice for political institutions persisted, then the notion of political justice would, for precisely this reason, remain indeterminate and empty. In that case, we would either have to forgo the attempt to establish institutions that are morally binding for all or continue on the basis of a mere *modus vivendi*. Hence the contractualist conception of justice presupposes that there are at least some basic principles and norms that are beyond reasonable disagreement.

But even if one were to succeed in identifying publicly recognized principles of justice, it would be mere fancy to expect that the reasonable consensus obtained could be extended to cover the whole range of norms and institutional arrangements that constitute a particular political order, let alone to cover each and every single political decision. Even under the admittedly idealized condition that the process of collective decision-making be fully rational and reasonable, we must face the fact that in many cases justified differences of opinion will continue to exist as to how social relations should be regulated as expediently and fairly as possible. In other words, we must take into account the possibility of *reasonable* disagreement at all levels of political argument and decision-making. Let us say that, as a matter of ideal theory, we have a situation of reasonable disagreement if the following asymmetry obtains: all parties involved have sufficiently strong rationally and morally sustainable reasons to support their respective claims and positions, but no party is capable of putting forward generally acknowledged reasons strong enough to eliminate all competing claims and positions of the other parties. Given reasonable pluralism, any contractualist political or moral theory that proceeds from the idea of publicly justified norms must, therefore, accommodate this fundamental possibility and incorporate *non-argumentative* forms of collective decision-making in order to meet the requirements of public justification.

Ex hypothesi in a situation of reasonable disagreement no further argument could yield a reasoned consensus on a contested question. Whenever an agreement not to agree would not do, because there is no way to avoid a collectively binding regulation, the argumentative deadlock in cases of reasonable disagreement is a reason to employ non-argumentative forms of collective decision-making (e.g., setting up a lottery or having a vote). In view of the contractualist requirement of public justification, this seems perfectly reasonable as long as the chosen non-argumentative procedure is sufficiently efficient and fair and finds the approval of those involved. Given the omnipresence of reasonable disagreement and given the unavoidability of a collectively binding decision, all parties involved have a reason to accept fair and effective forms of non-argumentative decision making and to recognize the resulting decisions as publicly justified and binding. The contractualist idea of public justification thus includes argumentative and non-argumentative parts, the former being concerned with questions of political justice, the latter with questions of legitimacy.

If all moral and political disagreement could, at least in principle, be traced back to factual errors or logical inconsistencies, a non-argumentative procedure like voting could, with regard to the moral justification of rules, never be more than a pragmatic way of dealing with ignorance, irrationality, or limited resources of other kinds. Sure enough, given the constraints of real life, voting even then would provide us with a morally attractive way of dealing with disagreements and conflict. Normally, voting is morally preferable to having a fight, and most of the time the attractions of secession are limited too. Taking a pragmatic perspective, however, the mere fact that a vote with a certain result was taken would, *by itself*, not make the result, say a particular regulation, a morally appropriate or correct result. If we proceed from the idea of reasonable disagreement, however, voting as a non-argumentative step in collective decision-making becomes a necessary part of the public justification of social arrangements and does indeed endow these arrangements with moral standing and normative authority.

The notion of what is politically legitimate, as distinct from what is politically just is hence only partially determined by rational argumentation. As far as constitutional democracies are concerned, its content is fixed to a much greater extent by *voting*, typically by majority decision. As a result, political legislation may in many cases be put legitimately into effect, against which reasonable objections can be raised, at least on the part of some citizens. Such controversial decisions cannot be fully justified on the basis of substantive argument alone but only by appealing to the fact that they are the result of a fair decision-making process, recourse to which appears publicly justified under the given conditions.

A conception of normative legitimacy, therefore, presupposes an account of the conditions under which collectively binding decisions can be reached by the factual working of non-argumentative procedures such as voting. To say, then, that a norm is legitimate (normatively speaking) is to say not only that the norm meets certain requirements of basic justice but also that it has a certain *factual pedigree*. The factual or pedigree element is crucial for a concept of normative legitimacy and hence shared by all conceptions of normative legitimacy, be they as far apart as the dynastic conception of legitimacy of, say, a Talleyrand and the radical democratic conception of a Rousseau.

Still, the procedural, non-argumentative part of legitimacy and its argumentative, non-procedural part that relates to the basic requirements of political justice do not have equal standing. Given the contractualist idea of public justification, rational argumentation is prior to all non-argumentative forms of decision-making. Whether a particular political procedure (say majority vote) is a fair procedure and meets the requirements of political justice is not itself to be settled by voting. It is to be settled by arguments that involve substantive notions of political justice. The public justification of social norms and institutional arrangements by means of non-argumentative procedures thus presupposes a reasoned consensus on the principles of justice that specify ideas of political equality, determine the rights of political participation, and also define the bounds within which collective decisions may intervene with individual liberty.

Proto-rights

Having discussed the concepts of justice and legitimacy in the last section, we are now in a position to apply the distinction between the two concepts to a notorious difficulty found in liberal theories of constitutional democracy. It is the function of the *constitution* of a democratic society to set up an institutional framework for collective decision-making and to enunciate the conditions under which voting as a non-argumentative procedure may issue in legitimate legislation, i.e., in political decisions that have normative authority and impose corresponding obligations or liabilities. The contractualist ideal of political legitimacy would then be realized only to the extent that concrete political decisions are arrived at in conformity with a constitution that can be publicly justified. See, e.g., Rawls's *liberal principle of legitimacy*:

> our exercise of political power is fully proper only when it is exercised in accordance with a constitution the essentials of which all citizens as free and equal may be expected to endorse in the light of principles and ideals acceptable to their common human reason. (Rawls 1993, p. 137)

A serious flaw of this formulation of liberal legitimacy is that it already presupposes a constitution as a given framework for the legitimate exercise of political power. The principle thus fails to account for what gives legitimacy to the political constitution of a society itself. Moreover, Jürgen Habermas has pointed out that there is an unresolved tension here between the principle of popular sovereignty and the idea (found in the work of Rawls and others) that – as a matter of political justice – there are certain constitutional liberties and rights that have a normative authority irrespective of popular sovereignty (cf. Habermas 1995). Indeed, if we assume – in line with the mainstream of contemporary political philosophy – that for the most part the requirements of political justice are given by a set of basic civil and political liberties, we have to conclude that being part of the content of political justice, the content of these basic liberties cannot be fixed by vote or any other form of non-argumentative decision-making. Questions of justice are to be settled by argument and not by vote. This, however, would mean that the most important elements of modern liberal constitutions – the basic political and liberal rights incorporated in these constitutions – remain excluded from the processes of democratic decision-making and hence out of reach of popular sovereignty. The philosopher kings, it seems, have taken over the *pouvoir constituante,* leaving the democratic sovereign nothing but to work out the legal details of political organization.

It seems possible, however, to address the misgivings of Habermas by denying that the rights and liberties guaranteed by Rawls's first principle are actually *constitutional* rights. (Keep in mind, though, that Rawls takes these basic rights and liberties to be constitutional rights: 1993, pp. 228f) Pursuing this line of argument, I propose to distinguish between *proto-rights* and *constitutional rights*. Proto-rights are part of the content of principles of justice and can be established within a theory of political justice solely by substantive philosophical argument. Constitutional rights, on the other hand, are those (rights) familiar from the political constitutions of liberal democracies. They have been established by the procedures of democratic legitimization and hence may be seen as a result of the exercise of popular sovereignty. Proto-rights and constitutional rights differ in various regards.

First, proto-rights are moral and not legal rights. Individuals have them independently of whether these rights are publicly and institutionally recognized in their society or not. *Second*, proto-rights are established solely by means of substantive philosophical argument and not by any kind of a legislative procedure that involves non-argumentative steps of collective decision making. *Thirdly*, proto-rights are non-institutional rights in the sense that individuals can have them even though these rights are not backed up by institutional structures that guarantee their appropriate administration and enforcement. *Finally*, proto-rights are less specific than constitutional rights in the sense that different constitutional rights (say, of freedom of speech) may guarantee the same proto-right.

As opposed to the proto-rights incorporated in first principles of political justice, constitutional rights are (1) legal rights that are (2) based not only on arguments but also on procedures of constitutional law-making that (in a democracy) typically involve voting as a non-argumentative way of collective decision-making. Furthermore, (3) constitutional rights are institutional rights backed up by a framework of legal structures that guarantee their appropriate administration and enforcement. And (4) they are more specific than proto-rights in the sense that different constitutional rights may protect the same proto-rights.

The last point deserves our special attention because it allows to resolve the alleged conflict that radical democrats such as Jürgen Habermas see between the claim of political philosophy that the content of political justice – insofar as the basic liberties are concerned – is to be fixed solely by substantive moral argument, and the claim of popular sovereignty that it is the people who determine (say, in a constitutional convention) the specific scheme of basic liberties for its own political order. If we assume that schemes of constitutional rights are always more specific than the proto-rights of political justice, then these schemes cannot be fully specified by means of those arguments providing the basis of the proto-rights. Furthermore, if all the constitutional schemes that incorporate the proto-rights of political justice are supposed to be equally just schemes, then there may be reasonable disagreement as to which specific scheme should be established in a particular society. In order to give normative authority to any such scheme, we therefore need a non-argumentative way of collective decision-making which, if we believe that there are equal proto-rights of political participation in a society of free and equal moral persons, will be a procedure of democratic decision-making.

Freedom of speech

I shall now illustrate the legal and philosophical relevance of the distinction between proto-rights and constitutional rights by discussing briefly the constitutional rights of freedom of speech in the US and in Germany. Freedom of speech and freedom of the press is guaranteed in plain words and without restriction by the US constitution's First Amendment of 1791: 'Congress shall make no law [...] abridging the freedom of speech, or of the press'. The formulations in Article 5 of Germany's *Grundgesetz* of 1949 are more differentiated. They reflect the technological advances that have changed the forms of public exchange since the eighteenth century. Article 5, paragraph 1, guarantees the right to free expression and dissemination of opinions ‘in speech, writing and pictures’, freedom of press and freedom of ‘reporting by means of broadcasts and films’ as well as freedom to ‘inform oneself without hindrance from generally accessible sources’. The German *Grundgesetz* (the constitution of the Federal German Republic), however, does not give a guarantee without qualifications. Article 5, paragraph 2, specifies as ‘limits’ to these freedoms the general laws, the protection of young persons, and the right to personal honour.

Nevertheless, the obvious differences in the wording of the two constitutional texts do not in themselves justify the conclusion that the constitutional rights guaranteed therein are not the same. In comparing the constitutional rights of different countries, we must take into account not only the relevant constitutional documents but also established institutional practices of law interpretation and law enforcement. If we do this, it appears there are, indeed, important commonalties between the US and the German rights to freedom of speech, but it also becomes obvious that significant differences exist.[7]

Even though the First Amendment does not mention broadcasts and films, the US Supreme Court did interpret the term ‘speech’ in the twentieth century consistently in a way that included the expression of opinion in films, radio, and also in television (cf. Brugger 2001, pp. 157f.). Moreover, freedom of speech does not enjoy absolute protection in the US constitution, either. In *Virginia vs. Black et al.* (538 US 1ff., 2003), the Supreme Court rules, for example, that speech aiming at harassment or intimidation of fellow citizens does not enjoy the protection of the US constitution.

Three congruencies of US and German constitutional freedom of speech rights seem to be of particular importance in this context. *First*, in both constitutions, freedom of speech occupies a prominent position, and the extensive protection of public speech is regarded as an indispensable prerequisite of a free and democratic society. *Second*, in both constitutional orders freedom of speech is treated not only as a necessary condition of democratic self-government but also as an indispensable prerequisite for the development of the human personality, while, in the reasons stated in court decisions, it is the importance of freedom of speech for democracy that is often privileged.[8] *Third* and last, it holds for both orders that restrictions on freedom of speech in concrete cases may not be justified directly by the content of speech but require that hazards for other constitutional values – e.g., the public order or (in Germany) human dignity – be proven to be immediately involved. In particular, speech may not be restricted only because it expresses controversial political opinions or is critical of government.

Without going into greater detail here, these commonalties support the idea that, both in the US and in Germany, the same proto-right of freedom of speech is protected by constitutional regulations. These important commonalties go along, however, with a number of equally important discrepancies.

Freedom of speech together with freedom of conscience and religion introduce the American Bill of Rights and are clearly brought to bear in the standing jurisdiction of the Supreme Court as a paramount constitutional value. In the ordering of the German *Grundgesetz*, however, freedom of speech is subordinate to human dignity as protected in Article 1. Indeed, the Federal Constitutional Court treats protection of freedom of opinion (like the protection of all other basic freedoms as well) as an aspect of the right to human dignity. But freedom of speech is thereby just one aspect among many, and it is often restricted on the basis of other human dignity considerations (especially the protection of personal honour and reputation) in a way that would be unconstitutional in the US (cf. Nolte 1990; Grimm 1995, p. 1703). In 1987, the Federal Constitutional Court ruled, for example, that it was an undue violation of Franz Josef Strauß' (a German-Bavarian politician) personality rights to portray him as a pig copulating with other pigs wearing judicial robes. Around the same time, however, the Supreme Court, in *Hustler Magazine vs. Falwell* (485 US 46, 1988), ruled that a caricature of the Reverend Jerry Falwell (in those days a political leader of the so-called 'Moral Majority'), in which he was portrayed as drunk and having sex with his mother in a garden shed, was an exercise of the freedom of speech protected by the Bill of Rights.[9]

In the US – contrary to Germany – substantially defamatory statements regarding political opinions are protected even if they are false on factual counts, as long as they are not made in bad faith. Thus – as the Supreme Court states in *New York Times vs. Sullivan* (376 US 254, 1964) – the critical faculty of the press which is essential for a democratic public is ensured even in marginal cases (cf. Tribe 1988, pp. 862ff).

Whereas something like the defamation of groups is unknown in US constitutional law, freedom of opinion has been repeatedly restricted by the jurisdiction of the German Constitutional Court in order to protect the personality rights of members of minorities against libel and slander that are not aimed directly at individuals and their rights but at groups. The threat of punishment – which is in accordance with the German constitution – for the *corpus delicti* 'incitement' (*Volksverhetzung*) in §130, German penal code, belongs also to this context.

A further important difference concerns the expression and dissemination of radical political beliefs. The German *Grundgesetz* embodies the concept of a 'militant' or 'well-fortified' democracy (*streitbare Demokratie)*. After the experience of the breakdown of the Weimar Republic and the atrocities of the National Socialists, individual liberties shall, in case of emergency, be subordinated to the exigencies of defending a free and democratic basic order. In the American/US system, even seditious libel and propaganda of revolutionary and subversive doctrines fall under the protection of freedom of speech. A statutory or judicial ban of national socialist propaganda – as it has been practiced in Germany since the end of World War II – could not be sustained before the US Supreme Court (cf. Eberle & Kommers 2002, p. 202).

What these comparisons illustrate is that the constitutional right to freedom of speech protected by positive law in the US – notwithstanding the mentioned commonalties – can obviously not be the same constitutional right as the one which – under the same title – is protected by the German Constitutional Court. For the set of actions, or rather of action types, that are protected in the two law systems, respectively, are not coextensive – even though they overlap in central areas. The comparisons also show to what degree the constitutional design of proto-right notions of freedom of speech in the two countries depend on specific national experiences and circumstances. What this suggests is that the equal right to freedom of speech that, as part of Rawls's first principle, is a requirement of political justice cannot be identical with the rights of freedom of speech familiar from liberal democratic constitutions. All we can say at the moment (at least if all the involved constitutions are just) is that citizens who enjoy the US or the German constitutional right of freedom of speech also enjoy the right that is part of the content of Rawls's first principle of justice. If we conceive of constitutional rights as *bundles of more specific rights,* we may say that the US and the German 'freedom of speech bundle' overlap and that all specific freedom of speech rights that are necessary prerequisites of political justice lie in the overlapping section.

Conclusions

Political justice and democratic legitimacy are two equally necessary and mutually dependent components of a well-ordered society that is effectively regulated by publicly justified principles and norms. Given the fact of reasonable pluralism, the proto-rights of political justice, which are identified by means of moral argument, are an insufficient basis for the public justification of constitutional rights and other specific social norms. By themselves, they do not provide a basis for endowing constitutional rights and other norms with legitimate normative authority. The process of the public justification of norms has to be a two-level procedure that incorporates argumentative and non-argumentative ways of collective decision-making. There can be no legitimate constitution with normative authority that does not contain the proto-rights of publicly justified principles of political justice. And there cannot be a legitimate constitution that has not been subject to an adequately framed democratic process which involves voting procedures as a fair and rational way of resolving reasonable disagreements in matters of political justice and expediency.

It is beyond the scope of this article to discuss in any detail the extent to which the US and German constitution actually meet the demands of political justice with regard to their freedom of speech clauses. It seems clear to me, however, that, in principle, as far as freedom of speech is concerned, both constitutions may be considered to be basically just constitutions, notwithstanding the fact that they do not contain the same constitutional rights of freedom of speech. Given the distinction between proto-rights and constitutional rights, both constitutions are just constitutions if, and only if, they effectively protect the same proto-rights that partly define political justice the content of which is not subject to the procedures of political decision-making. Constitutional rights, on the other hand – such as the freedom of speech rights we find in the US and German constitutions – may be seen as institutionalized proto-rights in need of democratic legitimization. Their constitutional specification is highly dependent on the historical, cultural, and institutional context of a particular political society and hence goes beyond what could be justified solely in terms of arguments that do not allow for reasonable disagreement. To respond to the misgivings Habermas expressed about Rawls's understanding of constitutional democracy, we are now in a position to say that constitutional rights – along with all other legal rights – obtain normative authority only by means of a process of political legitimization, but only on the assumption that this process meets the demands of the proto-rights which are part of the content of political justice, which, in turn, is not subject to the outcomes of political procedures.

Notes

1. The explicit distinction between 'concepts' and 'conceptions' has been introduced by John Rawls (1993, p. 14n; 1999, p. 5) who gives credit for it to Herbert Hart (1994, p. 160).
2. For a general account of authority, see Joseph Raz (1979, 1986, part one). Note, however, that Raz takes authority to be a 'normative power', viz. the capacity of an agent to change the 'normative situation' of others. Given this understanding of authority as a power, it goes without saying that only agents can have authority. Throughout this paper I shall use 'authority' in a broader sense, as explained in the text, and ascribe authority not only to agents but also to other things such as rules, principles, and decisions.
3. In saying this, I am well aware of the fact that in academic discussions or public political discourse 'legitimate norm' is rarely used and that 'legitimate government', 'legitimate authority', or 'legitimate ruler' are far more common expressions. Still, for reasons indicated in the text and because of the specific account of legitimacy outlined in this paper, I take norms to be the elementary bearers of legitimacy.
4. For the basics, see Weber (1922, Kap. 1, §§ 5–7). A detailed discussion of Weber's conception is beyond the scope of this paper.
5. Robert Dahl makes the same point when he distinguishes between an ethical and a psychological sense of 'legitimacy' and explains that the latter simply is 'a belief in the rightness' of a decision or process of decision making (Dahl 1956, p. 47, see footnote; cf. for the same point also Lipset 1958, p. 86). Note, however, that Beetham's empirical conception goes beyond subjective belief and also involves contextually defined substantive criteria of legitimacy (1991, ch. 1).
6. See Rawls (1993, lectures I & VI; 1999, p. 115); Hinsch (2002, chap. 5).
7. My still rather rhapsodic comparison between the constitutional law of free speech in the USA and Germany has greatly benefited from Tribe (1988, pp. 185ff.), Kommers (1989, pp. 366ff.) Grimm (1995), and Eberle and Kommers (2002).

8. For Germany see the discussion of these two aspects of freedom of speech in Glaeser (1972, esp. pp. 83f.) and Grimm (1995, p. 1698).
9. See the comparison of the Strauß decision of the German constitutional court with *Hustler Magazin vs. Falwell* in Nolte (1988) and Eberle and Kommers (2002, pp. 207f).

References

Beetham, D., 1991. *The legitimation of power.* London: Palgrave Macmillan.

Brugger, W., 2001. *Einführung in das öffentliche Recht der USA.* 2nd ed. München: C. H. Beck.

Dahl, R.A., 1956. *A preface to democratic theory.* Chicago: University of Chicago Press.

Eberle, E.J. and Kommers, P., 2002. *Dignity and liberty: constitutional visions in Germany and the United States.* London: Greenwood Press.

Flathman, R.E., 1993. Legitimacy. *In:* R. Goodin and P. Pettit, eds. *A companion to contemporary political philosophy.* Cambridge: Blackwell, 527–533.

Glaeser, W.S., 1972. Die Meinungsfreiheit in der Rechtssprechung des Bundesverfassungsgerichts. *Archiv des öffentlichen Rechts,* 97, 60–123 (Part 1) and 276–298 (Part 2).

Grimm, D., 1995. Die Meinungsfreiheit in der Rechtssprechung des Bundesverfassungsgerichts, *Neue Juristische Wochenschrift,* 27, 1697–1776.

Habermas, J., 1988. Law and morality. *In: The Tanner lectures on human values VIII.* Salt Lake City: University of Utah Press, 217–279.

Habermas, J., 1995. Reconciliation through the public use of reason: remarks on John Rawls's *Political liberalism. The journal of philosophy,* XCII, 109–131.

Hart, H.L.A., 1994. *The concept of law.* 2nd ed. Oxford: Oxford University Press.

Hinsch, W., 2002. *Gerechtfertigte Ungleichheiten. Grundsätze sozialer Gerechtigkeit.* Berlin: Walter-de-Gruyter.

Kommers, D.P., 1989. *The constitutional jurisprudence of the Federal Republic of Germany.* Durham, NC: Duke University Press.

Lipset S.M., 1958. Some social requisites of democracy. *American social science review,* 53, 69–105.

Luhmann, N., 1969. *Legitimation durch Verfahren.* Neuwied: Suhrkamp.

Nolte, G., 1988. Falwell vs. Strauß: Die rechtlichen Grenzen politischer Satire in den USA und der Bundesrepublik, *Europäische Grundrechtszeitschrift,* 14, 253–259.

Nolte, G., 1990. *Beleidigungsschutz in der freiheitlichen Demokratie.* Berlin: Springer.

Rawls, J., 1993. *Political liberalism.* New York: Columbia University Press.

Rawls, J., 1999. *A theory of justice.* 2nd ed. Cambridge, MA: Harvard University Press.

Raz, J., 1979. *The authority of law: essays on law and morality.* Oxford: Oxford University Press.

Raz, J., 1986. *The morality of freedom.* Oxford: Oxford University Press.

Tribe, L.H., 1988. *American constitutional law.* 2nd ed. Mineola, NY: Foundation Press.

Weber, M., 1922. *Wirtschaft und Gesellschaft. Grundriss der verstehenden Soziologie.* Tübingen: Mohr.

Why equality? On justifying liberal egalitarianism

Paul Kelly

London School of Economics, London, UK

The debate over the nature of egalitarianism has come to dominate political philosophy. As ever more sophisticated attempts are made to describe the principles of an egalitarian distribution or to specify the good or goods that should be distributed equally, little is said about the fundamental basis of equality. In virtue of what should people be regarded as equal? Egalitarians have tended to dismiss this question of fundamental equality. In the first part of the paper I will examine some of these strategies of marginalisation and assess whether the issue of fundamental equality matters. Jeremy Waldron has criticised this strategy of avoidance in his recent book *God, Locke and equality*. He argues that Locke's turn to a theistic grounding for fundamental equality provides a better approach to the problem than the approach taken by contemporary liberals such as John Rawls. I will examine Waldron's critique of Rawls and show that it is wanting. I will conclude by suggesting that Rawls's approach to the issue has a bearing on the way in which equality should be understood as a political value. This argument for the primacy of a political conception of egalitarianism has a bearing on the interconnection between core liberal values and the idea of the state that has been emphasised by Rawls, Dworkin and Nagel.

Defending egalitarianism

It is customary to credit Rawls with resurrecting normative political theory with the publication of *A theory of justice* in 1971. Others might make a case for Brian Barry's *Political argument* of 1965. However one wants to explain it, it is clear that something happens in the late 1960s or early 1970s that marks a move away from the modest application of linguistic philosophy to the analysis political concepts, and towards the form of normative theorising we find dominant today. Political philosophy has come to be associated with the development of liberal egalitarian theories associated with the names of John Rawls, Ronald Dworkin, Brian Barry and their criticism by the likes of G.A. Cohen. Egalitarianism provides the backdrop to increasingly technical questions about responsibility and choice versus circumstances, on the one hand and resources, access to advantage or primary goods on the other. Egalitarianism of the form we find in Rawls provides the paradigm within which normal political philosophy is carried on. Various summaries of these debates are provided under such headings as 'Equality of what?'[1] or 'On the currency of egalitarian justice'.[2] Each suggests that the real issue is the question of what should be equalised – income, resources, primary good, rights, welfare or opportunities for advantage. There is no doubt that these are serious questions deserving of attention from political philosophers and theorists. For example, does it make sense to describe oneself as an egalitarian without some clear idea of what one thinks should be equalised and what should not? But some philosophers such as Ronald Dworkin have suggested that these are not only important questions, but in some sense these are the fundamental questions for egalitarians. The reason for this is that a more fundamental sense of equality is assumed by all the rival candidate theories that one finds in modern politics. The differences between such theories are not differences between those who regard mankind as equals and those who believe in racial or hierarchical political theories; rather, they are differences over how equality of the relevant kind may be achieved. In this general sense every serious candidate theory is concerned with equality, the interesting differences between theories concern answers to questions such as 'Equality of what?' or 'The currency of egalitarian justice'.[3] Some will argue that the only goods to be distributed equally are basic rights to life, liberty and property; others will focus on social primary goods without which no decent life is possible; others still will try and specify the conditions of a valuable life in terms of a bundle of resources which individuals can use differently in pursuing their preferred conceptions of the good life. On this Dworkinian view the broad commitment to equality of concern and respect is the only game in town; what matters for politics and for political theorists is which candidate theory of egalitarianism can see off its opponents. This insight seems to capture an important aspect of the practice of political philosophy where theory construction and criticism is what political theorists do.[4] But, more importantly, Dworkin's argument shifts the meaning of egalitarian from those who believe in basic equality (as he claims that pretty much everyone believes in equality now) to a more specific answer to the 'currency' and 'equality of what' questions. For Dworkin liberal egalitarians are those who endorse the idea of equality of resources; for non-liberal egalitarians such as G.A. Cohen, egalitarians endorse the idea of equality of access to advantage.

The main consequence of the trend that Dworkin identifies and advocates is that it pays scant attention to more traditional questions about the basis of fundamental equality, or why we should be interested in equality in the first place. Some philosophers have cast a sceptical eye at Dworkin's account of the terms of political debate amongst liberals; in particular, Joseph Raz has made much of the supposed emptiness of the Dworkinian account of equality of concern and respect, yet Raz's warning seems to have been largely side-stepped (see Raz 1986, ch. 9). This is no doubt in part because Raz does not think much can be made of the idea of basic or fundamental equality as anything other than a principle of closure around a group of 'equals'. As such equality is secondary to the substantive characteristic shared by the group of 'equals' such that, again, the real issue is one of significance (what matters) and only then, of how it is distributed. And what matters is usually person-hood specified in terms of autonomy.

Most contemporary political philosophers seem to accept either Dworkin's position or a variation of Raz's. Barry, for example, assumes fundamental equality as the starting point of his 'Scanlonian contractualism', but says nothing about why we should accept it (Barry 1995, p. 70; Barry 1998). For Barry, basic equality is an axiom from which other things can be deduced or inferred and the success or attractiveness of these inferences is what will confirm and support the initial axiom. Such an approach has some commonsense plausibility in that anyone who seriously objects to the equal claims of other human beings is unlikely to be worried about the nature of social justice, much less reading Barry's books.

The other common approach to the problem of basic equality in the literature, which can be illustrated by the example of T.M. Scanlon, is the abandonment of the search for a single unified conception of equality as a value characteristic shared by all individuals and instead its replacement with a re-description of what egalitarians want in terms of a cluster of distinct but related moral commitments. These moral commitments can be illustrated by the diversity of reasons for rejecting inequalities (Scanlon 2002). Scanlon provides subtle and insightful discussions of what is wrong with suffering and severe deprivation, stigmatizing differences in status, unacceptable domination, procedural unfairness and unfair outcomes. These diverse faces of objectionable inequality depend on values other than basic equality of concern and respect, and suggest that it is particular types of inequality that are wrong and not necessarily inequality per se. This approach is shared by many philosophers, who agree with Scanlon that it is both more sensitive to our moral experience whilst allowing us to challenge objectionable social and political practices.

What both approaches suggest is that not much turns on the idea of basic equality – or that in virtue of which we are worthy of equality of concern and respect – and therefore that political theory can proceed without paying the idea much attention. What really matters is the internal analysis and critique of particular theories in the attempt to converge upon a position that merits support because it has seen off all of the available contenders. This strategy has some attractions in terms of how we do political theory. If every time we wished to address what is wrong with unjust social arrangements or policies we had to build a theory from the ground up, we would never make any contribution to wider political and moral debate. To demand this fully foundationalist approach of political philosophers seems to make no more sense then requiring biologists or chemists to do fundamental work in basic physics before advancing any hypotheses in their own fields of enquiry. So political philosophers can seek to make some progress in debates between luck-egalitarians, sufficientarians, prioritarians and humanitarians by the internal analysis and criticism of their arguments, presuppositions and implications. This is one strategy employed by many political philosophers.[5] Yet the question remains whether it is ultimately insufficient as a complete defence of a political principle that may be used to justify coercion in the real world of politics, or at least will claim to justify such coercion. The reason for this is that showing that a particular perspective can withstand a critical engagement with other theories cannot show its uniqueness as the right basis for social cooperation and political coercion. This is because a theory's unique ability to withstand critical challenge depends upon its being able to set limits to the range of possible rival candidate theories. In the case of arguments for egalitarianism, these rival theories will not only be alternative egalitarian theories up to and including utilitarianism, but also the whole range of non-egalitarian arguments and theories. Just as the strategy of internal analysis and criticism will not single out the uniqueness of egalitarianism amongst its rivals, so similarly it will not support the idea of fundamental equality, as there is no non-question begging sense in which egalitarianism must win out over non-egalitarian theories.

Do we need an account of basic equality?

A question we might ask ourselves at this point is whether it really matters that we do not provide a justification or defence of fundamental equality. I am interested in the question of why we should regard other (all?) human beings as equals. My interest and the point of this question is not the search for a universal motivation to act morally, although clearly if we can find a ground for regarding other human beings as moral equals this will have a bearing on questions of the scope and demands of our obligations. Rather, I am concerned with why we should be concerned with basic equality in the first place and what an appropriate concern for basic equality would look like. This question is certainly concerned with the scope of our obligations and this does seem to be central to the concerns of contemporary political philosophy. So at least in this sense the issue of basic equality does seem to matter and the question to be answered is, what is basic equality and how does it have a bearing on scope?

There are three main reasons why the question of basic equality might well matter and therefore why it should merit attention amongst those political philosophers who regard themselves as egalitarian.[6]

The first reason is the most obvious and concerns the ability of egalitarians to engage effectively with anti-egalitarians, Nietzscheans and the defenders of natural aristocracy. Although most contemporary political philosophy is conducted against the background of a weak commitment to equality of concern and respect, it is certainly not the case that everyone accepts this premise. It is certainly not the case that in the wider world egalitarianism is the norm, whatever Dworkin might claim. As well as the unattractive claims of racists, misogynists and homophobes, many people do think that there are ethically relevant differences between people that undermine the idea of basic equality. These anti-egalitarian claims can be based on prejudice but it is not a sign of prejudice as such that one rejects basic equality, as many egalitarians deny that all departures from equality are morally significant. Some inequalities can be egalitarian.

The rejection of egalitarianism can take many forms. Some might argue that there are no grounds for attributing equal worth to persons in any respect, because there are no grounds for attributing moral worth to persons as such. Followers of Nietzsche fall into this group. They see the claims of equality as part of the 'slave morality' legacy of Christianity, which in its attempt to overcome natural hierarchy undermines the status of any ethical values and leaves us with nihilism (Nietzsche 2003). For the nihilist anything goes because every claim to value is the assertion of the will to power. The Nietzschean challenge is similar to the challenge of the amoralist, to whom perhaps no general answer to the question 'why be moral?' can be given. But the challenge for the egalitarian is also different, because even if we can give some kind of ethical response to the Nietzschean, of the sort that he too is involved in a kind of ethical practice, it does not follow that this response will result in equal concern and respect.

Not all anti-egalitarians are nihilists or Nietzsche-inspired relativists. Some philosophers take a realist but anti-egalitarian view. A good example is John Kekes. Kekes rubbishes basic equality on its own grounds by claiming that because egalitarians do not take seriously the issue of evil they are unable to see why some people are less worthy of moral consideration than others and hence are not in the relevant sense equals. He gives the examples of torturers, murderers and concentration camp guards as the sort of people who show through their actions that they are less worthy of consideration than others (Kekes 2003). Kekes's argument is important, in at least this respect, in that he argues against prescriptive or moral equality, whilst potentially conceding the case in favour of descriptive equality. Thus all people may satisfy some natural criterion of equality as human beings (all having interests) yet fail to satisfy the relevant criteria of moral equality because of the repugnance of their acts and motives. It is at least arguable that certain kinds of person are not worthy of equal consideration even if we decline to deny them any protection of the law. We might, for example, find some people so repugnant in their acts (torturers are a good example) that we deny them equal concern and respect in any meaningful sense, and the only reason we do not allow them to become total moral outlaws is the concern not to demean ourselves rather than any concern for their status.

Without some criterion of basic equality we have no way of responding to the challenge of anti-egalitarians and this fact is perhaps more pressing today because of the unfortunate consequences of the so-called war on terror and the clash of civilisations thesis. It is too easy to dismiss such people as beyond the pale and therefore not deserving of serious consideration. If egalitarianism is only of interest to other egalitarians, then it is unlikely to have much impact beyond the confines of the seminar room.

Yet the problem is not simply that egalitarians will have little to say to the wider world of anti-egalitarianism. The problem is also one of consistency. Egalitarians cannot accuse anti-egalitarians of missing a crucial point of moral significance if they are themselves going to avoid any justification and explanation of the grounds of equal treatment. The Dworkinian view is to reject as candidates for serious consideration principles and policies that are systematically anti-egalitarian, such as racial discrimination, on the grounds that they fail to acknowledge a basic parameter of ethics. Yet this argument is seriously weakened if there is no attempt to explain and defend the basis of that ethical parameter. If one steps-back from righteous indignation and asks dispassionately what is the anti-egalitarian missing, we find the importance of making some case for basic equality. The anti-egalitarian can want many of the things that egalitarians want, but differ only in that he wants them for the morally worthy. This is not quite the position taken by Kekes, who wants to reject substantive egalitarianism as well, but it is one that could be based on his anti-egalitarian argument from evil. There is no good reason for the anti-egalitarian to reject the idea that once one has weeded out all the torturers and other evildoers, amongst the remainder equality might be the appropriate grounds of moral and political recognition. This is not unlike the idea of equality between equals that we find in Aristotle's *Nicomachean ethics*. Here the idea is that amongst those sharing the appropriate quality or excellence there should be equality of treatment, so that, for example, amongst able violinists, violins should be equally distributed. This form of egalitarianism is consistent with most forms of elitism and political systems such as aristocracy.

This brings us to the third reason for providing an account of basic or fundamental equality, namely the problem of scope. As we have just seen, some of those who claim to reject egalitarianism could with consistency accept a form of egalitarianism as equality amongst equals. The question of the scope of egalitarian principles is therefore very important, as how we define the scope of basic equality seems to have a direct bearing on the nature of egalitarian principles. Just as we could reconstruct the anti-egalitarian argument of Kekes so that it is consistent with allowing egalitarianism amongst a suitably circumscribed group of worthy individuals, so in the case of most other egalitarian principles we could circumscribe the group to whom they are supposed to apply. This is not merely an unintentional consequence of egalitarian arguments, for one of the central debates in liberal political theory concerns the question of the scope of liberal egalitarian political principles. If we take Rawls's theory as an example, we can see how the argument of *A theory of justice*,[7] was assumed to have a broadly cosmopolitan scope, yet that in *Political liberalism* and *The law of peoples*, the egalitarian principles of 'justice as fairness' are clearly supposed to apply to the members of 'a people' rather than to all people as such. Some have accused Rawls of apostasy in moving from his cosmopolitan conception of liberalism to a communitarian one, but arguably Rawls always claimed that equality in the relevant sense is something appropriate to those who share in the same scheme social cooperation and he is not alone amongst egalitarian liberals in holding such a view.[8] So at the heart of modern liberalism we already have ethical distinctions between individuals. Some of these distinctions can no doubt be explained via the institutional division of labour between political equality, which clearly presupposes membership of a polity; economic equality, which assumes some form of social and economic cooperation; and more basic forms of equality, which simply depend on common humanity. But that is not sufficient if we are to prioritize the respective claims of these various forms of equal treatment. Do the claims of individuals as such, to be equals, trump the claims of co-operators or members of the same ethical community? As this issue is precisely what separates cosmopolitan from other kinds of egalitarian, I do not see how we can make much in the way of progress without addressing the basis and character of fundamental equality.[9] The issue of the scope of equality versus ideas that may be more fundamental, such as humanity, is precisely what is being debated amongst defenders and critics of cosmopolitan egalitarianism.

For all of the reasons given above it is clear that the issue of basic equality is something that egalitarians should not ignore as it affects the scope and therefore the plausibility of the arguments they make about 'currency' and 'distributive principles'. One of the few political philosophers who have sought to address head on the issue of basic equality is Jeremy Waldron. He writes;

> Basic equality is so fundamental to innumerable aspects of our ethical outlook that it requires a special sort of defense – at once transcendent and powerful – so that it can both underpin what are usually taken to be the starting points of public justification and also prevail in the face of the various temptations that invite us to start drawing distinctions between types and grades of human being. (Waldron 2002, p. 14)

In the next section of the paper I propose to examine Waldron's argument based on his reading of Locke and his use of this to mount a critique of the treatment of basic equality in contemporary liberalism, such as that of John

Rawls. Before turning to Waldron's argument it is worthwhile reminding ourselves of the point of turning to basic or fundamental equality. The issue is, in virtue of what are human beings deserving of equal consideration and respect? My point will not be to provide an unchallengeable defence of equality; rather, the point will be to identify the nature of the claim to basic equality as only then will we be in a position to determine the requirements of any defence or justification of that claim.

Basic equality – Christian or liberal?

Waldron's discussion of basic equality is developed in the context of his reinterpretation of Locke's moral and political philosophy. One of the distinctive features of his argument is that Locke should be read as a philosopher who has potentially interesting things to say about fundamental philosophical problems and not merely as an historical curiosity. As such he challenges the interpretation of Cambridge historians such as Peter Laslett and John Dunn, who both argue that because of Locke's seventeenth-century theological views there are no issues of contemporary political relevance about which we can learn anything from Locke (see Laslett 1988, Dunn 1969). This means both that we can learn something about basic equality from Locke's arguments and also, more controversially, that we do not have to discard Locke's theological beliefs in order to learn from him. For Waldron, the discussion of basic equality is not merely a side issue in an historical discussion of a past political thinker: we can learn something about the 'shape' of basic equality from Locke that has a bearing on how we judge secular contemporary discussions of basic equality such as that notably offered by John Rawls in *A theory of justice*. I do not intend to say anything here about Waldron's methodology of historical enquiry or his critique of Cambridge historicism, other than to note that I am in broad agreement with him. Our primary concern is what we can learn about the 'shape' or nature of the criteria of fundamental equality.

Locke is interesting for Waldron because he has a conception of the fundamental equality of all mankind in the *Second treatise* as the bearers of rights and therefore of ethical significance. In this sense Locke too seems to fall into Dworkin's claim that equality is the only game in town. What makes Locke interesting is how he seeks to cash out that claim. Locke seems both to reject a straightforward species-based naturalism and to appeal to the idea of the species as the principle of closure of his conception of moral significance.

Human beings are not equal because they belong to the same species, Man. And the reason for this argument is to be found in Locke's account the concept or term species in his *Essay concerning human understanding* (Locke 1971, Book III, ch. vi). In the *Essay* Locke rejects species terms as what he calls nominal essences. Nominal essences are collections of ideas derived from sensation and experience derived from nature. However, they are not based on real distinctions between objects of experience and therefore cannot provide the basis for real distinctions between species, and more importantly, between mankind as a species and other kinds of species. The point about this is that our use of species terms cannot draw a real distinction between one species and another, although it can identify some natural features of creatures which are not shared by all. How we distinguish these criteria is largely based on convention and practice, and it is for that reason that species terms will not provide the right kind of distinctions and discriminations. We can see an intimation here of the kind of arguments used by defenders of animal rights or animal welfare such as Peter Singer. He would certainly not deny any differences between what we call species, but, rather like Locke, would deny the significance of these basically conventional distinctions for real and morally relevant distinctions between classes of being (Singer 1993). What we focus on in making such distinctions will draw the boundaries of moral significance and therefore who or what counts as an equal. Appealing to the idea of a common species will not do the relevant work because the classification is conventional though based in nature, but it is not given directly by nature. Names will not help us here.

So much for the argument of the *Essay*, yet in the *Two treatises* Locke does use the idea of the human species as the principle of closure of his account of ethical significance. This sets up an interesting historical question about the consistency of Locke's works which I do not intend to pursue.[10] Waldron suggests that Locke overcomes this apparent contradiction by weakening the status of the species-based claim in the *Two treatises*.

According to Waldron, Locke does not assert the strong claim about species identity as the boundary marker of significance for the reasons he sets out in the *Essay*. Instead, he falls back on the less ambitious claim that the perceptible qualities that make up the nominal essence of the species Mankind do actually contain some real resemblances that allow us to draw a boundary around the group of equals as the group of human beings. The key features that he picks out are that human beings are corporeal beings and that they have the capacity to think rationally or (what he takes to be the same thing) abstractly. The emphasis on corporeal beings is important because it suggests that Locke is concerned with human selves or persons and not souls, despite his obvious religious commitments. This criteria distinguishes human persons from any other kind of non-corporeal entity should they exist and whatever they might happen to be. This choice has the important implication for Locke that, despite his theological presuppositions, the scope of his conception of morality is definitely humanist.

The second characteristic that Locke identifies is the capacity for abstract thought or rationality. This immediately suggests one standard objection to all naturalistic attempts to ground ethical equality, namely, that not all of those we might include amongst 'humankind' possess the capacity to think abstractly. One simple response would be to robustly deny that those who do not manifest that characteristic are moral equals. Thus infants, most children up to a certain age, many elderly people as well as those with mental disabilities, those in comas etc., would seem to fall outside the scope of moral equality. Yet many of these people are precisely the kind of people we would want to protect by according them moral equality. Locke does not take this view. Instead, according to Waldron, he uses the capacity to exhibit abstract rational thought as a range-property, an idea derived from Rawls which seems to fits Locke's arguments about the scope of the capacity for abstract thought (Rawls 1999a, p. 444). The point about a range-property is that it allows for differences of degree within a range. Waldron illustrates Rawls's point with the example of being in New Jersey (Waldron 2002, p. 77). Both Hoboken and Princeton fall within the range concept, though they differ in the degree to which they fall within the State of New Jersey. Hoboken is on the border with New York. It falls within the range that matters for Waldron and Locke and not the degree. So although people differ in the degree to which they exhibit the capacity for abstract thought, this does not matter from the point of view of identifying the relevant criterion of equality.

But even if we can use the idea of the capacity for abstract thought amongst corporeal beings, Waldron's account of Locke's theory of basic equality seems to fall foul of the other standard criticism of naturalistic theories of ethics, namely how ethical significance is derived from what Locke concedes is a natural capacity, or how we move from descriptive to prescriptive equality. It is here that Locke's argument takes a theological turn and it is at this point that Waldron also argues that the significance of the appeal to God becomes important for making sense of equal status and value.

The argument works in the following way: the capacity of abstract reasoning is identified as significant, not simply because it is widely shared (though to differing degrees) by all human beings. Instead, the significance of abstract reasoning is that it enables each person to understand themselves as a part of the created order and from this they can reason to their obligation to preserve that order, including other moral equals, as part of the basic moral obligation we have to God. The idea seems to be as there is something rather than nothing there must have been a creator and therefore, a purpose to that creation of which human agents are a part. As soon as they ask themselves why have they been endowed uniquely with this capacity for abstract thought they will begin an easy process of reasoning to the idea of a created order that gives a purpose and therefore a meaning to the possession and exercise of these capacities.

There are a number of important points to note from Waldron's account of Locke's theory. Firstly, a straightforward appeal to a natural property will not be sufficient to ground basic equality. Secondly, natural capacity is a range property that admits of significant differences in degree. Thirdly, the appeal to God provides an important account of the significance of this capacity – what Waldron calls the 'shape' of basic equality. It is important, according to Waldron, that Locke's appeal to God is not for the traditional natural law idea of an authoritative sanction of our basic moral obligation. Clearly, for Locke, God does sanction the basic moral law of equal respect, but that is not the key point. The appeal to God, and therefore to a transcendent authority, provides the meaning and significance of the real resemblances (corporeality and capacity for rationality) on which moral equality is based. Thus the appeal to God in the defence of basic equality is not merely a contingent fact of Locke's historical circumstances that can be bracketed off from his 'proper' philosophical doctrines; it is central to his defence of equality. Yet Waldron also rejects the obvious contemporary response, which is that, if the defence of equality depends upon an appeal to God, so much the worse for equality. It is hard enough trying to defend egalitarianism without having to defend the existence of God as Locke conceives him. It is precisely this source of transcendence that is significantly missing, according to Waldron, in contemporary liberal theories of basic equality, and it is perhaps the embarrassment at having no such transcendent significance that causes liberals to fall back on either silence or a muted appeal to individuals as bearers of interests.

Precisely what we are supposed to make of Waldron's argument is carefully ambiguous. One could take the view that he is merely repeating the standard criticism of liberal theories to the effect that the bracketing strategy and the avoidance of substantive philosophical or metaphysical commitments is unsustainable.[11] This is certainly part of Waldron's critique of Rawls in this account of the Lockean alternative. But this familiar, though perhaps important, point is not all that Waldron is offering us. Although he provides a defence of Locke's view that civil society cannot accommodate atheists, he does not expressly say that a belief in God is essential for those who count as moral equals – a view that is not so alien in modern democracies. Yet because Waldron wants to take Locke's argument seriously, it does seem as though he endorses the need for God and the transcendent to make sense of our commitment to basic equality. Without it we are no better than the Nietzscheans who have no interest in equality or morality.

Where Waldron's challenge to contemporary liberalism is most clear is his suggestion that Rawls's defence of basic equality fails because it lacks the 'shape' or transcendent account of meaning and significance that basic equality needs. There is no alternative to substantive philosophical, metaphysical and even theological arguments in providing a defence of basic equality. Is Waldron right about Rawls and what does this tell us about the nature of fundamental equality?

Let us remind ourselves what, according to Waldron, Locke's appeal to God does in respect of justifying basic equality. His key point is that the appeal to the idea of God and a divine purpose provides the sources of an interpretation of the natural capacities of corporeal rationality, which gives them their special status amongst the range of other possible real resemblances amongst mankind. It is the meaning of the natural capacities that matters.

Rawls offers us an account of basic equality in terms of two features of moral personality: the capacity to form and pursue a conception of the good and the capacity for a sense of justice (Rawls 1999a, p. 442). These capacities are natural capacities but for Rawls they are also range properties; indeed, as we have seen, it was Rawls who introduced the notion. Consequently, people can manifest these capacities to a greater or lesser degree, thus covering the question of natural differences in intelligence and ability. It is also interesting that Rawls's characterisation of the two basic characteristics of moral personality as range properties answers Kekes's challenge about the egalitarians ability to take account of evil. Even Kekes's examples of torturers and murderers still have these capacities despite attempting to overcome or ignore their importance. It is for this reason that Rawls and liberal egalitarians see no one as beyond the protection of the law, however heinous their crimes may be. In this Rawls's position is also superior to that of Locke, who, as we have seen, leaves atheists outside the law.

So far, Rawls's position seems to mirror that attributed to Locke. Where they differ is on the issue of significance and meaning. Waldron claims that Rawls's account of moral personality has no shape as Rawls rejects the idea of appealing to some transcendent significance of these characteristics of moral personality. But this argument seems hasty. Rawls does provide an interpretation of the significance of moral personality, but in so doing he does not appeal to some external source of authority or significance. Instead, Rawls's interpretation of the significance of moral personality is spelled out through the articulation of a full theory of equal treatment appropriate to the kind of persons who find themselves in the initial choice situation of his theory of justice as fairness. This is similar to the strategy of analysis and criticism of candidate theories of egalitarianism that I identified in the first part of the paper. But the strategy of Rawls employs here is rather different in that Rawls sees part of the task of theory construction as specifying the nature of basic equality whilst the appeal to basic equality places constraints on the character of that theory construction. Theory construction and the strategy of reflective equilibrium are obviously important parts of Rawls's account of the characteristic features of moral personality. The meaning and significance of the two basic features of moral personality is provided by the role they play in making sense of a just social order. Waldron's challenge is whether the process of explaining basic equality in this way is sufficient. But in order to answer his challenge we need an account of, sufficient for what?

Waldron's demand cannot be that Rawls sees off all challengers to his account of basic equality, as Waldron's own Lockean theory is hardly likely to fare as well as Rawls's. For if Waldron's argument is not merely for the development of a philosophical anthropology before we can do political theory, but the more demanding claim that we need to take theology seriously, then his position would seem far more precarious than Rawls's. His argument does seem to play into the hands of the Nietzscheans by saying that equality depends upon a conception of God, but as we have no good arguments for belief in God we cannot sustain a conception of equality. Locke may well be providing us with an argument for basic equality but it is hardly one we should take very seriously. Rawls does not set the barrier of justification quite so high, so the idea of self-sufficiency in his account of basic equality must count as an advantage over Waldron and Locke. If the question is the role and purpose of basic equality, it is not obvious that Waldron's turn to the transcendent is necessary, although clearly some argument beyond the identification of a natural property is important. Where Waldron's argument ultimately differs is on the issue of the sanction of basic equality, or why we should respect it. But this is a different question to how we identify the meaning and significance of basic equality, and it is one that depends on the existence of God for its answer. And this is something that Waldron does not prove.

The question is whether Rawls's approach is sufficient to address the claims of why basic equality matters. His approach certainly offers something to say to the anti-egalitarian about the nature of basic equality. Using the idea of a range property he is able to address anti-egalitarians such as Kekes or others who deny the idea that there can be natural properties that include sufficient numbers to meet the aspirations of egalitarian theories. By providing an interpretation of the basic capacities of moral personality Rawls's theory meets the demands of consistency in addressing alternative non-egalitarian theories. Finally there is the issue of scope. Here Rawls's account of basic equality takes an interesting turn. He develops the idea of moral personality in the initial situation of establishing fair terms of social cooperation (Rawls 1999a, p. 442). The point seems to be that basic equality exists first and foremost amongst those engaged in constructing a fair scheme of social cooperation. What is not developed in this argument but which is increasingly clear in Rawls's work is that basic equality is primarily a political notion that is articulated against the backdrop of a certain kind of political society – a just state. This certainly goes some way to explaining why liberal egalitarian theories see equality as primarily a 'sovereign virtue' that expresses the relationships that exist between members of a just political community and its structures of power and authority. In the absence of political society the issue of basic equality would not have the same significance. But one should not conclude from this that Rawls confines the scope of equal recognition to fellow citizens. There are, after all, two basic features of moral personality; the capacity for a sense of justice is only one of them. All individuals share the capacity for a conception of the good, and it is no doubt in virtue of this that some form of cosmopolitan harm principle can be constructed. What is clear is that Rawls does not provide a simple answer to the issue of the scope of basic equality. At one level the capacity for a conception of the good is broad enough in range to encompass most of humanity. Yet at the level of a capacity for justice, it is not obvious that this entails relationships that are, at the political level, cosmopolitan in scope. The point here is not just one of a division of labour, but rather the more substantial claim that some of the relationships that consitute political equality are derived from membership of the appropriate kind of political community, namely a state regulated by the two principles of justice. This approach to basic equality is developed in Rawls's later works such as *The law of peoples*, but even if one does not follow Rawls's argument fully in this direction it is clear that he offers at best a 'statist' version of cosmopolitanism.

What can we conclude from the above? Rawls does not provide the only possible route to the justification of a liberal egalitarian perspective, but his approach to the issue of basic equality is insightful because it does not wholly marginalize the issue in the way that Dworkin's rival theory of liberal egalitarianism appears to. Furthermore, Rawls's theory connects the specification of basic equality to the context of a special form of political association but does not subordinate equality to the issue of the internal structure of a just state. In more general terms we can also see that whilst the defence of basic equality forms an important part of the defence of substantive egalitarian theories of distributive justice, one can overstate the importance of defending basic equality along the lines suggested by Waldron. Where this leaves us is with a defence of the status quo in terms of how political philosophers should proceed. The analysis and critique of rival theories of egalitarianism has an important role in the wider defence of basic equality. What we should not expect is a basic natural property in virtue of which people become moral equals, but neither should we lament the absence of such a property. The appeal to basic equality is important in making sense of the egalitarian project, but the account of basic equality is not a straightforward first premise from which all else must be derived. It is a central part of the process of egalitarian argument in so far as it forces us to concentrate on the issue of the scope of our principles, and this is something that can be lost in a preoccupation with issues such as the currency of egalitarian justice. But in making the defence of basic equality depend on the articulation of an egalitarian theory of the just political community we open up scope not only for philosophical arguments but also establish opportunities for other forms of political theorising to assist in providing representations of the core idea of basic equality and the forms of social relationships on which it depends. Although Waldron's account of Locke proved to be unhelpful in providing the foundation of basic equality, perhaps there is scope for marshalling past historical thinkers and modes of thought in defending basic equality. Perhaps I could suggest Tom Paine.

Notes

1. Taken from the title of A. Sen's 'Tanner lecture on human values' (1980).
2. The title of an equally famous article by G.A. Cohen (1989).
3. The exploration of this Dworkinian idea forms the principle narrative of W. Kymlicka (2002, pp. 2–5).
4. A fact that is lamented in Barry (2005). Barry suggests in this book that too much political theory is narrowly inward-looking and that egalitarians would be more profitably employed looking at how real equality can be achieved in modern democratic societies such as the UK and the US.
5. Indeed it is a strategy I have used myself in Kelly (2004). It can also be found in Jeremy Bentham's attempt to provide an informal justification of the primacy of the principle of utility in *An introduction to the principles of morals and legislation*. See the discussion in Harrison (1983, pp. 187–188).
6. I am not suggesting that there should be a complete redirection of attention from questions about the currency of egalitarian justice or the nature of what should be distributed. All I am suggesting is that some attention should be given to this fundamental question as well, and that certainly seems to be lacking in the contemporary literature.
7. See especially the interpretation of Rawls's theory in Beitz (1999).
8. See, for example, Nagel (2005). Although I have not be able to find a clear statement in his writings, Ronald Dworkin claimed in a conversation with the author that there was no such thing as international justice. Presumably the point is that whatever equality exists beyond borders is different from what exists amongst those within a political community.
9. I am aware that most cosmopolitans will answer that they do have a conception of basic equality which gives priority to humanity over other forms of ethical relationship, on the grounds that they are concerned with humanity's equal status as the bearer of interests. This is, however, too quick as the idea of human interests is still controversial; indeed, it is partly what theories of egalitarian justice try to explain. Some accounts of basic interests might actually presuppose membership of certain kinds of communities, such as juridical states, in order for people to enjoy freedom.
10. Laslett (1988) argues that Locke made no attempt to make the arguments of the *Essay* and the *Two treatises* consistent, and to seek such consistency is to force interpretations upon Locke's works that they ultimately will not sustain.
11. A version of this argument can also be found in Taylor (1989). Taylor is concerned with the way in which the resources from which our modern conceptions of selfhood, such as the free and equal subject of democratic citizenship, are under threat in the early twenty-first century. His concern is that what he calls 'horizontal secularism' is in danger of undercutting the support of values we cherish. This is precisely what Nietzsche predicted in his *Beyond good and evil* and the *Genealogy of morality*.

References

Barry, B.M., 1995. *Justice as impartiality.* Oxford: Clarendon Press.
Barry, B.M., 1998. Something in the disputation not unpleasant. *In:* P. Kelly, ed. *Impartiality, neutrality and justice.* Edinburgh: Edinburgh University Press.
Barry, B.M., 2005. *Why social justice matters?* Cambridge: Polity Press.
Beitz, C., 1999. *Political theory and international relations.* Rev. ed. Princeton, NJ: Princeton University Press.
Cohen, G.A., 1989. On the currency of egalitarian justice. *Ethics,* 99(4), 906–944.
Dunn, J., 1969. *The political thought of John Locke: an historical account of the argument of 'Two treatises of government'.* Cambridge: Cambridge University Press.
Harrison, R., 1983. *Bentham.* London: Routledge.
Kekes, J., 2003. *The illusions of egalitarianism.* Ithaca, NY: Cornell University Press.
Kelly, P., 2004. *Liberalism.* Cambridge: Polity Press.
Kymlicka, W., 2002. *Contemporary political philosophy: an introduction.* 2nd ed. Oxford: Oxford University Press.
Laslett, P., 1988. Introduction. *In:* J. Locke, *Two Treatises of Government,* ed. P. Laslett. Cambridge: Cambridge University Press.
Locke, J., 1971. *An essay concerning human understanding,* ed. P.H. Nidditch. Oxford: Clarendon Press.
Nagel, T., 2005. The problem of global justice. *Philosophy & public affairs,* 33(2), 113–147.
Nietzsche, F., 2003. *Beyond good and evil.* Harmondsworth: Penguin books.
Rawls, J., 1993 *Political liberalism.* New York: Columbia University Press.
Rawls, J., 1999a. *A theory of justice.* Rev ed. Oxford: Oxford University Press.
Rawls, J., 1999b. *The law of peoples.* Cambridge, MA: Harvard University Press
Raz, J., 1986. *The morality of freedom.* Oxford: Oxford University Press.
Scanlon, T.M., 2002. The diversity of objections to inequality. *In:* M. Clayton and A. Williams, eds. *The ideal of equality.* Basingstoke: Palgrave, 41–59.
Sen, A., 1980. Equality of what? *In:* S. McMurrin, ed. *The Tanner lectures on human values, vol. 1.* Salt Lake City, UT: University of Utah Press.
Singer, P., 1993. *Practical ethics.* 2nd ed. Cambridge: Cambridge University Press.
Taylor, C., 1989. *Sources of the self.* Cambridge: Cambridge University Press.
Waldron, J., 2002. *God, Locke and equality.* Cambridge: Cambridge University Press.

Luck, equality and responsibility

Keith Dowding

Research School of Social Sciences, Australia National University, Canberra, Australia

Egalitarians claim that inequality in society is only justified to the extent that it results from choices freely and responsibly made. Inequality resulting from brute bad luck is not justified. I argue that luck, and therefore responsibility, are defined in terms of the reward structure. Luck and responsibility are epiphenomena of the incentives that people have to choose from the opportunity sets available. To that end egalitarians should look more directly at the degree of inequality that is acceptable and examine more closely the classes of actions they want to leave to individual responsibility even though these will lead to greater inequality. State action should concentrate upon reducing inequality between classes of people; it cannot be expected to reduce all inequalities between people even though many of these will have only peripheral relationships to responsibility.

> Talk about 'differences that are a matter of luck' and 'differences for which people are not responsible' and people being 'worse off through no fault of their own' has been engaged in uncritically, without adequately examining what it could mean. (Hurley 2003, p. 204)

Introduction

Responsibility has become a central issue in egalitarian debates. Many egalitarians argue that the only justifications for inequalities in society are those which result from the choices responsibly and freely made by individuals. If one person is less well off than another, not due to the choices each makes, then the first has a legitimate claim of injustice. The label 'luck' has been attached to the generation of inequalities that do not derive from choice responsibly and freely made. So luck is the other side of responsibility. For luck egalitarians all inequalities deriving from luck should be expunged from the just society. Or rather more carefully, they feel inequalities deriving from brute luck should be expunged from the just society.[1]

Taking responsibility for the outcomes one receives has long been a clarion call for those on the right of the political spectrum. For egalitarians to give a central role to responsibility allows them to avoid the charge that equalizing outcomes will deny responsibility by removing the expression of individual agency. By distinguishing the vagaries of life over which we have no control (brute luck) from those which we do (option luck) is the route some egalitarians have taken to overcome such a critique. After all, it is easy to demonstrate that in today's society inequality does not map onto responsibility (Barry 2005). I will argue, however, that the neat trick of taking responsibility for outcomes out of the right-wing camp does not work as well as it might for egalitarians. The distinction between brute and option luck is not easy to maintain outside of simple examples and reducing brute luck can reduce the scope of individual responsibility. Rather we need to decide what levels of inequalities are acceptable and let agents act within those bounds.

Considering how unequal society should be, given responsibility for outcomes, requires a decision over the object of equality. I do not discuss that difficult subject here, though note that some potential objectives sit less well with the discussion of responsibility and luck than others. In this paper, I tend to assume that the objective of equality is material benefits (money). Despite sophisticated discussion over the 'equality of what?' question, most of the examples given in the literature concerning luck and responsibility seem to rely upon material benefits as the object of equalization. I point out what broader accounts might entail and show that moving beyond material benefits only exacerbates the problems I identify.

Responsibility

Despite the title of the paper I am not intending to discuss in any depth the thorny issue of responsibility. The paper does discuss what we might mean by 'luck' in some detail as I believe that concept has been taken somewhat for granted. One of the aims of the paper is to argue that we cannot distinguish luck and responsibility in either theory or practice to the degree theorists have assumed. I take a minimal approach to responsibility.

A great deal of the literature on responsibility deals with the issue of freewill and determinism. I am not concerned at all with this literature. The approach to responsibility I adopt is compatible, I believe, with either a free will or a deterministic approach to responsibility (that is a deterministic approach which still allows the assignation of responsibility to people; see, for example, Dennett 2003).

I assume we assign responsibility to people dependent upon how much control we believe they have over their course of action. Bracketing out the freewill-determinism issue allows us to suggest that people have more control over the outcomes dependent on their actions based upon (a) the number of viable elements in their opportunity set, and (b) the relationship between the actions they perform and the outcomes those actions lead to.

On the first aspect it is obvious that if an opportunity set had only one element in it then we cannot assign responsibility for 'choosing' that alternative. However, it is not clear that we assign more responsibility for any chosen element the more elements there are. In the formal freedom of choice literature the elements in an opportunity set are simply given. However, in real life there may be alternatives available that people might feel ought to be chosen, but the costs are such that they choose another element. When assigning responsibility for actions we take account of the potential costs of actions as well as their likely outcomes. We assign responsibility given the number of viable alternatives in an opportunity set.

However, individuals must be able to distinguish the alternatives. If there is no diversity amongst the alternatives then we cannot expect a person to accept responsibility for the particular alternative chosen. If the alternatives all appear identical – matches from a matchbox – then people will pick rather than choose (Ullman-Margalit and Morgenbesser 1977). To the extent that there are no reasons for picking one rather than another we cannot assign responsibility for one alternative (such as a match from a box) being picked rather than another. Diversity here needs to be an objective characteristic of the alternatives. When challenged over why one has chosen one course of action rather than another, it is not sufficient to say that one is indifferent to each since to oneself they are indistinguishable. If one course of action affects others greatly then responsibility can be assigned to the picker no matter that she is indifferent to the outcomes.

Not being able to distinguish the alternatives can be offered as an excuse against responsibility for outcomes if one did not have sufficient information. Not being aware that one course of action would deleteriously affect others can be an excuse against being held morally responsible for the outcome especially where, given the circumstances, one cannot be expected to have had that information.

The importance of information shows the limits to the number of alternatives in an opportunity set. Assuming that there are costs to collecting information then an optimal opportunity set will be finite. If there are too many alternatives or there is too much information to process about the alternatives in an opportunity set then rational choice becomes more rather than less difficult (Dowding and van Hees 2008). Again the amount of information that we can expect someone to have processed in a decision is important for the assignation of responsibility.

Finally there is the relationship between the actions we perform and the outcomes that result. Again, in the formal literature on freedom of choice, the elements of an opportunity set are thought to be well-defined in the sense that choosing them leads directly to that element. Action and outcome become the same thing. In real life, however, the actions we choose in order to bring about an outcome and the outcome itself are not so directly correlated. How far we assign responsibility to someone for the outcome itself depends upon how we view the relationship between the action and the outcome. We may not blame someone for a bad outcome given what she (and we) might have expected to happen given the actions taken. This leads us back into the idea of luck.

Three types of luck

Dworkin (1981, 2000) first made the distinction between brute and option luck in relation to his insurance market justification for equalizing resources. One way of making the distinction is expressed by John Roemer (1996, p. 248):

> Option luck is the outcome of a gamble explicitly taken, while brute luck is an outcome in which no gamble was entered into. Being struck by lightning when no insurance was available against that calamity is brute luck: being struck by lightning if insurance was available, whether or not you were insured, is a matter of option luck. … Thus the presence of insurance markets transforms events of brute luck into events of option luck. Dworkin's view is that it is fair for person to suffer the consequences of option luck, for persons decide how much to insure against those kinds of event. Brute luck, however, is a morally arbitrary (and hence unfair) way of distributing resources.

The basis of the distinction as given in the quotation from Roemer is that someone cannot complain about the bad consequences that may follow from a risk that one has chosen to take. After all, failing to insure against some bad outcome allows one to keep the money that would otherwise have been invested in the insurance. An attempt to gain advantage over those who do insure has been thwarted by events, but events that one can predict with some probability.[2]

Brute luck is not normally used in quite this manner, however. Rather than describing chance events for which there was no prediction or insurance, brute luck is often used to describe the conditions in which one find oneself from birth. This is a necessary condition of life from each person's point of view, though the distribution of life-chances in any society can be known given other known facts about that society. I will make a distinction between two forms of brute luck: 'Contingent Brute Luck' describing events as in the quotation from Roemer; and 'Personal Identity Brute Luck' (or more simply 'Personal Identity Luck') (Dowding 1991, pp. 64–65) to describe the conditions one has from birth. Of the second Cohen (1995, p. 229) suggests 'no luck is bruter than than of how one is born, raised and circumstanced'. Some are born with different qualities (such as beauty or the capability to develop certain types of skill or talent), or with disabilities; and people are born into different positions in the social and economic structure. To the extent that the position one is born into naturally necessitates (dis)advantages – be they institutional, such as caste systems; or economically, such as class systems; or socially such as caste and class systems; or educationally such as the (dis)advantages children have given the social, economic or educational attainments of their parents and so on – these constitute Personal Identity Luck. Some (dis)advantages might be inherent in our very genetic makeup – such as physical or mental impairments; beauty and so on.[3] They might be attached to someone of any social class. Others might come with the class – but in either case they constitute Personal Identity Luck. Contingent Brute Luck is constituted of the events which occur during one's life not correlated with social class that (dis)advantage one. These are completely outside one's control. The kind of simple bad luck that might hit anyone – such as being struck by lightning; or having some disabling disease and so on.[4]

We should note in passing that whilst contingent brute luck can be turned into option luck with the right insurance scheme, it requires the insurance scheme to be operable and in operation, otherwise option luck to contingent brute luck is like Kaldor-Hicks compensation is to no compensation. A bad day at the office matters when the work that day is an examination for promotion. And even then, identical outcomes do not follow from identical efforts when the normal bounds of marking entail that the same scripts might have reversed marks on different occasions.

I leave aside these distinctions between types of luck to be returned to below. First I want to interrogate the notion of luck itself. What precisely do we mean by 'luck'?

Interrogating luck

In contrast to 'responsibility' and 'choice' there is relatively little writing devoted to the precise meaning of the concept of 'luck'. Perhaps this is because the idea of 'luck' seems straightforward. In the egalitarian literature luck is usually thought of as those events which are outside of one's control. However, luck cannot straightforwardly be defined in terms of control for three reasons. First, 'control' is not a binary relation. There are not events which are completely in our control and those which are completely out of our control: even events we ordinarily think of being completely in someone's control occur with some probability between zero and one, even if that probability often approaches one. But other events considered to be in our control occur with probabilities much less than one. Events often do not turn out entirely as we intended even when we consider ourselves to be controlling them successfully. Secondly, most if not all of our efforts require joint action – if not others actively cooperating with us then at least not actively opposing us. Thirdly, not all events outside of our control are normally considered to be part of our luck. The sun rising each morning is outside of our control, but we do not normally consider ourselves to be lucky each day-break (Pritchard 2005).

It might seem obvious that luck has something to do with probabilities. And in the case of option luck, one could have insured against the (low) probability of calamity, but one preferred to keep one's money. If the calamity had not befallen one then one would gain advantage over those similarly placed who had insured. However, once calamity strikes then one is worse off than those who had insured. One entered the game, played the odds, and what results results. We might point out that risk takers sometimes win big against the odds; and sometimes they lose. That is life. Everyone can choose to be a risk taker, or behave conservatively. Taking responsibility for one's actions is to accept the consequences that follow. It is not merely option luck that concerns us here, but whether the acceptance of responsibilities includes the playing out of contingent brute bad luck following choices freely and responsibly made.

We can question the relationship between luck and probabilities. We might suggest that luck is not so much to do with probabilities as expectations. One may not expect one's house to be struck by lightning. When it is we call this bad luck. Not insuring one's house (at the correct odds for the likelihood) is not bad luck. One has not insured against the expectations properly constituted. That is why there is no justified claim for failures to insure.

But again, luck is not simply the difference between our expectations about what might occur and what actually occurs. A premiership club losing to a conference team may be against my expectations but has nothing to do with my luck if I am completely indifferent to the football results. Luck has to be measured in losses or gains, not simply in failures in expectations. Consider two lotteries. One with a ten million to one chance of winning a thousand pounds (for, say, a one-penny stake) and one with a million to one chance of winning a million pounds (for, say, a one-pound stake). Consider two people each with one ticket for each of the lotteries. Is the winner of the first lottery luckier than the winner of the second? The winner of the first lottery must have had lower expectations of winning (one in ten million) than the winner of the second (one in a million). But surely we think of the second winner as the luckiest, since his gain is the greater.

What matters then is the difference in rewards for the two individuals, each of whom behaved similarly with similar insurance, but for one person things worked out well and the other badly. How lucky or unlucky we think of either of the individuals depends upon the difference in the value of the respective outcomes. The contingent working out of the probabilities has determined who was lucky and who not, but how lucky one is considered to be is determined by the difference in the value of the outcomes. I will refer to the economic and social system of rewards as the 'reward structure'.

I will say more about what might be meant by the reward structure below. It could be considered to be equivalent to what Rawls (1971) calls the 'basic structure' – that is the major social institutions of government and regulation of trade and personal relations. However, it could also be given an expansive interpretation to cover those other elements that Cohen (1997, 2000) believes need to be covered by egalitarian concerns namely: the conventions that non-coercively govern our actions; the social ethos that shapes our attitudes to what is right and wrong; and the personal choices that people make.

How might one measure luck? We could view the amount of luck one has as a relationship between the expected outcome and the actual outcome. A measure of luck could be thought of as something like $AV - EV$, where EV is the expected value of the outcome and AV is the actual one. Over a series of trials, we would expect AV to approach EV. However luck is often associated with events that only happen once in a lifetime. My expected monetary payoff (EV) in a £1m lottery with a million to one chance of winning and where my ticket costs $1 is 0. We should note the seemingly odd consequence of examining 'luck' in this sense is that my actual payoff will never equal my expected payoff. For I either win: getting £999,999 (£1 million minus my stake); or I do not win: with a payoff of –£1. Thus the monetary payoff equals my luck in the lottery.

It seems naturally odd to consider someone who does not win a million to one lottery as 'unlucky' even to the extent of –£1, since their not winning is, with high probability, precisely what we expect. Perhaps it is better to consider luck as being related to the distribution of outcomes. We do not expect to win the lottery, so the expected outcome is –£1, and only if we do win, do we want to apply the term 'luck' to it. Bad luck is then only associated with outcomes that are unexpected. There are no unlucky losers in the lottery, only lucky winners. Such an interpretation requires an analysis of rational expectations of the odds of an event happening, but I will take this analysis no further here.[5]

In a similar vein Pritchard (2005, ch. 5) places two conditions on an event being lucky.

> (L1) If an event is lucky, then it is an event that occurs in the actual world but which does not occur in a wide class of the nearest possible worlds where the relevant initial conditions for that event are the same as in the actual world.
>
> (L2) If an event is lucky, then it is an event that is significant to the agent concerned (or would be significant, were the agent to be availed of the relevant facts).

We might see option luck or contingent brute luck in these terms. We cannot view personal identity luck in quite these terms. Personal identity luck is not subject to the first condition. It is only subject to the second. No person has any expectations about how they are to be placed in society prior to their birth, though given our knowledge of any society we can have expectations about the distribution how people will be placed in that society.[6] The only way in which we could apply the type of formula suggested above (p. 567) if expectations were to be taken as some average on the distribution of rewards. However, I will argue that even for choices made, whilst we ordinarily think of luck as something not expected, or being of low probability, it is the second condition that is most important in our calculation of how lucky someone is.[7]

One consequence of equating luck with the reward structure is to suggest that luck egalitarians are wrong to say that inequalities are unjustified to the extent they derive from brute bad luck:[8] though by this statement I do not mean any criticism of luck egalitarianism. Since luck is defined in terms of the reward structure it is the reward structure that creates unjustified inequality and it is by examining the reward structure that we must justify inequality rather than by the luck it creates. Luck is simply the label we paste on to unjustified inequalities as determined by the reward structure.

To the extent that there is a clear distinction between option and brute luck then the conclusion might follow that brute bad luck needs to be abolished and inequalities justified by decisions responsibly made. If the distinction is hard to maintain beyond some clear examples, then such an analysis is more problematic. If attention needs to be directed towards the correct reward structure, then different views about just rewards, the ends of the good life, and how far we want to encourage responsibility as opposed to equality become significant. This is because we cannot hold the concept of 'responsibility' static any more than we can the concept of 'luck'. Changing the reward structure will not only affect the differences in luck, it will also affect incentives to behave in one or another manner, which will reflect upon how responsible people are. That is, there is not a fixed amount of luck or responsibility in a society. Rather the reward structure will determine how much luck *and* responsibility there is for each person in that society.

We need to examine the relationship between luck and probabilities a little more closely to see how difficult it can be to distinguish brute and option luck; and to examine the relationship between the reward structure and responsibility.

Luck and probabilities

Imagine a simple Bournelli trial of coin tosses. In each trial we have a pattern of outcomes with probability p (success) and $1 - p$ (failure). What patterns do we describe as good/bad luck and what do we describe as 'to be expected'? For each trial we know the probability of heads is 0.5 and for tails is 0.5. Let us concentrate upon the probability of getting heads as success. Each time the coin comes down heads, we see this as success. If the coin comes down heads on a trial we can see this as good luck. Sometimes winning the toss can be very important to an outcome. In cricket, winning the toss can, at times, virtually decide the outcome of the match. But in any coin toss, with a fair coin, coming down heads has a probability of 0.5. Once more we can see that how much luck we assign to any given coin toss is determined by the reward. Tossing a coin in a laboratory to, say, generate a random set of outcomes, involves no luck. Tossing the coin to see who gets the £1 million does.

Now consider a sequence of tosses. If we toss the coin 100 times, we should expect there to be sequences where it comes down heads more often than 50% of the time. We could look at the sequence 6–15, and see eight heads, and the sequence 53–62 and see only two heads. Both *sequences* are expected in the sense that we can assign the same probability to each sequence occurring. Again however, if we are betting on the coin coming down heads, the first sequence might be called lucky, the second unlucky. But how much luck do we assign to each sequence? The question is how can one empirically apply the concept of luck to a sequence of coin tosses? We know that the 50–50 split will not necessarily be seen in a short sequence. We can work out the probability of any given split that we do see. However, if we see someone tossing a coin and the heads-to-tails split seemed to favour heads when he bets on heads, and tails when he bets on tails, then we might begin to think that the coin is not fair. If it is established that the coin is fair then we might think it is his tossing that is not fair. We might begin to think that the sequence is determined by skill. The question is at what point would we think the sequence was determined by skill? We have a hypothetical answer about expectations about sequences, and we have an actual set of sequences. The actual set does not fit our expectations, yet we also have an expectation about how often such a set of sequences would not fit our expectations.

We have an under-determination problem. We can extrapolate from the evidence either that the agent is skilfully tossing the coin to get heads (or tails) more often than we should expect, or for the set of sequences we have witnessed, the agent has been lucky. On one account he is lucky, on another he is skilful. How can we determine which our case is?

In the following I will be suggesting that this simple example of judging luck or skill in coin tossing shows the difficulty of judging whether someone has ended up where they are through contingent brute luck or through option luck. That is, whether they can be judged to be responsible for their position in life or whether it is down to luck. I ignore personal identity luck here, to be returned to later.

Path dependency

We have seen the difficulties of understanding luck in simple sequences of coin tosses and then considered how we might view luck with regard to level of skill at coin tossing. One way of judging skill would be to examine independent evidence. We might glean this by looking at the total population and examining the correspondence between how people look when tossing the coin, and the types of sequences they reach. For example, for any group of coin-tossers who seem to have better luck than others we could examine the manner in which they toss coins to see if we can tell how they are able to generate more heads than the unlucky group. Correlating success with some evidence independent of success – such as the manner of the coin-tosser – might allow us to judge skill. If we are correct in our inferences we could then teach that skill to enable others to correctly toss heads more often than we would expect by chance.

The analogy is to how players look when playing sports. We develop theories about good batting at cricket, hitting at baseball, golf swings and using a tennis racket. Our theory about how to play, together with how well people do, can teach us some of the differences between skill and luck. But even here, we know that 'looking right' and getting the right results are not perfectly correlated. Some good players manage to break the rules, and many people 'look right' yet do not gain good results. Nevertheless, the coincidence of results and the way people seem to play allows us to make some judgements about how skilful people are at sports and what constitutes a lucky break. Does the relationship of skill at sports teach us anything about contingent brute luck and responsibility in other areas of life? It can perhaps teach us something about path dependency and how luck affects responsibility.

One important aspect of doing well at sport is temperament. Temperament both enables us to work hard at training and also affects the outcome of matches. In some sports temperament is the key to success. There are many good snooker players playing in clubs, but to keep one's form in high-tension matches requires a nerve that some people do not seem to have. This is so in other sports too. Some players in tennis are thought to have the 'big match temperament' whilst others are seen as 'chokers' who play well but do not win as much and all too often lose the big games. Sometimes the player who appears less skilful wins because she seems to have the 'big match temperament'. She may be beaten more often than not by her opponent, until it comes to the big tournaments and then she seems to always prevail. We might think this 'big match temperament' is a type of skill. We might hope to find some material manifestation of this skill independently of the results one achieves due to it. For example, we might think it appears in some DNA sequence. However, given what we know about the manner in which genes are switched on and off by environmental conditions this is likely to be a forlorn hope since the big match temperament is likely to be highly path dependent.

One player, Martha, may be thought to have the big match temperament, whilst another, Cherie, may be a 'choker'. These are genuine facets about their play, but each may have developed those temperaments fortuitously. Perhaps the first time, they met in a final, Cherie was off colour and lost. The second she was on form, but Martha had a couple of lucky calls and edged out Cherie. Now Martha has a winning sequence of two, and Cherie a losing sequence of two. This fact about their history of matches that occurred because of luck rather than skill (by supposition) – now affects future matches. Perhaps in their third match Cherie starts to play badly as she closes on victory, in part caused by her losing the two previous finals. Then she loses a fourth time through the run of the ball (luck). By now she can never beat Martha in big final because she is, indeed, a choker.

In fact what we have with regards to the early sequence of Martha and Cherie's matches is an outcome space that is typically patterned into different subsets and that patterning gains its significance from how it is perceived. It was chance really that Martha beat Cherie twice, but the fact that the pattern matters to them affects they way they play in future finals, which then alters future patterns of the outcome space. Future patterning would have its own contingent brute luck without the past patterning affecting today's play. But players' behaviour has been altered by their perception of the past patterning. The patterning of a subspace of sequences of coin tosses gains significance depending upon what was riding on each sequence. Similar sequencing has occurred between Martha and Cherie, but with the added difference that previous sequencing (by supposition caused through brute luck) has affected subsequent sequencing by the choices made by the players. Cherie may not be as aggressive as she normally is in her play because of the 'choking effect' and this affects the subspace she currently occupies. Brute luck is affecting her choice – choice otherwise made with full responsibility.

In other words contingent brute bad luck affects the nature of choices one makes, not simply now, but forever. But that means that it affects our attitudes towards risk and so how we make choices when faced with options. Past contingent brute luck also affects one's reactions to future option luck: but by how much?

How unlucky has Cherie been in continually losing to Marie in the final? We have considered the probabilities in terms of the patterning of outcome subspace and how that affects future patterns. But that does not determine how unlucky she has been. Luck depends on the reward structure and the nature of what we feel should be equalized. If money is the object of equality, how unlucky Cherie is depends upon the relative difference between first and second prize. If respect and status is important then it depends upon how much respect and status rides for each on the results of their finals.

The degree that chance played in creating the sequences of losses for Cherie against Martha plays a role in our judgement of their respective luck. But how unlucky Cherie is, and how lucky Martha, depends upon the rewards that were consequent upon the sequence of outcomes. If the rewards for winning are only marginally superior to those of losing then Martha has only had a little bit of good luck and Cherie a little bit of bad luck. If the rewards are very different then the amount of luck each had – dependent upon the playing out of chance and its subsequent effect upon future behaviour – will be consequently higher. An egalitarian should then want the rewards consequent upon winning not to be too great. But how much is too great?

A radical egalitarian would want the rewards for winning and losing to be the same. Though precisely what we include in rewards is important. We might imagine the monetary rewards of winning and losing to be identical. But can we imagine the entirety of rewards being equal? Some lists of the relevant thing to be equalized include 'respect' or the 'social bases of respect'. Can we really imagine no difference in how the players or spectators would feel about winning or losing? If two players compete, then their very nature will determine that there are rewards for winning – or there would be no competition. There has to be some motivation for them to compete; tennis is not simply patting a ball over a net. So there will be some inequalities.

One argument for Rawls's difference principle is that inequalities are justified to the extent that they exist for the benefit of the worst off group in society. One incentive argument suggests that in order to motivate people to do well greater differences in 'prizes' for succeeding are required than, say, merely greater respect. Material rewards generate greater output of goods and services, and with the correct tax and transfer schemes this greater output can be to the advantage of the worst off.

All would agree that current reward structures do not exist for the worst off groups, and the degree of inequality that exists cannot be justified by the difference principle. There is disagreement, however, over whether this is because markets are inherently bad at generating the correct incentive schemes, or whether we simply do not have working labour markets. Certainly, few could seriously maintain that we have a labour market rather than a privileged self-serving club for remuneration of company executives. Some maintain that with a finely tuned basic structure, labour markets could operate for the worst off by creating the right incentives for rewarding talents and hard work.[9] Quite how egalitarian such a society would be – whether the economic rent demanded by the high producers would mean great inequality even if their productivity made the worse off better off in terms of our measurement device; or whether making the worse off according to our measurement device would entail that such economic rents must be relatively low is not something we can judge without a clear understanding of both the measurement device and empirics about the incentive effects of the economic in terms of that device. I do not wish to get into that discussion here. Rather I want to examine the how the nature of reward systems affect responsibility in egalitarian schema.

Patterns and responsibility

We assign responsibility according to the amount of control that individuals have over the outcomes that result from their actions. The number of viable alternatives in their opportunity set limits their choice of actions. The assignation of responsibility given any opportunity set depends on how diverse is the choice and the relationship between the action and the outcomes. Here I concentrate upon the latter problem. The sporting analogy was designed to show how difficult it might be to assign responsibility in some cases. We can assign expectations over the likelihood of sequences of heads and tails (what I refer to as a 'pattern') in finite series of coin tosses. However, if an individual appears to get heads more often than we should expect over a long enough sequence, we might expect that the pattern is not random. However, often the data will underdetermine whether a pattern is random or forced in some manner.

Furthermore, given that confidence (or temperament) is important for successfully instigating particular types of patterning of outcomes, past outcomes affect one's present skill levels. As long as luck is assigned to chance events, and responsibility to those more under one's control (skill) then our assignation of responsibility will depend upon our judgements about the conditioning of confidence and temperament.

This demonstrates, however, that present responsibility for outcomes might well be based upon past contingent brute luck. If we recognize that inequalities are justified by the degree of responsibility that people have to outcomes (based on their behaviour now) we will not be removing brute luck entirely from the reward structure. And we should not. Contingent brute bad luck is something that enables character to develop, just as contingent brute good luck might.[10]

How do we judge individual responsibility in relation to patterns in behaviour dependent upon choices made? To return to the sporting analogy: it was suggested that temperament is important in sporting events. We would ordinarily place temperament within the ambit of personal responsibility. Learning how to develop a big match temperament is something that coaches try to train in their protégés. Certainly we might see it not only as an aspect of but an integral part of personality. I have argued, however, that it is also something that might be developed through contingent brute luck. If we try to reduce the element of luck in our egalitarian society by reducing the differences in rewards for winning and losing, we are also likely to affect the development of temperament. The greater the differences between winning and losing the more likely that features of temperament will emerge. If there is little at stake in a game then 'choking' is less likely to emerge. If we make the results too egalitarian we lose elements of responsibility. Would this be a general feature?

If the sporting analogy has any utility for life more generally the problem it illustrates for the luck egalitarian is that we need incentives to enable choice and responsibility that will not exacerbate the effects of contingent brute luck.

To return to the characterization of responsibility above (pp. 562–563), we assign responsibility to the extent that people have a viable set of distinguishable alternatives. To make responsible choice those alternatives must be distinguishable. If it makes no difference whether one wins or loses a tennis match, or becomes a lawyer, doctor or gardener, because any potential difference is compensated for, then there is no distinction and therefore no responsibility. Of course, there has to be a difference between winning and losing in tennis as long as we keep score. There are, of course, distinguishing features of lawyers, doctors and gardeners outside of any material rewards. But to the extent there are these distinguishing features there are incentives to choose one job or profession over the others. Those incentives include the nature of the job, one's fitness to take it on, reputational effects and material benefits. We might want to equalize many of those different incentives. However, if we equalize over all of them, then we are left with no choices – only 'picks' or 'assignments' – and no responsibility for choices. In other words, the attempt to distinguish responsibility and luck for differential outcomes does not allow us to bring responsibility into the conception of equality rather than as a rival desideratum.

Perhaps the situation is not so bleak for egalitarians. In order for individuals to be motivated to choose alternatives from opportunity sets, they need to be able to find them distinctive. This does not imply that everything must be the same for everyone. That would only be so if all humans were stirred by precisely the same motivations. But people have different desires, talents and so on. If there were the perfect niche for each person to fulfil their lives, and each niche were equally socially valued, then we could have responsible choosing of niches with equal social valuation. Individuals would maximize for themselves and equalize across society. We could not be assured however, that such a fitting of people into niches would be socially optimal. No one might want to clean the streets.

Incentives

Given there is no reason to think that people naturally want to fill all available niches, incentives are required for people to choose some occupations rather than others. Some egalitarians have argued that Rawls's difference principle must be applied to moral psychology as well the basic structure (Narveson 1996, 1998; Cohen 2000). Cohen has argued that we need to understand that it is not enough for the basic structure or constitution of society to be geared towards equality if other interdependent factors are not also egalitarian in character. The conventions of society, the social ethos that shapes people's attitudes and the personal choices that people make must all be geared towards egalitarian aims. It is not my aim to criticize Cohen's account in any detail. Estlund (1998), Williams (1998), Pogge (2000) and others have done so. It is sufficient to say that I believe the best way of changing personal choices towards greater fraternity and equality is to turn the social ethos and the conventions of society towards those aims. And those are most easily manipulated in that direction by the institutions of the basic structure (the argument of Pogge (2000)). Rather we need to understand what such an argument means for responsibility. We could simply define the just society as one where everyone does what is best. There are indeed social niches and everyone responsibly works out where their niche is and fills it. Or we could think more seriously about the need for incentives.

I began the paper by suggesting that the object to be equalized was very important for the discussion of how we are to view the issues addressed in the paper. Throughout I have assumed, usually in the background, sometimes in the foreground, that the object of equality is material benefits or simply more money. I do not believe, as it happens, that human psychology will ever allow us to equalize across possible jobs the equalization of income, let alone wealth. But for the sake of argument, we can imagine a society where the reward structure materially equalizes across all positions. Unless the state directs what people do, we can still imagine a labour market of sorts. There will be numerous positions to be filled. There can be objective criteria for filling these positions – based upon qualifications gained, human capital and so on. However, if someone is qualified for several jobs, what would be their reasons for choosing one over another? If Martha had the capability to be a doctor, an architect or a gardener, and there are no material incentives for one over the other, then she will choose in terms of the satisfaction she expects to gain. So she chooses to be a gardener. This will means one fewer gardening jobs going, so Michael, who could have been a gardener, gets a job working in a restaurant. He gains less satisfaction from that position than as a gardener. Now it might be said that Martha should have taken a job as a doctor, leaving the gardening job for Michael. That might maximize the position of the least well-off person – Michael. Though if material rewards are equalized then Martha, unhappy as a doctor, becomes the least well off and Michael, happy as a gardener, should perhaps take the job in the restaurant. In other words, once material rewards are equalized then incentives for responsible choice must come from somewhere else. Do these need to be equalized too? If so, we may have problems since we have reduced what we can trade for those rewards. And we cannot be assured that everyone ideally fits into a particular niche for social optimality. If we are to leave room for responsibility we must leave some room for inequalities somewhere.

We do not get rid of contingent brute luck in such a situation either. Someone may choose a career because of the interest it might bring, but, through no fault of their own, discover that the nature of the job changes over time. An academic may choose a career in what she thinks will be an exciting research programme, but regrets the choice as someone else soon makes all the exciting discoveries and now there is only tedious follow-up work.

Fully functioning perfect labour markets are supposed to materially reward talent and effort, and oil some of the differences in job satisfaction. Of course, supposing that this occurs is almost as fantastical as expecting each person morally to find their perfect niche. 'Talent' is a term taken for granted in much of the egalitarian literature. As we have seen, judging the degree of talent is difficult. Talent may include some genetic predisposition or capabilities, but is largely a result of development involving luck as well as training. We may judge relative talents within disciplines reasonably well. We may be able to make judgements about who constitutes the best sets of lawyers, doctors, academics, road-sweepers, sportspeople and so on. That is, talents (together with associated luck) may emerge within labour categories, but we can only judge across categories when we have some currency by which to measure the judgement. Salary and respect are two obvious candidates. However, we cannot be assured that either work well. Perhaps perfect labour markets might provide relative salary levels on which to place such judgements. We can be assured that current labour markets signally fail. Brute luck comes into effect with salary levels as shortages or fashion, or technological change may destroy the carefully reasoned grounds for job choice. Trading the interesting career as an academic for the better paid though boring accountancy job might end up a poor decision as academia becomes a minefield of administration rather than research. In other words, there may be some relationship between talent and effort and rewards through well-functioning labour markets. But there is a lot of luck involved too.[11]

All this is by way of repeating that whilst responsible choosing is involved so will contingent brute luck. They go together. That is not to say that the effects of luck cannot be reduced. Formal equal opportunities and ensuring the respect of rights will do so. Ensuring that job satisfaction can remain as high as possible through labour laws will do so. And setting the terms of material rewards so the highest and lowest paid do not have such great disparity will do so.

I have been arguing that to place emphasis on responsibility and luck in justifying levels of inequality is to examine the epiphenomena of problem. The reward structure largely determines the degree of both. Egalitarians need to answer crucial empirical questions about what levels of inequality are acceptable, including: How great should the differentials be between the highest and lowest earners? What is the highest sustainable level of basic income? What level of disability might require extra help? Historically there have been suggestions as to the relevant differentials that might be justified. The manifesto group of the British Labour Party in the early 1980s suggested differentials of top to bottom earners of something like 10:1 whilst Proudhon suggested a 4:1 ratio. However, picking ratios out of the air may not be the best procedure. What we can be assured, however, is that current levels of inequality are unjustified. And a start towards working out justified inequalities would be to pick off the unjustified ones first.

Personal identity luck

I set aside personal identity luck as a form of brute luck. If luck is measured as some form of relationship between expected outcomes and actual outcomes, then lowly returns from a lowly position in life can hardly be called bad luck. After all, if one is in a lower class, with uneducated parents, poor upbringing and so on, then the poor outcomes one receives can hardly be unexpected. If we measure luck something along the lines suggested on page 77 then two people on their deathbeds may have had identical luck, but one might have lived a life of relative poverty in relation to the other. Of course, the point at which we measure brute luck at birth is not from one's circumstances at birth, but from some imagined original position behind a veil of ignorance. And what we are measuring with personal identity luck at birth is the social structure as measured by expected rewards of birth into different social classes.

Seen in this manner, personal identity luck is a measurement of social class and caste; and a measure of expected lifestyle for people with different capabilities (such as 'natural talents' or disabilities).[12] To that extent the best hope we can expect to measure the differences in personal identity luck by looking at the outcomes of difference classes or what John Roemer (1998) calls 'types' of people using his Equality of Opportunity (EoP) measure. Roemer believes his measure captures the effects of brute luck. I think that is too broad a claim. Rather, it captures the average effects of personal identity luck across type.

We can see why Roemer's approach does not capture responsibility from his response to one of the early criticisms of his EoP measure (Roemer 1998, pp. 21–22). Roemer's measure is designed to capture autonomous effort – or responsibility. He does so by selecting his types by a vector of characteristics outside of the control of people (personal identity luck) with each member of a type sharing similar characteristics. The assumption is that each type faces similar opportunity sets, and how well they do through their choice of elements within the sets is a measure of their responsibility. So we can look at the average salary of each centile in two types (men and women) and the differences across the types will show the difference in opportunity to earn money between the two types.

Now an underlying assumption of such statistical analysis is that the residual we are trying to capture (and other error terms) are equally normally distributed within each type. That is, any factor that affects the selection of variable within opportunity sets not contained in the data, affects each type in precisely the same manner. For that reason choice of types is important.[13] Brian Barry constructed an example of two types: an academic and an Asian type, who, as it happens, have identical success at education.[14] However, the Asian group got there through sheer hard work caused by their cultural milieu, whereas the academic type breezed through with little effort. If we want to reward effort, Barry suggests, the Asian type should receive higher rewards than the academic type, but Roemer's formula treats both types equally. Roemer (1998, pp. 21–22) responds that if indeed the pain of hard work is what is to be rewarded then Barry is correct, but he is trying to capture autonomously taken effort. The comparison in autonomously taken effort is between Asian children within type, not in comparison with another (academic) type. In itself this is a reasonable response. What it reveals is the assumption that autonomously chosen effort is assumed to be equally normally distributed across types.

What reason do we have for making such an assumption? To continue the education example, it may be that the top centile in each group is successful not due to autonomous choice, but because their parents are pushy relative to other parents of that type. The difference between the Asian type and a non-Asian type might be tracking relative parenting pushiness across types (culture), but the differences within both the Asian and non-Asian groups could be capturing relative parenting pushiness within each type. Or again, we can capture systematic factors across types affecting health (bad personal identity luck), but relative health levels within types may be capturing the effects of contingent brute luck rather than autonomously chosen life-styles. Moreover, however we define types, and whatever it is we measure, whilst there are inequalities (captured by dividing the types into centiles) these problems will emerge.

This criticism of Roemer's EoP measure is directed at his interpretation of what it measures. It is not directed at the measure itself. EoP measures the systematic effects of personal identity luck as captured by relevant social and ethnic classes as well as by gender. Using such a measure to reduce relative inequalities across such types would be a massive step forward for equality. I do not believe, however, that the inequalities that would be left – those captured by placing individuals into centiles within types – would simply be those left by personal responsibility for the reasons argued in this paper.

Conclusion

I have examined the claim that inequality can only be justified in terms of choices freely and responsibly made and that egalitarianism requires the effects of brute bad luck to be removed. On the face of it this seems a very reasonable egalitarian claim. I have argued, however, that luck is largely defined in terms of the reward structure. That in itself should not be a problem for egalitarians. Changes in the reward structure will reduce brute bad luck. However, changing the reward structure will, as those on the right of the ideological spectrum claim, affect the degree of responsibility that people can take for their choices. Luck and responsibility is an epiphenomena of the incentives that people have to choose from the opportunity sets available. One conclusion is that egalitarians need to take a closer look at what reasonable rewards should be. They need to make empirical claims about how great the differential rewards for different types of behaviour should be.

I have also shown that luck and responsibility are more closely bound than often imagined. Our personalities and characters are created by our history and that will include past contingent brute luck. Luck will reverberate throughout our lives and we cannot hope to remove bad luck entirely from the rewards we receive. Some may now make better (more responsible) decisions than others simply because of luckier decisions in the past. It is hard to disentangle luck and responsibility.

We can measure, as John Roemer has importantly shown, average differences in personal identity luck based on types of individual. We can work to reduce the inequities that exist across those types. I have argued, however, that we cannot be assured that his measure captures responsibility as opposed to luck within types. Contingent brute luck may be equally normally distributed within each type, as are autonomously derived effort levels.

We do want to assign responsibility to people. We do want to reward people who have, through their own efforts, done well. At the individual level, both in our personal and professional lives, we can seek to ensure that that happens. Governments can seek to reduce inequality and should utilize the results of social research that demonstrates systematic effects creating inequities. It should seek to reduce the inequalities across types and classes of people. Governments should not seek to reward responsibility but leave that to others. Rather it should seek to reduce inequalities and welfare losses dependent upon failures in responsibility. We know there are many failures in human rational action. We know people systematically under-insure against calamity. We know people under-insure against infirmity. We know evolution has fitted people to like fatty, salty and sugary foods that are now in super-abundance in the developed world. We know children are not the best judges of their educational needs; that parents will fight to give advantage to their own children; and that the distribution of good family backgrounds is not equitable. Government can regulate to try to overcome all of these problems and more. It should not be concerned to reward the distribution of responsibility over decisions within these areas, but rather, should try to raise the threshold of poor decisions where we know they are systematically deficient.

Acknowledgements

This paper was presented at the 'Choice Group', London School of Economics, November 2005; the British Academy on 16 December 2005; and the Political Ideas conference, St Catherine's College Oxford, on 3 January 2006. I would like to thank audience members for their comments, especially Chris Armstrong, the late Brian Barry, Richard Bradley, Alex Brown, Ian Hampshire-Monk, David Owen, Adam Swift, Simon Tormey, Alex Voorhoevre, and Andrew Williams, although I admit I have not made as many changes to the text as their comments deserve. I would also like to thank Martin van Hees and Christian List for the many conversations we have had about luck prior to the writing of this paper.

Notes

1. Dworkin's distinction between 'option' and 'brute' luck is considered below.

2. The literature assumes that the insurance market is efficient and correctly judges the probabilities of chance events. However, if one is subject to the vagaries of life against which one cannot insure, then no blame can be attached to one.
3. Though even here, of course, what counts as beauty or mental impairment depends upon the nature of society (its structure and culture).
4. In fact elements of the genetic side of Personal Identity Luck might also be correlated with class – if 'beauty' is inherited and enables upward social mobility then it too will be correlated with class. Similarly, inherited susceptibilities to disease may be more likely to emerge where social conditions are more stressful, again hitting the lower social classes to a greater extent. Even lightning might strike those who are out in the field more so contingent brute luck may not be completely contingent. I ignore that possibility here and assume contingent brute luck is equally normally distributed amongst all social classes. That is, it is the normal distribution of such brute luck that makes it contingent brute luck rather than personal identity luck
5. We cannot assume that luck is the difference between the actual outcome and the most probable one, as Richard Bradley pointed out to me. Whilst this seems to be a reasonable account of luck when the most probable outcome is highly likely, it is not when the differences between the outcomes are small. Consider the lottery where you have a one in six chance of winning each of £10, £20, £30 and £40 and a two in six chance of winning nothing. The most probable outcome is nothing, but we might describe someone who won nothing as unlucky. Perhaps it depends on how the outcomes are described – winning nothing or winning something.
6. For that reason such personal identity brute bad luck might be better termed 'fortune' and certainly that phrase is closer to natural English. I make nothing of the linguistic point; what matters is the conceptual analysis and what it entails.
7. Pritchard's analysis of luck is written with regard to problems in the theory of knowledge and how to analyze epistemic luck, that is, the luck that associated with 'knowing something' by chance, as in the Gettier (1963) examples. How I analyze luck here is not meant as any form of criticism of his analysis in the context in which he is writing.
8. Developed, for example, by Arneson (1989, 1999); Cohen (1989, 2000); Roemer (1996, 1998).
9. Some argue that the operation of markets leads to inequalities that luck egalitarianism allows but that are surely wrong (Anderson 1999, Scheffler 2003). However, I am querying the neat option luck–brute luck distinction that such a claim relies upon.
10. In the comedy science fiction TV series *Red Dwarf*, what Rimmer (one of life's 'losers') thinks was good luck in not being held back a year at school, he discovers was bad luck when he meets his superhero self from the possible world where he was held back a year and which led him to transform his attitude to life.
11. This was well understood by the management guru W. Edwards Deming who argued that performance pay outside of strict confines was illusory as there is so much random variation in performance.
12. I use the term 'capability' in its dictionary definition as a 'potential ability' rather than Sen's (1984, 1987a, 1987b, 1993, 1999) and Nussbaum's (2000) preferred use of it to mean 'ability'. See Morriss (2002) and Dowding (2006).
13. As far as I can see most of the criticisms of Roemer's EoP approach (for example, Phillips 2006) merely give examples where this assumption clearly cannot be satisfied. This means that his formula cannot be used in those cases; it is not a criticism of the formula itself.

14. Brian Barry constructed the example at the American Political Science Association conference in 1996, and is discussed by Roemer (1998, pp. 21–24).

References

Anderson, E., 1999. What is the point of equality? *Ethics,* 109 (2), 287–337.

Arneson, R.J., 1989. Equality of opportunity for welfare. *Philosophical studies,* 56 (1), 77–93.

Arneson, R.J., 1999. Equality of opportunity for welfare defended and recanted. *Journal of political philosophy,* 7 (4) 488–497.

Barry, B.M., 2005. *Why social justice matters.* Cambridge: Polity.

Cohen, G.A., 1989. On the currency of egalitarian justice, *Ethics* 99 (4), 906–944.

Cohen, G.A., 1995. *Self-ownership, freedom, and equality.* Cambridge: Cambridge University Press.

Cohen, G.A., 1997. Where the action is: on the site of distributive justice. *Philosophy & public affairs,* 26 (1), 3–30.

Cohen, G.A., 2000. *If you're an egalitarian, how come you're so rich?* Cambridge, MA: Harvard University Press.

Dennett, D.C., 2003. *Freedom evolves.* London: Allen Lane.

Dowding, K., 1991. *Rational choice and political power.* Aldershot: Elgar.

Dowding, K., 2006. Can capabilities reconcile freedom and equality? *Journal of political philosophy,* 14 (3), 323–336.

Dowding, K. and van Hees, M., 2008. Freedom of choice. *In*: P. Anand, C. Puppe and P Pattaniak, eds. *Oxford handbook of rational and social choice.* Oxford: Oxford University Press.

Dworkin, R., 1981. What is equality? Part 2: Equality of resources. *Philosophy & public affairs,* 10 (3), 283–345.

Dworkin, R., 2000. *Sovereign virtue: the theory and practice of equality.* Cambridge: Cambridge University Press.

Estlund, D., 1998. Liberalism, equality and fraternity in Cohen's critique of Rawls. *Journal of political philosophy,* 6 (1), 99–112.

Gettier, E., 1963. Is justified true belief knowledge? *Analysis,* 23 (6), 121–123.

Hurley, S.L., 2003. *Justice, luck, and knowledge.* Cambridge, MA: Harvard University Press.

Morriss, P., 2002. *Power: a philosophical analysis.* Manchester: Manchester University Press.

Narveson, J.F., 1976. A puzzle about economic justice in Rawls' theory. *Social theory and practice,* 4 (1), 1–27.

Narveson, J.F., 1978. Rawls on equal distribution of wealth. *Philosophia,* 7 (2), 281–292.

Nussbaum, M., 2000. *Women and human development: the capability approach.* Cambridge: Cambridge University Press.

Phillips, A., 2006. 'Really equal': opportunities and autonomy. *Journal of political philosophy,* 14 (1), 18–32.
Pogge, T., 2000. On the site of distributive justice: reflections on Cohen and Murphy. *Philosophy & public affairs,* 29 (1), 137–169.
Pritchard, D., 2005. *Epistemic luck.* Oxford: Oxford University Press.
Rawls, J., 1971. *A theory of justice.* Oxford: Oxford University Press.
Roemer, J.E., 1996. *Theories of distributive justice.* Cambridge, MA: Harvard University Press.
Roemer, J.E., 1998. *Equality of opportunity.* Cambridge, MA: Harvard University Press.
Scheffler, S., 2003. What is egalitarianism? *Philosophy & public affairs,* 31 (1), 5–39.
Sen, A., 1984. *Resources, values and development.* Oxford: Blackwell.
Sen, A., 1987a. *Commodities and capabilities.* New Delhi: Oxford University Press.
Sen, A., 1987b. The standard of living: lecture II, lives and capabilities. *In*: G. Hawthorn, ed. *The standard of living: the Tanner lectures, Clare Hall, Cambridge, 1985.* Cambridge: Cambridge University Press.
Sen, A., 1993. Capability and well-being. *In*: M. Nussbaum and A. Sen, eds. *The quality of life.* Oxford: Oxford University Press.
Sen, A., 1999. *Development as freedom.* Oxford: Oxford University Press.
Ullmann-Margalit, E. and Morgenbesser, S., 1977. Picking and choosing. *Social research,* 44 (4), 757–784.
Williams, A., 1998. Incentives, inequality and publicity. *Philosophy & public affairs* 27 (3), 225–247.

Coercive redistribution and public agreement: re-evaluating the libertarian challenge of charity

Clare Chambers[a] and Philip Parvin[b]

[a]*Jesus College, University of Cambridge, Cambridge, UK;* [b]*Trinity Hall, University of Cambridge, Cambridge, UK*

In this article, we evaluate the capacity of liberal egalitarianism to rebut what we call the libertarian challenge of charity. This challenge states that coercive redistributive taxation is neither needed nor justified, since those who endorse redistribution can give charitably, and those who do not endorse redistribution cannot justifiably be coerced. We argue that contemporary developments in liberal political thought render liberalism more vulnerable to this libertarian challenge. Many liberals have, in recent years, sought to recast liberalism such that it is more hospitable to cultural, religious, and ethnic diversity. This move has resulted in increased support for the claim that liberalism should be understood as a political rather than comprehensive doctrine, and that liberal institutions should draw their legitimacy from agreements made among members of an appropriately conceived deliberative community, rather than from controversial liberal principles like individual autonomy. We argue that, while this move may indeed make liberalism more compatible with cultural diversity, it also makes it more vulnerable to the libertarian challenge of charity. Not all versions of liberalism are troubled by the challenge, but those that are troubled by it are increasingly dominant. We also discuss G.A. Cohen's claim that liberal equality requires an 'egalitarian ethos' and argue that, if Cohen is right, it is difficult to see how there can be an adequate response to the libertarian challenge of charity. In general, our argument can be summarised as follows: *the more that liberalism is concerned accurately to model the actual democratic wishes and motivations of the people it governs, the less it is able to justify coercively imposing redistributive principles of justice.*

Egalitarian arguments in favour of redistribution have attracted criticism from libertarians. Robert Nozick's *Anarchy, state, and utopia* set the scene for debates about the legitimacy of taxation, social justice, and self-ownership which dominated Anglo-American political philosophy throughout the 1970s and early 1980s. More recently, however, the debate has shifted. Debates about redistribution now tend to centre on the luck egalitarian approach, with its issues of choice and responsibility, rather than on justifying the redistributive state. Meanwhile, many liberal thinkers have chosen to focus on a very different set of issues, primarily those of identity, community, citizenship, and culture.

Communitarian critics of liberalism focused on fundamental questions about the conception of the individual that lay at the heart of the Rawlsian model. These critiques yielded insights into the nature of the self which forced many liberals to re-think their commitments to principles such as individuality and autonomy. Many liberals felt the need to demonstrate how liberal principles could be compatible with individuals' rootedness in cultural, religious, and other communities which shape their preferences and conceptions of the good (Sandel 1982; Walzer 1985; Taylor 1992; MacIntyre 1996). While liberals such as Joseph Raz and Will Kymlicka (who we might describe as adopting a 'comprehensive' understanding of liberalism) controversially sought to ground individuals' capacity for autonomy precisely in these memberships (Raz 1986; Kymlicka 1989), many other liberals sought to empty liberalism of its substantive commitments on the grounds that liberalism should be as neutral or impartial as possible between rival understandings of such fundamental matters as identity and autonomy.

This trend became even more pervasive in the wake of debates about multiculturalism and minority rights (which largely grew out of earlier debates between liberals and communitarians). For many, it would seem, the most pressing issue facing liberal political theory is not whether and how social and political institutions should distribute benefits and burdens, but how liberalism might be re-interpreted in order that it accommodate cultural, ethnic, and religious diversity.

This political or impartialist approach to understanding and justifying liberal justice is now the dominant form of liberalism. The claim that liberalism should not seek to ground its conception of justice in controversial liberal conceptions of the good but in the common agreement of all those diverse individuals who are to be bound by them has been advanced by a growing body of thinkers including John Rawls, Charles Larmore, William Galston, and many others. All claim that liberalism should – as far as possible – shun the justification of liberal justice in substantive, controversial principles in favour of agreements derived from appropriately configured public deliberation in the interests of deriving a conception of justice which takes seriously the claims of cultural and religious minorities.

It is our contention that, even if these reinterpretations of liberalism render liberalism more hospitable to communitarian or multiculturalist concerns, they leave it more vulnerable to libertarianism. We focus on one libertarian claim in particular: that *coercive* redistribution is neither required nor justified. One of Nozick's arguments against state redistribution is that the duty we have to help the poor is a moral duty to perform acts of charity, not a political obligation to comply with state redistribution. We call this claim *the libertarian challenge of charity*: why should principles of redistributive justice be coercive?[1]

We argue that, while some forms of liberal egalitarianism can answer the libertarian challenge of charity fairly straightforwardly, others cannot. In general, we argue that liberals who care about establishing a regime of coercive principles which underwrite redistributive initiatives aimed at alleviating poverty should think twice about adopting the political liberal model, for it may be that in doing so they undermine their ability to rebut the libertarian challenge of charity. We begin in section 1 by outlining three kinds of responses that liberal egalitarians might provide to the libertarian challenge (in favour of principles being coercive): responses of *disagreement* about the principles of justice; of *unreasonableness* on the part of some individual members of the polity to engage with others on fair terms; and problems of *motivation* to act justly. We then discuss, in the following sections, which kinds of liberalism contain the normative resources to appeal to these responses. We assume throughout that the normatively weakest response to the libertarian challenge is that of problems of *motivation*, and that all liberals are able to appeal to this response. However, in the final part of the chapter we explore in depth the arguments put forward by one particular egalitarian thinker – G.A. Cohen – who believes that this response is not open to liberal egalitarians. We discuss Cohen's argument at length because, if true, his conclusion would have profound implications for liberalism, and if our wider argument holds, for political liberalism in particular. We also argue that Cohen's arguments have a surprising implication: despite his explicit anti-libertarianism, his defence of an egalitarian ethos leaves him unable to refute the libertarian challenge of charity.

We therefore make two main claims. Firstly, we argue that recent developments in liberal theory have led to the weakening of liberals' response to the libertarian challenge of charity, and that this is a problem. Secondly, and relatedly, we argue that Cohen's argument for egalitarianism is potentially very damaging to a Rawlsian justification of redistribution and, in particular, to political liberalism, but that – under close inspection – Cohen's claims leave his own form of egalitarianism entirely open to the libertarian challenge. In general, our argument can be summarised as follows: *the more that liberalism is concerned accurately to model the actual democratic wishes and motivations of the people it governs, the less it is able to justify coercively imposing redistributive principles of justice.*

Reasons for coercion

Libertarians do not challenge state coercion *tout court*. Coercion is required to maintain the minimal state, which secures law and order, enforces contracts and defends society from external aggressors. Libertarians are wary of state coercion when it is used to enforce particular moral codes or when, as we focus on here, it is used to compel people to donate some of their resources to assist others. For Nozick, this compulsion is analogous to forced labour, violating individuals' rights of ownership over themselves and the fruits of their labour.

An important part of the egalitarian response to libertarianism has been to rebut this libertarian critique of compulsory redistribution. In order to do so effectively, we suggest, liberals need to show not only that redistribution of resources is required in order to secure equality. They must also show why it is legitimate to use *coercion* to bring about that goal. Egalitarian liberals value liberty as well as equality and often, as in the case of Rawls, prioritise liberty. It is therefore necessary for liberals to explain why liberty can justly be constrained using the heavy hand of the state. If equality can be achieved by other, less coercive means, liberals ought to prefer those to the use of law.

We can identify three general liberal justifications for coercion, which function as responses to the libertarian challenge of charity: *disagreement, unreasonableness* and *problems of motivation*. These responses can be offered individually or in various combinations, and stand as placeholders for specific arguments made by particular philosophers.

The first reason why redistributive justice might require coercion is if it is controversial and thus subject to *disagreement*. If members of a society do not agree on what the principles of justice are, such that a proportion of them deny that the prevailing understanding of 'justice' is in fact just, it will be necessary to enforce those principles coercively. This response, we suggest, is the most robust against the libertarian challenge. In section 2 we discuss this response further and argue that, within liberalism, it is available unproblematically only to comprehensive liberals, for only comprehensive liberals are untroubled by substantive disagreement about justice.

The possibility of disagreement about the principles of justice prompts the Rawlsian distinction between reasonable and unreasonable disagreement. Even if all reasonable people agree on the principles of justice, any society may contain unreasonable people who do not wish to co-operate with others on fair terms. The second reason why coercion might be required, then, is that some people are *unreasonable*. This response is available to most forms of liberalism. However, it may not be easy to distinguish the *unreasonable* members of society from those who *disagree* about what justice is. In Rawls' work, unreasonableness is defined as an unwillingness to co-operate fairly with others under conditions of diversity, and is thus intended to stand apart from any comprehensive conception of the good. However, an understanding of reasonableness as willingness to co-operate fairly is an understanding that relies on a particular (liberal) account of justice. If this is true, then an unreasonable person could also be someone who disagrees about the principles of justice. As we point out in section 3, this conclusion is rather problematic for political liberals and those who support deliberative democracy, and makes unreasonableness a rather precarious response to the libertarian challenge.

Even if all people within a society agree on the principles of justice, however, there still may be a role for coercion on the grounds of *problems of motivation*. A society may have unanimity on the principles of justice, and no unreasonable people. Thus everyone might agree that justice requires a certain level of redistribution. Without coercion, however, people may fail to give the amount of money that justice requires as a result of selfishness or weakness of will. Coercion might thus be required merely to enforce the duties that people agree they have. This response appears to be available to liberals; however, in section 4 we discuss Cohen's claim that Rawlsian liberal justice requires that people are motivated to obey the difference principle in their everyday lives, not only when compelled to do so by law. If Cohen is right, we argue, there can be little or no response to the libertarian challenge.

Finally, note that it is not a response to the libertarian challenge to point to the need for a central institution to co-ordinate redistribution. One role the state plays is to calculate how much money is required for redistribution overall, and to inform people how much each is required to pay to meet that end. Without the state (or some other institution) to perform this role the demands of justice could never be met, for even the most perfectly motivated individual would be unable to work out what justice demands she give or who the recipient of her donation should be. Some co-ordinating institution is required, then, but there is no need for it to be coercive. In a society containing perfectly motivated citizens who agree on the principles of justice, all that would be required from the co-ordinating institution would be calculations of each person's just contribution and a fair distribution mechanism. Citizens would be informed of their personal contribution amount, and would then be legally free to donate or not donate it as they pleased. Of course, in the circumstances described, everyone would donate exactly as justice required.

With this typology of responses to the libertarian challenge of charity in place, we now consider which responses are available to which forms of liberal egalitarianism.

The response of *disagreement*

The response of disagreement – the claim that redistributive justice can be coercively enforced because not all citizens will agree with its demands – is most easily available to comprehensive liberals. Comprehensive liberals believe that liberalism embodies a commitment to certain substantive ethical principles (such as individual autonomy or equality) and that it is the role of the state to encourage or enforce these values. For these thinkers, liberalism represents an ethical system rooted in the supremacy of certain principles which are taken to express something important and evaluative about the particular ends and ideals that individual persons pursue, and the ends to which the state should be directed. Galston calls this 'Enlightenment' liberalism as it embodies a general commitment to principles such as individual autonomy and equality that we find in Enlightenment thinkers such as Constant and Condorcet (Galston 2002). Contemporary advocates of this form of liberalism include Raz, Steven Wall, Kymlicka, and the early Rawls, who in general invoke the principle of personal autonomy to underwrite a powerful defence of egalitarianism, equality, and redistribution (Rawls 1971; Raz 1986; Kymlicka 1989; Wall 1998).

Given all this, the comprehensive liberal response to the libertarian challenge of charity is straightforward. Liberalism does not exist merely to operationalise the preferences of all individuals. Instead it must promote only those goals and preferences which are congruent with the ethical principles on which liberalism rests. Comprehensive liberalism is rooted in a commitment to individual autonomy which in turn rests on a commitment to *all* persons possessing those resources necessary to reflect upon, and pursue, those ends which give their lives value. This right of individual autonomy is one shared by all persons equally, and so it is the responsibility of a liberal state to ensure that all persons equally possess the substantive capacity for autonomy (by ensuring that everyone has access to all those resources necessary for autonomous reflection and free choice). This right trumps any interest that any individual may have in withholding their resources: the redistribution of resources from those who have them to those who do not arises directly from an appeal to the basic principles of equality and individual autonomy which comprehensive liberals take to be at the heart of liberalism. Hence, people may not accept that justice requires them to give up their claim on certain resources in order that they be redistributed to others, but for comprehensive liberals they are simply mistaken: justice *does* require this, and so these people can be legitimately coerced into contributing to redistributive initiatives.

Political liberals reject this comprehensive approach, citing its foundational principles as too controversial to sustain liberal justice in a world characterised by pluralism. Political liberalism thus eschews as far as possible the comprehensive liberal strategy of grounding its normative prescriptions in particular substantive claims, and seeks instead to establish a free-standing, procedural account of justice capable of providing an ethical framework within which those conflicts arising out of moral and political diversity can be appropriately resolved. As Brian Barry states, liberal principles of justice are not 'designed to tell us how to live … [but] rather how to live together, given that we have different ideas about how to live' (Barry 1995, p. 77). Or as Charles Taylor puts it, they focus on 'what it is right to do rather than what it is good to be, on defining the content of obligation rather than the nature of the good life' (Taylor 1992, p. 3). If we are to find truly effective and reasonable grounds for arbitrating between different ends without violating the deeply held self-understandings and beliefs of those involved, political liberals argue, then we must reject comprehensive accounts of the good (and of the self) and establish instead a political conception of justice which stands independent of, and prior to, our more substantive ideas about ourselves and the world. We must, in Charles Larmore's words, define 'the common good of political association by means of a minimal moral conception' (Larmore 1995, p. 123).

We therefore find in political liberalism a shift in the way liberal principles and institutions are justified. No longer are we to appeal to particular 'comprehensive doctrines'. Rather, we are to appeal to agreements made by citizens in some appropriately modelled account of public reasoning. In doing so, we acknowledge the partial and controversial nature of liberal principles like individual autonomy, and respect the different understandings and perspectives of all those in society who are to be bound by the principles of justice. This shift in the method of justification appears to bar political liberals from providing the first response in our typology. Coercion can no longer be justified on the grounds that some people will disagree with the principles of justice, because such disagreement would invalidate those very principles. That is, the validity of particular principles cannot be established independently of what people think of them, because for political liberals the validity of principles of justice is precisely determined by the common agreement of all those who are to be bound by them.

This response on its own leaves political liberalism particularly vulnerable to the libertarian challenge of charity.[2] After all, if we can no longer ground liberal justice on an appeal to the overarching supremacy of certain substantive values but must ground it instead on widespread common agreements made by diverse individuals or groups through a process of public reasoning, then libertarians are surely justified in suggesting that the need for coercion is weakened. If liberal justice is based on principles which gain their legitimacy precisely from public agreement then it need not be coercive, since justice will be rooted in the expressed preferences and commitments of those involved. Coercion becomes unnecessary.

Of course, most political liberals understand the process of public reason as a hypothetical or ideal one, not one which actually occurs between situated individuals. The more that agreement on liberal principles is understood to be hypothetical, the greater the role for coercion in enforcing those principles. For liberals who ground their redistributive principles in ideal agreements can still argue that actual preferences in the non-ideal real world may not map on to those ideal agreements. Thus the response of disagreement remains available if redistributive principles require only *hypothetical* agreement.

However, for some theorists the process of agreement must be more concrete. There is a third group of broadly liberal thinkers who extend the arguments put forward by political liberals about the importance of agreement and public deliberation into a much wider normative approach to justifying coercive principles. Consider, for example, Amy Gutmann and Dennis Thompson. 'The process of mutual reason-giving', they say, 'is not equivalent to the hypothetical justifications proposed by some social contract theories. Such justifications may constitute part of the moral reasoning to which some citizens appeal, but the reasoning must survive the test of actual deliberation if it is to ground laws which actually bind all citizens' (Gutmann and Thompson 2002, p. 157). Importantly, this deliberation 'should take place not only in the private homes of citizens or the studies of philosophers, but in public political forums' (p. 157). This approach clearly builds on the so-called deliberative turn in liberal theory, which saw thinkers such as Rawls and Larmore replace hypothetical contracts with a more fluid, inclusive form of public reasoning about justice that they felt was more capable of incorporating the different conceptions of the good of diverse populations of liberal democratic states. However, it descends from the realm of the hypothetical and describes the actual conditions under which principles of justice are decided and 'fair terms of political cooperation' are set (p. 153). In this sense, it represents perhaps the most explicit attempt to ground the justification of principles of justice in agreements among individuals rather than wider controversial principles.

Deliberative democrats vary in the extent to which they ground justice in actual agreement. Some, such as Gutmann and Thompson, do introduce regulative principles into the deliberative process in order that the outcomes satisfy requirements of fairness and equality. However, it is important to note that even these substantive principles are considered morally and politically provisional in the sense that 'both procedural and substantive principles are systematically open to revision in an ongoing process of moral and political deliberation' (Gutmann and Thompson 2002, p. 154). Substantive deliberative democrats like Gutmann and Thompson therefore recognise the importance of modelling public deliberation according to certain principles, but regard these principles as provisional in the sense that they might themselves be rejected by those involved. Other deliberative democrats, such as Iris Marion Young, emphasise even more firmly the role of *actual* agreement in grounding principles of justice. For Young, democratic debate must be circumscribed only by basic procedural fairness, with justice itself emerging from debate rather than being set in advance (Young 2000).[3]

This form of deliberative democracy is particularly vulnerable to the libertarian challenge of charity since, like political liberalism, it is unable to use the response of disagreement. If principles of justice gain their legitimacy from the fact that they are justifiable to all those within a polity who are to be bound by them, it is not possible to argue that coercion is required because some people are unconvinced. If controversial principles are not accepted by some members of society, this is a problem not of enforcement but rather of legitimacy. In other words, if redistributive justice requires coercion then its normative foundations are undermined.

The response of *unreasonableness*

Nonetheless, both deliberative democrats and political liberals are able to provide alternative responses to the challenge of charity. Political liberals, for example, can provide the response of *unreasonableness*. This response is rooted in the possibility that certain members of the polity might be unreasonable in the sense that they do not wish to cooperate with others on fair terms. While all reasonable people might agree to the principles of justice (arrived at through an appropriately modelled and constrained process of common deliberation), the polity might still contain a proportion of 'unreasonable' people who do not wish to co-operate or engage in the kind of public reasoning demanded by political liberalism. In this sense, political liberals invoke an important distinction between false or *mistaken* forms of reasoning and *unreasonable* forms of reasoning. Comprehensive liberals are able to claim that those who disagree with the principles of justice are merely wrong in the sense that they have a misguided notion of what justice requires. Political liberals, on the other hand, avoid such claims (because of their controversial nature) and appeal instead to the notion of reasonableness, defined as this willingness to cooperate on fair terms and derive principles of justice in the appropriate way. In doing so, political liberals seek to avoid having to impose controversial ethical principles or conceptions of the good from the top down. Instead, they seek to establish a process of public reasoning and deliberation which constructs principles of justice from the bottom up (from the reasonable agreements of those bound by them).

The problem, however, is that it is not clear how effectively the political liberal definition of 'reasonableness' avoids the presupposition of substantive, controversial liberal values. That is, it is not clear how successful the distinction between 'unreasonable' forms of reasoning and 'mistaken' forms of reasoning is, when we realise that reasonableness is defined by appeal to controversial liberal principles. This is an important issue, and there exists a significant body of work exploring the extent to which political liberalism succeeds in distancing itself from controversial, comprehensive principles like autonomy.[4] It is not possible to go into detail here, then. However, it is important to note that political liberalism (in particular the varieties argued for by Larmore and the later Rawls), like the impartialist liberalism of Barry, is no more a mechanism for merely operationalising the desires and preferences of citizens than comprehensive liberalism. The kind of public reasoning about justice presented by political liberals such as Rawls and Larmore would appear to be structured and constrained in such a way as to produce agreements which are in line with traditional liberal principles of equality and autonomy. Indeed, Rawls accepts that his form of political liberalism is applicable to only liberal societies, and thus accepts the contingency of its fundamental premises of political freedom and equality (Rawls 1993). It seems, then, that while political liberals might seek to reinterpret the grounds of liberal justification away from overarching, controversial accounts of value, they succeed only in moving it into a process of agreement and public reasoning which itself embodies precisely those same controversial principles. In defining what kinds of reasons and arguments participants in public dialogues about justice might and might not legitimately engage in, and in requiring that all individuals should have access to these deliberations on a basis of equality, political liberalism can be seen to embody substantive commitments to controversial values in the same way as comprehensive liberalism. Political liberalism cannot avoid invoking the value of political equality and individual autonomy because it is important to political liberals that the process of public reasoning about justice is conducted in a particular way, subject to particular constraints, between people understood to be free and equal.

Consequently, the political liberal response to the libertarian critique is actually similar to the comprehensive liberal response. Because political liberals require that we understand the process of public reasoning to be constrained by basic liberal principles of freedom and equality, their account of public reasoning effectively represents a mechanism for filtering out non-liberal arguments and, hence, non-liberal outcomes. In the sense that political liberalism seeks to justify liberal justice in public agreements, and then defines the process by which these agreements are legitimately made as circumscribed by comprehensive liberal principles, political liberalism ultimately grounds the justification of liberal justice in those same substantive liberal values as comprehensive liberalism.

Political liberals may not accept this, of course, for in doing so they jeopardise their wider aim of establishing liberal justice independently of controversial principles. Political liberals are therefore faced with a choice. They could accept that their justification for liberal justice rests on appeals to controversial principles, in which case they are able to respond as robustly to libertarians as comprehensive liberals by appealing to those principles (at the expense of their wider aim of establishing political justice independently of such principles). Alternatively, they could cling to their original aim of establishing liberal justice independently of controversial principles and accept that in doing so their response to the libertarian challenge of charity is weakened. In response to the latter option libertarians might reasonably suggest that if political liberals drop their more controversial claims about the way in which people should engage in public reasoning, and ground principles of justice in agreements about what people actually do want, then the argument for coercion is weakened. Libertarians would be right about this, as in this event, political liberals would be forced to appeal only to the third (much weaker) response of *motivation*.

The response of *motivation*

We have assumed that the thinkers discussed so far are able to make use of the third response to the libertarian challenge of charity: the response of *motivation*. In other words, the various forms of liberal egalitarianism so far considered can argue as follows: 'The principles of distributive justice under consideration may well be those that everyone agrees with, or cannot reasonably reject, or accepts actually to be just. Nonetheless, it is still necessary to enforce those principles coercively, since people may lack the *motivation* to do that which they accept they ought. In short, state coercion is needed to overcome weakness of will.'

Indeed, we have suggested that political liberals and deliberative democrats need the response of motivation, if they are to succeed in grounding justice independently of any appeal to controversial conceptions of the good. Their alternative response of *unreasonableness* risks collapsing into the response of *disagreement*, and this latter response is available to only comprehensive liberals. However, G.A. Cohen's recent work suggests that egalitarian liberals *cannot* make use of the response of motivation since what he terms an 'egalitarian ethos' is crucial to egalitarianism.

This claim is of critical importance. If Cohen is right that justice requires an egalitarian ethos, it must also be the case that the libertarian challenge of charity is correct and that coercive enforcement of redistribution is at least unnecessary and at most unjust. It also suggests that those political liberals who do not wish to give up their wider project of establishing liberal justice independently of controversial liberal principles are not – in the absence of the response of motivation – able to rebut the libertarian challenge of charity. It is therefore important to discuss Cohen's claims in detail in order to determine, firstly, how damaging they are to political liberalism and, secondly, how susceptible these arguments themselves are to the libertarian challenge.

In a number of recent works Cohen considers what sorts of inequalities are permitted by Rawls' difference principle. The difference principle allows inequalities only if they are necessary to benefit the worst off, and is based on the thought that it is better to have more primary goods than fewer, even if one can have more only at the expense of increased inequality. The question then becomes when and why an inequality would benefit the worst off, and thus be justifiable.

An inequality in primary goods might benefit the worst off in two main ways. First, it might be necessary to pay people more in order for them to perform work that is extremely socially beneficial. If no one were to do this sort of work everyone, including the worst off, would suffer. So, for example, the difference principle might justify paying people more to become doctors if, without the increased salary, there would be insufficient doctors to meet everyone's healthcare needs. It is usually thought this situation will occur in highly skilled jobs, where employment vacancies can be filled by only a few people. Note, however, that there is no necessary connection between this sort of income inequality and skilled work. It is possible that some unskilled jobs could be so unpleasant that no-one would be willing to perform them without extra wages (refuse collection or abattoir work, for example). In actual societies the threat of unemployment and poverty suffices to induce some people to take such jobs without extra income. In a Rawlsian society, however, the baseline of equality means there are fewer desperate people, and thus it is more likely that unpleasant but socially necessary unskilled jobs would warrant higher salaries.

The second main way in which an inequality might benefit the worst off is through some version of the trickle-down effect. On one version of the trickle-down effect it does not matter what work the person with the higher income is doing, or even if they are doing any work at all. Since wealthy people spend more money and pay higher taxes, their increased consumerism contributes to employment and welfare for those who are less wealthy. On another version of the trickle-down effect, the worst-off are benefited by the work the wealthy are doing. This applies if increased income for some encourages entrepreneurial activity that directly creates employment opportunities for the worst off. Thus a person might be tempted to start up a new business, creating jobs for others, if she is thereby able to enjoy increased income from the business's profits. If such increased income were not available she might choose alternative work that does not create jobs.

Note one important difference in these justifications of inequalities. In some cases – the unskilled socially necessary jobs and the increased consumerism trickle-down effect – it does not matter who is given the extra money. In the case of the unskilled jobs, any able-bodied person who is *willing* to perform them is *able* to perform them, and thus the extra income is available to anyone. In the case of increased consumerism, it is not necessary that the extra income be allocated in relation to work at all. Allocating it to random lottery winners would have the same effect. However, in the remaining two cases – the skilled socially necessary jobs and the entrepreneurial trickle-down effect – the extra income is available only to those people who have the necessary skills to perform the skilled labour or generate the extra jobs. These considerations might make a Rawlsian individual in the original position happier about the first sorts of inequalities than the second. For the first sorts of inequalities are, in principle, available to everyone, whereas the second sorts of inequalities are confined to those who are lucky that their particular skills are socially valuable.

Cohen does not make this distinction or separate these four sorts of inequalities. He does, however, highlight another ambiguity in the difference principle. The principle states that inequalities are just only when they are 'necessary' to benefit the worst-off, but it does not explain what it means for an inequality to be necessary. On what Cohen calls the 'strict' reading of the difference principle, extra income is justified only if the work in question *cannot* be performed without extra income, perhaps because it is particularly burdensome. If it were to be paid at the same rate as other work, the extra burdens would leave the worker in a disadvantaged position compared to others. Unpleasant or particularly difficult jobs fall into this category. Cohen does not criticise this strict form of the difference principle (Cohen 1991, p. 296).

On the 'lax' reading of the difference principle, on the other hand, an inequality is justified simply if it is needed to *persuade* or *induce* someone to perform work that benefits the worst off (or to perform more work so as to increase productivity and benefit them that way). Cohen terms this the incentives argument, and writes that he will 'mainly be interested in the case where a talented rich person puts it forward' (1991, p. 278) Cohen's claim is that when talented rich people put forward the incentive argument they resemble kidnappers who are able to hold others to ransom (1991, p. 278). Since only some people are able to perform the skilled socially necessary jobs, these talented individuals are able to demand more than is necessary to compensate them for any extra burden. This is not the case with the unskilled socially necessary jobs: since everyone could in principle perform them, there is no scope for some to demand more income than offsets the extra burdens (market forces should result in an equilibrium between income and burden).

Cohen's argument runs as follows. If citizens agree that Rawls' principles of justice are indeed just, then they affirm the principle that inequalities should be permitted only if they benefit the worst off. However, if a talented person demands more money for performing a socially necessary skilled job (more than others are getting, and more than is needed to offset the burdens of that job) then she is acting in a way that contradicts the difference principle. By demanding an extra incentive, she is demanding a payment that is not strictly *necessary* in order to benefit the worst-off. It is entirely within her control to perform the work without demanding the inequality. It would therefore be possible for her to act in such a way as to benefit the worst-off without thereby creating an inequality and, if she really is committed to the difference principle, this is what she would do. As Cohen puts it:

> It is generally thought that the difference principle would be used by government to modify the effect of choices which are not themselves influenced by the principle, but, so I claim, in a society of wholehearted commitment to the principle, there cannot be so stark a contrast between public and private choice. Instead, citizens want their own economic behavior to satisfy the principle, and they help to sustain a moral climate in which others want the same. (1991, p. 312)

Should we assume that a society will nurture 'wholehearted commitment to the principle'? For Cohen, it is true of both Rawls' writings and of egalitarian theories of justice in general that society must contain such commitment. It is true of Rawls since he states that his theory is intended to apply to a well-ordered society, one in which citizens know what the principles of justice are, agree that they are indeed just, and are motivated to comply with them (Cohen 1991, p. 318). In *If you're an egalitarian, how come you're so rich?* Cohen argues that it is also true of egalitarian theories in general:

> If, as I now believe, how selfish people are affects the prospects for equality and justice, then that is partly because, as I now also believe, justice cannot be a matter only of the state-legislated structure in which people act but is also a matter of the acts they choose within that structure, the personal choices of their daily lives. I have come to think, in the words of a recently familiar slogan, that *the personal is political.* (Cohen 2001, p. 122)

If Cohen is correct, then egalitarians cannot make the response of *motivation* against the libertarian challenge, for they cannot claim that citizens who accept the principles of justice will lack the necessary motivation to implement them. However, we also want to show that Cohen's arguments go further. If an egalitarian ethos is a requirement of justice, it follows that coercive enforcement of redistribution is unjustified. We make this argument in three stages. First we discuss how the ethos might be a *necessary* condition for justice. Second we argue that, if it is necessary for justice, then the ethos must be *sufficient.* Finally we argue that, if the ethos is sufficient, then coercion is both unnecessary and *unjustified.*

Is the ethos necessary?

We have seen that Cohen is committed to the idea that the ethos is necessary for justice. However, the scope of this claim is unclear. Presumably all egalitarian theorists can agree that an egalitarian ethos is necessary if society is to be ideal or utopian. To put this thought another way: an *ideally* just society will need coercion for neither redistributive nor criminal justice, since no-one will be motivated to shirk their obligations or violate the rights of others. Any egalitarian can agree that such a situation is desirable and that any society that lacks such an ethos is *pro tanto* non-ideal. Thus, if the claim 'the egalitarian ethos is necessary for justice' means 'the egalitarian ethos is necessary for a utopian, ideal society', all egalitarians can agree. But such a claim is not very significant since we are unlikely ever to reach utopian, fully ideal conditions and since Rawlsians are unlikely to find it problematic that Rawls offers no considerations as to how to achieve such conditions.

Cohen's arguments lack force, then, if they simply point out that a society cannot reach utopia without an egalitarian ethos. The question then is whether utopia is the same as justice; in other words, whether it is possible for a society to be just and yet non-utopian. To put this issue in a different way: Cohen's arguments are most significant if they indicate that justice of any sort is impossible without an ethos or that, without an ethos, a society is seriously deficient. Cohen does seem to hold this position: he writes that 'a just society is normally impossible without [an egalitarian ethos]' (Cohen 1991, p. 316). This claim might be justified in one of two ways. It might be based on the idea that justice is an all-or-nothing concept, such that a society is either fully, ideally just, or else hopelessly unjust, with no normative distinction between levels of injustice. This position is implausible: it is perfectly possible to say that some societies are more just (or less unjust) than others, according to such considerations as the proportion of positions of advantage that are filled according to the equal opportunity principle and rewarded according to the difference principle. On the other hand, then, the claim of necessity might be based on the idea that justice *is* a matter of degree but that, without an egalitarian ethos, the 'level' of justice that a society can obtain is significantly deficient.

Samuel Scheffler rejects the idea that a society cannot reach (an acceptable level of) justice without an egalitarian ethos. Scheffler argues that Cohen fails to demonstrate that Rawls's theory requires an egalitarian ethos since it is compatible with Rawlsian justice that the state simply forbid any increased salaries that are incentives rather than compensation for special burdens. As Scheffler puts it, 'an ethos of justice would not actually be *necessary* to produce an economic distribution satisfying the strict [difference] principle – such a distribution *could* be achieved by the coercive structure alone' (Scheffler 2006, p. 118).[5] If Scheffler is right then the distinctiveness of Cohen's position is lost. In order to rebut Scheffler and maintain his own position Cohen must assert that the ethos is necessary: the coercive state cannot bring about equality without it (and thus the state is not a sufficient condition).

Support for this position is found in the following passage from Cohen:

> We are left with the strict difference principle, which government cannot by itself implement. For the strict difference principle to prevail, there needs to be an ethos informed by the principle in society at large. Therefore, a society (as opposed to its government) does not qualify as committed to the difference principle unless it is indeed informed by a certain ethos, or culture of justice. Ethoses are, of course, beyond the immediate control of legislation, but I believe that a just society is normally impossible without one, and Rawls himself requires that there be a nurturance and cultivation of appropriate attitude in the just society that he describes. (Cohen 1991, pp. 315–316)

Cohen is committed to the view that the ethos is necessary for justice, then. However, this claim does not yet concede the libertarian challenge. For that, we need to show that the egalitarian ethos is *sufficient* for justice.

Is the ethos sufficient?

The ideal that the ethos is necessary suggests that it is also sufficient. For Cohen's very idea of an egalitarian ethos is that it is a property of individual citizens that leads them to be motivated to forego personal gain in order to bring about distributive justice. If people are willing to forego personal gain in the incentives case (in other words, if they are willing to do socially necessary work without demanding extra pay so as to benefit the worst-off), then there seems no reason why they would not also willingly donate their 'tax' burden without it being coercively demanded by the state. We noted at the start of this chapter that it would be possible for the state to take on a non-coercive co-ordinating role, calculating everyone's fair burden but not demanding that they pay it. If citizens have an egalitarian ethos of the sort Cohen thinks they need, there is no reason why they would not pay their fair share freely and happily. There is no need, in other words, to enforce coercive taxation laws since citizens will contribute willingly without.

Thomas Nagel offers an argument against this idea that something like an egalitarian ethos is sufficient for justice. In a piece aimed explicitly at rejecting the libertarian challenge of charity Nagel argues that 'a person who is willing and, indeed, eager to contribute through taxation might be unwilling to give off her own bat' (Cohen 2001, p. 169). Nagel's thought is that one might agree on the principles of justice but lack motivation, and thus coercive taxation is justified. Cohen devotes several pages to arguing against Nagel's position, since he rightly identifies Nagel's claim as undermining the need for an egalitarian ethos. Cohen's argument rests on a distinction between difficulty and cost. Firstly, donating voluntarily and donating via taxes are equal in *cost*. That is to say, if one does the calculations correctly (or if they are done by a central co-ordinating institution), the amount due will be the same under both systems. The only reason to prefer coercion over donation, then, is that the two systems are not equal in their *difficulty*: it is more difficult to spur oneself to voluntary action since one faces constant temptation to defect in the name of self-interest. However, Cohen argues, one can 'avoid such recurrent difficult voluntary decisions' (Cohen 2001, p. 171) by setting up a standing order with one's bank. Thus, Cohen concludes, 'we have not been supplied with a reason for not giving off our own bat what we would be willing for the state to take' (2001, p. 172).

Having thus refuted Nagel, Cohen does not consider the original context of Nagel's argument: an attempt to rebut Nozick's libertarian challenge. Cohen thus appears not to notice that his refutation of Nagel is also a defence of this aspect of libertarianism. For if there is no need to supplement the egalitarian ethos with coercion in order to overcome difficulties in contributing, what could be the role of coercion?

One possible role for coercion even if an egalitarian ethos prevails is as a solution to assurance problems. An individual might be motivated to comply with the principles of justice only if all other members of her society are also complying, and it might be only coercion that assures her of this universal (or near-universal) compliance. But this suggestion raises a number of questions. The first is whether it is reasonable for an individual with an egalitarian ethos to insist on being assured of near-universal compliance. The second is whether coercion would in fact be necessary to provide this assurance.

It is clear that assurance is problematic in societies that are *not* characterised by an egalitarian ethos, but this is not the matter under consideration here. If assurance is indeed to be a reason why the ethos is not sufficient, then assurance problems must remain even when the ethos is universally shared. And it seems possible for assurance problems to remain even under conditions of a universal ethos only if members of a society lack information about the extent to which the ethos is in fact shared. In a society where citizens had perfect information about others' propensity to egalitarianism, individuals would have no grounds on which to withhold their contributions for lack of assurance. And, while state coercion is one possible means of solving assurance problems, it is not the only such means. Cohen notes that 'The beauty of a state-imposed duty, *or of a general ethos of giving*' (2001, p. 175, emphasis added) is that *either one* can solve assurance problems. It follows that 'for assurance reasons, equality is, necessarily, a *social* project' (2001, p. 176) – but it does not follow that it need be coercive.[6]

An alternative reason why an egalitarian ethos might be insufficient for justice is that coercion might be required to *create* an egalitarian ethos. Just as forcing children to eat with good manners fosters an ethos of etiquette when they are adults, so too citizens might develop an ethos of giving voluntarily only if they are first forced to do so by the state. In other words, Cohen might be wrong when he claims that ethoses are 'beyond the immediate control of legislation' (Cohen 1991, pp. 315–316). Certainly it is at least plausible that ethoses are affected by state action.[7] But note that, if the egalitarian ethos is to retain any significance, direct coercion cannot be needed permanently. It may be that individuals newly liable to contribute to redistribution must be coerced for a time in order to develop an ethos. This period would like the general justified coercion of children: necessary in order for them to become autonomous moral citizens. But if citizens need ongoing coercion in order to maintain their ethos it is not clear in what sense they really have one. The arguments of this paper still apply, then, to those who have become autonomous citizens.

Is coercion justified?

The final stage in our argument is to show that, if the egalitarian ethos is both necessary and sufficient for justice, then coercion is *unjustified* and the libertarian challenge of charity stands. Indeed, the importance of liberty to liberal conceptions of justice means that if principles of justice do not *need* to be enforced coercively it is *unjust* to use coercion. Not only does coercion imply that the society is not in fact well-ordered and thus not just, it also involves the use of force where none is needed. And using force where none is needed seems to violate the equal basic liberty principle (and other similar statements of the liberal value of freedom), since it would be possible to increase everyone's liberty while threatening no-one's. Cohen must, therefore, succumb to the libertarian challenge and accept that the principles of justice (or, at least, the principles of distributive justice) *need not* and *should not* be coercively enforced.

Coercion is only needed and justified, therefore, when a society lacks an egalitarian ethos. According to Cohen's arguments, this will occur only when people do not support the principles of justice. But saying that coercion is justified because people disagree about what justice requires is already to concede a fair amount to the libertarian challenge, since it is to concede that coercive redistribution is *required* because people do not agree that it is *justified*. Cohen is thus left with the unpalatable conclusion that coercion is required only if citizens do not feel that it is justified and, since the ethos is necessary for justice, despite the fact that it will not bring about justice. Cohen's own arguments thus suggest the appeal of the libertarian call for leaving redistribution to the voluntary acts of individuals.

At one point, however, Cohen does state that his aim is not to deny the need for a coercive state, but rather to deny that there is a justification for rejecting the egalitarian ethos. Thus he writes:

> That I know or fear that I would not give off my own bat is indeed a reason for me to prefer redistribution through the state, but it is not what we are looking for, which is a *justification for not giving* if the state does not force me to. It can't be a justification for not giving when the state does not force me to that I *would* not give unless the state forces me to. (Cohen 2001, p. 170)

Cohen thus suggests that an individual might well prefer to be coerced into giving. But if he concedes this point, Cohen must concede several others. First, he must reject the priority of the equal basic liberty principle. For, if it is possible for individuals to comply with the demands of justice without coercion then there is no good reason to limit liberty by introducing coercion simply for the sake of convenience. Second, if Cohen concedes that the egalitarian ethos can be insufficient to bring about egalitarian outcomes, such that state coercion is justified, he is vulnerable to Scheffler's critique of his position discussed earlier. If the state can bring about justice in cases where the ethos has failed why, *pace* Scheffler, can it not do so in all cases? Why, in other words, would the ethos be needed at all? It seems that, in order to survive Scheffler's critique, Cohen must retract the implication of the passage quoted above in favour of the intuitively appealing claim that a necessary ethos is also sufficient. After all, if the egalitarian ethos means that people willingly sacrifice their own self-interest in the name of equality above and beyond what the state can practically or legitimately achieve, it makes sense to think that they will be even more willing to do so in cases clear enough to ground coercion.

Cohen's approach thus cannot rebut the libertarian challenge of charity. If an egalitarian ethos is required for distributive equality then state coercion is unnecessary and therefore unjustified. To put it another way, if people not only agree with the principles of justice but are also motivated to comply with them there is no role for redistributive taxation.

Conclusion

It is now possible to pull together the threads of the argument, and emphasise how the first part of the chapter on comprehensive liberalism, political liberalism, and deliberative democracy connects with the second part on Cohen. Earlier in the chapter, we argued that certain forms of liberalism can offer more (and better) responses to the libertarian challenge of charity than others. We suggested that the most coherent and powerful response can be provided by comprehensive liberalism, which can state that coercive redistribution is simply a requirement of justice irrespective of whether people actually believe it to be. The coercive redistribution of holdings from the most advantaged to the least advantaged is simply required by liberal commitments to individual autonomy and equality, and hence, it is just. We suggested that political liberals are less able to rebut the libertarian critique as a consequence of their unwillingness to appeal to controversial principles. The political liberal approach of deriving regulative principles of justice from agreements made between individual citizens rather than the stated good of principles like individual autonomy or equality undermines the liberal justification for coercion, and presents political liberals with a choice. They can either structure the agreement process such that it can only produce outcomes which are consistent with comprehensive liberal principles, in which case their rejection of comprehensive liberalism is rendered hollow, or they can commit themselves to a deliberative process which is not weighted towards liberal outcomes, and which genuinely seeks to model the preferences of the people involved. If the latter option is taken, then political liberals must be willing not only to bear the costs of this more democratised form of liberalism (in the sense that outcomes may violate wider liberal principles) but to make use of the weakest response to libertarianism of all: the response of motivation.

Consequently, liberals who are able to make the response of disagreement have the strongest normative justification for coercion, since they can deny that disagreement (which is what makes coercion necessary) undermines the legitimacy of justice. Justice is justice, regardless of the views of the citizenry. The response of unreasonableness is weaker since it admits that assent to the principles of justice is generally important and thus that the requirement of coercion is suboptimal. Finally, the response of motivation (offered on its own) is the weakest of all, since coercion is justified by expediency alone. However, if Cohen is right about motivation and the egalitarian ethos, then the response of motivation is not really a response at all. Cohen's arguments are important for two reasons. The first is that they undermine the response of motivation, and thus leave those political liberals who do not wish to appeal to comprehensive liberal accounts of the good without an adequate reply to the libertarian challenge of charity. The second is that they imply that distributive justice cannot legitimately be coercively enforced. They thus concede the libertarian challenge.

What Cohen's argument suggests is that any form of liberalism which relies on the response of motivation to rebut the libertarian critique of coercive redistribution will not, in fact, be able to rebut this critique. This is a problem because the dominant trend in contemporary liberal thought is to reject the comprehensive approach and adopt a more deliberative approach, more capable of establishing a conception of justice in societies characterised by cultural, ethnic, and religious diversity. As liberals have increasingly turned their gaze *away* from longstanding debates between libertarians and liberal egalitarians about the rightful distribution of resources and goods and *towards* issues arising out of multiculturalism, they have argued in ways which have left their liberal egalitarian premises vulnerable to much older, much more established critiques advanced by libertarians. If our argument in this chapter holds then, in seeking to determine the appropriate conduct of social and political institutions through agreements made between citizens rather than prior values like autonomy and equality, political liberals and deliberative democrats are less able to defend egalitarian claims for redistribution than they otherwise think. Indeed, if Cohen is right, then it would seem that they are not able to defend egalitarian claims at all, without first rejecting their wider aim of establishing a free-standing conception of political justice.

Acknowledgements

Previous versions of this paper were presented at the American Political Science Association annual meeting in Chicago, Political Theory Research Seminars at the Universities of Edinburgh and Manchester, and Philosophy Research Seminars at the Universities of Bristol and Glasgow. We are very grateful to the participants for their extremely helpful comments. We should also like to thank Steven Montgomery and Adam Tebble for written comments.

Notes

1. One way that Nozick phrases this challenge is as follows: 'Any persons who favor a particular end-state pattern may choose to transfer some or all of their own holdings so as (at least temporarily) more nearly to realize their desired pattern' (1993, pp. 232–233). Nozick makes a mistake, of course, when saying that 'Any persons' may do this, since those who feel that they should have *more* resources under their preferred distribution cannot act unilaterally without violating the entitlements of others. However, Nozick's claim is true of all those who would be subject to

coercive taxation under an egalitarian scheme. Nozick's general discussion of what he calls 'Philanthropy' occurs on pp. 265–268.

2. Alan Carter has gone further, arguing that political liberalism lacks the resources needed to justify a state that is coercive in *any* area, not just redistribution. For more on this, see Carter (2006a, 2006b).
3. For a critique of this view see Chambers and Parvin (forthcoming).
4. We have explored this issue in more depth elsewhere. See Chambers and Parvin (forthcoming). For an interesting discussion of the problem of compliance in Rawls's work, and the inability of political liberalism to provide a unique and coherent response to illiberal diversity, see Carter (2006a, 2006b).
5. Scheffler has further arguments against Cohen, but it is only his argument about the potential of state coercion to replace an egalitarian ethos that concerns us here.
6. Note that it is by no means obvious that individuals have grounds to refuse to contribute without coercion even if they lack information about others' ethoses. There is a large literature, which cannot be discussed here, arguing against the idea that individuals have duties of justice only when their society is characterised by perfect compliance.
7. For an extended analysis and defence of the thesis of social construction see Chambers (2008).

References

Barry, B.M., 1995. *Justice as impartiality.* Oxford: Oxford University Press.

Carter, A., 2006a. The evolution of Rawls's justification of political compliance: part 1 of the problem of political compliance in Rawls's theories of justice. *The journal of moral philosophy,* 3 (1), 7–21.

Carter, A., 2006b. Political liberalism and political compliance: part 2 of the problem of political compliance in Rawls's theories of justice. *The journal of moral philosophy,* 3 (2), 135–157.

Chambers, C., 2008. *Sex, culture, and justice.* University Park, PA: Penn State University Press.

Chambers, C. and Parvin, P., forthcoming. What kind of dialogue do we need? Gender, deliberative democracy and comprehensive values. *In*: J. Browne, ed. *Dialogue, ethics and gender identity*.
Cohen, G.A., 1991. Incentives, inequality, and community. *In:* G. Peterson, ed. *The Tanner lectures on human values*. Salt Lake City, UT: University of Utah Press.
Cohen, G.A., 2001. *If you're an egalitarian, how come you're so rich?* Cambridge, MA: Harvard University Press.
Galston, W., 2002. *Liberal pluralism: the implications of value pluralism for political theory and practice*. Cambridge: Cambridge University Press.
Gutmann, A. & Thompson, D., 2002. Deliberative democracy beyond process. *The journal of political philosophy*, 10 (2), 153–178.
Kymlicka, W., 1989. *Liberalism, community and culture*. Oxford: Clarendon Press.
Larmore, C., 1995. Political liberalism. *In* C. Larmore, *The morals of modernity*. Cambridge: Cambridge University Press, 121–151.
MacIntyre, A., 1996. *After virtue: a study in moral theory*. London: Duckworth.
Nagel, T., 1991. *Equality and partiality*. Oxford: Oxford University Press.
Nozick, R., 1993. *Anarchy, state and utopia*. Oxford: Blackwell.
Rawls, J., 1971. *A theory of justice*. Oxford: Oxford University Press.
Rawls, J., 1993. *Political liberalism*. New York: Columbia University Press.
Raz, J., 1986. *The morality of freedom*. Oxford: Clarendon Press.
Sandel, M., 1982. *Liberalism and the limits of justice*. Cambridge: Cambridge University Press.
Scheffler, S., 2006. Is the basic structure basic? *In*: C. Sypnowich, ed. *The egalitarian conscience*. Oxford: Oxford University Press.
Taylor, C., 1992. *Sources of the self*. Cambridge: Cambridge University Press.
Wall, S., 1998. *Liberalism, perfectionism, and restraint*. Cambridge: Cambridge University Press.
Walzer, M., 1985. *Spheres of justice: a defence of pluralism and equality*. Oxford: Blackwell.
Williams, A., 1998. Incentives, inequality, and publicity. *Philosophy & public affairs*, 2 (3), 225–247.
Young, I.M., 2000. *Inclusion and democracy*. Oxford: Clarendon Press.

Human rights and moral cosmopolitanism

Charles Jones

Department of Political Science, University of Western Ontario, Canada

What does it mean to defend moral cosmopolitanism in terms of human rights? I outline 'human rights cosmopolitanism', explain the role of equality in giving content to this conception, and defend the liberal view of human rights against the restricted view by considering – and responding to – several arguments for remaining neutral between a range of cultural and ideological perspectives on the demands of social justice and political legitimacy. I defend the liberal view that a conception of human rights should not remain neutral on controversial questions of justice and legitimacy.

The aim of this paper is to clarify what is claimed and implied by a cosmopolitan moral perspective framed in terms of human rights. I begin by describing the meaning of both moral cosmopolitanism and human rights. After briefly describing the view I label 'human rights cosmopolitanism', the bulk of my discussion is taken up with a critical analysis of two different distinctions between conceptions of human rights: the first distinguishes orthodox from practical conceptions, while the second distinguishes the full or liberal view from the restricted view of human rights. Although the distinctions are themselves different, they are both found in the recent work of Charles Beitz (2001, 2004).

One central motivating concern here is to understand the role of equality within the view I wish to defend. What are the links between cosmopolitanism, human rights, and equality? I focus explicitly on the question of the alleged minimalism of human rights, and on the place of equal consideration of all individuals in the conception and justification of these rights. I conclude that minimalism, in either of its main forms, is not a plausible implication of moral cosmopolitanism.

Moral cosmopolitanism

My starting point is moral cosmopolitanism, so it is important to distinguish this perspective from some related views. The most general typology should distinguish between political, cultural, and moral versions of cosmopolitanism. While I do not focus on the political and cultural variants here, I will briefly mention each one since they are important related strands of contemporary thought. Political cosmopolitanism is the view that political authority should be shifted from individual states to supranational political institutions. It is not necessarily committed to the idea of a world state, but it does require reforms of economic and political institutions, usually with the aim of overcoming problems created by a state-centric world. If states are, in part, causally responsible for war and for the failure to address global environmental crises, political cosmopolitans hold out the hope that supranational politics can address these issues.

Cultural cosmopolitanism is the idea that individuals can live a good life both within and beyond the confines of particular cultural traditions. In this view, individual identities can be shaped and developed by a range of cultural frameworks. Cultural cosmopolitans disagree with the claim that human beings can live good lives only within one particular national or cultural tradition. The cosmopolitan label is explained by the fact that this view is open to the entire range of distinctive practices that exist across the world. If a political 'world citizen' questions the assumption that political communities should be territorially limited in their scope, a cultural 'world citizen' questions the particularistic assertion that lives have value only when lived within one dominant culture (Scheffler 2001, p. 116).

Both of these views are linked, I believe, to the view I wish to consider, but I will not presuppose any view about these interrelations. I begin from cosmopolitanism as a moral conception (Barry 1998). Moral cosmopolitanism affirms the equal moral worth of each individual person, regardless of sex, race, ethnicity, religion, nationality, or any other form of group membership beneath the level of the class of all human beings. It is, thus, a form of moral individualism that assigns priority in moral reasoning to the interests of individuals rather than groups. And it assigns *equal moral value* to each individual, denying hierarchy or favoritism at any basic level of ethical thinking. This moral cosmopolitan requirement to regard persons as equals also suggests an appropriate perspective from which to consider persons, their interests, claims, and obligations to one another. This perspective is an impartial one, a viewpoint from which each person's rightful claims are given a fair hearing.

I am interested in moral cosmopolitanism as a tool for judging the legitimacy of social and political institutions and practices, rather than as an all-encompassing moral theory. The moral cosmopolitan point of view is more plausible as applied to this narrower yet still vital set of concerns. And I interpret its egalitarianism as demanding that each person is entitled to a justification of those institutions and practices in which his or her standing is on a par with that of any other person.[1] The view is, then, a moral perspective from which to evaluate institutions, and it demands that institutions are justified only if each person affected can be given a rationale consistent with their equal moral status. This last requirement is important to keep in mind, especially because its implications are potentially quite radical.

Finally, I affirm here a moderate moral cosmopolitanism, which means *both* that there are basic obligations that each of us must recognize toward all other human beings, *and* that particular affiliations – to family, nation, state, and so on – give rise to special duties whose justification, if plausible, is explicated independently of any supposed instrumental value for promoting the good of humanity. The legitimacy of associative duties, on this view, is derived not from our universal duties to human beings in general but from some other feature of the particular association itself. I cannot argue for the moderate position here, but I will investigate the implications of this view for human rights and the duties of global justice.

The meaning of human rights

I take human rights to be protections for basic interests of persons against standard threats to those interests. They are claims linked to the dignity and moral status of individual human beings, and they generate duties that must be recognized by all other human beings, though it is essential to assign these duties to institutions rather than individuals. If justice is the primary institutional virtue, and human rights describe the entitlements of each person that must be protected and promoted by the main social, political, and economic institutions under which they live, then we can see human rights as 'the basic requirements of global justice' (Beitz 2003, p. 44). While one might hope that domestic institutions would do the job of rights protection, the scope of concern for human rights cannot be limited to the domestic sphere.

So, on this view, human rights gain their rationale from a concern for individual persons and their basic interests in such goods as the capability to obtain shelter, food, and a say in how their lives go. But these interests are best protected through a combination of particular actions and an effective institutional framework.

It will be helpful here to mention a distinction made by Charles Beitz between orthodox and practical conceptions of human rights (Beitz 2004, pp. 196–201). According to the orthodox view, human rights are akin to natural rights in that they possess three features: they are pre-institutional in the sense that they would obtain in a pre-political 'state of nature'; they are possessed by all persons simply in virtue of their common humanity rather than their 'merely contingent social relationships'; and they are timeless, or justifiably claimable by all human beings regardless of time and place. The practical conception of human rights, on the other hand, takes seriously the practical political role of human rights as part of contemporary international human rights doctrine, which includes the attempt 'to describe social conditions conducive to the living of dignified human lives' (Beitz 2004, p. 199).

Accordingly, it limits the content of these rights to those that could be accepted by individuals regardless of their cultural background and assumptions, and it enables political cooperation between international actors to commit themselves to action in defense and enforcement of human rights (Beitz 2004, pp. 204–205).

My view is that Beitz's distinction is suggestive, as is his argument for favoring the practical conception of human rights. But in his eagerness to distance himself from the orthodox or traditional view, he underplays some aspects of its legacy that we should retain. In fact, I wonder whether the orthodox/practical dichotomy is an instance (or several instances) of the fallacy of incomplete disjunction, i.e., it offers us two alternatives from which to choose, when there is a third option that is better than either of these. Let me explain.

On the question of the 'pre-institutional' character of rights as traditionally conceived, my first idea is that we need to distinguish two senses in which a human right may properly be called 'pre-institutional'. In the first sense, a right is pre-institutional when it exists 'before' institutions, in a state of nature. Someone who affirms human rights in this sense believes that 'they could exist in a condition where there are no institutions' (Beitz 2003, p. 41). We should agree with Beitz that this view is implausible. Many human rights, such as the right to a fair trial, actually implicate institutions in their very description. But, in the second sense I want both to distinguish and defend, a human right is pre-institutional in that it does not derive its legitimacy *from* institutions. Rather, human rights provide the grounds for *creating or reforming institutions* to promote morally important human interests. The whole point of outlining and defending human rights is to provide reasonable grounds for an institutional framework, including the territorial scope of that framework. Human rights talk, properly understood, should always include normative discussion of institutions. If we accept this distinction between senses of 'pre-institutional', we should reject this aspect of the orthodox view while still affirming that human rights are morally prior to institutions, and that their role is to provide reasons for setting up particular sorts of institutions and doing so in a particular way. My own view is an interest-based, institution-generating conception of human rights. The present point is that human rights can represent legitimate claims even where the required institutions do not exist.

My second idea is that we need to be more careful when asking, *In virtue of what* do individuals possess human rights? When answering this question, Beitz says we have a choice between (1) common humanity, and (2) contingent relationships between persons and societies. It seems to me that this choice is not forced upon us, and that instead we should affirm that there is something important about shared humanity that generates a legitimate human rights claim, but that this is not sufficient to ground that claim without some systematic kind of relationship to which we can point. It seems neither possible nor desirable to give up the 'common humanity' premise of the traditional or orthodox conception of human rights, given its role in justifying these rights. The common humanity claim rules out any attempt to limit basic rights only to those sharing some feature such as shared citizenship. But this does not preclude recognition that this shared moral status generates particular claims only in the context of links between persons that might have been otherwise.

One persuasive element of the orthodox view is that it captures the idea that it is aspects of a person's humanity that play a key role in justifying human rights claims. Often the best way to protect these rights is by using the enforcement capacity of states; so, citizenship rights can be partly instrumental in promoting the rights-based interests of human beings. Nonetheless, human rights cannot be derived from, or justified by appeal to, citizenship rights. After all, many who need the protections affirmed by universal human rights lack any kind of citizenship. Refugees do not lack human rights because they lack citizenship rights; rather, their stateless plight is precisely what identifies them as vulnerable people whose human rights demand attention.

My third claim is much more sympathetic to Beitz's own view. Here I agree that it is a mistake to assume that human rights are timeless, and I assert that the practical implementation of human rights makes sense only in a context of advanced political and socioeconomic development such as (part of) the world has now achieved. But this is not a question of the meaning of human rights; it is instead a matter of the social conditions in which these rights become candidates for practical implementation. In any case, the issue of time-sensitivity is less important than the fact that we live in a world in which the rights of billions of individual human beings are threatened while the social means to protect and promote those rights lie within our reach.

Human rights cosmopolitanism

Moral cosmopolitanism comes in many forms, including contractualist, utilitarian, and neo-Kantian. But I want to describe a cosmopolitan view elaborated in terms of human rights, both because I believe this to be a plausible position and because it seems a promising way to develop an account of the political implications of moral cosmopolitanism, given the significance of human rights language in contemporary political practice.

A view counts as morally cosmopolitan if it satisfies the criteria of moral individualism, egalitarianism, and impartial concern. There are, accordingly, several varieties of moral cosmopolitanism. Utilitarianism can be understood to meet these criteria while interpreting them in a manner that specifies the human good and requires its maximization. Contractualism can take a global form in which principles are acceptable if no one – regardless of nationality, citizenship, sex, and so on – could reasonably reject them as the basis for informed, unforced agreement (Scanlon 1998). Neo-Kantianism, likewise, specifies its moral cosmopolitanism by demanding that maxims of human action are acceptable only if they are universalizable, i.e., if everyone could act on them.

The view I am describing here, *human rights cosmopolitanism*, provides a particular interpretation of the central moral commitments to judge institutions from an impartial perspective and to treat all individual persons with equal consideration and respect. As I have said, the view emphasizes the dignity of individual human beings, the fundamental importance and urgency of the basic claims these individuals may make on one another, and the universality of correlative duties to which these claims give rise. Human beings possess these rights in virtue of their humanity, and the rights in turn generate the main arguments for assessing and transforming the main social, economic, and political institutions under which they live. But the claims gain traction only when individuals are linked by institutions in a concrete sense, as is the case in our world of advancing globalization. One important aspect of the connection between persons is the impressive legal and political tradition, especially since the middle of the twentieth century, in which human rights themselves have been specified and affirmed in international fora and – to a lesser extent – protected and promoted in international practice.

Human rights, equality, and minimalism

In what sense is a commitment to human rights an expression of minimalism about political morality? Thomas Scanlon maintains that human rights are a class of especially important moral considerations whose violation represents 'a case of falling below *minimum* standards required of institutions' (Scanlon 2003a, p. 113, emphasis in original). 'Minimum' standards need not mean 'undemanding' or 'not extensive' or 'limited in scope to co-members of nation-states'. But there is a tendency to conceive of human rights as somehow broader in scope yet shallower in content than other rights. This is a puzzle that demands our attention.

If human rights express a commitment to *equal* concern for every human being, why is this often taken to imply more limited obligations across borders than those applying to fellow citizens of a state? The answer might appeal to the particular meaning of equality as part a conception of human rights. What kind of equality is tied up with a commitment to human rights? At the very least, any view of human rights is inseparable from the idea that each person is due equal consideration or equal respect. This gets us beyond the claim that there are classes of person with varying degrees of moral worth depending on their class membership. Men are not to be valued more highly than women, there are no natural slaves, and a person's national membership does not entitle him to greater concern than anyone else. Equal consideration is a fixed point of modern moral argument, but it does not by itself entail any strong substantive view of equal well-being or equal outcomes (Scanlon 2003b, p. 202). Equality of concern does not entail equal distribution, but nor does it tell us whether equal distribution is the proper goal.

One common view of human rights is that their enforcement protects all persons against the most extreme and objectionable forms of interest-violation. Individuals have interests in obtaining practically effective guaranteed access to enough food, shelter, and basic freedoms to enable them to live a life worth living. This can be linked to a claim in the literature on egalitarianism that has been called the *sufficiency* view, because it says that once each person has enough, inequalities beyond that point are of no moral consequence (Frankfurt 1988, pp. 134–135). On this view, it is objectionable that, in our world as we know it, so many millions of people live in such deprivation, unable to meet their most elementary needs, while at the same time millions of others have so much more than they need and could eradicate most or all of the deprivation without incurring unreasonable costs. The claim is not that each person should have the same income, wealth, or even general life prospects, but that it is fundamentally unjust to allow such *radical inequalities* in the protection of basic interests. It should be added here that the sufficiency view is inadequate if it is blind to the consequences of the inequalities it allows. For example, highly unequal distributions of wealth correlate with significant inequalities of power, and these should be the concern of moral cosmopolitans from their perspective of impartial concern for each person.

But does a correct interpretation of human rights pull in a more egalitarian direction? There are several reasons to think so. First, if we adopt the practical conception, it is clear that contemporary human rights doctrine is not minimal in its content or demands. The Universal Declaration of Human Rights (UDHR) and the associated Covenants touch on 'nearly every dimension of a society's basic institutional structure, from protections against the misuse of state power to requirements for the political process, health and welfare policy, and levels of compensation for work' (Beitz 2003, p. 39).[2] Human rights claims seem to be maximal in their content, even if they remain incompletely justified by supporting reasons. Secondly, human rights are not minimum standards that apply globally but which more local arrangements must go beyond. They are themselves, it seems, potentially quite demanding in calling for large international transfers of wealth and perhaps significant changes to institutions, including reform and creation of regimes with enforcement capacity to protect the individual interests in question (Buchanan 2005, p. 76).

The view of human rights I have just described denies that they are minimalist tools of moral argument. But to understand and evaluate the alleged minimalism of human rights, even on a cosmopolitan conception of them, we need the distinction between types of minimalism (Cohen 2004).[3] The first type is called *substantive minimalism*, 'which is a position about the content of human rights and, more broadly, about norms of global justice' (Cohen 2004, p. 192). Joshua Cohen, who coined this term, understands substantive minimalism as limiting human rights to protections of negative liberty or, even more minimally, protecting individuals against 'forcible intrusions on bodily security'. I think it is helpful here to think of a spectrum of positions, from minimal to maximal, ranging from protections against physical attack at one end to distributive egalitarianism at the other. But the minimalist requirement does not correspond to the demand to recognize only negative duties towards rights-holders, since even the most minimal protections, if they are really to secure individuals' interests, require positive action by duty-bearers. We should guard against the idea that there is a neat division between negative rights and positive rights, since no right is protected without positive action. In fact, the need for police protection and law courts suggests that rights are best protected not only by recognizing a range of positive duties but also by setting up institutions through which those duties may be met.[4]

Cohen's substantive minimalism focuses on the *content* of human rights claims: rights protect security of the person but not much more. However, this seems to be only one sense in which substantive claims can be more or less minimal. Another sense is not content but *scope* of application, where a minimalist view is limited in its focus to fellow nationals while a maximalist view is global in scope. This sense is perhaps less important when one is discussing human rights because the global reach is implicit in the very language being used. So it is understandable that Cohen should emphasize the content of human rights claims in this context.

The second type is called *justificatory minimalism*, which suggests that a conception of human rights should be presented so as to acknowledge pluralism and affirm toleration (Cohen 2004, p. 192). On this view, human rights should be defended independently of any particular comprehensive, religious, or philosophical conception, in order to encourage and enable agreement in a world of ethical and religious pluralism. The idea of this sort of minimalism is to allow people from different traditions of thought to find their own reasons for affirming the common standards represented by human rights. While this strategy excludes one possible obstacle to agreement on human rights, it does not tell us anything precise about the content of reasons that might be acceptable as grounds for agreement.

My position on justificatory minimalism is that it is acceptable only if each of the different argumentative strands leading to the shared list of human rights affirms the equal moral worth of each person regardless of sex, race, religion, and so on. This is best seen as a constraint on the types of reasons that are acceptable in defending a list of human rights. It is important that the reason be shared, but it is equally important that nothing should count as a reason in this domain unless it recognizes the equal worth of human beings. I take this to be a requirement of political argument deriving from morally cosmopolitan commitments. If one accepts this constraint on acceptable justifications of human rights *and* one rejects the 'negative liberty' minimalist view, then it is unclear why any sort of *substantive* minimalism should be accepted. In other words, liberal egalitarians who defend demanding theories of distributive justice for co-citizens cannot rationalize different and less demanding treatment for outsiders without some additional argument. And the cosmopolitan constraint of equal concern for all human beings suggests that such an argument will have to be quite strong. I will not assess the range of arguments that have been presented on that score; instead I want to discuss in more detail the issues surrounding the question of justification.

Human rights: two views

We have seen Charles Beitz's thought-provoking distinction between orthodox and practical views of human rights, but he also offers a different sort of classification between two conceptions of human rights (Beitz 2001, p. 270). On this account, what differentiates one conception from the other is the presence or absence of a link between human rights on the one hand and contested views about social justice or political legitimacy on the other. According to the *neutral/nonpartisan/restricted conception of human rights*, such rights are neutral between the various cultural and ideological perspectives in the world on the substantive questions of social justice and political legitimacy. Human rights are not partisan in disagreements between reasonable persons about justice and legitimacy, and the conception is restricted in the sense that it conceives human rights as (merely) political standards on which people may agree despite continuing – and perhaps unending – ideological and cultural conflicts about the demands of justice. Let us call this the *restricted view* (RV) for short; this view maintains that 'human rights represent the common element in a range of views about social justice or political legitimacy found among the world's cultures' (Beitz 2001, p. 270).

RV can take several forms. One variant regards human rights as the 'thin' moral core that may be extracted from the various 'thick' local moralities to be found across the world. Following Michael Walzer, we may speak of the universality here as a 'reiterative universalism', the common moral norms repeated from within each of the many otherwise distinctive community-based moral frameworks (see Walzer 1994, Chs. 1 and 2). On this interpretation, the content of human rights depends on the 'thin' common element derivable from the *actual commitments* of local communities. A different variant of RV conceives of human rights hypothetically, as 'the objects of a possible agreement among the world's political cultures. … A value could count as a genuine human right even if it were not explicitly present in every culture, just in case members of each culture could reasonably accept it as consistent with their culture's moral conventions' (Beitz 2001, p. 273).[5] Despite the differences between this version and the Walzerian position, both views defer to a culture's evaluative beliefs in identifying and elaborating on a list of basic human rights.

A third version of RV is exemplified by John Rawls in *The law of peoples* (Rawls 1999). Rawls believes that societies can be 'decent' and minimally legitimate despite failing to fulfill the requirements of liberal justice: hence, there are distinct levels of legitimacy in the international sphere. To be minimally legitimate, a society must recognize and protect 'human rights proper', but such legitimacy is consistent with the denial of basic liberal democratic rights. (I briefly return to Rawls's account, and its rationale, below.)

By contrast with RV and all of its subvariants, the second view is the *nonneutral/partisan/liberal/full conception of human rights*. On this view, human rights are non-neutral and partisan in the sense that they provide standards by which to judge the justice or legitimacy of any society's social, political, and economic institutions, even in cases where the standards conflict with those prevailing in a given society. Notice that the sense in which the liberal conception is partisan should not be confused with the sense of that adjective according to which allegiance is more or less blind or unreasoned. In the present instance, partisan adherents are simply those who take a position on disputed questions of justice and legitimacy, seeking not to abstract from disagreements in the name of reaching consensus. Accordingly, nonpartisans in this case are those who seek such abstraction. Let us call this second conception the *liberal or full view* of human rights (LFV), according to which 'the advocate of human rights takes a stand on controverted questions of political theory' (Beitz 2001, p. 270).

One might argue that it is potentially misleading to label this second conception 'liberal', since there are grounds for thinking that both conceptions represent opposing understandings of liberalism, where RV emphasizes toleration and LFV stresses the links between liberal normative premises and core claims about political legitimacy and social justice. On this interpretation, the dispute is not between a restricted view and a liberal view; rather it opposes a restricted conception with a full conception, where the distinguishing feature is the willingness of adherents to take a position on controversial questions of justice. But to the extent that liberalism suggests that *individuals* are the fundamental units of moral concern regardless of their group membership, whereas some versions of RV may legitimize collective wholes of various kinds at a basic level, then there are good grounds for identifying LFV as a liberal view. One type of proponent of RV mentioned earlier, namely, John Rawls in *The law of peoples*, explicitly defends an account of international political justice according to which 'liberal peoples' and 'decent hierarchical peoples' may coexist in a spirit of mutual toleration (Rawls 1999, p. 79). Rawls thinks that liberal societies should tolerate such decent hierarchical societies that are non-liberal in the sense that they take an associationist form. This means that 'the members of these societies are viewed in public life as members of different groups, and each group is represented in the legal system by a body in a decent consultation hierarchy' (Rawls 1999, p. 64) In a sense, this variant of RV abstracts from the moral individualism of traditional liberalism; hence there is some reason for labeling it something other than liberal.

Beitz's distinction between what I am calling the restricted view (RV) and the liberal or full view (LFV) somewhat oversimplifies a rather complex set of oppositions between a range of liberal views on the one hand and, on the other hand, various characteristics by reference to which we may identify conflicts about social justice and legitimacy. Most importantly, RV might come in a wholesale form that seeks neutrality between all cultures and ideologies or it might take a more discriminating form, remaining neutral only between culturally based disagreements but not all ideological conflicts, or vice-versa. Nevertheless, Beitz has identified the core of the issue at stake between conceptions of human rights: should human rights be conceived so as to be neutral between competing cultural or ideological views about justice and legitimacy, or should they be understood as norms that function as criteria for taking stands on disputes between competing cultures and ideologies on fundamental questions of legitimacy and justice? Beitz's way of framing this issue is to ask whether the existence of ideological and cultural pluralism in itself should 'limit the scope of a plausible doctrine of international human rights' (Beitz 2001, p. 270). We need to understand why someone might maintain that it should, and why, in the end, there is sufficient reason to conclude that it should not.

'International human rights' here signifies those rights enunciated in the United Nations' International Bill of Rights, which includes the Universal Declaration of Human Rights (1948), the International Covenants on Civil and Political Rights (1966), and the International Covenant on Economic, Social, and Cultural Rights (1966). These include rights of the person (rights to life, liberty, security, property, freedom of thought and religion, freedom from slavery, torture and degrading punishment), 'rule of law' rights (rights to equality before the law, impartial justice, presumption of innocence, freedom from arbitrary arrest), political rights (rights to participation in government, voting, freedoms of speech, association, and assembly), economic and social rights (rights to an adequate standard of living, security when unemployed, union participation, free education, social security), and community rights (rights to self-determination and protection of minority cultures).[6]

It is most plausible to interpret this list of human rights on the liberal or full view as committing its defenders to substantive positions concerning justice and legitimacy. This should be evident when one considers that – among other things – these rights generate (1) a list of conditions for legitimate state action, (2) justice-relevant limits on the scope of market economic activity, and (3) legitimacy-relevant conditions for political processes. But the defender of RV can offer an alternative interpretation of the universality of human rights, according to which they ought to be seen as the common concern of everyone in the world, even those who reject some of the substantive conditions explicitly or implicitly laid out in the UDHR and the two covenants. One important implication of RV that should be emphasized, in my view, is that the received list of human rights must itself be pared down to a set of minimum commitments that can be accepted by peoples with culturally based positions that reject one or more of the rights on the received list. For instance – to take one example more or less at random from a very long list of countries one could discuss here – if Saudi Arabia is to be included as a human rights-respecting country, the list of universal human rights must not include the right to join labor unions, since the Saudi Arabian government expressly prohibits the establishment of unions.[7] Further rights that would have to be rejected include the right to equality before the law,[8] along with freedoms of speech, the press, assembly, association, religion, and movement.[9] Other human rights are violated in practice, despite their being legally recognized. One glaring example is the right not to be arbitrarily arrested.[10] Consequently, if RV is to be accepted, its defenders have the burden of identifying precisely which rights should be regarded as the cross-culturally common commitments of all the countries in the world.

What does it mean to say that human rights are not neutral? One way to explain the sense in which the liberal or full view (LFV) is non-neutral or partisan is to identify what it excludes. Here we may note that LFV excludes beliefs and practices that violate civil and political rights, reject basic economic entitlements, or deny the equal status of women and men. Rather than combining different cultural beliefs and practices into a shared yet restricted conception of human rights, LFV explicitly opposes certain beliefs and practices (and supports others), regardless of ideological or cultural origin, whenever they conflict with its core normative commitments. Of course, from the fact that no culture is monolithic it follows that it is always possible to engage in internal criticism of the dominant interpretation of a culturally condoned practice or belief. But the proponent of LFV bases her rejection of such a practice or belief not on the views of cultural insiders but on the universal scope and legitimacy of the human rights violated by the practice or belief in question, and in turn defends those rights by appealing to arguments thought acceptable to all reasonable persons regardless of their cultural membership.

The restricted view of human rights: evaluating the arguments

Why should rights be conceived restrictively? Here the main justificatory arguments appeal to a set of distinct values: toleration, anti-paternalism, the avoidance of parochialism, and pluralism itself.[11] Let us take each of these arguments in turn, explaining the reasoning that supports RV (or rejects LFV) and outlining responses to this reasoning.

Toleration

As Beitz notes, 'many people will think that the restricted conception is the more plausible because it seems to embody a tolerance of culturally embedded moral differences that is missing from the liberal [or full] view' (Beitz 2001, p. 270).[12] This argument says that we should accept a 'principle of cultural deference', according to which the conventional morality of a society determines the acceptability of criteria for judging the legitimacy of that society's political morality (Beitz 2001, p. 274). The full, liberal view of human rights contradicts this principle of deference; therefore we should favor a restricted view consistent with the wide cultural variation in the world that often rejects 'Western' liberal democratic human rights norms. I will not argue in any detail against such conventionalism here, but it is worth mentioning that the critical power of moral argument will be diminished significantly if we conceive of political morality in this way: there simply is no good reason to limit one's argumentative resources for evaluating social practices to the norms that happen to be widely accepted within any given society or culture. Moreover, it is implausible to argue that social acceptance itself constitutes a right-making property; rather, if a practice is right (i.e., permissible or required), this is due to properties of the practice itself or to the consequences of the practice.[13]

This cultural toleration argument also trades on a propensity to overlook the internal complexity of cultures themselves. If there is an Indian tradition of encouraging women to be obedient, subordinate, and self-sacrificing to men, there are also Indian 'countertraditions of female defiance and strength' in which the 'turbulent voice of protest' is raised against male domination (Nussbaum 2000, pp. 41–42). And, of course, the same cultural heterogeneity applies to so-called 'Western' culture, so that in the end it is difficult to maintain there is a single culture that deserves to be tolerated. If the position is amended to take account of this complexity, so that it now says we should defer to the dominant moral norms in a given society or culture, it is relevant to ask why 'dominance' should carry normative weight in a dispute over contested values. Consequently, the toleration argument fails because it *either* stems from an unacceptable conception of the proper way to defend moral norms, *or* is difficult (if not impossible) to explicate coherently due to its crude understanding of culture.

Anti-paternalism

Perhaps some form of RV is the default position we are left with if we take a stand against paternalism. According to the anti-paternalist objection, LFV is paternalistic because it imposes itself on those who do not accept it, and it does so *for the good of those on whom it is imposed*. If this were straightforwardly true, it would be a classic case of paternalism, since it would seek to benefit people for their own good, regardless of the wishes of those people allegedly being benefited. Of course, the legitimacy of paternalism is itself a matter of some controversy, so the charge of paternalism does not bring closure to the discussion. More importantly, however, it is misleading to describe the universal promotion of LFV as paternalistic, because there is a vital complicating factor that differentiates LFV-promotion from textbook cases of state paternalism. Accordingly, even if it is agreed that paternalism is unjustifiable, that is irrelevant to the legitimacy of LFV.

In the textbook case of paternalism, the state restricts the freedom of action of individual citizens in order to make those individuals better off than they would be without the restriction. But in the LFV case, state action is contemplated with the aim of infringing some people's liberties 'in order to protect the human rights of others' (Beitz 2001, p. 273). Imagine that agents of the state act to deny me my human right to participate as an equal citizen in the governing of my country. The liberal or full view of human rights identifies this action as illegitimate. We might even describe this as a conflict of freedoms, where the freedoms of some to exercise unequally distributed, effective control of the political process conflicts with the freedoms of others to have a roughly equally effective say in that process. What is *not* happening here is the straightforward infringing of the liberty of some for their own good; rather, the liberty of some is infringed, the liberty of others is promoted (where it previously had been denied), and the reason for infringing the liberty of some is not (only) that it would produce benefits for those whose liberty is infringed, but rather that this infringement is entirely legitimate as a means to bringing about the equal freedoms recommended by the liberal or full view of human rights.

Beitz suggests that any initial plausibility of the anti-paternalism objection stems from a tendency to think of states as akin to individual persons, with the resulting failure to recognize that persons are separate moral agents and states are, at best, 'aggregates of separate persons with wills and interests of their own' (Beitz 2001, p. 273). The entire objection from paternalism, then, seems to depend on the seriously flawed assumption that John Rawls identified in his critique of utilitarianism: to borrow Rawls's phrase and apply it to the present case, we may say that the anti-paternalist objection to LFV 'does not take seriously the distinction between persons' (Rawls 1971, p. 27).

In some cases, the argument from anti-paternalism is self-defeating, for example, when it is applied to the case of democratic rights, where members of the society in question reject such rights yet defenders of LFV want to promote them for everyone, even those who reject them. In this case, the argument both (1) rejects imposing norms on people whom it quite properly regards as free agents, and (2) denies full democratic rights to those free agents. The self-defeatingness consists in simultaneously affirming people's freedom yet failing to affirm the democratic rights needed to give proper expression to that freedom.

The avoidance of parochialism. John Rawls's defends his conception of universal human rights in part by arguing that it is not parochial (Rawls 1999, p. 65).[14] Liberal democratic understandings of human rights are parochial in that they are limited in their range to liberal democratic societies; they set out a list that goes beyond those rights that any decent society must recognize in order to be an equal member in good standing in the society of peoples. As Rawls understands his 'law of peoples', decent societies protect universal human rights that 'express a special class of urgent rights, such as freedom from slavery and serfdom, liberty (but not equal liberty) of conscience, and security of ethnic groups from mass murder and genocide' (Rawls 1999, p. 79).[15] Rawls's view has significant normative purchase, since it requires that a range of rights must be protected by any decent society, liberal or otherwise, including the human right to subsistence, which Rawls understands as including 'minimum economic security' (Rawls 1999, p. 65) Rawls's preferred version of liberal egalitarianism would protect all of the universal human rights as he understands them, along with a further list of rights such as the right to democratic political participation. There is an interesting question here concerning the way Rawls would classify other, 'libertarian' liberal positions that deny human subsistence rights on the grounds that such rights are 'positive' and therefore for that very reason not claimable by all human beings.[16] The implication would seem to be that libertarian societies should not be classified as *decent* societies because they deny human rights to subsistence. In any case, Rawls's main point is that there can be 'decent hierarchical societies' that protect 'human rights proper', even though they deny certain rights that liberal democrats would want all human beings to possess.

The charge of parochialism is clear enough, but in Rawls it remains undefended. We can make sense of the distinction between liberal peoples and decent but non-liberal peoples, and we can understand that Rawls's own version of the restricted view of human rights (RV) would have us think of them only as the 'human rights proper' that can be accepted by non-liberal peoples. But Rawls's account remains question-begging at this stage, because he has explained how he understands the claim that what we are calling the liberal or full view of human rights (LFV) is limited to liberal democratic societies, but he offers no argument whatsoever to answer the following question that might be put by a proponent of LFV: even if we grant that it is better for societies to be decent than not decent, why should some decent societies be considered legitimate when they deny several core human rights, for example, equal rights to political participation, specifically when women are excluded from formal participation in state decision-making?

Perhaps we can understand better the need to avoid parochialism if we change tack and consider the issue from a methodological perspective. Joseph Chan makes an interesting distinction in terms of alternative methods of justifying human rights. The first method justifies human rights by appealing to universal principles acceptable to all reasonable persons. The second approach sounds very much like the second variant of RV outlined earlier: this approach is 'ecumenical' in that it 'tries to seek consensus on human rights from within cultural perspectives'.[17] According to Chan and Daniel A. Bell, this 'interpretative approach' is the best way to justify human rights in a Chinese context.

Why should one adopt the interpretative approach? One answer is that it is the most promising strategy for promoting human rights globally, i.e., in a world where many dominant local cultural traditions lack the notion of human rights and are likely to be brought to recognize them only if the local traditions themselves are built on rather than challenged (Bell 1998, p. 567). There is no point in condescending to the locals from an allegedly superior vantage point that refuses to engage with locally endorsed moral beliefs. As a strategic point, this seems to me quite reasonable. But Bell seems to want to maintain something more, namely, that as a matter of preferred moral method the 'ultimate justifications' of shared human rights norms will remain in dispute, and that non-Western traditions in some cases should change the content of those rights themselves. Consider the following ambiguous passage from Bell:

> The point here is that 'cultural interpretation' is not just a strategic matter of finding local resources for the promotion of human rights: it may be equally important to recognize the possibility that in certain areas, non-Western traditions may justifiably differ from 'international' human rights norms and to suggest ways in which those traditions can contribute to the international discourse on human rights, changing it from what it is today. (Bell 1998, p. 579)

The passage is ambiguous because it is not clear whether Bell is arguing for one or other, or both, of two different things. Least controversially, he supports changes in 'the international discourse on human rights' by way of the inclusion of non-Western traditions. Even if we stick to the point about strategy, there is no doubt that the *discourse*, by which I presume Bell means the *arguments offered in support of human rights*, will change as more discussants from a wider range of cultural traditions enter the debates on fair terms. We might say, therefore, that introducing non-Western perspectives into the debate formalizes a commitment to discursive pluralism. This is an entirely positive development, and anyone who would reject it leaves himself open to accusations of cultural imperialism and denial of a voice to many whose traditions were overridden, denigrated, and neglected for centuries. But this first point about the discourse of human rights is quite distinct from another point that Bell seems to be making here, namely, that international human rights norms themselves may be rejected on the grounds that certain aspects of non-Western traditions reject those norms. This is how I interpret Bell's claim that 'in certain areas, non-Western traditions may *justifiably* differ from 'international' human rights norms' (emphasis added). The substance of Bell's position is that, in some instances, one should defer to cultural traditions when they conflict with universal human rights. This is an interesting suggestion, but it cannot be evaluated in the abstract.

In any case, the core of Bell's objection to the stereotypically Western liberal approach to justice and human rights is that it is a species of 'parochial universalism', i.e., it attempts to 'put forward a universally valid theory of justice that draws only on the moral aspirations and political practices found in liberal Western societies' (Bell 1998, p. 568). Parochial universalism, as exemplified in Bell's opinion by Brian Barry's *Justice as impartiality*, constitutes an arrogant dismissal of non-Western cultural particularities. It is claimed that such an attitude is likely to do less for human rights than the interpretative approach favored by Bell and Chan.

The correct response to Bell's accusation points to the need for what Evan Charney has called 'nonparochial universalism' in defending human rights (Charney 1999, p. 840). Charney draws attention to Bell's apparent openness to rejecting certain universal human rights in the face of pressure from local cultural moral norms, and raises searching questions about it: 'But if fundamental human rights norms identify a basic minimum of rights that all persons possess simply in virtue of their common humanity, how could there be any justification for departing from them? How could cultural particularity provide a justification for violating those norms that by their very nature presumably transcend cultural particularity?' (Charney 1999, p. 840). I think Charney correctly questions the extent of the pluralism allowed by the doctrine of universal basic human rights. What I have called 'discursive pluralism' is not at all threatened by the members of different cultural traditions participating in discussions about universal human rights. But if Bell is thinking of rejecting some candidate right on the grounds that the dominant Chinese cultural tradition – Confucianism – rejects it, much more needs to be said. It is important to point out that there may be a huge number of different ways of implementing these rights in different times and places, and here the role of cultural traditions can and may loom large. Nevertheless, to say that (a) the practical realization of human rights may take different forms on the grounds that cultural pluralism favors distinctive ways of implementing, protecting, and promoting what is held universally in common, is quite different from saying that (b) some basic human rights may be overridden when they conflict with strongly held conflicting, culturally based moral views. The first claim places the recognition of global, cultural diversity at the center of its account of the best way to understand human rights in the international context, while the second claim amounts to nothing more than the cultural deference view.

Pluralism itself

The restricted conception of human rights might appeal to the intrinsic value of pluralism or diversity as such. What makes our world valuable, according to this argument, is that it contains a diverse set of cultures. The liberal or full view of human rights, it might be thought, would threaten this pluralism by imposing its univocal Western liberal-democratic bias so as to wipe out the many flourishing practices that its dictates reject.

We should distinguish between two kinds of diversity or pluralism that one might defend: (1) diversity of values and practices *as such*, and (2) diversity of values and practices within a universal framework that limits pluralism within a range consistent with the recognition and protection of fundamental interests and rights. Diversity *as such* is neither appealing nor defensible, since it would condone a range of morally objectionable practices, from wife-beating to stoning and beyond (Nussbaum 2000, p. 51). But once we recognize this basic point, 'pluralism as such' cannot be the basis for rejecting LFV in favor of RV, because the defender of 'pluralism as such' is incapable of explaining why some uncontroversially abhorrent practice ought to be rejected.

Accordingly, a wise proponent of RV will limit his claim to the following: within the constraints imposed by protections for the core universal human rights, it is better to live in a world characterized by diverse ethical and political practices than in one where a single, Western, liberal-democratic model is imposed on everyone regardless of cultural or ideological background. A shrewd defender of LFV will request clarification of the type of imposition being contemplated. After all, there is no single liberal-democratic political model: there is a large variety of electoral systems, representative institutions, interpretations of property rights and rights such as freedom of speech, all consistent with LFV. Consequently, it is more accurate to describe a world in which all countries accept and enforce the liberal or full view of human rights as a world characterized by a variety of political, social, and economic institutions falling within a broad range. On the other hand, if LFV is defensible as a general way of understanding human rights, its defenders should not shrink from wanting to see it 'imposed' in cases where, say, the vast majority of citizens of a given country are denied the right to vote or speak freely or associate with others at the level of civil society. Diversity is not a value when it requires the denial of fundamental freedoms to which every human being is entitled in virtue of their humanity.

There is, in fact, a link between valuing diversity on the one hand and, on the other hand, supporting democracy as a universal political norm. Once we recognize, as I think we should, that diversity is an important value (subject to the constraints mentioned above), we are led to ask a further question: where diverse practices are permitted, what is the best way for different societies to determine their preferred mode or direction? One plausible answer is that democratic decision-making processes provide the best procedures here, especially since they are morally motivated by the norms of respect for the equal dignity of individuals that provide part of the rationale for respecting diversity in the first place.

The connection between human rights and justice

We have seen how each of the four main supporting arguments for the restricted view of human rights contains problems that suggest the relative superiority of the liberal or full view. But can LFV be defended more directly? In particular, can one argue for LFV as the better conception on the grounds that human rights identify part of the requirements of justice, so that RV suffers from something like a conceptual inadequacy by omitting a feature of any coherent conception of human rights? I do not think LFV can declare victory so easily, for this argument mischaracterizes RV. Any restricted view tries to combine (1) an account of human rights with (2) silence on much that is controversial about the demands of social justice. LFV differs from RV not in its commitment to justice, since RV's rights must be considered to be elaborations on the core commitments of justice. Rather, LFV's defenders see no principled reason to remain silent on anything but a minimal, common core of human rights. It is, therefore, the *extent* of justice commitments that differentiates LFV from RV. Despite Beitz's description of it, the restricted view is not entirely noncommittal concerning the requirements of justice. Instead, it is the content of RV's human rights that is determined by whatever can, in fact, be described as universally, cross-culturally shared rights norms. For this reason, RV is bound to be limited in its list of human rights. There is no alternative, in that case, to case-by-case analyses of particular rights claims, aimed at explaining why a given right should be included in a cross-cultural list of basic human rights.

No account of basic human rights encompasses a complete description of the requirements of justice, since variations in the distribution of certain valued goods (such as income and wealth) are compatible with universal rights protection, even where rights are understood in terms of the liberal or full view. Any satisfactory theory of social justice must include protections for individual interests provided by human rights, but it will mention also either (a) further specifications on the legitimate range of inequality of basic goods, and/or (b) elaboration of the character of the processes by which distributive decisions may be made. This latter task aims to explain how legitimate decisions can be reached, and why decision-making that takes a given form is for that reason legitimate.

Conclusion

Moral cosmopolitanism is a powerful normative perspective within which to expound a conception of human rights. These rights protect the basic interests of individuals as part of an institutional framework that provides protections against standard threats to those interests. In both content and scope, there is good reason to reject minimalist interpretations of human rights. Most importantly, a comparative critical evaluation leads to the conclusion that the liberal view of human rights can generate objections to the restricted view and that this liberal conception is more faithful to the fundamental normative commitments of moral cosmopolitanism.

Notes

1. For this formulation, see Beitz (2005, p. 17).
2. Beitz even suggests that we should understand human rights as asserting 'something more like necessary conditions of political legitimacy, or even of social justice' (Beitz 2003, p. 39).
3. See also, Buchanan (2005).
4. For a clear argument in support of the claim that all rights are positive, see Holmes and Sunstein (1999).
5. Beitz identifies this as an 'overlapping consensus' view, though I avoid that label here in order to prevent confusion with the different use of that phrase in the political liberalism of John Rawls.
6. See the helpful summary at Beitz (2001, p. 271) on which I draw here.
7. The relevant information may be found in US Department of State (2001). For the prohibition of unions, see section 6, 'Worker rights'.
8. US Department of State (2001), section 5, 'Discrimination based on race, sex, religion, disability, language, or social status' says that in Saudi Arabia 'there is legal and systemic discrimination based on sex and religion', that 'the Shi'a religious minority suffers social, legal, economic, political, and sectarian discrimination', and that in a Shari'a court, 'the testimony of one man equals that of two women'.
9. US Department of State (2001), Introductory section.
10. US Department of State (2001), section 1d, 'Respect for the integrity of the person, including freedom from arbitrary arrest, detention, or exile'.
11. Nussbaum (2000, pp. 41–59) discusses three of these four arguments (culture, diversity, and paternalism) as reasons for rejecting universal, cross-cultural moral norms. My discussion is influenced by Nussbaum, but I focus here only on the sense in which we should understand *human rights* as universally valid norms.
12. Beitz's own position, however, is that it is paradoxical to 'stop short' of the full liberal view, given that one is engaged in a description of 'evaluative standards for social and political institutions'.
13. For further elaboration of the problems with relativist reasoning of this sort, see Jones (1999, ch. 7, especially pp. 175–176), and Nussbaum (2000, pp. 48–49).
14. Rawls (1999, pp. 59–60) also defends his view by appealing to the value of toleration.
15. Rawls says that Articles 3 to 18 of the Universal Declaration of Human Rights count as 'human rights proper' (Rawls 1999, p. 80).
16. In Jones (1999, ch. 2, especially pp. 62–66), I explain why the distinction between 'negative' and 'positive' rights cannot withstand serious scrutiny.
17. J. Chan, 'A Confucian perspective on human rights for contemporary China', cited in Bell (1998, p. 567).

References

Barry, B.M., 1995. *Justice as impartiality.* Oxford: Oxford University Press.

Barry, B.M., 1998. International society from a cosmopolitan perspective. *In:* D. Mapel and T. Nardin, eds. *International society: diverse ethical perspectives.* Princeton, NJ: Princeton University Press, 144–63.

Beitz, C., 2001. Human rights as a common concern. *American political science review,* 95 (2), 269–282.

Beitz, C., 2003. What human rights mean. *Daedalus,* 132 (1), 36–46.

Beitz, C., 2004. Human rights and the law of peoples. *In:* D. Chatterjee, *ed. The ethics of assistance.* Cambridge: Cambridge University Press, 193–214.

Beitz, C., 2005. Cosmopolitanism and global justice. *The journal of ethics,* 9 (1–2), 11–27.

Bell, D.A., 1998. The limits of liberal justice. *Political theory,* 26 (4), 557–582.

Buchanan, A., 2005. Equality and human rights. *Politics, philosophy & economics,* 4 (1), 69–90.

Charney, E., 1999. Cultural interpretation and universal human rights: a response to Daniel A. Bell. *Political theory,* 27 (6), 840–848.

Cohen, J., 2004. Minimalism about human rights: the most we can hope for? *The journal of political philosophy,* 12 (2), 190–213.

Frankfurt, H., 1988. Equality as a moral ideal. *In:* H. Frankfurt, *The importance of what we care about.* Cambridge: Cambridge University Press.

Holmes, S. and Sunstein, C.R., 1999. *The cost of rights.* New York: Norton.

Jones, C., 1999. *Global justice.* Oxford: Oxford University Press.

Nussbaum, M., 2000. *Women and human development.* Cambridge: Cambridge University Press.

Rawls, J., 1971 *A theory of justice.* Oxford: Oxford University Press.

Rawls, J., 1999. *The law of peoples.* Cambridge, MA: Harvard University Press.

Scanlon, T., 1998. *What we owe to each other.* Cambridge MA: Harvard University Press.

Scanlon, T., 2003a. Human rights as a neutral concern. *In:* T. Scanlon, *The difficulty of tolerance.* Cambridge: Cambridge University Press, 113–123.

Scanlon, T., 2003b. The diversity of objections to inequality. *In:* T. Scanlon, *The difficulty of tolerance.* Cambridge: Cambridge University Press, 202–218.

Scheffler, S., 2001. Conceptions of cosmopolitanism. *In:* Samuel Scheffler, *Boundaries and allegiances.* Oxford: Oxford University Press, 111–130.

US Department of State, 2001. Country reports on human rights. Released 4 March 2002. http://www.state.gov/g/drl/rls/hrrpt/2001/nea/8296.htm.

Walzer, M., 1994. *Thick and Thin.* Notre Dame and London: University of Notre Dame Press.

On the interrelations between domestic and global (in)justice

Peter Koller

Institute of Legal Philosophy, Sociology of Law and Legal Informatics, Karl-Franzens- University of Graz, Austria

My paper consists of two parts. The first part deals with the fundamental normative standards of domestic social justice on the one hand and global justice on the other, standards that are requisite in order to identify injustices on both levels. On this basis, the second part focuses on the interrelations between domestic social justice and global justice with particular attention to the interdependencies between domestic and global injustices.

The demands of domestic and global justice

Kinds of justice

In contrast to unconditionally universal requirements of morality, such as the commandment not to hurt other people without justification, the demands of *justice* are context-dependent in the sense that they always refer to certain social relationships among the parties concerned. There are, however, a great many social relationships subject to justice which differ so much that it seems pointless to look for a single basic principle of material justice that would apply to all of these relationships alike. So it will be useful to differentiate between different forms of social interaction in order to see whether there are any standards of justice which fit with them. This strategy was already pursued by Aristotle when he proposed the distinction between two sorts of justice that are usually named ‘distributive’ and ‘commutative’ justice (Aristotle 1954). Although this classification leads to the right direction, it is too rough to illuminate the most significant demands of justice. In my view, it is necessary to distinguish between four kinds of justice each of which refers to a particular elementary type of social relationships:

(1) distributive justice => communal relationships
(2) transactional justice => exchange relationships

(3) political justice => power relationships
(4) corrective justice => wrongness relationships

I think that this classification enables us to identify a number of widely shared and reasonable, though rather weak demands of justice that apply to the rules and institutions of social life. Each type of social interaction includes specific conflicts whose fair resolution requires appropriate principles of justice. I would like to sketch the kinds of justice and their respective demands briefly (Koller 2001, pp. 19 ff, 2003).

Distributive justice applies to *communal relationships.* These are interpersonal constellations whose participants have a common claim to certain goods or are bound to bear some common burdens. In short: individuals entertain a communal relationship when and insofar they share some common goods or common burdens or both. Justice demands that common goods and burdens are to be distributed in a way that is reasonably acceptable to all participants. There is one general principle of distributive justice that works for all distributive problems, even though the specific criteria that apply to them vary with their special features. It can be put as follows: the goods and burdens of a common enterprise are to be distributed *equally* among its members unless an unequal distribution is justified by reasons that are acceptable to all parties concerned from an impartial point of view. This principle – the *principle of equal treatment* – is the basic demand of distributive justice within modern moral and political thinking based on the idea that every human person is to be respected equally. Taken alone, the principle of equal treatment is rather weak and abstract, but it acquires significant strength when it is combined with further relevant information (see Bedau 1967; Rawls 1971, p. 62; Feinberg 1973, pp. 99 ff; Miller 1976, pp. 24 ff).

Transactional justice focuses on *exchange relationships*, i.e. contractual transactions through which independent persons, each of whom is endowed with particular rights, voluntarily agree on a mutual transfer of some of their rights to each other. Justice demands that such transactions occur in a way which ensures that they are to the benefit of all parties involved, so that none of them has a legitimate reason to complain about the outcome. In developed societies, exchange transactions usually are regarded as just, if the parties involved voluntarily agree on them under conditions which enable them to pursue their best interest. In particular, these conditions require that all parties involved have equal legal competence, enough knowledge of the relevant facts, and sufficient capacities of rationality in order to make choices in their well-considered interest. To this end, contractual agreements must be performed in a way that no party is able to dictate the terms of trade. Since these conditions, if met, make sure that exchange relationships will lead to optimal outcomes about which no party can reasonably complain, they define the basic requirements on *fair* exchange relationships (Roover 1958; Hayek 1976, pp. 73ff; Lucas 1980, pp. 208 ff).

Political justice deals with *power relationships* that occur when a person or collective body effectively claims the power to determine the ways or circumstances of conduct of other people through binding decisions backed by the threat of force. There are good reasons to assume that, at least in large social unions, some forms of power are necessary in order to secure a just and efficient social order. Since such power involves significant dangers too, it is subject to certain requirements of justice in order to keep it within acceptable limits. It is generally agreed that power is not an end in itself, but a means to achieve a rightful and efficient social order. Accordingly, power is deemed to be just only if it serves *legitimate purposes* and is exercised in an appropriate way. Its purposes are twofold: on the one hand, enforcing the legitimate claims and obligations of individuals and, on the other, facilitating projects of social cooperation to the benefit of all people involved, such as the provision of public goods. And its exercise must be *impartial* on the ground of general rules that apply to all parties involved alike (Höffe 1987, pp. 62ff).

Corrective justice applies to *wrongness relationships*. These occur when people commit wrongdoings by flouting binding social norms, violating the rights of other persons, or breaching their duties toward others. This constellation demands a correction of the committed wrongs in order to restore the social order by compensating the victims or punishing the wrongdoers for severe crimes. The ways and forms of correcting wrongs are the object of *corrective justice*, which includes two parts: on the one hand, *restitutive* justice which deals with the just compensation of damages, and, on the other hand, *retributive* justice that focuses on the question as to when and how wrongdoings ought to be sanctioned by punishment. Both sorts of corrective justice raise a number of problems as to the *appropriateness* of corrective measures. In this context, however, it is neither possible nor necessary to enter in a discussion of these problems (Sterba 1980, pp. 63ff; Coleman 1992, pp. 179ff).

So much to the elementary kinds of justice each of which includes particular demands. In social reality, however, these kinds are not independent, but connected to each other. First of all, human interaction actually occurs within complex networks of social relationships, such as families, neighbourhoods, political communities, that combine the types of social relationships and their respective demands in manifold ways. A family, for instance, usually combines all types of interaction: communal relationships in view to the common assets and burdens; power relationships between parents and children; exchange relationships when its members perform transactions about things to which they have separate rights; and wrongness relationships when a member commits a wrong that requires correction. Secondly, there are conceptual relations among the different kinds of justice and their respective demands: most significant in this context is the fact that distributive justice has priority to all other kinds of justice, because transactional as well as political and corrective justice presuppose a just initial distribution of the particular rights and duties of the parties involved in exchange, power and wrongness relationships. On the basis of this preliminary sketch of the demands of justice in general, I want to explain the notions of domestic social justice on the one hand and global justice on the other.

Domestic social justice

Domestic social justice is a rather complex concept which includes a plurality of demands. Let us say that it comprises the *totality of demands of justice that apply to a society's social order*. It seems plausible that such an order is subject to *all* kinds of justice previously mentioned: it is subject to distributive justice insofar as it represents a sort of communal enterprise whose members have common claims to certain goods or share certain burdens; to transactional justice to the extent in which it empowers individuals to coordinate their relationships by contractual transactions; to political justice insofar as the societal order needs or makes use of authorized power; and also to corrective justice, because any societal order has to deal with wrongdoings that call for correction. These kinds of justice are interconnected in various ways, one of which is of particular importance: the fundamental role of *distributive* justice relative to the other demands. Distributive justice has *priority* to all other kinds, since transactional, political, and corrective justice necessarily presuppose a previous arrangement of individual rights and obligations that itself is subject to distributive justice. So distributive justice is indeed the core of the idea of domestic social justice, and this explains why most discussions on social justice are about distributive matters (Koller 2003; Barry 2005, pp. 27ff).

To the extent in which a society is to be considered a *community* the members of which share common claims or burdens, its order is subject to distributive justice with its basic principle of equal treatment, which can be sharpened in regard to societal orders as follows: All members of a society ought to have an *equal share* of the common goods and burdens unless their unequal distribution appears justified for generally acceptable reasons. So there are three questions which have to be dealt with in order to come to more specific requirements of social justice: first of all, the question as to whether and in what respects a society may be understood as a community; secondly, what goods and burdens are common to the members of a society; and thirdly, what reasons, if any, may justify social inequalities. As to the first question, it is helpful to differentiate between three types of community: ownership communities, cooperative communities, and solidarity communities (Koller 1993).

An *ownership community* is a relationship among people who commonly own certain goods, because, for example, they have inherited them jointly or produced them through their cooperative work. It seems pretty clear that each society is such a community with regard to two sorts of goods to which all members have a common claim: these are the society's natural resources on the one hand, and its cultural heritage on the other. This assumption implies that all members of a society have a claim to a fair share of the natural and cultural goods in the sense that they must have sufficient access to their benefits (Steiner 1994, pp. 231ff). A *cooperative community* is a constellation where people cooperate in order to produce certain goods by submitting themselves to respective burdens. It is also obvious that, to a certain extent, each society is a cooperative community. This is even true of a traditional society that consists of independent and self-sufficient families, since it could not secure a peaceful social order unless its members submit themselves to a number of negative duties at least. A modern society, however, is a cooperative community to a much greater extent, because its highly differentiated division of labour connects the members to a much closer network of mutual cooperation in which everybody is, in some way, affected by and dependent on the others. Consequently, every member of the society has a claim to access to social cooperation and a fair share of its outcomes (Rawls 1971, pp. 520ff). Finally, people form a *solidarity community* to the extent in which they are mutually responsible for taking care of the well-being of their fellow-members. One may question whether a large society represents a community of this sort. Yet, modern societies have become such communities to a certain degree due to the fact that smaller social units which, in previous times, were responsible for the sick, the handicapped, and the elderly, have collapsed. So a modern society is to be regarded as a sort of solidarity community, too (Koller 2007).

As a result, a society is subject to distributive justice in regard to all social goods and burdens that emerge from these communal features. This conclusion raises the question as to the particular things which are common to the members of a society and, therefore, require just distribution. In general, one may say that these things consist of the goods and burdens of social coexistence and cooperation whose social distribution is of fundamental importance for the opportunities and prospects of the individual members and can be effectively controlled by the society's institutional order, in short: the *basic social goods and burdens* (Rawls 1971, pp. 90ff). What things qualify as such goods and burdens partly depends on contingent circumstances, particularly the stage of societal development. In a modern society, however, the basic social goods apparently include the following five sorts of individual assets: (1) general rights, (2) civil liberties, (3) political participation, (4) social opportunities, and (5) economic prospects. On the level of a society's institutional order, these assets take the form of individual *rights* connected with respective *obligations* which represent the basic social burdens. Accordingly, the social order ought to arrange the distribution of these assets in a way that all members enjoy them equally, unless there are generally acceptable reasons that justify inequalities.

This leads to the final question as to whether such reasons exist at all, and if so, which inequalities may be justifiable to what extent. In spite of far-reaching disagreements on this question, I guess that most people would admit that there are some reasons which, in principle, make social inequalities acceptable. This is particularly true of considerations that focus on the following aspects: the merits, contributions and achievements of individuals, their vested rights and liberties, and their urgent needs (Frankena 1962; Honoré 1970; Hare 1978). I think that such considerations are plausible, if the inequalities in question are contributing to or resulting from a generally advantageous social order, so that they are, in the long run, to the benefit of all people concerned, including those who fare worse. This condition can be transformed to a *general principle of justifying inequalities* that runs as follows: social inequalities are justifiable, if and only if they are necessarily connected to a societal order that, in the long run, is to the benefit of all members, including the worse-off (Rawls 1971, pp. 65ff). Admittedly, this principle is not only very vague, but also needs a lot of empirical information in order to become applicable to social reality. But I think it sets a rough frame for the discussion about social inequalities.

If the principle of justifying inequalities is applied to the fundamental social goods previously mentioned, we arrive at five fundamental demands of domestic social justice which, in principle, are widely accepted in most advanced societies, although there are considerable controversies about their precise interpretation: (1) *legal equality*, i.e. the rule of law and equal protection of the laws; (2) *civil liberty*, understood as equal individual liberty with the basic liberties in its centre; (3) *democratic participation*, namely equal access to collective decision-making processes on public affairs; (4) *equal opportunity*, i.e. equal access to unequal social positions that entail different degrees of income, power, influence, and reputation; and (5) *economic equity* in the sense that economic inequalities are to be limited to the extent up to which they appear justifiable from an impartial point of view. These five demands represent the core of the presently dominant public conception of domestic social justice. Even though there are considerable disagreements on what they mean and require in detail, they are not empty phrases which can be interpreted arbitrarily in any way (Koller 2003).

At any rate, from those demands of domestic social justice flow a number of widely acknowledged *basic rights* of individuals against their respective society and its institutions, namely the well-known liberal, political, and social rights, such as the rights to life, bodily integrity, and private freedom, the rights to political activity and participation, and the rights to social subsistence, work, education, and health care (Nickel 1987; Donnelly 2003). These basic rights may be taken as minimum demands of domestic social justice that a societal order has to meet in order not to be unjust. Thus, severe and frequent violations of those basic rights represent obvious *injustices in the domestic sphere*, even if the more demanding aspects of social justice are under dispute. Accordingly, a great many societies in our present world suffer from extreme injustices, while only a minority of them appear to do better. In my opinion, however, virtually all of them are, more or less, unjust (Barry 2005, pp. 37ff, 169ff).

The idea of global justice

The idea of global justice is difficult to grasp, because it is has not yet developed to a widely shared moral-political concept with a fairly stable profile. That the recent debate on global justice reflects the rapid changes of our world that are addressed in the talk about *globalization* is evident and does not require further explanation (Held 2000; Lechner and Boli 2004; Koller 2006). Nor do I intend to deal with various approaches to global justice that are discussed in contemporary philosophy (Luper-Foy 1988; Nardin and Mapel 1992; Pogge 2001; Kohler and Marti 2003). Instead, I want to make an attempt to clarify the idea of global justice with the help of the proposed classification of elementary kinds of justice.

For a first approximation to the notion of global justice, I want to pursue a similar strategy as in the case of domestic social justice. Accordingly, global justice is to be understood as the *totality of demands of justice that can be reasonably applied to international relations and the global order*. And I think that again all kinds of justice come into play, namely distributive, transactional, political, and corrective justice. Since this may appear not so clear in view to distributive justice than in the other cases, I would like to take first a glance at these cases, before I deal with distributive justice.

The global order is subject to *transactional justice* when different nations as a whole or their members maintain trade and exchange relationships. Transactional justice requires that international trade relations and global market processes take place under *fair rules and framing conditions* which ensure that all participating peoples and nations can derive benefit from them. To this end, those rules and framing conditions must ensure that no nation is mighty enough to dictate unilaterally the terms of trade to its own advantage, and that international exchange transactions are balanced to the effect that they are not distorted by asymmetrical market restrictions (Franck 1995; pp. 413ff; Beviglia Zampetti 2006; Kapstein 2006, pp. 45ff; Stiglitz and Charlton 2006).

The demand of *political justice* applies to international and global affairs to the extent in which these affairs actually include or require authorized power. In order to circumvent the difficult question as to the form of such power, I want to point to two rather weak and obvious implications of political justice in view to the global order: First of all, an appropriate global order ought to be capable to *prevent the two most significant evils* of our present world: (i) gross and massive violations of fundamental human rights, such as genocides, ethnical cleansing, and avoidable famines (Buchanan 2004, pp. 118ff; Chwaszcza 2007), and (ii) an irreversible extermination of global natural resources, such as the destruction of oceans, earthly climate conditions, and rain forests (Kaul *et al.* 1999). Secondly, power in international affairs ought to lie in the hands of inter-, trans- or supranational authorities that have *sufficient strength and independence* in order to enforce the rules of international law in an *impartial* way (Franck 1995, pp. 173ff; Buchanan 2004, pp. 233ff).

The demand for *corrective justice* enters in the agenda of international relations when nations or some of their members commit severe wrongdoings against other peoples or their individual members, wrongdoings that require compensation or retribution. But how can corrective justice be achieved in international affairs, if it applies at all? In principle, it seems evident that it does apply. For why should a nation be exempt from the obligation to render appropriate compensation, if it has inflicted gross wrongs or harms on another nation? However, one may quarrel about the weight and the consequences of this demand. There is not only the problem of how to determine the scale of the compensation that would be appropriate to the committed wrongs, but also the danger that the project of reversing those wrongs would be causing international conflict rather than peace. Therefore, I think that corrective justice in international affairs should not be regarded as a matter of primary importance, even though it is certainly not irrelevant. Since, in most cases, it overlaps with the demands of transactional, political, and distributive justice, it can support and strengthen these other demands (O'Neill 2000, pp. 129ff; Meyer 2005, pp. 135ff).

Now I want to turn to the most contested issue of global justice, the question as to whether and to what extent international relations and the global order as a whole are subject to *distributive justice* (Buchanan 2004, pp. 191ff). A number of thinkers, including Rawls (1999, pp. 113ff), advocate the view that distributive justice does not have any significance in the context of international or global justice. I want to contradict this view and argue for a complex concept of global justice that integrates distributive justice in a differential way. Accordingly, distributive justice applies to international relations to the extent in which the international or global order has distributive effects in regard to the communal affairs of different nations or humankind as a whole. On the basis of this interpretation, the impact of distributive justice on international relations clearly depends on *contingent facts*, namely the actual structure of the world, especially the degree of international and global interdependencies. The more individual nations and peoples become mutually interconnected and interdependent in their activities, the greater is the domain of their communal affairs that create problems of distributive justice. When we consider the present situation of the world, we find at least three issues that evoke the demand for distributive justice: the extent of the nations' political autonomy within the global order; the negative effects of societal activities across borders; and international economic cooperation based on division of labour.

The first issue, *the extent of the nations' political autonomy within the global order*, is already present in a world where the national economies are relatively separate, but it increases with the process of globalization. I assume that a just international order ought to grant to each nation the right to political self-determination to the greatest extent that is compatible with a peaceful and mutually beneficial global order (Koller 2000; Moellendorf 2004, pp. 102ff). The second issue, *the negative effects of societal activities across borders*, results from the fact that the social and economic activities of individual societies increasingly have negative effects on other countries and even the whole world. This fact raises the demand for a just distribution of the benefits and costs of border-crossing social and economic activities: the costs must be distributed in proportion to the benefits which individual nations derive from those activities. When such a distribution cannot be achieved by market regulations, corrective justice requires that the nations who fare better have to pay appropriate compensation to those who are worse off (Barry 1989; Singer 2002, pp. 14ff). Thirdly, there is the issue of *international economic cooperation based on division of labour*. Individual nations increasingly converge into comprehensive units of social and economic cooperation based on division of labour, in which all contribute to the production of earthly wealth, but also become more and more dependent from each other. Even though this cooperation essentially operates on the basis of market transactions, it creates a problem of distributive justice, since market processes alone cannot secure a just distribution of their outcomes. Consequently, distributive justice also applies to the benefits and burdens of international cooperation based on division of labour.

As a result, the idea of global justice combines a variety of demands that flow from all elementary kinds of justice. Even though these demands are rather vague, it is fairly obvious that the present international order fails to meet them to a high degree. In fact, this order suffers from extreme injustices in the light of each demand. The demand of *transactional* justice is grossly violated by the prevailing systems of global trade and international finance, at least as far as the relationships between rich and poor countries are concerned. The trade system highly favours the interests of the rich countries to the disadvantage of the poor, and the international credit system operates in a way that there is a permanent flow of wealth from the poor to the rich countries (Woods 1999; Oxfam International 2002; Hertz 2004; Stiglitz 2006). Nor does the present international order accord to the demand of *political* justice. When we only look at the global level, we encounter a peculiar situation: on the one hand, there is a legal international power, the United Nations (UN), which suffers both from ineffectiveness and distorted decision-making mechanisms; on the other hand, there is a very small group of real super powers, particularly the USA, whose governments are mainly led by their national self-interest rather than the common good of the international community (Höffe 1999, pp. 267ff; Czempiel 2002).

Last but not least, the present world system is also in contradiction to *distributive* justice. As to the first issue, it greatly fails to meet the requirement that every nation's political autonomy is compatible with a peaceful global order, since it concedes to state governments two rights or privileges: the right of exercising control of its country's natural resources at will, including selling them, and the right of raising credits in behalf of its country that bind future governments. These two rights – the 'resource privilege' and the 'borrowing privilege', as Thomas Pogge (2002, pp. 112ff, 146ff) calls them – entice corrupt regimes to enrich themselves at the cost of the people by disposing of their land's resources and raising credits. Furthermore, the present order violates the demand for a proportional distribution of the costs and benefits of societal activities across borders, because the rich nations derive the lion's share of benefits from the use of natural resources belonging to the common heritage of humankind at the cost of the poor countries and future generations (Redclift and Sage 1999; Singer 2002, pp. 14ff). And finally, the existing form of international economic cooperation is also not defensible, for it works in a way that some nations take the benefits, while others are left with empty hands (Oxfam International 2002).

Interrelations between domestic and global justice/injustices

Kinds of interrelation

In most discussions where the relationships between domestic and global justice come up, the emphasis usually lies on the alleged *tensions* between the two spheres. For instance, it is often said that the prevailing systems of liberal welfare state are endangered by the ongoing process of globalization through which less developed nations will gain a larger share of earthly wealth at the cost of the developed world. This view seems highly questionable to me for two reasons. First of all, even if the current process of globalization entailed a redistribution of earthly riches in favour of some developing countries, it would not necessarily lead to a better global order, as long as inequalities in developing countries and the number of global poor continued to grow, as is the case. And secondly, existing liberal welfare democracies in the Northern world would not conform to a defensible conception of domestic social justice, if they were based on global inequalities that prevent other peoples from achieving a just domestic order. The interrelations between the two spheres can be divided in two kinds: conceptually necessary interrelations on the one hand and causally contingent interrelations on the other.

There are some *necessary interrelations* between domestic and global justice that flow from the very concepts of both spheres of justice and their fundamental normative demands. So far, I have not said anything about the relationship between the two spheres. I have merely presupposed that each of them exists by its own right without scrutinising the fact that the world is split into a plurality of relatively autonomous political communities or different nations whose internal affairs ought to comply with the demand of domestic social justice, while their external relationships raise the problem of international and global justice. Thus, the necessary interrelations between domestic and global justice depend on the question as to whether and to what extent the division of the world in a variety of different peoples or nations, who form relatively separate societies, is justifiable from a moral point of view. Since this rather complex and contested matter cannot be discussed in detail here, I will sketch my own proposition very briefly.

First of all, the existence of a plurality of separate societal communities may be understood, apart from its mere factuality, as a form of *moral division of labour*, i.e. a social arrangement establishing particular units whose members have special rights and obligations toward each other in order to enable them to cope with their demands better than otherwise. Understood in this way, the separation of humankind in various societies aims to enable human individuals to cope with their problems of existence and coexistence, since societal communities with personal and territorial limits may facilitate the establishment of effective social orders better than completely open and unlimited social relationships. Secondly, from the viewpoint of a universal morality that takes into consideration the fundamental interests of all human beings regardless of nationality and membership, such a moral division of labour appears universally acceptable only if it meets two requirements that are targeted to make sure that the division of the world in a plurality of societal units is to the benefit of all humans: every society's social order, including its political and economic structure, must be arranged in a way that is, on the one hand, *internally well-ordered* in the sense that it is in the well-considered interest of all members; and, on the other, *externally universalizable* in the sense that it is acceptable as a general practice. Consequently, the activities of a society must not cause negative externalities to others that would make a peaceful and beneficial coexistence among peoples and nations impossible if these activities were carried out by all nations.

If so, then it becomes obvious that domestic justice and global justice are mutually interrelated through their very concepts. In fact, they are conceptually interrelated in both ways: on the one hand, *domestic justice is framed by global justice*, because a just societal order must be compatible with the demands of global justice; on the other hand, *global justice is dependent on domestic justice* in the sense that a just global order must enable all individual societies to achieve domestic justice. These interrelations have important normative consequences for the specific interpretation of the demands of domestic social justice and global justice: they exclude any conception of domestic social justice that necessarily relies on the maintenance of significant global injustices, and they also rule out any conception of global justice that entails or fosters considerable domestic injustices within individual societies.

Furthermore, there are also various *contingent interrelations* between domestic and global justice, which may appear more interesting, though they are not so easy to determine in a general way. These interrelations do not result from their respective normative demands alone, but are based upon causal interdependencies between domestic and global affairs that are judged as just or unjust. Thus, in order to determine the contingent interrelations between domestic and global justice or injustice, it has to be shown that domestic orders qualified as just or unjust have causal impact on the global order's propensity to being just or unjust, or the other way round.

Before I take a closer look at these matters, I would like to put forward two conjectures which I am going to examine and substantiate in the following section: first of all, *domestic justice facilitates and promotes global justice*, since gross injustices in individual societies nourish international injustices and obstruct the development of a just global order; and secondly, *global justice facilitates and promotes domestic justice*, because unjust international affairs nourish domestic injustices and undermine the stability of just domestic orders. Accordingly, the causal interrelations between domestic and global justice also operate in both ways.

Patterns of contingent interdependency

Now, I want to specify the causally contingent interrelations between domestic and global justice a bit further. To this end, I'll proceed in two steps and mainly focus on injustices in domestic and global affairs: firstly, I am going to describe the causal interdependencies between domestic and global injustices in general, and then deal with some conspicuous mechanisms in the current process of globalization that instantiate the general patterns in the context of our present world system. There are a number of general patterns of contingent interdependency between domestic and international injustices running in both directions. Since most of them are well known, I can restrict myself to sketchy hints.

As far as the track *from domestic to international and/or global injustices* is concerned, there are at least three typical patterns: stabilising indefensible domestic orders by provoking external conflict; pacifying internal conflicts by exploiting or plundering other nations; and preserving the privileges of ruling elites in different societies through their international cooperation.

The first pattern, *stabilising indefensible domestic orders by provoking external conflict*, is a very common strategy of state governments and ruling classes to remain in power, cope with internal opposition, and protect the social status quo. External conflict usually not only mobilizes the citizens' loyalty to their government, but also enables the government to restrict civil rights and submit the citizens to rigid control (Coser 1956; Krippendorf 1985). The range of feasible means to this end reaches from violent aggression and threats, such as war and arms race, to non-violent forms of striving for national superiority, such as national chauvinism and international economic competition. I just want to mention a few examples: the outbreak of World War One, that was provoked by Austria's and Germany's political and military elites in order to preserve their indefensible political systems against growing internal opposition by national and labour movements; the occupation of the Falkland islands by Argentina's military regime which, thereby, attempted to safeguard its contested authority, and whose quick defeat by the British forces helped Prime Minister Margaret Thatcher to win the subsequent parliamentary elections; and President Bush's project of a 'war on terror' that provided him an excellent opportunity to present himself as a national leader, while his government was able to limit civil rights, cut down social welfare programs, and weaken the tax burdens of the rich.

The second pattern is *pacifying internal conflicts by exploiting or plundering other nations* (Chomsky 1993; Kleinschmidt 1998, pp. 263ff). This strategy is promising for national elites who face internal problems, since it adds to the advantages of the first pattern further benefits, namely a transfer of wealth and riches to the own population at the cost of other nations. This can be managed by different means, which include wars of conquest, colonial rule, predatory imperialism, and unfair trade relationships. An extreme case is Nazi Germany's war policy, which was mainly targeted at the conquest of 'more space' for the sake of the German nation in Eastern Europe and eventually lead to World War Two. A less martial, though not at all harmless example, are strategies of direct foreign investment by transnational companies in developing countries: even though such investments are mostly welcomed by poor countries, their long-term effects are often damaging, since the companies, striving for maximal profits, press the wages and labour conditions of their workers to the lowest possible level, while the profits flow to their shareholders in wealthy countries, with the result of a constant transfer of capital from the poor to the rich (Oxfam International 2002, pp. 175ff).

The third pattern, *preserving the privileges of ruling elites in different societies through their international cooperation*, is less conspicuous, but not infrequent. Very often, the political and economic elites in various nations have common interests which they, much better than other social groups, can promote or protect through appropriate forms of international agreements that range from political treaties and institutions to informal rules of social distinction. A famous case is the so-called 'Holy Alliance' of 1815 by which the political ruling classes of dominant European powers established a system of mutual cooperation to the preservation of repressive monarchical regimes in order to defend their privileges against the rise of liberalism and democracy (Bobbitt 2002, pp. 144ff). A recent example is the attempt of a powerful international lobby of transnational companies to put forward an agreement on 'Trade-Related Aspects of Intellectual Property Rights' (TRIPs) that would endow the companies with very comfortable and long-lasting patents not only on new inventions, but also on traditional techniques, securing them a permanent inflow of payments at the expense of users all over the world, including poor peoples whose inherited knowledge has been expropriated through the companies' patents (Kapstein 2006, pp. 71ff).

As to the reverse track *from international to domestic injustices*, I again want to point to three typical patterns of causal impact: domestic injustices may result from hegemonic power structures in international relations, from the absence or failure of international governance, and from distorted decision-making in international institutions. All these patterns are ubiquitous in the international world and well-known.

The first, the preservation or creation of domestic injustices through *hegemonic structures in international relations*, can take various forms, including puppet regimes, corrupt power elites who benefit from collaborating with external powers, and warlords that are financed by external powers with the aim of overthrowing a country's legitimate government. The history of international affairs offers plenty of instances for each case (Kleinschmidt 1998, pp. 318ff). The same is true of the second pattern, the occurrence of domestic injustices as a result of the *absence or failure of international governance*: it is an outstanding feature of classical as well as modern international law that it relies on effective domestic power irrespective of whether or not it meets at least minimal normative requirements, such as respecting basic human rights. As a result, international law favours any nation's ruling elite, for instance, by ascribing to it the resources and the borrowing privileges that enable it to remain in power by means of brute force because of its disposal of the nation's inherited resources and future assets (Pogge 2002, pp. 146ff). And we are also quite familiar with the third pattern, the promotion or enforcement of domestic miseries by *distorted decision-making mechanisms in international institutions*. We are confronted with instances of this pattern almost daily when we collect information about the current debates and decisions international organisations, such as the UN, the International Monetary Fund, or the World Trade Organisation (Stiglitz 2002; Oxfam International 2002, pp. 207ff; Singer 2002, pp. 51ff).

The effects of globalization

The general patterns of interaction between domestic and global injustices manifest in numerous instances in the context of contemporary globalization. Globalization leads to a rapidly growing multiplication and intensification of social interdependencies all over the world as a result of manifold changes in all spheres of social life, including technology, economy, politics, and ecology (Held 2000, Lechner and Boli 2004). This process has significant impact on injustices both on the domestic and on the international level, since it often contributes not only to traditional and new injustices, but also to a faster or wider diffusion of their negative consequences. In order to illuminate some significant features of interacting domestic and global injustices, I want to take a closer look at three cases: political repression, world poverty, and erosion of politics.

Political repression: Many countries are governed by repressive and predatory regimes that rule with brute force, grossly violate basic human rights, and plunder their countries. The scale of human rights violations ranges from frequent disregard of civil rights and violent suppression of political opposition to genocide. Most of these countries suffer also from severe poverty and backwardness, because their ruling regimes obstruct social and economic progress. In turn, these miseries cause migration streams on a huge scale towards countries with favourable living conditions (Dasgupta 1993; Opitz 1997; Przeworski *et al.* 2000). Furthermore, there is sufficient evidence to assume that such miseries, under certain additional conditions, provide the breeding-ground for international terrorism. The political and social evils in countries ruled by repressive regimes create a constantly reproducing pool of potential political rebels who recruit from various disadvantaged groups. When the rebels, who often get support from foreign countries, cannot cope with the police and military forces of the regime under consideration, they may see one feasible strategy to achieve their goals: terrorism on a global scale. This strategy may appear promising to them for several reasons: terrorism all over the world, particularly in wealthy countries, as it not only attracts enormous attention, but also hurts the nations of the Northern world which are deemed to be jointly responsible for the miseries in their native countries (Kitschelt 2006).

Though this constellation is not completely new, it gains increasing significance that concerns both its consequences and causes. Due to new technologies of information and communication, people are increasingly aware that any repressive regime is not only a grave evil for the individuals directly concerned, but for humankind as a whole. This fact evokes the demand for a global policy that obstructs the emergence and preservation of such regimes as far as possible. However, before trying to develop such a policy, we need to examine the causes of repressive regimes. Among the causal factors which contribute to the emergence and survival of such regimes, international relations play an important role, all the more so as global interdependencies grow. Under present conditions, predatory regimes can emerge and survive only because they are tolerated by international law and promoted by other nations. The prevailing system of international law facilitates the existence of such regimes by conceding to them the resources and the borrowing privileges previously mentioned, as these privileges enable them to get the means of remaining in power with the help of foreign governments and firms who themselves can derive considerable benefits from trading with those regimes (Pogge 2002, pp. 146ff; Boris 2005).

In view of this fact, a more effective policy of global human rights protection would require a mixture of measures. First of all, there is a need for a sufficiently strong and independent global institution, preferably in the context of the UN, that would screen the human rights situation on a worldwide scale and impose appropriate sanctions on countries that grossly violated basic human rights. Such an institution would have to operate on impartial and transparent decision-making procedures in order to gain international credibility (Donnelly 2003, pp. 127ff; Eide 2000). Secondly, a global human rights regime will hardly work if the privileges of every country's government to dispose of the land's natural resources and future assets remain unconditional. Therefore, these privileges ought to be restricted and bound to the condition that a government complies with minimal requirements of human rights protection (Pogge 2002, pp. 162ff). Thirdly, a global human rights policy will achieve its end only if it is supplemented and supported by effective regional systems of human rights protection which go together with economic opportunities. A paradigm example of such a system is the European Convention for the Protection of Human Rights whose success is based on two elements: its backing by an independent and easily accessible jurisdiction (the European Court of Human Rights), and its association with a much more comprehensive project of economic and political integration (the European Union) which requires of the – present and future – member states to comply with the Convention's requirements (Greer 2006; Merli 2007).

World poverty: In human history, there have always been rich and poor societies, and in most of them we find considerable inequalities and even gross poverty. In the context of present globalization, however, social inequalities and poverty become a much more serious problem, because they are not only increasing both among nations and within most societies, but also producing international conflicts through their border-crossing effects. Even though economic globalization has helped a group of developing countries to improve their economic performance and to reduce their domestic poverty considerably, it has also led to a deepening marginalization of many regions of the world whose populations suffer from extreme poverty (Stewart and Berry 1999, Wade 2003). About 40% of the world population is doomed to live on less than \$2 purchasing power per day, and about 20% is below even \$1 a day (World Bank 2007). There is no general agreement on the causes of this constellation, but I think that there are convincing reasons to assume that it has a lot to do how the liberalization of global markets has been managed in past decades. I will now mention a few factors which, in my view, obviously play a role (Woods 1999).

First, the very rapid transition to open markets that has been carried out by many developing countries, mostly pressed by the loan conditionality of the International Monetary Fund, has severely damaged their economies, particularly their agricultural and low-skill labour-intensive industrial sectors, because they were and still are not competitive with subsidized imports from richer countries (Oxfam International 2002; Stiglitz 2002).

Second, a large number of poor countries have fallen into a catastrophic debt trap because of their governments' policy of borrowing credits on international finance markets. While these credits mostly have been used to the benefit of the ruling elites, they have made the foreign trade relations of those countries a permanent loss-making business, since annual expenditures on interest often exceed by far the entire income from export, with the result that there is a constant transfer of wealth from poor to rich countries (Hertz 2004).

Third, the financial institutions associated with the United Nations – the World Bank and the International Monetary Fund, which are both dominated by the rich countries – have made their loans dependent on the condition that borrowing countries not only open their markets to imports, but also pursue rigid cost-cutting policies which mostly decrease their expenditure on education, health care, social security, and public services at the cost of the lower classes of the population, particularly the poor (Stiglitz 2002).

Fourth, the World Trade Organization, which was established to enforce the rules of free trade, operates in a way that systematically favours the interests of the rich and powerful countries to the disadvantage of the poor, because it provides rich countries with free access to the markets of the poor, whereas it allows them to protect their own economies against international competition by import restrictions and export subsidies, particularly in sectors where the poor countries would have significant competitive advantages, as in agriculture and low-skill industries (Oxfam International 2002, pp. 207ff; Singer 2002, pp. 51ff).

These observations raise the demand for a new global economic order that supports the legitimate claim of poor countries to development and to a fair share in the benefits of global economic cooperation. In my view, the most realistic and promising track to such an order is a sort of 'global governance', namely a set of global and regional institutions endowed with appropriate means to regulate the dynamics of the global economy in favour of the developing countries in general and the global poor in particular (Nye and Donahue 2000; Held and McGrew 2002). At any rate, the policy of such global governance had to pursue the following steps: first of all, the provision of fair trade relationships by the abolition of protectionist import restrictions and export subsidies on the part of developed countries; secondly, the promotion of the poor countries' economic competitiveness by helping them to improve their educational systems, infrastructure, health systems, and technology; thirdly, the prevention of corrupt and predatory governments by denying them access to foreign financial support; and fourthly, the correction of gross inequalities resulting from market failures by redistributive measures, such as transfers financed by a Tobin tax, i.e. a tax put on financial transactions across borders (Pogge 2002, pp. 196 ff; World Bank 2002; World Bank 2005; Stiglitz 2006).

Erosion of democracy: increasing international interdependencies in the course of globalization create considerable problems and challenges which escape appropriate political control, because they can no longer be met by nation states' domestic politics, nor can they be handled on the international level, where sufficient procedures of political decision-making do not yet exist. This leads to a deepening erosion of politics and democracy by the dynamics of unregulated social power. As far as I see, this constellation results from mutually reinforcing circumstances.

(1) The international mobility of capital involves the national societies in a harsh race for economic competitiveness, which forces them to a cut of taxes and social standards in order to attract investment. As a result, social inequalities are growing almost everywhere, and with them social problems and conflicts, while the political capacities to cope with them are shrinking (Krugman 1996, pp. 35 ff; Kirchgässner 2006). (2) Many social activities, made possible by advances in technology, economy, traffic and communication, result in a constant increase of negative border-crossing effects among various societies, causing numerous agenda for political action. Examples are international migration streams, global warming, the hole in the ozone layer, deforestation, the destruction of the seas, and so on. Yet, for the time being, there are no appropriate political regulation mechanisms to deal with those problems (Kaul *et al.* 1999; Nordhaus 2000; Grubb 2000). (3) Since the end of World War Two, a considerable number of international political arrangements have already emerged, such as the United Nations and its many associated organisations, such as the World Bank and the IMF, the GATT and the WTO, the Kyoto Protocol, and many others. Most of these arrangements, however, are minimally effective, and some of them even seem to aggravate the problems under consideration rather than solving or reducing them. Outstanding examples are the IMF and the WTO, which both mainly serve the interests of the mighty and wealthy countries by which they are dominated (Stiglitz 2002; Oxfam 2002; Kapstein 2006).

The resulting erosion of politics and democracy provokes the demand for a new type of global politics that is capable of regulating the ongoing process of globalization to benefit all the peoples of the world. What such a global politics could and should look like, however, is a highly contested matter. I tend to the idea of a 'transnational politics without a global state' based on a differentiated network of relatively independent, but interconnected international institutions, which ought to have sufficient powers to make binding decisions on particular issues on the basis of a division of labour and powers (Held 1995; Held and McGrew 2002; Zürn 1998). Clearly, in order to create an improvement, these institutions would have to distinguish themselves from the present ones in various respects: greater transparency in their decision-making procedures, the appropriate representation of the nations concerned, and impartiality in their executive measures. Although the building of such a system of transnational politics will not eradicate the enormous injustices of our world, it is, I believe, the only way of alleviating and reducing them.

References

Aristotle, 1954. *Nicomachean ethics,* ed. David Ross. Oxford: Oxford University Press.

Barry, B.M., 1989. The ethics of resource depletion. *In:* B. Barry, *Democracy, power and justice: essays in political theory.* Oxford: Oxford University Press, 511–525.

Barry, B.M. 2005. *Why social justice matters.* Cambridge: Polity.

Bedau, H.A., 1967. Egalitarianism and the idea of equality. *In:* J.R. Pennock and J.W. Chapman, eds. *Equality* New York: Atherton, 168–180.

Beviglia Zampetti, A., 2006. *Fairness in the world economy.* Northampton, MA: Edward Elgar.

Bobbitt, P., 2002. *The shield of Achilles: war, peace and the course of history.* London: Allen Lane.

Boris, J.P., 2005. *Commerce inequitable. Le roman noir des matières premières.* Paris: Hachette.

Buchanan, A., 2004. *Justice, legitimacy, and self-determination: moral foundations for international law.* Oxford: Oxford University Press.

Chomsky, N., 1993. *Year 501: the conquest continues.* London: Verso.

Chwaszcza, C., 2007. *Moral responsibility and global justice: a human rights approach.* Baden-Baden: Nomos.

Coleman, J., 1992. *Risks and wrongs.* Oxford: Oxford University Press.

Coser, L. A., 1956. *The functions of social conflict* Glencoe, IL: RKP.

Czempiel, E.O., 2002. *Weltpolitik im Umbruch.* München: C.H. Beck.

Dasgupta, P., 1993. *An inquiry into well-being and destitution.* Oxford: Oxford University Press.

Donnelly, J., 2003. *Universal human rights in theory and practice.* 2nd ed. Ithaca: Cornell University Press.

Eide, A., 2000. Universalizing human rights: the process and challenges in the age of globalization. *In:* W. Krull, *ed., Debates on issues of our common future.* Weilerswist: Velbrück, 30–45.

Feinberg, J., 1973. *Social philosophy.* Englewood Cliffs, NJ: Prentice Hall.

Franck, T.M., 1995. *Fairness in international law and institutions.* New York: Oxford University Press.

Frankena, W.K., 1962. The concept of social justice. *In:* Richard B. Brandt, *ed. Social justice.* Englewood Cliffs, NJ: Prentice Hall, 1–29.

Greer, S., 2006. *The European Convention on Human Rights: achievements, problems and prospects.* Cambridge: University Press.

Grubb, M., 2000. Governing the global commons: an assessment of Kyoto. *In:* W. Krull, *ed., Debates on issues of our common future.* Weilerswist: Velbrück,, 155–170.

Hare, R.M., 1978. Justice and Equality. *In:* J.A. Arthur & W.H. Shaw, *eds. Justice and economic distribution.* Englewood Cliffs, NJ: Prentice Hall, 116–131.

Hayek, F.A., 1976. *Law, legislation and liberty,* Vol. 2: *The mirage of social justice.* London: Routledge and Kegan Paul.

Held, D., 1995. *Democracy and the global order: from the modern state to cosmopolitan governance.* Cambridge: Polity.

Held, D., ed., 2000. *A globalizing world? Culture, economics, politics.* London: Routledge.

Held, D. and McGrew, A., eds, 2002. *Governing globalization: power, authority and global governance.* Cambridge: Polity.

Hertz, N., 2004. *I.O.U. The debt threat and why we must defuse it.* London: Fourth Estate.

Höffe, O., 1987. *Politische Gerechtigkeit.* Frankfurt a.M.: Suhrkamp.

Höffe, O., 1999. *Demokratie im Zeitalter der Globalisierung.* München: C.H. Beck.

Honoré, A.M., 1970. Social justice. *In:* R.S. Summers, ed., *Essays in legal philosophy.* Oxford: University Press, 61–94.

Kapstein, E.B., 2006. *Economic justice in an unfair world: toward a level playing field.* Princeton, NJ: Princeton University Press.

Kaul, I. *et al.* eds, 1999. *Global public goods: international cooperation in the 21st Century.* New York: Oxford University Press.

Kirchgässner, G., 2006. Wirtschaftliche Globalisierung: Konsequenzen für die Wirtschafts-und Sozialpolitik. *In:* P. Koller, ed., *Die globale Frage. Empirische Befunde und ethische Herausforderungen,* Wien: Passagen, 275–312.

Kitschelt, H., 2006. Staatsversagen, Globalisierung und Regimekonflikt. Ursprünge des heutigen internationalen Terrorismus im Nahen Osten. *In:* P. Koller, ed. *Die globale Frage. Empirische Befunde und ethische Herausforderungen,* Wien: Passagen, 131–199.

Kleinschmidt, H., 1998. *Geschichte der internationalen Beziehungen.* Stuttgart: Reclam.

Kohler, G. and Marti, U., eds, 2003. *Konturen der neuen Welt(un)ordnung. Beiträge zu einer Theorie der normativen Prinzipien internationaler Politik.* Berlin: Gruyter.

Koller, P., 1993. Gemeinschaft und Gerechtigkeit im Disput zwischen Liberalismus und Kommunitarismus. *In:* A. Balogh and J.A. Schülein, eds. *Soziologie und Gesellschaftskritik,* Wien: VWGÖ-Verlag, 75–109.

Koller, P., 2000. Westfälisches System oder globale Friedensordnung? *Politisches Denken: Jahrbuch 2000* Stuttgart – Weimar: J.B. Metzler, 96–118.

Koller, P., ed., 2001. *Gerechtigkeit im politischen Diskurs der Gegenwart.* Wien: Passagen.

Koller, P., 2003. Soziale Gerechtigkeit – Begriff und Begründung. *Erwägen Wissen Ethik,* 14 (2), 237–250.

Koller, P., ed., 2006. *Die globale Frage. Empirische Befunde und ethische Herausforderungen.* Wien: Passagen.

Koller, P., 2007. Solidarität und soziale Gerechtigkeit. *In:* H-J. Große Kracht, *et al.*, eds. *Das System des Solidarismus. Zur Auseinandersetzung mit dem Werk von Heinrich Pesch SJ.* Berlin: LIT, 179–205.

Krippendorf, E., 1985. *Staat und Krieg. Die historische Logik politischer Unvernunft.* Frankfurt a.M.: Suhrkamp.

Krugman, P., 1996. *Pop internationalism.* Cambridge, MA: MIT Press.

Lechner, F.J. and Boli, J., eds, 2004. *The globalization reader.* 2nd ed. Oxford: Blackwell.

Lucas, J.R., 1980. *On justice.* Oxford: Oxford University Press.

Luper-Foy, Steven, ed., 1988. *Problems of international justice.* Boulder, CO: Westview Press.

Merli, F., 2007. Rechtsprechungskonkurrenz zwischen nationalen Verfassungsgerichten, Europäischem Gerichtshof und Europäischem Gerichtshof für Menschenrechte, *Bundesstaat und Europäische Union zwischen Konflikt und Kooperation, Veröffentlichungen der Vereinigung der Deutschen Staatsrechtslehrer,* vol. 66, 392–422.

Meyer, L.H., 2005. *Historische Gerechtigkeit.* Berlin: Gruyter.

Miller, D., 1976. *Social justice.* Oxford: Oxford University Press.

Moellendorf, D., 2002. *Cosmopolitan justice.* Boulder, CO: Westview Press.

Nardin, T. and Mapel, D., eds, 1992. *Traditions of international ethics.* Cambridge: Cambridge University Press.

Nickel, J.W., 1987. *Making sense of human rights.* Berkeley, CA: University of California Press.

Nordhaus, W.D., 2000. Global public goods. *In:* W. Krull, ed. *Debates on issues of our common future.* Weilerswist: Velbrück, 143–154.

Nye, J.S. and Donahue, J., eds, 2000. *Governance in a globalizing world.* Washington DC: Brookings Institution Press.

O'Neill, O., 2000. *Bounds of justice.* Cambridge: Cambridge University Press.

Opitz, P.J., ed., 1997. *Der globale Marsch: Flucht und Migration als Weltproblem.* München: C.H. Beck.

Oxfam International, 2002. *Rigged rules and double standards: trade, globalisation, and the fight against poverty.* Oxford: Oxfam.

Pogge, T., ed., 2001. *Global justice.* Oxford: Blackwell.

Pogge, T., 2002. *World poverty and human rights.* Cambridge: Polity Press.

Przeworski, A., Alvarez, M., Cheibub, J.A. and Limongi, F., 2000. *Democracy and development: political institutions and well-being in the world, 1950–1990,* Cambridge: Cambridge University Press.

Rawls, J., 1971. *A theory of justice.* Cambridge, MA: Harvard University Press.

Rawls, J., 1999. *The law of peoples.* Cambridge, MA: Harvard University Press.

Redclift, M. and Sage, C., 1999. Resources, environmental degradation, and inequality. *In:* A. Hurrell and N. Woods, eds. *Inequality, globalization, and world politics.* Oxford: Oxford University Press, 122–149.

Roover, R., 1958. The concept of the just price: theory and economic policy. *The journal of economic history,* 18 (4), 1097–1111.

Singer, P., 2002. *One world: the ethics of globalization.* New Haven: Yale University Press.

Steiner, H., 1994. *An essay on rights.* Oxford: Blackwell.

Sterba, J.P., 1980. *The demands of justice.* Notre Dame, IN: Notre Dame University Press.

Stewart, F. and Berry, A., 1999. Globalization, liberalization, and inequality: expectations and experience. *In:* A. Hurrell and N. Woods, eds. *Inequality, globalization, and world politics.* Oxford: Oxford University Press, 150–186.

Stiglitz, J., 2002. *Globalization and its discontents.* New York: Penguin Books.
Stiglitz, J., 2006. *Making globalization work.* New York: W.W. Norton.
Stiglitz, J. and Charlton, A., 2006. *Fair trade for all: how trade can promote development.* New York: Oxford University Press.
Wade, R. H., 2003. The disturbing rise in poverty and inequality: is it all a 'big lie'? *In:* D. Held and M. Koenig-Archibugi, eds. *Taming globalization: frontiers of governance.* Cambridge: Polity, 18–46.
Woods, N., 1999. Order, globalization, and inequality in world politics. *In:* A. Hurrell and N. Woods, eds. *Inequality, globalization, and world politics.* Oxford: Oxford University Press, 8–35.
World Bank, 2002. *Globalization, growth, and poverty: building an inclusive world economy.* Washington DC: World Bank.
World Bank, 2005. *World development report 2006: equity and development.* Washington DC: World Bank Publications.
World Bank, 2007. *World development indicators* 2007. Washington DC: World Bank Publications.
Zürn, M., 1998. *Regieren jenseits des Nationalstaates.* Frankfurt a.M.: Suhrkamp.

Cultural diversity and biodiversity: a tempting analogy

David Heyd

The Hebrew University of Jerusalem, Israel

What makes diversity valuable? The axis of the discussion will be the analogy between cultural diversity and biological diversity, an analogy which may prove enlightening in exposing some of the deep reasoning behind the value of diversity as well as point to the fallacies and dangers in the attempt of proponents of both types of diversity to draw support from the analogy itself. There is an extensive literature on cultural diversity on the one hand and on biodiversity on the other, but very little on the relations between the two.

The paper analyzes the difficulties in the conception of diversity as an intrinsic value, especially in non-essentialist and non-teleological views of the natural and the social world. The issue of diversity also raises the deep divide between a 'person-affecting' and an impersonal conception of value and the logical problem in the idea of 'a right to an open future' (especially in deciding *how* open it should be).

It is doubtful whether 'reservations' (both biological and cultural) can be thought of as preservations of diversity.

The culture of diversity

The heated debate about multiculturalism is primarily political. It usually takes up the issue whether cultural differences or cultural identity should be recognized as the basis for group rights, for autonomous status, or even for separatist claims. The debate takes place mostly in the context of the modern, culturally heterogeneous state and revolves around the question whether the politicization of cultural identity would lead to the promotion of justice, equality and rights or rather undermine them. Does democracy consist of the reinforcement of culturally based groupings or rather in the creation of a common civic identity which would leave cultural characteristics to the private sphere?

There is, however, another, perhaps more peripheral argument for multiculturalism, which is typically non-political. It has to do with the value of diversity. This does not mean that diversity cannot serve political goals and ideals, but proponents of diversity often advocate it as an intrinsic value, something which is good in itself. So, for example, globalization, inasmuch as it promotes cultural uniformity, is bad independently of the issues of inequality, exploitation, violation of rights and other political wrongs. This paper is concerned with the idea of diversity as a general philosophical (or axiological) issue, although it obviously may have direct political bearings on the dispute between universalism and particularism or that between global and domestic conceptions of justice.

The aim of the paper is to critically examine a widespread belief in today's liberal culture that diversity is good and should be maintained, even promoted. The axis of the discussion will be the analogy between cultural diversity and biological diversity, an analogy which may prove enlightening in exposing some of the deep reasoning behind the advocacy of diversity as well as point to the fallacies and dangers in the attempt of proponents of both types of diversity to draw support from the analogy itself.

Diversity is nowadays 'doubly PC', that is to say, both politically and philosophically correct. Historically, the culture of diversity (unlike cultural diversity as a social fact) is a relatively new phenomenon, having developed during the 1980s and the 1990s. Cultural diversity is but one manifestation of the culture of diversity, the other being biodiversity. It is by no means a coincidence that despite the different origins of the two movements, their evolution took place more or less simultaneously. The call for cultural diversity has its roots in the sense of crisis of the traditional, homogeneous nation-state and in the fear of globalization as a potential threat to domestic distinctions.[1] The fast-growing movement of biodiversity was the response, emerging more or less at the same time, to the rapid process of the extinction of species, the disappearance of old habitats, and the disastrous ecological effects on both the natural and the human world. Multiculturalists and friends of the earth are not necessarily the same people, although it has often been argued that some social and environmental ills have common causes and that only by preserving old cultural practices can the integrity of the planet be protected from an ecological doom.[2] The two movements have followed separate political courses and have grounded their respective ideologies in different philosophical reasoning. Nevertheless, they share a common underlying structure, which is the deep value of diversity as such.

Even the term 'diversity' is relatively new in the contexts of ecology and political philosophy.[3] Biological science has been for a long time concerned with the role of 'variety' or 'variability' in the evolutionary process, and liberal politics considers 'pluralism' as a fundamental fact of modernity. Diversity, as we shall shortly see, is a more recent idea, roughly two decades old, which, unlike its two value-neutral predecessors, conveys an intended positive connotation. Variability and plurality are purely descriptive attributes of groups of entities, referring to the sheer number or quantity of different specimens in a group. Diversity is associated with the quality of the distinctions between the entities, the richness and complexity of the group in question, the value the plurality has for us – as scientists or aesthetic evaluators – or for the group itself. Diversity is a kind of variety which is either interesting (for us) or which enfolds in it the potential for renewal and development (of the group of which it is an attribute).[4] In the sphere of human action we expect a diversity of options, not just a plurality of objects of choice. For example, in a consumer society we aspire to a diversity of commodities that provide us with real choice (as well as possible significant changes in our choice) rather than a large number of different items of more or less the same kind from which we can at most pick one in an arbitrary way. We try to achieve 'diversified' workplaces or university student bodies, since the qualitative variety of people acting in those institutions is thought to be meaningful to their operation, productivity, and potential development.

In a comprehensive study of the history and culture of the concept of diversity in American society, the anthropologist Peter Wood notes the wide gap between real diversity and invented or concocted diversity and argues that the culture of diversity in contemporary America is of the latter form. Unlike the experience of real diversity in the early history of the European encounter with native Americans, which was characterised by awe, excitement, disgust and delight, the present plea for diversity is a superficial expression of lazy open-mindedness, which is typically widespread in university campuses (in both admissions and hiring policies). According to Wood's scathing critique, diversity is used nowadays to trump the traditional constitutional principles of liberty and individual equality in the name of group rights and is based on the dubious hypothesis that diversity promotes the better functioning of institutions (learning at universities, productivity in the workplace). Much of what is hailed as cultural diversity is connected with the racial history (and guilt) of America which explains the crucial role of the 1978 *Bakke* case that gave a tremendous push to the rhetoric of diversity (Wood 2003, pp. 13–14, 73, 81). It is interesting to note that although Peter Wood's lengthy book deals with a wide array of expressions of the culture of diversity (in the campuses and curricula, in religion, in the world of business and consumer behaviour, in the arts and in the law), it does not deal with *biodiversity*. This is surprising since from a cultural point of view of the kind taken by the author, biodiversity is clearly a typical manifestation of the general fixation with diversity.

Philosophically speaking, all order is constituted by some form of unity in plurality. The two extreme cases, which verge on meaninglessness, are accordingly boundless plurality with no unifying principle (complete chaos) and absolute unity with no distinctions (a Parmenidean One). How to describe the relationship between unity and variety, and to what extent the plurality of phenomena is real or apparent, is a metaphysical issue on which there is much debate. But diversity is an axiological issue, which is introduced in contexts where plurality is perceived as a value, not just as a given fact that calls for explanation. One such context in the sphere of metaphysics is Leibnizian theodicy: evil is explained as a necessary accompaniment of plurality in the created world. Evil could have been avoided only if the world was a unity with no distinctions, but axiologically speaking, this would not have been the best of all possible worlds. The value of ontological diversity is the underlying principle of the whole tradition of the 'great chain of being' and the principle of plenitude.

But when the question of diversity is viewed not only as a matter of value but also as a moral guiding principle, human power and control over the desirable degree of variety must be assumed. On the ontological level, we do not exercise such control, since we cannot change the degree of variety of inanimate objects in the world and have to accept it as given – both as scientists and as metaphysicians. On the level of art, which in a way is the opposite of the ontological, we can be said to have unlimited control over the degree of diversity of the elements which we use in the making of works of art, since we create the elements themselves. But the degree of uniformity and plurality in art is a purely aesthetic matter. It is of no moral concern since it implies no cost outside the realm of art. But between the spheres of ontology and art lie the biological and cultural spheres over which we have *some* measure of control and in which the issue of diversity involves morally relevant costs (even if the considerations for the preservation of diversity itself are often, as we shall see, of aesthetic nature). In both spheres, human beings have gained in modern times the power to destroy diversity, but also to preserve it. This is why the concept of diversity as a moral question is most typically exemplified in ecological policies on the one hand and in the politics of culture on the other.

Yet, beyond these very general remarks about diversity, the manner in which the concept is deployed by environmentalists and multiculturalists, should be carefully examined, since its context of application is similar but also distinct in important ways. Two United Nations declarations may provide a good starting point for this comparison: The Universal Declaration on Cultural Diversity (2001) and The Convention on Biological Diversity (Rio de Janeiro, 1992). Article 1 of the cultural diversity document explicitly introduces the analogy between the two kinds of diversity, trying to reinforce the claim for cultural diversity on the more scientifically based grounds of biological diversity: 'As a source of exchange, innovation and creativity, cultural diversity is as necessary for humankind as biodiversity is for nature.' And the biodiversity document, from its perspective, also wishes to connect the value of biodiversity with that of the preservation of traditional cultures, stating in Article 10(c): 'Protect and encourage customary use of biological resources in accordance with traditional cultural practices that are compatible with conservation or sustainable use requirements.' The connection here is bi-directional: the preservation of biodiversity is often dependent on the protection of traditional cultures which know how to maintain the environmental balance; and the possibility of preserving certain cultures and ways of life is crucially dependent on the protection of their natural habitats.

The two documents are responses to the threat of loss or reduction in diversity, primarily associated with globalization with its unifying and homogenizing effect. Implicitly, they are attempts to check the process of an anthropocentric domination of nature (which disregards other species or the environment at large) and the process of Eurocentric cultural domination of other societies in the world (which violates the rights of people to pursue their traditional ways of life). Explicitly, the two documents register their double concern, the forward-looking and the backward looking. On the one hand, the imperative of the conservation of diversity is the only means of safeguarding 'sustainable development', both biologically and culturally. On the other hand, it is an expression of respect for the 'heritage' of the past, again both biological and cultural. Both documents point out in their opening section that diversity is inherent to the kind of value they wish to protect: culture is constituted by plurality, and diversity is crucial to evolution. 'Creativity and innovation' are repeatedly mentioned as the goals of the preservation of cultural diversity, and 'maintaining life sustaining systems of the biosphere' is the declared purpose of the convention on biodiversity.

This short reference to the two UN documents is meant only to highlight the main features of the common rhetoric of diversity since the 1980s and the attempt to connect the biological and cultural forms of diversity. UN declarations do not contain philosophical argumentation. The purpose of this article is to examine the analogy between the two ideals of diversity in a critical manner. It should be noted that although there is a vast literature on both biodiversity and cultural diversity, there is surprisingly little examination of the analogy between them.

Levels and degrees of diversity

Like any ontological taxonomy, diversity is a category-relative concept: it always raises the question, diversity *of what*? Since, as we have noted, diversity is not mere plurality, but plurality associated with some value, there is always a normative principle in the identification of diversity within a category of entities. In the biological sphere, diversity may refer to either the intra-species or the inter-species level. Within a species, diversity may refer to the existence of different sub-groups (or 'populations'). Within the human species, diversity refers to the plurality of races or ethnic groups. On the inter-species level, biological diversity applies to the overall variety of species in a particular environment or in the world at large.[5] Here the normative guiding principle is not the prospect of a particular species but the survival of an ecosystem. This kind of diversity relates to some overall equilibrium of various species living side by side, such as the one giving rise to a food chain.

When this diversity is reduced, the ecological balance is upset, putting at risk the integrity of the environment and the chances of survival of the species living in it. But as biologists have noted, it is not the preservation of the quantitative variety of species that is the decisive factor, but rather the taxonomic and local differences between them. Thus, diversity of genera is more significant than that of species, or biological rarity and complementarity of species are the relevant standards for diversity (Sarkar 2002, p. 148).

The cultural counterpart reveals a similar two-level distinction. We often speak of the value of diversity within a given society, that is to say, the contribution of the heterogeneity of cultural or ethnic sub-groups to the overall prosperity or adaptability of that society. As a parallel to biological inbreeding, there is a view that 'closed' societies, which are too homogeneous, are at risk of stagnation and degeneration. Then there is the higher level of what may be called 'global diversity', in which the question of differences is judged from the point of view of humanity at large or of human history. From this perspective, cultures can survive and develop in a given environment only through mutual relations of influence, conflict, and 'cultural trade'. Multiculturalism may accordingly be understood as describing either the manifold identity of a given society or the degree of cultural variety in the world as a whole.[6]

Ecosystems are not necessarily global. When a 'foreign' species invades a territorially isolated ecosystem, it can overturn the ecological equilibrium and undermine its integrity. Something similar often happens when a powerful culture invades a relatively isolated society, destroying its traditional identity and inner social cohesion. Typically, the term 'migration' is often used to describe these changes in both the biological and the human world. Yet, although significant migration changes the existing equilibrium in a particular ecosystem or society, it remains a matter of evaluative judgment whether this is for the better or for the worse. White settlement of the Americas is seen by some people as a change for the better and by many as a disaster. The same applies to changes of the natural landscape in remote uninhabited territories when human beings first move into them. My general argument is that variety as such cannot decide the normative dispute.

A deep problem of circularity arises from these considerations. Diversity is used as an argument for supporting certain forms of natural habitat or social organization, but identifying those habitats or organizations as 'diverse' or contributing to diversity presupposes that the richness or variety of their constitution is good and desirable. In other words, the concept of diversity cannot be fully naturalized. The principle of 'the more, the merrier' makes sense only relatively to particular kinds of entities and in the light of their function, operation, or purpose. There is no a priori way to ascribe diversity to a system. Hence, there is no way to measure diversity and its degree independently of some normative principle. In ontology there is no way to decide in which of two rooms there are more entities (or objects) since we need a principle of individuation of entities to make such a comparison possible. This principle may relate to some pragmatic or epistemological purpose. In the context of diversity, it is an axiological principle. Diversity is relative to some normative expectation. For example, one supermarket may offer more kinds of soups; the other may display a larger variety of brands of fewer kinds of soups. Again, there is no absolute measure to determine which supermarket offers more variety.

This non-essentialist picture of diversity seems more appropriate to the cultural than to the biological domain. Cultures lack rigid identity and are 'imagined' rather than natural, constructed and constantly re-constructed, and also inherently mixed (with elements of other cultures).[7] Biological diversity seems to be rooted in natural distinctions, such as the biological taxonomy of species and the role of genetic variability in evolution. But as in the cultural analogue, biodiversity is relative: it could apply within a habitat or between habitats (Norton 1986, p. 112). The two forms of diversity do not necessarily coincide, and the choice between them is value-laden. Furthermore, the human selection of species for preservation is guided by cultural or normative principles. These are aesthetic or commercial, scientific or sentimental, rather than purely biological.

The desirable extent of diversity is therefore indeterminate. There is no *optimum* level of diversity as there is no optimum population size in demography (see Heyd 1992, pp. 140–153). There are various, incommensurable 'optima', each guided by a different view of the function or goal this variety serves for either present or future people and species. Intra-species diversity may be beneficial for the prospects of survival and adaptability of that species; inter-species diversity may be good for the ecological equilibrium of an environment (a habitat or the ecosystem). The same can be said about the value of a multicultural society vs. the value of the preservation of cultures in the world at large. The desirable degree of diversity is fixed from *within* the system, be it biological or cultural. It is consequently impossible to judge whether system A's diversity is more extensive than, let alone superior to, system B's diversity. And to the extent that the value of diversity is projected by *us* onto the system, it cannot be said to be inherent to the system but rather a reflection of our own needs and interests.

Synergism

Diversity is often associated with synergism, that is, with the belief that a certain quality of plurality guarantees a richer outcome than the sum of the elements constituting that plurality. Take, for example, J.S. Mill:

> Whatever really tends to the admixture of nationalities, and the blending of their attributes and peculiarities in a common union, is a benefit to the human race. Not by extinguishing types, of which, in these cases, sufficient examples

> are sure to remain, but by softening their extreme forms, and filling up the intervals between them. The united people, like a cross breed of animals (but in a still greater degree, because influences in operation are moral as well as physical), inherits the special aptitudes and excellences of all its progenitors, protected by the admixture from being exaggerated into the neighbouring vices. But to render this admixture possible, there must be peculiar conditions. The combinations of circumstances which occur, and which effect the result, are various. (Mill 1968a, p. 364)[8]

In those years of the development of evolutionary theory, Mill is quick to draw the analogy between the biological and the cultural benefits of cross-breeding, which of course requires the maintenance of some level of diversity. It is said that variability and chance are the power engine of natural evolution. Mill alludes to the same factors (a variety of combinations of circumstances and what he calls 'peculiar conditions') in the cultural sphere. Note also that the synergistic effect of such 'admixtures' is, according to Mill, more conspicuous in the cultural case than in the biological, since it is of a moral nature, that is, it is mediated by self-aware considerations and choice of desirable attributes. This is a very important point, since in biological hybridization there is indeed no guarantee that the new, combined attributes will be overall more beneficial than harmful.

The last three paragraphs of Chapter 3 of *On liberty* consist of a well-known plea for diversity. Mill first argues that on the individual level, 'the unlikeness of one person to another' draws our attention to the possibility of 'combining the advantages of both, of producing something better than either'. But then he immediately proceeds to suggest that diversity on the collective level has the same value. What preserved Europe from stagnation (for which China is Mill's example) is not any inherent excellence in it, but the 'remarkable diversity of character and culture'. Mill warns that although Europe owes its success to 'plurality of paths' and 'many-sided development', it is now under the threat of the uniformity of public opinion and the ideal of 'assimilation' (Mill 1968b, pp. 129–130). With a prophetic sense anticipating today's discourse about globalization, Mill mentions democratic education, with its levelling effect, easy communication and growing international commerce as the main causes of the creation of sameness in humanity. He associates individuality with cultural identity, both being dependent on conditions of diversity.

I would like to suggest that the synergistic value ascribed to diversity both in evolutionary thinking and in Mill's philosophy is conceptually connected to their anti-teleological character. Life, both biological and social, is a constant process, but with no pre-given direction. It is accordingly impossible to list in advance the conditions for the future existence of species and cultures in general. Biological and cultural processes are projections from present conditions into the future rather than the realization of a timeless design. Having no essential nature, organisms and cultural beings evolve in ways which are not fully determined by what they are. We might point to the analogy between the central role of chance in biology and freedom in human culture as the non-teleological force that moves life processes into an unpredictable future.

One way to interpret evolution is ameliorative or progressive. Mill certainly believes that diversity (cultural and individual) will lead to better forms of life and that uniformity means stagnation and degeneration. Although, as we have seen, there is no way to specify the particular sense in which future society will be better, due to the absence of essentialist or trans-historical criteria, sheer diversity guarantees an openness to further development which *is* ultimately the value standard. This view is not accepted, however, in modern evolutionary theory. The idea of the survival of the fittest by no means implies that in the later stages of evolution, species will be 'better' than, or superior to, past ones. It only means that adaptability is the major factor in the future of a species. From our contemporary point of view, which is much less optimistic than Mill's, this non-progressive concept of evolution is true also for cultures. However, since future conditions of the environment, both natural and social (political, economic), cannot be foreseen, the degree of adaptability cannot be ascribed to a species or a society as one of its intrinsic or essential attributes.

In the language of the liberal philosophy of education, the fundamental principle in a non-teleological and non-essentialist conception is 'the right to an open future', i.e. to conditions of survival and development. Since this open future is connected in nature with the unpredictability of evolution and in human culture with the scope of free choice, we cannot specify the content of this future. It is interesting to note here that the concept of 'sustainable development' has become a catchword in the rhetoric of environmentalists, and is the natural parallel to the right to an open future in human affairs. Its merit is that it circumvents the issue of the substantive direction of the desirable development by defining sustainable as 'a development that meets the needs of the present without compromising the ability of future generations to meet their own needs' (whatever they are) (World Commission on Environment and Development 1988).

One important implication of this perception is that 'health' must also be characterized in the same open-ended, non-teleological vein. Biodiversity is very often identified with a healthy environment and a culturally diverse society (or workplace, student body) as a healthy society. But note that this notion of health is explicated by locutions such as 'vitality' and 'adaptability'. These are typically all linked to the potential to maintain life and pass it on to the future even in adverse external conditions. This minimalist concept of health is very different from the Platonic idea based on the correspondence of a particular human body or soul with its essential, pre-given nature, or, in the cultural analogue, from the conditions which manifest 'the spirit of the people' within a particular culture. Like the idea of 'an optimum', health seems to be a system-relative concept. It relates to the function of an organism or a social system in terms of its relations with other systems or its place in the world. Consequently it makes no sense to apply the concept of 'health' to the world as a whole, natural or human, or to compare its relative health to counterfactual conditions of natural evolution or human history.

Respect or affirmation

Mill hailed diversity as a condition of cultural development and vitality. But there is another major strand in liberal thought which views cultural plurality as simply a given fact, an outcome of contingent modern historical processes.[9] For Isaiah Berlin, pluralism is the resigned response to the incommensurability of values and is more of a tragedy of modern man than a lever of progress. Pluralism, even if not desirable as such, must be acknowledged and respected. The ultimate grounds of this respect are often formulated in individualistic terms. Since culture plays a constitutive role in the identity of individuals and in their ability to pursue a way of life of their choice, cultures, at least of significantly large minorities, should be protected from assimilationist pressures. This is a right-based argument for cultural diversity, an argument which is expanded by communitarians to include also views that hold that collectives or groups have cultural rights independently of the individuals composing them. But the whole point of rights is that the interests they protect are considered worthy of such protection partly because they are adopted or chosen by people rather than due to their objective value. In that sense, the object of respect is not cultures but individuals (or groups of individuals) and their will, choice and interests.

However, articulating the interest of people in maintaining their cultures is philosophically problematic. Although it is obvious that individuals need certain cultural conditions for leading their own lives successfully, it is far from clear whether it is in their 'interest' that these conditions necessarily persist into the future, for example for their children, and whether these interests should be protected by *rights*. Even if my identity is 'culturally bound', it does not mean that my descendants' identity can be considered to be bound in the same way. For this identity is still not 'given' and its perpetuation is exactly the issue when the long-term prospects of a disappearing culture are debated in the political sphere. Thus, even if the existence of Yiddish newspapers was in the interest of first-generation eastern European Jews immigrating to America, it is not clear whether it could be said to be in the interest of their children. If there were no such newspapers when these children eventually became media consumers, their identity would have developed as English readers who had no interest in Yiddish material (which is indeed what actually happened).[10]

The right-based argument for cultural diversity is not easy to apply in the biological domain. Nevertheless, some environmentalists, often known as 'deep ecologists', insist that the language of rights must be extended to the natural sphere. Some of them confidently speak not only of the rights of cats and dogs but also of flowers and trees. Their arguments are not easy to comprehend, but I will not engage in criticising them here. What should be noted in our context is that the problematic extension of rights to the non-human world does not lie merely in the ascription of interests and rights to non-rational creatures which lack consciousness (and hence free choice), but in the transition from the individual to the species level. Few environmentalists would respect the rights of a particular panda bear to lead its traditional way of life. It is the panda bear as a *species* which calls for protection. One might suggest that the protection of species is analogous to the preservation of human cultural communities in their collective ontological status. But it must be noted that the abovementioned idea of justifying cultural rights in terms of group rights maintains that the rights carriers are human beings capable of making decisions based on preference. This does not hold for natural species. The conclusion is that from the liberal point of view, the principal obstacle in the analogy between biodiversity and cultural diversity is that in the environmental sphere the collective right of the species cannot be reduced to the rights of individual members of the species in the way it can be in the human sphere.

What's good about diversity?

According to scientific speculation, 99.9% of the species that have existed in the history of the world have disappeared. Why are we so obsessed with the threat of disappearance of species in our lifetime? If we do not regret the extinction of the dinosaurs, why should we be concerned by the possible disappearance of the panda bear? A similar question arises regarding the disappearance of cultures or languages in the shorter history of civilised humanity. So many expressions of various past cultures have completely vanished without leaving a mark. Is this a tragedy? One may of course argue that the significant problem in our time on both the biological and the cultural fronts is the *pace* of extinction, when slow, long-term processes of evolution or cultural change are compressed into a few decades. But even if this is true, why should such an acceleration of change create moral concern? Well, say the anxious, such fast change is not 'natural': it is controlled by human beings and by direct political and economic decisions which are self-interested and prejudiced. But even if this too is true, the question remains whether it is wrong to let biodiversity and cultural diversity decline. Having set aside the arguments for protecting species and cultures in terms of rights, we turn now to the examination of arguments supporting diversity as such.

The 'person-affecting' argument: Diversity may have extrinsic, 'utility' value. This is more obvious in the biological than in the cultural realm. The preservation of species may be of much value in agriculture and medicine, but it is more debatable whether the protection of cultures has a similar utility value. David Ingram argues that cultural diversity may not only have such utility value but may be 'a matter of physical survival', since globalisation may deprive local habitats of their traditional practices that satisfy their subsistence needs (Ingram 2000, pp. 257). This radical argument (appealing to the famous case of the African tribe of the Ik) is controversial. Empirically, it may be challenged by alternative interpretation of the evidence. Philosophically, we might argue that the chances of survival of cultural communities are better advanced by policies of adjustment and adaptation to modern conditions than by protective policies which strive to perpetuate them in their traditional form.

But even if diversity has no extrinsic value, practical or utilitarian, its intrinsic value may be viewed as still deriving from its being the object of human evaluation, from the way it 'affects' human interest, curiosity, aesthetic appreciation, etc. In other words, it is not an 'impersonal' value in the sense of being independent of the way humans relate to it. It would be accordingly senseless to say that biodiversity was valuable before the emergence of the human species or will be after its extinction. Like the treasures of the Louvre, natural diversity has no value in a human-less world. But this does not mean that now, when human beings exist and appreciate diversity for their own reasons, diversity should not be considered a value. And with regards to cultural diversity, Barry, following Weinstock, takes that person-affecting approach when he argues that there is no more value *per se* in a more culturally diverse world, since the question is always *for whom* the world is richer in options and who will benefit from that greater variability. Even if there was an objective way to measure degrees of diversity, the comparison between two (non-related) societies differing in the extent of their diversity would make little sense, since the identity of the individuals composing the two societies would be different and accordingly *their* way of appreciating what amounts to valuable diversity of options would be different (Weinstock 1997; Barry 2001, pp. 134–135). The person-affecting approach to value leads here to cultural relativism with regards to the value of diversity.

Impersonal value: Being person-affecting does not mean that the value of diversity cannot be intrinsic. Albert Musschenga, for example, maintains that beyond and independently of the adaptive value of cultural diversity, cultures are valuable in their contribution to the richness of human life. They maintain beauty and elegance, simplicity and uniqueness, even when they lose the evolutionary battle with other cultures (Musschenga 1998). Does this apply to biodiversity? Musschenga does not believe it does, since the analogy between cultures and organisms is implausible. However, Ronald Dworkin believes it does, suggesting that it would be 'a shame' if we let certain species die, even if they can be shown to have no aesthetic or scientific value for us (Dworkin 1993, p. 75). But then, we should note, Dworkin's justification of the intrinsic value of diversity becomes explicitly 'impersonal' rather than 'person-affecting: it is a cosmic shame' if we, with our own hands, cause the disappearance of species. Typically, Dworkin's view is presented in his chapter on sacredness, which hints at a transcendental realm lying beyond human interests. This impersonal justification of diversity, particularly of natural diversity, is typical of metaphysical approaches of the kind advocated by Leibniz or of traditional religious views about human beings serving as stewards of the natural world. It is also the conceptual framework of 'deep ecology'. Since human cultures are not metaphysically 'essential' or the direct creation of God, impersonal justifications of cultural diversity are much less common.

Achievement: Dworkin considers the analogy between the value of the two forms of diversity as based on the similarity between the creative process leading to the formation of works of art and the evolutionary process leading to the formation of natural species. According to this approach, even though the evolutionary process is essentially random, the adaptation of a newly created life-form is an 'achievement' (1993, p. 76). Although Dworkin is not himself committed to this 'conservationist' view, he urges us to take it seriously. But I am not sure we should. Achievement is the result of intentional effort. It may be the object of our respect, but only as part of our respect for the achiever. Random evolutionary processes cannot be viewed as 'nature's investment which should not be wasted', and there is no person to whom respect is owed for the end-result. In nature things just happen.

The justification of diversity in terms of achievement is backward-looking. It consists of a duty we feel towards maintaining past 'creations'. The best expression for this kind of justification is the term 'heritage', which is common to both environmental and cultural discourse. It appeals both to the sense of awe we have towards the very long time it took for the biological world to develop into what it currently is, and to the sense of obligation we feel towards our ancestors who formed ways of life, languages and art which they held important for themselves but also wished to perpetuate. But awe and respect should be held distinct, especially in their normative implications. Dworkin himself speaks of a sense of shame rather than of a duty to preserve endangered species, but the difficulty in this romantic view is that this sense of shame does not apply to domesticated species, on the one hand, and to small or harmful species (like bacteria or rats), on the other. This indicates that the preservation of species is sought for other reasons. Cultures could be said to have an interest in their perpetuation; species do not have such an interest. Furthermore, as we have already noted, we do not feel sorry for the past extinction of the huge number of species that have disappeared 'naturally' in the history of evolution.

Beauty and rarity: We are again forced back to a more human-centred perspective in which biodiversity is celebrated for its aesthetic value. Variety, multiplicity and heterogeneity under some principle or order are indeed conditions of beauty. Routine and uniformity are boring. Curiosity and wonder are the products of being exposed to variety. Upon encountering a strange animal, Jews bless God for 'having made creatures diverse' as a sign of admiration and respect for God's glory. And as already mentioned above, we are aesthetically attracted to the rare and the extraordinary and struggle to preserve species that look to us striking or unique. In that sense, it is not quantitative variety but qualitative and distinctive differences which inform the ideal of diversity. As in art, it is the way distinctions appeal to our perception which makes them valuable. The aesthetic value of diversity is itself culture-dependent and the current preference for multiculturalism is connected to the general (postmodernist) opposition to uniformity, hierarchy and domination.

The archival motive: The human thirst for knowledge demands also the preservation of whatever can produce knowledge. This explains the motivation to record, document and physically conserve not only ideas and thoughts but also material evidence. Dworkin's sense of shame in the irreversible loss of disappearing species may be explained in these terms of 'keeping for the record'. We are concerned with the preservation of natural and cultural forms of life just because they were there, that is independently of any particular direct potential benefit. It is no coincidence that the term 'reservation' is used in salvaging both endangered species and declining cultures. However, the archival motive aspires to a very limited notion of diversity. It accepts the fact that the form of life in question has disappeared as a natural or social *living* entity, and can at most be preserved in a museological or documentary sense. Zoos, genetic banks and artificial tribal reservations serve our curiosity but at the same time attest to the decline in actual diversity.

Autonomy and self-awareness: One moral argument refers to diversity as a necessary condition for the exercise of autonomy. From his liberal point of view, Raz rejects what I have called 'the archival justification' of diversity and claims that there is no reason for the preservation of fossilized or ossified cultures which cannot serve their members (Raz 1994, pp. 166–167). Variety as such has no value. It must contribute to the exercise of the meaningful choice of individuals. This means that the options should be worthwhile and also that they should be sufficiently distinct, that is, in our terms, diverse. But we have already noted that there is no objective standard of diversity, since what is considered a meaningful menu of options for choice changes with cultural conditions and values. Raz tries to address this relativistic challenge by characterising the spectrum of worthwhile options in terms of human virtues (which are more universal than culture-dependent values) but does not indicate what should be considered as its adequate scope. Furthermore, diverse forms of life, which express different (respective) virtues, may often belong to the same culture. Personal autonomy requires a variety of options within a culture rather than access or exposure to different cultures.

Multicultural society is justified by Raz in terms of the rights of individuals to membership in a culturally defined community. Without such cultural identity, a person cannot hope to exercise autonomous choice, to have freedom and dignity, and hence to flourish. But this, of course, is only an argument for diversity in societies whose members *happen* to have different cultural backgrounds. It is not a plea for cultural diversity as such, i.e. the value of a mixture of cultures in a given society as a way to promote the autonomy of all its members. For Raz the potential of conflict and tension between competing cultures in a particular society is clearer than the beneficial effect it might have for individual autonomy for the simple reason that choice is typically guided by culturally bound practices and norms. But for Biku Parekh, the value of cultural diversity lies beyond its contribution to the free choice of individuals. Even if a neighbouring culture in my society is not a real 'option' for me (as is usually the case since it lies beyond my cultural identity), it provides me with a critical perspective about my own culture. Parekh offers a wider justification for cultural diversity, grounding it in enlightened self-awareness rather than in the practical exercise of autonomous choice. Parekh's fundamental idea is that no culture can express the whole spectrum of human values and capabilities and necessarily suppresses or neglects many of them. Cultures complement each other and widen our horizons, making us aware of alternatives to our own life forms and their limitations. Being provided with an external point of view on our culture, we become less dogmatic (Parekh 2000, pp. 167–168).

This looks like a compelling argument not only for multicultural diversity but also for a conservationist policy. Its major advantage over the narrower liberal argument in terms of individual rights is that it is not restricted to living cultures or practical options and hence explains the value of conservation as such. Within a society, the co-existence of diverse cultures fosters cultural tolerance and modesty. In the inter-social sphere, it allows us to experience completely different systems of belief and practice. After all, isn't this exactly the deep value of tourism, which in the modern world enables large numbers of people not only to read about distant cultures or view their material expression in museums but to actually encounter them as living communities, even if they are not actual options of choice for themselves?[11]

Experimentation and open future: A typical nineteenth-century argument for diversity is the constitutive value of experimentation in the formation of both individuals and cultures. In a non-teleological world, all development is the product of experimentation with different options in changing contingent conditions. Experimentation is a condition of vitality and renewal and in its absence biological and cultural systems are condemned to degeneration. This is the case for both Nietzsche and Mill. Variability of conditions is necessary for meaningful experiments.

However, the experimentation model is problematic in both its cultural and natural applications. Experimentation in the strict sense involves intentional design, a devised programme controlling the relevant variables with the purpose of gaining new insight or knowledge. Nature does not evolve through such a design. Furthermore, cultures too cannot be viewed as designed experiments in human possibilities, and in that respect their evolution is closer to that of natural species than to scientific or personal experiments of the kind Mill and Nietzsche had in mind. Diversity of options is important indeed for the individual who wants to check the boundaries of experience and human capacities, and a rich culture serves that purpose. But this does not necessitate a diversity of cultures.

A milder form of the argument from experimentation is that of the value of an open future. Variability is good since it leaves open various courses of development for an organism or a habitat, thus enhancing its potential for survival and renewal. Bryan Norton further argues that diversity augments diversity and hence promotes the chances that new species, which might be beneficial to humans, evolve.[12] In the philosophy of education there is a common argument about the child's right to an open future. This is associated with forms of non-dogmatic ways of raising children, leaving them as much free choice in the future as possible. One typical use of this argument, which connects the natural with the moral, is the alleged right to an open genetic identity.[13] Cloning is often considered an unacceptable restriction on the way the identity of a future child is formed and is accordingly considered a violation of this principle of openness, or rather the natural, uncontrolled process of the formation of human life. Clones are perceived as a primordial threat due to their uniformity and their predictable character which leaves no room for either free choice or natural chance. Although there is something intuitively appealing in this argument, it is based on a simple mistake: the genetic determination of the life of a naturally created animal or human being is no less fixed than that of a clone animal or human being. Furthermore, due to the well-known non-identity problem, originally articulated by Derek Parfit, there is no *subject* to this right to a genetic open future (e.g. not to be cloned) since the alternative of being what one is (e.g. a clone) is to be someone *else*. And as I have noted elsewhere, this critique of the argument for the right to an open future applies in the context of education, especially in the sphere of the formation of the deep, 'identity fixing' characteristics of children after they have been born (Heyd 2008).

Preferential treatment: Diversity is often mentioned as the goal of inverse discrimination in admissions policy to universities or in strategies of hiring employees. The assumption here is that gender, religious, ethnic and racial plurality is good. But is it good as such, or is it good in terms of the particular ends and function of the institution in question? Most sorts of variety are either insignificant or potentially harmful to the goals of the institution. George Sher has correctly noted that even if diversity is a beneficial policy of admission or employment, preferential treatment in its name is justified only when it can be shown that the preferred groups have been discriminated against in the past. In that context the argument from diversity is necessarily backward-looking. The intrinsic aesthetic value of diversity cannot serve as the basis for a social policy of preferential treatment (Sher 1999, pp. 85–104). It must be emphasised that Sher does not talk about the conservation of cultural diversity *per se*. But his argument can be extended to that level, since there are voices that call for extra investments for sustaining cultures that are under threat. Policies which actively support cultural diversity are usually motivated by guilt for past injustice and suppression rather than by an abstract ideal of diversity for its own sake.

It is interesting to draw the analogy here to biodiversity. Although we do not use the concept of preferential treatment in this context, ecologically sensitive societies make particular efforts to protect those species about which they feel guilty for having endangered them to the point of extinction – eagles, panda bears, elephants, buffalos. Obviously, this priority cannot be considered a matter of justice. Conservation is not a policy of compensation for past violation of rights (if indeed animals and animal species have rights!). But it is perceived as containing a moral dimension. The species that merit special concern are not just declining in a natural evolutionary manner, but are 'victims' of base human behaviour, usually associated with greed or plain cruelty. Such motives of biological preservation should be considered, like preferential treatment, as corrective measures rather than as serving diversity as such. Giving an equal chance of survival to these species is considered as justifying extra human investment.

Nature and culture

The temptation to use the same philosophical discourse in discussing biodiversity and cultural diversity has well-known origins. We tend to view cultural distinctions and development in natural terms belonging either to essential, 'built in' properties of peoples or to their determination by the non-human, physical and biological environment (climate, type of land, or access to natural resources). But we are equally inclined to 'moralize' our environmental discourse, ascribing value to natural phenomena.

Herder's famous plea for the preservation of national cultures is based on a naturalized concept of culture. He says that nature 'placed in men's hearts inclinations towards diversity', but at the same time made us satisfied with what we actually are by hiding from us most of the alternative options. It is thus a sign of decline when cultures aspire to resemble foreign cultures (Herder 1969, pp. 186–187). Herder's anti-universalist view about the uniqueness of particular cultures is based on his naturalistic view of the importance of climate in the identity of peoples and in his belief that the historical evolution of humanity is grounded in the diversity of cultures and the 'manifold flowering' of man (1969, p. 223). He upholds cultural diversity on the vertical, historical axis, that is, as part of the essential conditions for the development of humanity. On the horizontal axis this diversity is hidden, and particular cultures flourish only when they manifest the uniformity of their natural identity. Contrary to the progressivist views of the Enlightenment, Herder's romantic conception of history is open-ended, in a way similar to biological evolution. It fits well into the current double apprehension of global uniformity (which is the outcome of globalization) and of over-heterogeneity of national societies (which is the outcome of mass immigration).

From the opposite direction of the analogy, Elliott Sober examines the moral and aesthetic value of the preservation of species (Sober 1986, pp. 173–194). The utility of some species for human purposes is obvious, but there is no utility value in such preservation for its own sake, since even Benthamite utility can be ascribed only to individual animals rather than species. But the aesthetic argument seems to confirm the analogy between natural species and works of art (or, for our purposes, cultures). Both are unique and un-imitable; rarity enhances their value; we want to preserve them in their 'natural' setting (context, habitat); and both have no value independent of human appreciation. Sober's general view is that the value basis of cultural and environmental diversity is the same, since the distinction between the natural and the artificial, the wild and the domesticated, is morally irrelevant.

The natural and cultural perspectives seem to reinforce each other in the plea for diversity. It is hard to avoid holding products of long natural evolution as having some moral status; hence terms of awe, shame, and even responsibility and guardianship, guide much of the environmental discourse. It is symmetrically tempting to view the long-term cultural achievements of human beings as part of some grand plan of nature. This explains the attraction of the analogy between the ideals of biodiversity and cultural diversity. But both the value of diversity itself and the analogy between its natural and human forms are typically culture-relative, as is manifest in some dominant ideologies of our time.

However, as our examination has shown, there are serious pitfalls to this analogy. If *awe* in the face of long-term natural development that is independent of humanity is the guiding principle of a 'do not touch' policy, then it can hardly apply to humanly created products like cultures and languages. That is to say, even if we are not allowed to interfere with processes that precede our existence and control, we may destroy our own creations or let them die. On the other hand, if we feel *respect* for past human effort, achievement, or cultural aspirations, this may serve to justify cultural diversity but it does not apply to biodiversity, which is not the consequence of a voluntary or purposeful design. The analogy between cultural and biological diversity holds only if we either regard the two respective spheres as guided by teleological principles or if we view them both as driven by causal-mechanical forces. But most of us hold that natural evolution is a blind causal process while human development is at least partly driven by choice and purpose.

Unlike the natural/artificial distinction, which seems to have no morally relevant consequences, the difference between the protection of species and the protection of individuals' interests is significant in its moral implications.

Since environmentalists are not concerned with individual animals or organisms but rather with species, the justification of biodiversity takes either the impersonalist line (appealing to the value of the existence of species 'for its own sake'), or a person-affecting direction (referring to the value of the species *for* human beings). But cultural diversity is supported in terms of the rights and interests of past, present or even future members of the culture concerned.[14] The impersonal sense of awe or reverence for nature is, as we have seen, too general and vague as a justification for biodiversity (we are selective in the kind of species diversity we strive to maintain). The human-centred justification is limited and often empirically dubious, since we know so little about the way current changes in biological and cultural diversity are going to affect the sustainability of future natural and historical development and, furthermore, we do not even know what future people would count as 'sustainable'.

It seems then that the natural (or should I rather say cultural!) temptation to view bio- and cultural diversity as analogical should be critically checked.

Notes

1. Anthony Appiah notes that the rhetoric of diversity, especially in the US, intensified in direct proportion to the actual decline of cultural diversity in American society. He also makes the interesting historical remark that cultural diversity is a concept based on the German concept of 'Kultur', which relates to the particular identity of 'Volk', rather than to the French 'civilization', which is associated with universal progress and which has fallen into 'conceptual disrepute' (Appiah 2005, ch. 4). As a commentator at the presentation of this paper at the Center for Human Values in Princeton University, Professor Appiah had some very helpful insights and suggestions for which I am much indebted.
2. For one of the many interesting studies of the value of cultural diversity for the preservation of biodiversity, see Wertz (2005). The native North Americans understood the value of biodiversity for themselves and for the environment and although they had no grasp of the scientific basis of their agricultural practices, we can learn much from respecting their culture about the way to preserve biological diversity.
3. A quick look in the *Philosopher's index*, under the entry 'diversity', provides compelling evidence to this general claim.
4. The Hebrew term for diversity (*givun*) is the equivalent of 'multicoloured', basically connoting the aesthetic satisfaction derived from such kinds of variety. The difference between the French adjective 'divers' and the English 'diverse' illustrates the distinction between the value-neutral and the value-positive meanings.
5. Strictly speaking, biodiversity refers exclusively to the latter, the inter-specific level, and hence, as Anthony Appiah suggested to me, cultural diversity is a *species* (rather than a full analogue) of biodiversity. It can be put as the analogy between the diversity of genes and that of memes. However, we should note that this hierarchy of the levels of diversity is valid only from the biological point of view (of the analogy between bio- and cultural diversity).
6. Anthony Appiah maintains a similar distinction between 'internal' and 'external' diversity. He salutes the former (on the condition that the richness of a given culture is associated with universal values rather than with values which are themselves

culture- or identity-dependent). As for the latter form of diversity, Appiah believes that it can be considered as good only from the point of view of a 'liberal spectator' (Appiah 2005, pp. 147–149). I am not sure that the liberal point of view holds on the global inter-cultural level (rather than to individuals or communities within a society) and hence see the value of global (external) diversity in terms of the productive impact it potentially has on the vitality of particular interacting cultures.

7. See, for example, James Tully (1995, p. 11). Tully is not concerned with the value or disvalue of diversity *per se*, but with the constitutional issues of the claim of cultures to gain political recognition in multicultural societies.
8. I follow Finlay's interpretation that, despite appearances, Mill should not be taken as an 'assimilationist' (Finlay 2002).
9. Philosophers have noted the distinction between the descriptive concept of multiculturalism and the prescriptive. Parekh (2000, p. 6) refers to the former as 'multicultural' and to the latter as 'multiculturalist'. Barry (2001, p. 22) warns against the uncritical shift from descriptive assumptions to normative political conclusions. See also Raz (1994, p. 158).
10. Thus, assimilation may sometimes be 'in the interest of a group of people', most typically when their culture is losing its vitality. Yet it is often difficult to distinguish between such inner decline and the disappearance of a culture as a result of external suppressive pressure (which cannot be in the interest of its members). See Appiah (2005, pp. 130–131).
11. Mass tourism is a highly complex modern phenomenon. It is, admittedly, often motivated by hedonic consumerism and merely superficial curiosity, but one cannot deny its indirect, though deep, effect on the cultural self-image of the tourists and their ability to recognize and acknowledge other forms of life.
12. Accordingly, by contributing to diversity, particular species that currently do not have a direct utility value to humans must be considered as indirectly beneficial to humans in the future (Norton 1986, p. 117).
13. Mill also suggests a naturalistic approach to human development. He compares human nature to a tree, which must be allowed 'to grow and develop itself on all sides' rather than a 'machine to be built after a model' (1968b, p. 117).
14. This line is similar to liberal justifications of respect for minority cultures in multi-ethnic societies (most notably, Kymlicka's) . It is difficult to justify the effort to save cultures whose members have lost interest in the future of those cultures.

References

Appiah, A., 2005. *The ethics of identity*. Princeton, NJ: Princeton University Press.

Barry, B.M., 2001. *Culture and equality*. Cambridge, MA: Harvard University Press.

The Convention on Biological Diversity (Rio de Janeiro), 1992. See http://www.ciesin.org/TG/PI/TREATY/bio.html

Dworkin, R. 1993. *Life's dominion*. London: HarperCollins.

Finlay, G., 2002. John Stuart Mill on the uses of diversity. *Utilitas,* 14 (2), 189–218.
Herder, J.G., 1969. Yet another philosophy of history. *In:* F.M. Barnard, ed., *J. G. Herder and political culture.* Cambridge: Cambridge University Press.
Heyd, D., 1992. *Genethics: moral issues in the creation of people.* Berkeley, CA: University of California Press.
Heyd, D., 2008. The intractability of the nonidentity problem. *In:* M.A. Roberts and D.T. Wasserman, eds. *Harming future persons: ethics, genetics and the non-identity problem.* Dordrecht: Springer.
Ingram, D., 2000. *Group rights: reconciling equality and difference.* Lawrence, KA: University of Kansas Press.
Mill, J.S., 1968a. *Considerations on representative government,* ed. Geraint Williams. London: Dent.
Mill, J.S. 1968b. *On liberty,* ed. Geraint Williams. London: Dent.
Musschenga, A., 1998. Intrinsic value as a reason for the preservation of minority cultures. *Ethical theory and moral practice,* 1 (2), 201–225.
Norton, B., 1986. The inherent danger of undervaluing species. *In:* B.G. Norton, ed. *The preservation of species: the value of biological diversity.* Princeton, NJ: Princeton University Press.
Parekh, B., 2000. *Rethinking multiculturalism: cultural diversity and political theory.* London: Macmillan.
Philosopher's index, http://webspirs.ziur.co.il/webspirs/start.ws?customer=hujiph.
Raz, J., 1994. Multiculturalism: a liberal perspective. *In:* J. Raz, *Ethics in the public domain.* Oxford: Clarendon Press.
Sarkar, S., 2002. Defining 'biodiversity'; assessing biodiversity. *The Monist,* 85 (1), 131–155.
Sher, G., 1999. Diversity. *Philosophy & public affairs,* 28 (2), 85–104.
Sober, E., 1986. Philosophical problems of environmentalism. *In:* B.G. Norton, ed. *The preservation of species: the value of diversity.* Princeton, NJ: Princeton University Press.
Tully, J., 1995. *Strange multiplicity: constitutionalism in the age of diversity.* Cambridge: Cambridge University Press.
The Universal Declaration on Cultural Diversity, 2001. See http://unesdoc.unesco.org/images/0012/001271/127160m.pdf
Weinstock, D., 1997. The graying of Berlin. *Critical review,* 11 (4), 481–501.
Wertz, S. K., 2005. Maize: the Native North American's legacy of cultural diversity and biodiversity. *Journal of agricultural and environmental ethics,* 18 (2), 131–156.
Wood, P., 2003. *Diversity: the invention of a concept.* San Francisco: Encounter Books.
World Commission on Environment and Development (The Bruntland Commission), 1988. See http://www.un-documents.net/wced-ofc.htm

Linguistic justice and the territorial imperative[1]

Philippe Van Parijs

Chaire Hoover d'éthique économique et sociale, Université catholique de Louvain, Belgium and Department of Philosophy, Harvard University, USA

The most massive example of linguistic injustice is arguably provided by the increasing dominance of English, both within Europe and worldwide. One dimension of this injustice can be characterised in terms of unequal dignity. In order to address linguistic injustice in this sense, the most promising strategy consists in implementing a linguistic territoriality regime, i.e. a set of legal rules that constrain the choice of the languages used for purposes of education and communication.

Justice, dignity, territory

Throughout the world, the ever growing and irreversible dominance of English is frequently perceived and sometimes indignantly denounced as being grossly unfair. It definitely raises issues of cooperative injustice, i.e., relating to the unfair spreading of the burden of producing the lingua franca between those who have to learn it as a foreign language and those who have it as their mother tongue. It also raises issues of distributive injustice, i.e. relating to the inequality of opportunities deriving from unequally valuable native competences. But these issues need not worry us unduly, as the development that produces them is accompanied by a self-corrective process, or at least by an easy opportunity for sufficiently astute non-Anglophone communities to trigger such a process. The free-riding of Anglophones on the language learning of non-Anglophones – cooperative injustice – can be significantly offset by the free-riding of non-Anglophones on unprotected or poorly protected information generated more than proportionally by Anglophones. And the language-based material and political advantage of native Anglophones – distributive injustice – will gradually get eroded and eventually be reversed by the cheapening of the learning of English as a result of intelligent policies such as an inexpensive ban on dubbing and of the very spread of the use of English in an increasing number of contexts.[2]

For many of those most incensed by the growing dominance of English, however, the measures that would effectively tackle linguistic injustice as cooperative and distributive injustice make it worse in a third and more fundamental sense: as unequal dignity. Plundering the web may provide a clever form of compensatory free-riding and a ban on dubbing an effective way of democratizing valuable language skills, but both will undeniably contribute to accelerating further the dominance of one language over all others. The primary, most fundamental injustice, it is often felt and claimed, resides precisely in what this dominance expresses: a lack of respect towards the 'dominated' languages and their native speakers, the ascription of an inferior, humiliating, insulting status to the people whose identities are closely tied to them.[3] Even if the burden of learning the lingua franca as a second language is shared fairly by the people who have the lingua franca as their mother tongue, even if second-language competence is widely and thoroughly spread or the residual handicap adequately compensated, there remains the painful fact that the language of one subset is being given a privileged standing far above all others.

For the resentment thus expressed to make ethical sense, justice must not only be a matter of distribution of outcomes or of opportunities, whether material or not. It may be the case that being regarded as belonging to an inferior category, whether caste, class or ethnic group, leads to discrimination or to a lack of self-confidence that reduces one's welfare or life chances. But the idea is here that, irrespective of such effects, justice requires people to be granted equal dignity.[4] In this light, linguistic injustice as unequal dignity can plausibly be claimed to constitute the most fundamental form of linguistic injustice, and may well turn out to be the one hardest to fix. To address it, recurrent demystification and the symbolic assertion of the equality of all languages can do some good, but as pragmatic considerations keep restricting the scope for the latter, the former will sound more and more like a spiteful and ineffective outburst against the ever more pervasive dominance of English.[5]

There is, however, a third, arguably far more credible way of expressing and thereby pursuing the equal dignity of the various languages concerned and the associated identities. It consists in allowing each of them to be 'queen' in some territory, large or small, thereby granting a privilege, within the limits of that territory, to the identity associated with the language to which that territory has been ascribed. Within those limits, it is that language, and not a lingua franca, that is given the top function, that operates as the official language of the population as a political community. This guarantees that it is not always the same who need to do the bowing. It allows each linguistic community in turn, depending on location, to be the special one. It inhibits arrogance by blocking universal supremacy. Of course, the territories claimed by the various languages will be far from equal. Some will be bigger than others, prettier, richer, more glamorous, more populated. But whether lavish or modest, there will be a place for every recognized language to be on top, and for the associated identities to be correspondingly honoured. The symmetry entailed in such a set up is the only really significant way in which linguistic justice as equal dignity can be implemented, consistently with the full acceptance of the systematic asymmetric bilingualism inherent in the adoption of a lingua franca.

Linguistic territoriality regimes

For this strategy to work, it must be realistic to expect those who settle on a particular territory to have the courage and the humility to learn the territory's official language if they do not know it already. Under present conditions – of comparatively high mobility and lingua franca spread – this requires the implementation of fairly strong versions of what I shall call a *linguistic territoriality regime*, i.e. a set of legal rules that constrain the choice of the languages used for purposes of education and communication. The total absence of a linguistic territoriality regime would correspond to a regime in which the choice of language in any context is simply demand-driven: a language will be allowed for a particular purpose if a sufficient number of people want it to be used, with all linguistic aspects of social life adjusting swiftly to people's preferences under the sole constraint of threshold levels imposed by a cost-conscious use of resources. Whether a linguistic territoriality regime is in place is therefore a matter of degree: it depends on how firmly legal rules constrain this 'spontaneous' choice of language within the confines of a particular territory.

In the sense in which I shall be using the expression, therefore, a linguistic territoriality regime is not simply a language regime that is determined by the authority that rules over a particular territory. Which language(s) one is allowed to learn at public expense, to speak and write while expecting to be understood by public officials, or to get public information or services in, is always specified, explicitly or not, by the legislation of the territorially circumscribed political entity in which one might wish to exercise these various rights. In this broad sense, all language regimes, like all legislation, instantiate a territoriality principle, just as they instantiate a personality principle in the general sense that the rights they create are ascribed to individual persons. As I shall use it here, the notion of a linguistic territoriality regime does not refer to how much power linguistically distinctive communities are given over linguistically relevant legislation, but to how constraining or, on the contrary, accommodating public practices are to the linguistic wishes of the people who happen to live within given borders, irrespective of whether the relevant legislative authority corresponds to these borders. The more linguistic practices are restricted for reasons irreducible to a lack of sufficient demand, the stronger the linguistic territoriality regime involved and the smaller the room left for what is sometimes called a linguistic personality principle in the specific sense of each user being entitled to freely use the language of communication in any context.[6]

Whether out of a concern for freedom, for privacy or for effective implementation, existing linguistic territoriality regimes tend to confine themselves to the coercive regulation of (state-organized, or state-subsidized, or most broadly state-recognized) education and to communication in public settings. The latter typically covers the internal working language of public administration and the language in which public officials communicate with the public, the language in which the courts operate and in which the public media broadcast, the language in which official information is displayed in public spaces, sometimes also the language of commercial messages in public spaces and of formal business in large private firms, and the language in which laws are published, elections organized and proceedings conducted in local, regional or national assemblies.[7]

In all these cases, the coercive rules that define the linguistic territoriality regime interfere with the spontaneous interaction of probability-sensitive learning and maxi-min communication, which would otherwise govern the dynamics of linguistic repertoires. Probability-sensitive learning refers to the fact that the main determinant of the speed and quality of the learning of a language is the probability with which one can expect to have to practise that language, and this both for motivational reasons (the cost of the investment must exceed the expected benefit) and for opportunity reasons (our language teachers are our speech partners and TV channels). Maxi-min communication refers to the fact that the language picked for communication between plurilinguals systematically tends to be not the language best known by the majority, or best known on average, but the language best known by the speech partner who knows it least well.[8] A territoriality regime typically imposes public education in the local language even when probability-sensitive parents would prefer to have their children taught in another language. Or it imposes administrative or judiciary procedures in the local language even in situations in which it is not the maxi-min language and in which, therefore, another language would better facilitate mutual understanding. As a result, more people will learn the local language, or will learn it more thoroughly, that if probability-sensitive learning had been left unconstrained, thereby increasing the frequency with which the local language will be the maxi-min language. At the same time, more interactions will occur in the local language than if maxi-min communication were given free rein, thereby creating both a stronger incentive and a wider opportunity to learn the local language. Consequently, the fact that the language of private communication should be immunized from the coercive grip of the linguistic territoriality regime does not mean that it is immune to its influence: which language is picked as the medium of schooling and public communication can obviously be expected to have a profound impact on linguistic competence and hence on the spontaneous (maxi-min-guided) choice of language even in totally uncoerced private communication.

In the standard case of a linguistic territoriality regime, one single language is imposed throughout the country concerned in the various contexts deemed in need of regulation. But in several cases, different languages are imposed in different parts of the same country. And in some cases, more than one language is imposed in part or the whole of a country (think, for example, of Catalonia and Luxemburg, respectively). Often applied unwittingly by nation states, the linguistic territoriality regime becomes salient when introduced, modified or strengthened as part of the formation of a new sovereign state (from Norway to Bangladesh and from Latvia to East Timor), but it has also been present from the start in the highly decentralised plurilingual Swiss Confederation and has been introduced, under strong pressure from the dominated linguistic communities, in a number of other plurilingual states such as Belgium in 1932 (with a number of explosive exceptions) and Canada in 1975 (with Quebec's notorious 'Law 101'). As democracy spreads or deepens throughout the world, especially in that majority of its states whose populations are more than marginally plurilingual, the linguistic territoriality regime will and – I shall be arguing – must play an ever more important role.

If the local language is a powerful language, which most immigrants spontaneously have a strong incentive to learn, the territoriality principle will hardly be felt, as only a very light constraint may be enough for the spontaneous interaction of differential learning and maxi-min communication to take over and keep that language firmly in place. But when this is not the case, when the spontaneous incentive to learn is weak, the enforcement of the territoriality principle will require perceptibly coercive measures, more or less visible, more or less effective, and more or less resented by parts of the population, non-natives and natives alike.

Laponce's law and the survival argument

Intelligently designed, a linguistic territoriality regime is both necessary and sufficient to keep competence in a local language sufficiently high and universal for that language to fulfil, legitimately and sustainably, the top function as the official language of the political community. And this in turn is necessary and, if anything is, sufficient, to secure equality of dignity between peoples whose identities are closely associated to a language. This is my central argument in favour of linguistic territoriality. I shall consider objections to it below, but want to consider first some related but distinct arguments which may add further strength to it under specific circumstances.

Firstly, the justice-as-equal-dignity case for a linguistic territoriality regime gains further strength once linguistic communities understand, and believe that the others understand, that in a high-mobility, high-communication context, a linguistic territoriality regime provides the only way of preventing the gradual erosion of their language that is not unacceptably coercive. This strengthening of the argument does not rely on anything like a holistic right of each language to survive, or to have a fair chance to survive. Nor does it appeal to the need to preserve the societal culture associated with a particular community's inherited language as a necessary component of the resources required for leading a meaningful life. It simply says that the argument for a linguistic territoriality regime on grounds of equal dignity becomes stronger once it is understood to be the only effective and acceptable way of preventing the gradual extinction of the language with which a community's identity is linked. To understand this, it is important to realize that there are two fundamentally distinct mechanisms that threaten the survival of languages.

One of them is top-down. It consists of a national political authority deliberately imposing the national language at the expense of local idioms, mainly through compulsory schooling and compulsory military service. As the transnational migration of individuals and families expanded, the same tool of compulsory education in the national language, routinely coupled with a stigmatisation of the immigrants' original languages, was massively used over the last century or so by all countries of immigration in order to secure the assimilation of immigrants and their offspring. Thus, the same basic process applied in one case to the linguistic assimilation of dialect users and national minorities stuck within the borders of a state with an official language different from their mother tongues, and in the other to the assimilation of ethnic minorities stemming from immigration. In both cases, it can be aptly described, using Gellner's (1993, pp. 139–140) telling metaphor, as one that gradually converts the linguistic map – and tirelessly re-reconverts it, as new stains appear – from a Kokoshka landscape into a Modigliani portrait, from a motley patchwork of coloured spots to a neat juxtaposition of smooth surfaces demarcated by firm lines.

However, this Gellner-type, top-down, state-driven mechanism does not constitute the only mechanism through which weaker mother tongues get displaced by stronger ones in a post-agrarian, frequent-contact, high-mobility context. There is another, bottom-up, people-driven type of mechanism, a soft brand of Modiglianisation as it were, which can be captured in what I shall call *Laponce's law*: the kinder the people, the unkinder the languages.[9] Languages can coexist for centuries when there is little contact or not at all between the parts of the population that speak it. But as soon as people start talking, trading, working with each other, courting each other, having children together, the weaker of the two languages will be slowly but inexorably driven out by the other, by the one which people have a stronger incentive to learn because of its being more prestigious or more widely spread.[10] This macro-law is nothing but one macroscopic reflection of the interaction of the two micro-mechanisms referred to earlier: probability-sensitive learning and maxi-min language use.

Quite often, the top-down and bottom-up mechanisms operate side by side and reinforce each other. But sometimes the Laponce-type mechanism is observable in a fairly pure form, for example in Quebec until 1975, in Flanders between 1898 and 1932, or in Brussels up to the present. In these areas and periods, officially affirmed bilingualism is supposed to have switched off the Gellner-type mechanism as regards the two recognised languages, while the dominant language (English in Canada, French in Belgium) keeps spreading at the expense of the weaker one through differential conversion rates of both native and immigrant families.[11] Because language is a means of communication, the weaker language is plagued by an intrinsic vulnerability that has no analogy in the case of other components of culture, such as religious practices or cooking habits. How quickly the stronger language will invade contexts previously occupied by the other will vary greatly as a function of such factors as the scope of immigration, the progress of urbanization, the degree of residential and educational segregation, etc. But once the linguistic communities involved become aware that laissez-faire leads to the gradual erosion of one of the languages, it is hard for those who identify with it not to feel despised, treated unjustly, denied equal dignity, if they are not allowed to use effective means to prevent this predictable agony.

Survival without territory?

According to perceptive observers of this process, such as Jean Laponce, effective means can only be provided by a linguistic territoriality regime.[12] But is there really no alternative? After all, if people do not want their language to die, it is simply up to them to use it. However, two features of the mechanism that leads to the erosion of a weaker language combine to prevent this voluntaristic alternative from holding much promise.

To start with, there is the standard collective action problem as it applies to the choice of language for both education and communication purposes. Consider education first. Parents may realize that if all send their children to dominant language schools, their own language will gradually be eroded and disappear, and want to prevent that. But if other native parents do not opt for the dominant language school, the language will not be eroded, and it is then in the interest of each family, taken separately, to send its own children to such a school. If others do defect in this way, on the other hand, no particular family will make a difference and each may therefore just as well send its children to such a dominant language school. Let us now turn from language choice in education to language choice in communication and consider, for example, the case of shopkeepers in an area with many customers who speak a dominant language different from the local one. Again, whether their competitors comply or not with the voluntary policy of deviation from the maxi-min in order to save their language, it will be in any particular shopkeeper's self-interest to try to gain or retain customers by defecting, i.e. by accepting to use the dominant language. To prevent individual rationality from defeating the attainment of an option preferred even by all members of a particular linguistic community, tireless collective mobilization would therefore be required. Whether in matters of education or communication, well-targeted legislation is so much less onerous that the strenuous informal monitoring and painful mutual sanctioning without which the voluntaristic strategy cannot durably succeed.

Secondly and even more crucially, one must remember that, in the terms I used to formulate Laponce's law, it is the kindness of the people that provides the stronger language with its unkind claws. Speakers of the weaker language can, in order to block the process leading to its disappearance, insist on speaking their own language and on pretending they understand nothing else in the many informal contexts in which the dominant language is the maxi-min language, and is therefore the one that makes communication most fluid and mutual understanding least problematic. Implementing the will to maintain one's language through this stubborn, exclusionary and hence 'unkind' insistence on using one's language unavoidably generates a permanent climate of face-to-face tension between members of the two linguistic communities. Coercively imposed rules, even imperfectly enforced, have the advantage of reducing – without suppressing – these strains: it is less 'aggressive', 'nasty', 'sectarian', 'unwelcoming', 'petty-minded' to say 'Sorry, I know it is stupid, but the law does not allow us to provide schooling, information or other services in your language' than to say 'Sorry, I refuse to listen or speak to you in your language, or to provide services in the language in which you would find it easiest to receive them, even though nothing but my bad will prevents me from doing so'.

Once it is admitted, for these two reasons, that voluntarism does not provide a serious alternative, and hence that some set of coercive rules regulating the teaching and public use of languages is required, it still does not follow that these coercive rules should take the form of a linguistic territoriality regime. The linguistic constraint needed to protect the weaker language could in principle either apply to all people in a specific place – the linguistic territoriality regime – or to specific people wherever they are. The latter option could be called a linguistic personality principle, interpreted this time in a coercive sense, not in the permissive sense mentioned above (section 2): people with a specific mother tongue would be obliged to learn or use it in specified contexts, wherever they happen to be inside the area in which the legislation applies. This second option is not as commonly used as the first one. The compulsory use of Hebrew, Latin or Arabic for liturgical purposes could be interpreted as approximations of it, and so can a rule briefly implemented in Brussels in the 1970s that forced people educated in Dutch to send their children to a Dutch-medium school, or the fact that the obligation placed upon Québecois parents to send their children to a French-language school is restricted to people who were not themselves educated in a Canadian English-language school.

Which of the two formulas offers a stronger guarantee of survival to a threatened language depends on the respective probabilities of the homeland running empty on the one hand and of the race losing interest in procreation (or intermarrying heavily) on the other. The former formula, however, has several decisive advantages over the second one, which jointly account for its far broader adoption. Firstly, it is arguably less coercive: one can change one's residence, not one's native tongue. Secondly, it is far easier to implement because of the place-bound nature of many of the services concerned (educational, administrative, judiciary, etc.). The third reason is more subtle, yet ultimately the most important. To understand it, let us remember the fundamental objective assigned here to the implementation of a linguistic regime. The aim is not, as such, to guarantee the survival of a vulnerable language, but to secure the equal dignity of the identity associated with it. And for this objective to be achieved, it is not enough that survival of the language should be secured. The latter must also be enabled to function in top position, i.e. as the public language of its native speakers' political community. At first sight, this could be achieved through a devolution of powers to non-territorial as well as to territorial linguistic communities. But this is not the case, for reasons that are worth spelling out.

The non-territorial linguistic federalism thus suggested was proposed by Karl Renner (1918), the Austrian social-democratic thinker and statesman who first set out to think systematically about how democracy could function in a multilingual context. In his elaborate proposal, each of the eight nations comprised in the Austro-Hungarian Empire (Germans, Czechs, Poles, Hungarians, Slovenes, Slovaks, Croats, Italians) were to be given their own Parliament and granted full autonomy in matters of culture, education and some aspects of social policy, with issues of joint concern settled through negotiation between the representatives of the various nations. The Austro-Hungarian Empire fell apart shortly after the book was published, and Renner's scheme was therefore never tried in the context for which it was meant. But some form of non-territorial federalism was tried elsewhere, for example, in Estonia in 1925, in Cyprus in 1960, or in South Africa in 1984, never with great success.

This is hardly surprising, as it has two intrinsic defects which territorial federalism avoids. One is that it is akin to racial apartheid in giving people living in the same places access to services that may be of greatly different quality, at least if the linguistic divide correlates with economic inequality, simply by virtue of a feature – one's mother tongue – which is hardly less a matter of arbitrary luck than one's race. Unequal rights in different places does not have the same humiliating, degrading nature. The other defect derives from the irreducibly spatial nature of any coherent, comprehensive project for a political community. There is a deep structural strain inherent in any set up in which distinct political communities elaborate and discuss their own projects separately and then need to negotiate and compromise with each other on countless issues, because they happen to share the same territory. Non-territorial political communities, therefore, are not the way to go.

Consequently, if Laponce's law is to be counteracted, territorial legal constraints are to be strongly preferred to personal ones, not only because they are less coercive and more convenient to implement, but also because they are far better suited to enable each protected language to function sustainably as a political language, and hence to be granted the corresponding dignity.

Laitin's *sons of the soil* and the pacification argument

In addition to the preservation of some degree of symmetry and the prevention of linguistic erosion, both directly relevant to the pursuit of linguistic justice as equal dignity, the pacification of inter-ethnic relations is also frequently invoked to justify linguistic territoriality regimes.[13] To spell out this argument, consider Fearon and Laitin's (2000) finding that most cases of civil violence in recent decades were the making of *sons of the soil*, i.e. of autochthonous populations that felt invaded by members of a distinct ethnic group moving in, either spontaneously or in organised fashion, from another part of the same multi-ethnic state, without trying to integrate into the local population, and in particular without bothering to learn the local language. Especially if they are gradually outnumbered – or fear being outnumbered – by the immigrants, without any legal means of preventing it, they see violence as the only way of preserving their legitimate interests. In a more or less acute form and with a more or less pronounced time lag, many of the inter-ethnic conflicts most familiar to us – from Ulster and Palestine to East Timor and Kosovo – illustrate the same basic pattern. In this light, a firm and unambiguous linguistic territoriality regime may be expected to have a pacifying impact, at least in those circumstances in which the unbalance of power is not such that sons of the soil spontaneously surrender to the 'invaders' and switch to the language of the 'colonizers', accepting their linguistic inferiority as one of the many facets of their subjection.

However, David Laitin (2004) also documented a significant positive correlation between the institutionalization of language rights – at least some of which can be assumed to consist in some linguistic territoriality regime – and the occurrence of inter-ethnic violence. This sounds like a refutation of the argument just sketched on behalf of linguistic territoriality regimes. But it is not. For Laitin's interpretation of this correlation is not that the institutionalization of language rights causes inter-ethnic violence, but rather that both are the consequence of the weakness of states. Hence, his analysis is consistent with the view that the concession of (the right sort of) linguistic rights is a way of taming inter-ethnic conflict, just as the strong correlation between the occurrence of flu and the absorption of flu medicine is consistent with a favourable healing impact of (the right sort of) flu medicine. Moreover, on the background of his own 'sons of the soil' thesis, it is worth distinguishing, among linguistic rights concessions, between 'territorial' and 'personal' ones, as only the former can be expected to contribute to pacification, whereas the latter should rather be expected to have the opposite effect.

That the linguistic territoriality regime may contribute to the pacification of inter-ethnic relations remains therefore plausible enough. And this fits in with its justification in terms of equal dignity. But the connection needs to be made cautiously. First of all, Laitin's data and analysis suggest that there is a surer way of stamping out ethnic conflict: strengthening the state without any linguistic concession. But even leaving aside that this is seldom a real option in the countries concerned, what is best for peace is not necessarily best for just peace. The case for a linguistic territoriality regime is that it provides a way of pursuing lasting peace in a way consistent with justice as equal dignity. This is particularly clear when the main impulse behind the violence of the 'sons of the soil' is their feeling of being humiliated by arrogant invaders who despise their language and culture.

However, it must be conceded that hostility towards newcomers speaking a different language may have other sources than a perceived threat to one's dignity. It may well stem chiefly from the fear of tougher competition for jobs, housing or public services, or from the fear of having one's community life impoverished. Thus, Jean Laponce (2004) stresses the negative externality that arises for a local community when natives of their language are replaced by non-natives who cannot or will not learn it. This negative externality is particularly onerous for local people poorly equipped for communication with aliens culturally quite different from themselves. All sorts of mutual informal services on which one routinely relies – from keeping an eye on each other's property to organizing child care or taking elderly people to the hospital – if not made impossible, are made significantly more difficult if communication and trust are impaired by the lack of a common language. An effective linguistic territoriality regime addresses such concerns, whether by having a dissuasive effect on the inflow, by accelerating the development of communication and trust between the old and the new, and by creating a realistic expectation that the newcomers will adjust to the locals rather than the other way around, thereby enabling the locals to retain at least a temporary advantage.

In addressing these concerns of the local population, the linguistic territoriality regime may switch off a process that could generate desperation and violence – in the worst case anti-immigrant racial riots – on the part of those who feel most threatened. Mechanisms of this sort establish a link between linguistic territoriality regime and pacification. However, the source of the violence to be averted is not always, or not always mainly, injustice interpreted as unequal dignity or in any other way. Indeed, the motive may be the fear of losing a privileged position, relative to disadvantaged intruders. Yet, the linguistic territoriality regime can be defended even then as a way of fostering peace consistently with justice: justice as equal dignity because of the counterfactual symmetry pointed out earlier, and distributive justice too to the extent that it is part of the core of an effective linguistic territoriality regime that it should efficiently equip newcomers and their offspring with proficiency in the local official language. Pacification, however is only a lateral aspect of the fundamental justification. The linguistic territoriality regime recommends itself on grounds of justice as equal dignity even, indeed perhaps especially, in those cases in which the 'sons of the soil' are too subdued or too intimidated or too peace-loving to threaten the public order.

Which languages, which borders?

Before the implementation of the linguistic territoriality regime can get off the ground, however, it is indispensable to tackle the prior question of which languages should be granted a territory and of which territory this should be. There cannot be a neat answer to this dual question, but the guiding idea should be that there must be a sufficiently large and geographically concentrated number of people who regard themselves as sharing the same language and are willing to pay the cost, if any, of implementing a linguistic territoriality regime.

It is important to clarify straight away the relationship between this guiding idea and something sometimes called the 'law of the soil', or the claim of an ethnic group to its ancestral land. It does not matter as such, when the linguistic territoriality regime is being put into place, for how long the linguistic community has been living on the territory concerned. It only matters indirectly as it is likely to be strongly correlated with the degree of geographical concentration of the population and may significantly affect the community's willingness to pay the cost of implementing the linguistic territoriality regime. Providing it is sufficiently large and concentrated, therefore, a population stemming from fairly recent immigration may qualify no less than one which has been living in the same place for millennia. It is in the very nature of the territoriality principle, however, that once it is in place a crucial distinction is being made between the 'locals' and the 'immigrants', who are expected to adjust linguistically to the local environment.

Fairness is respected to the extent that it can credibly be said: 'You need to learn our local language here just as we would need to learn yours if we settled in your own place.' Some people's place may be small or poor or very cold or very hot, and the probability of my ever settling there close to zero, but the symmetry needed for equal respect does not require equal attractiveness or equal probability.[14] For those allophone immigrants who do not have a protected linguistic homeland – the Kurds, the Arameans, the Baluba – the solution cannot consist in allowing them to grab a territory wherever they decide to migrate, but where their presence for centuries has made them sufficiently concentrated over a large area for an appeal to territorial protection to make sense. In many cases, no doubt, there will be disagreement about whether such a principle was tacitly in place and for how long: the English-Only movement in the US, for example, takes for granted that it was when the Hispanics arrived *en masse*, yet that it was not when the first Anglophones settled in Los Angeles or Nuevo México. This makes it all the more urgent to clarify the linguistic status of each place, using the above guiding idea to select the languages and draw the borders.

Unless these borders are just making explicit the linguistic territoriality regime inherent in much nation-building, they are bound to be contentious. Many compromises will need to be made between geographical coherence and linguistic homogeneity, between drawing borders so that they include as many natives as possible of the language concerned and as few natives as possible of the other languages. Whichever compromises are made, some people will be stuck on the 'wrong' side of the border. But this need not be a disaster. The vested rights of such linguistic minorities can be protected through special measures that will be phased out as the generation to which they belong dies out. Moreover, languages other than the official one can thrive and even get official support. The lines of the Modigliani painting entailed by the regime must be firm and the contrasts can be sharp, but the colours need not be dark. What matters is that the protective measures be powerful enough to keep promoting the official language into maxi-min position often enough for all permanent residents to have both the desire and the opportunity to acquire an adequate competence in the local official language. Failing this, the local language could not legitimately be given the highest function.

Net benefit or net cost?

The key condition, however, is that there must be, with regard to a particular language and particular borders, a community willing to bear the cost of implementing the linguistic territoriality regime on behalf of its language. What does this cost consist of? Most obviously, foregoing some economies of scale in the production and dissemination of educational material, legislation or administrative documents. How much is thereby being foregone chiefly depends on the respective sizes of the linguistic communities whose languages are being adopted or abandoned, respectively, as a result of the territoriality regime being implemented. This is why the existence of a critical mass of native speakers is a decisive consideration.

However, the loss inherent in scale-shrinking may be more than compensated by some positive efficiency effects of adopting the native language of a larger share of the population for educational and official purposes. Take the case of the Democratic Republic of the Congo, where an educational system (dys)functioning essentially in French produces generations of illiterates. Given the extreme dearth of resources now and in the foreseeable future, it is worth exploring the option of organizing primary and secondary education in the country's four recognized national languages (Kikongo, Swahili, Lingala and Ciluba) in the parts of the country in which they prevail, while making official use of those languages in public administration and political life, again in the corresponding areas. Of course, this would require the production of teaching material and administrative documents for a population averaging a quarter of the country's 50 million population, instead of producing it for the whole country or importing it from other 'francophone' countries. But the performance of a poorly equipped educational system could be expected to be enhanced if it were to function in languages in which, say, 90% of its pupils are competent, rather than in one in which 7% are. Moreover, the accountability of politicians and public officials, and hence the contribution of public decisions to the welfare of the population, could reasonably be expected to increase as a result of their having to function in a language understood by the majority of the citizens instead of just a tiny elite.[15]

In this light, it looks as if there may well be circumstances in which implementation of the linguistic territoriality regime generates a net benefit, rather than a net cost for the local population. This suspicion is further reinforced by the following consideration. With no linguistic territoriality regime in place (or, worse still, with a foreign language imposed), it is as if locals had to pay customs tariffs on their own soil, to use Benedict Anderson's (1993, p. 615) illuminating metaphor, by having to learn a foreign language and to communicate clumsily in it even in their own homeland. Once the principle is in place, it is for the non-locals to pay the 'customs tariffs' of language learning and uncomfortable communication. Obviously, the regions claiming this symmetry of 'customs tariffs' must feel sufficiently confident that the non-natives they could benefit from will bother to pay them, rather than just turn elsewhere.

It is one aspect of the general point metaphorically expressed in this last observation that constitutes arguably the main component of the cost intrinsic to any implementation of the linguistic territoriality regime under contemporary conditions. It consists in the growing asymmetric flow of human capital towards what I shall call the *ground floor* of the world, i.e. those parts of the world in which English, the worldwide lingua franca, is the official language, essentially the greater part of North America, the British Isles and Oceania.[16]

It is only recently that it has become possible to document with any statistical precision the existence of such an asymmetric flow. Thus, Docquier and Marfouk (2005, p. 23) observe that 'immigrants are particularly educated in Canada, Australia, New Zealand, the United States and the United Kingdom', i.e. in the world's five main Anglophone countries. Their estimates indicate that three of these countries (the US, Canada and Australia), totalling hardly more than 5% of the world population, house nearly 75% of the world's 'expatriate brains', defined as those graduates of higher education who are not currently domiciled in their country of birth. In 2000, the non-anglophone OECD countries had an aggregate net deficit of 2.1 million brains (down from 2.8 million in 1990), i.e. there were over 2 million more graduates born in those countries who were living elsewhere than there were graduates born elsewhere living in those countries. By contrast, the six anglophone OECD countries enjoyed a massive surplus of 13.9 million brains (up from 9.2 in 1990), 9.9 million of them in the USA alone (up from 5.9 million in 1990). Put paradoxically: out of the 12 million brains sucked into the rich portion of the planet, 14 million inhabit its Anglo compartment.

To understand what underlies this strong asymmetry, imagine you are thinking of moving abroad. Which country you seriously consider moving to will no doubt be affected by many factors, above all, by job opportunities. However, (1) which job opportunities you are likely to be best informed about will be significantly affected by whether or not you know the country's language; (2) which job opportunities you feel you would be (or could quickly become) suitable for will be affected by how well you master the country's language; (3) if you have a family, which country you would find it sensible to move to is bound to be influenced by which languages your spouse and children understand and speak, or could easily learn, or which it makes independent sense for them to learn;[17] and (4) how genuinely welcoming a country's local population is likely to be towards foreigners will also depend on how quickly and how well they can reasonably expect the newcomers to master their language, thereby avoiding the disruptive negative externalities mentioned above.

All of these considerations have some weight for migrations of all sorts, but there are four reasons why they can be expected to be particularly weighty for the migration of the highly skilled. (1) The high-skilled are more likely to have bearable job opportunities at home and can therefore afford the luxury (relative to the needs of sheer survival) of not inflicting too much of a linguistic adjustment cost on themselves and their families. (2) The jobs for which they would qualify generally have far greater linguistic requirements than unskilled jobs. (3) For the time being, the probability that highly skilled workers and their families already have, before migration, a good knowledge of at least one foreign language is far higher than for other workers. (4) Unlike the less skilled, the highly skilled are highly likely to have studied abroad, and where they have studied is bound to affect where they may later consider moving to, while being greatly affected not only by what languages they know, but even more by what language they find important to try to know better. Indeed, asymmetry in the net flow of students is at least as pronounced as in the net flow of graduates.

For all these reasons, as one language becomes ever better known abroad, and therefore also ever more useful to know better, the propensity for workers in general, but especially for highly skilled workers, to migrate to countries in which that language prevails, can only be growing – other things remaining equal. In a world in which a number of mother tongues have developed into regional lingua francas, the asymmetry just described can be expected to generate a number of regional attractor basins into which the highly skilled will tend to descend from the linguistic hills formed by countries whose languages are hardly known abroad. But in a world in which English is being snowballed into the one universal lingua franca, we can expect the formation of a huge ground floor visible from all the linguistic hills and mountains of the world, from all the upper floors in which more obscure, less penetrable mother tongues are being spoken, but in which the lingua franca is ever better known; a huge ground floor towards which the highly skilled of Finland and Hungary and also of Germany and France, will tend to wander more and more, without anything like a matching tendency for the highly skilled of the United States or Britain to climb up to the French plateau, let alone to the Hungarian peak.

Territoriality made cheaper

In an increasingly knowledge-based economy, it is not difficult to understand how heavy a cost this systematic net loss of highly selected, expensively trained people may mean in terms of economic dynamism. With further spreading of the lingua franca, one can expect a constant swelling of the pool of potential recruits for highly skilled jobs on the ground floor. With such a large pool, the countries concerned can allow themselves to be selective.[18] The more economic dynamism is boosted as a result, the more attractive these places become, language aside, and hence the greater the scope for more 'creaming off' from the highly skilled populations of the rest of the world.

For upper-floor populations, this chronic net outflow of human capital constitutes a significant cost likely to weigh far more than any economies of scale foregone. However, the outflow is necessarily accompanied by three epiphenomena, which may amount together to a huge discount in terms of long-term cost. First, there are the remittances sent back home by migrant workers to their close or more remote relatives. For various reasons, including the enhanced safety of transnational bank transfers and the dwindling cost of keeping in touch, the volume of these remittances has been growing steadily, to the point of outstripping the volume of development aid.[19] Secondly and probably more significantly as regards the highly skilled, there is the transfer of knowledge by those returning to their country of origin, whether by virtue of what they learned when studying, training and working in a foreign country, or by virtue of the network of trusted contacts they established during their stay abroad.[20] Thirdly, the presence on the ground floor of bright brains from all over the world makes the ground floor particularly vulnerable to the cheap worldwide spreading of whatever knowledge it possesses and produces. The spread of English as a lingua franca induces asymmetric free-riding on Anglophone intellectual production.[21] The presence of highly trained non-Anglophones on Anglophone soil greatly helps in making this information immediately identifiable, understandable and usable in the rest of the world, while the reverse is not true.

There is no doubt that these three mechanisms soften the blow, but not to the extent of preventing the gap from deepening between the ground floor and its ever wider and deeper attraction basin, in terms of knowledge and wealth creation. Hence, the net cost for the upper floors, in terms of steady relative or even absolute decline, is something they should worry about, perhaps even so much that they may wonder whether it makes sense to keep inflicting it upon themselves. After all, it is up to them to give up their linguistic territoriality regime. They could make settling in a non-Anglophone country linguistically as comfortable for the highly skilled of the world as settling on the ground floor, whether in terms of administrative procedures, schools or courts, and even in terms of political life. By doing so, they would go a long way towards cancelling the linguistic competitive advantage of the ground floor. In the process, however, they would also trigger a powerful mechanism which may look innocuous enough at first but will soon displace local languages in an increasing number of contexts. As argued above, this would amount to a surrender of linguistic justice as equal dignity – not simply to a gradual flattening of the linguistic surface of the globe.

Nonetheless, a carefully and firmly limited use of this strategy may make sense, and even prove essential to keep the cost bearable. It consists in lowering to ground floor level, not the whole of a non-Anglophone country, but duly circumscribed 'linguistically free zones', i.e. small areas in which the constraints of the linguistic territoriality regime are waived. The highly skilled and their families who settle in these zones, typically selected because of their high-tech vocation, would be relieved of the heavy 'tax' of having to learn the local language. As a consequence, the lingua franca would gradually rule within these enclaves about as imperially as it does on the real ground floor. The organization of a significant proportion of higher education and scientific research in the English medium constitutes a minimal component of the 'linguistically free zones'.[22] In the absence of such an exception to the linguistic territoriality regime, the spreading of competence in the lingua franca (and of the desire to improve it) would keep swelling the pool of students wanting to study in the higher education institutions of the ground floor, thereby enhancing the latter's ability to select the best and further improve the quality of its higher education at the expense of what can be achieved elsewhere – bearing in mind that 'quality' of one's peers is arguably the chief determinant of anyone's educational achievement.

Instead of lowering parts of the upper floors, one can try, secondly, to exploit the advantages of being on that floor. One potential advantage is that having a less widely spread language, by maintaining a distinctive culture, may make it easier to nurture a feeling of community and thereby to instil a sense of loyalty that will inhibit the opportunistic search for the highest net return among highly skilled workers henceforth made more mobile by their competence in English. Another potential advantage is that being a speaker of a less widespread language and having to learn at least one other language as a result enables those who have to make that effort to escape the arrogance and the insensitivity to cultural differences that come too easily to those who have never had to undergo that humbling process and are invariably in the comfortable position of being able to use their mother tongue. Without noticing, such arrogance and insensitivity trigger rancour, resentment, even hatred. This may prompt actions against whose risk one needs to protect oneself, sometimes at great expense. Being (perceived as) less arrogant is an asset which the upper floors of the world can intelligently exploit – and already do.

With the inbuilt discounts listed above and a judicious use of the strategies just sketched, a number of linguistic communities throughout the world will feel that it is worth shouldering the expected cost of sticking to a sufficiently effective version of the linguistic territoriality regime, the cost of saving their soul, of preserving their identity, of upholding their dignity. Of course, within the existing institutional world order, the more the lingua franca spreads, the more vulnerable the countries concerned become. But at the same time, the more the lingua franca spreads, the less unrealistic the prospect of creating the linguistic preconditions for a European and worldwide institutional order that will make such a choice less costly.

Notes

1. This chapter is a component of the draft of a book in progress under the title *Linguistic justice for Europe and for the world* (Oxford University Press). Some of the claims it takes for granted are being presented and defended in other components of this book, which will be referred to below as *LJ* followed by chapter or section number. A first rough formulation of the book's main claims can be found in Van Parijs (2004). A couple of sections of this chapter also appear in Van Parijs (2009).
2. See *LJ* 2 and *LJ* 3 on cooperative justice and distributive injustice, respectively, and on how best to address them.
3. It need not be assumed that people's collective identity is universally linked with a language, or that it is more often, or more strongly, linked with language than with religion or ethnic origin. What is special about languages is that a privilege needs to be given to one of them across borders in today's world (see *LJ* 1), whereas there is no analogous case for a privilege to one religion or one race. (There is an analogous case for the privilege a city must be given as the political capital of a supra-national political entity, but this is a privilege granted to a space where all citizens of this entity must be welcome, not to a particular group of people.)
4. It can be linked, for example, to the importance attached by Rawls (1971, pp. 178–179) to society's institutions being arranged so as to provide the 'social bases of self-respect', no matter what effect these may have on the distribution of

the social and economic advantages covered by the difference principle. Other theories of distributive justice may accommodate this idea differently. For example, prior to discussing which metric of distribution would be most relevant, they may require that all members of society must be given an equal status, that they cannot have their identity disparaged, ranked lower than that of others.

5. See Van Parijs (2009) and *LJ* 4.1 for a discussion of these first two strategies against linguistic injustice as unequal dignity and their limitations.
6. On this distinction (often misleadingly used), see Réaume (2003) and Patten (2003). I discuss below (p. 678) a coercive interpretation of the personality principle.
7. Here is, for example, the Slovenian version of the linguistic territoriality regime, as laid down in Slovenia's 2004 Law on the Public Use of the Slovenian Language: 'The law states that Slovenian shall be used orally and in writing in public life… It stipulates that the names of all state bodies, local administrations, public organizations, public companies, and political parties shall be in Slovenian. Public insignia as well as the names of private companies, premises and shops should be in the Slovenian language, too. All proceedings involving public and private companies should be carried out in the Slovenian language. Slovenian is also prescribed as the language of public notices, conferences, press releases, announcements, and product labelling and instructions. Contracts with Slovenian companies must be written only in Slovenian and only this version may be considered as an original. In addition, all companies and individuals under private law must communicate with their customers in Slovenian and only people with appropriate knowledge of Slovenian can be employed in jobs that require communication skills' (Kodelja and Krivic 2007, p. 9).
8. Suppose for example that You are a native English speaker with an excellent knowledge of Spanish and a rudimentary knowledge of French; that I am a native of French with an excellent knowledge of English and no knowledge of Spanish; and that She is a native of Spanish with a good knowledge of both English and French. You are the speech partner who speaks French least well (rudimentary), I am the one who speaks Spanish least well (none), and She is the one who speaks English least well (good). Since She knows English better than You know French and than I know Spanish, English is the language best known by the speech partner who knows it least well. The prediction is therefore that English will be spontaneously picked as the medium of conversation between the three of us. The description of both mechanisms (probability-sensitive learning and maxi-min communication) and their explosive interaction is refined and qualified in *LJ1*.
9. The phrasing is mine, but the process at work is perceptively described by Jean Laponce (1984, 1993, 2006).
10. See, for example, the statistics on the language prevailing in mixed (French/English) couples in Canada (Laponce 1993, pp. 34–35).
11. The realization of the steady progress of English in Montreal (despite the inflow and higher birth rate of Catholic francophones) and of the steady progress of French in Brussels and all major Flemish cities gave the key impulse to the demands for a linguistic territoriality regime as a more serious way of implementing the equal dignity of the two languages than the sheer formal assertion of equality and nationwide bilingualism. See Levine (1990) on Montreal and Nelde and Darquennes (2001, pp. 94–96) on Brussels.
12. Along the same lines in the Swiss context, see e.g. Papaux (1997, p. 133): 'it is absolutely necessary to determine the territorial domains of each language and to protect autochtonous linguistic communities, whether or not they are threatened, in their traditional spreading areas. For the persistence of national languages cannot conceivably be guaranteed without ascribing to each an exclusive territory'.

13. When comparing the three oldest multilingual democracies, for example, it is often said that the secret of Switzerland's greater linguistic peace, relative to Belgium and Canada, resides in its much earlier implementation of the linguistic territoriality regime: there has never been a Germanization of Geneva analogous to the Frenchification of Brussels or the Anglicization of Montréal.
14. Might equal dignity not be better expressed if the territories claimed by each language were equal in terms of size, population or wealth? This would have absurd implications. If the shares were equal and small (say, close to the current share of the smallest linguistic community), this would leave the bulk of the planet up for linguistic grabs, reducing the operation of the linguistic territoriality regime to a marginal museum-like phenomenon. If the shares were equal and big (say, close to an equal share of the total surface, population or wealth of the world), this would require converting to a different native tongue the bulk of the population of the world. And anything in between would combine both drawbacks in varying proportions. Moreover, this sort of formula would involve an inbuilt perverse incentive to multiply the salience of linguistic differences so as to be able to grab a larger territory.
15. On the linguistic situation in the Congo, see Mukash (2003). Obviously, assessing the likely sizes of the overall economic costs and benefits of such a four-language territoriality regime is bound to remain speculative. The role given to the Indian Union's 16 national languages provides a sensible basis for such speculation, even though the populations involved are more massive (Telugu alone has more native speakers than there are Congolese citizens). Less obviously relevant but more comparable size-wise are the Finnish and Flemish cases: would Finland and Flanders be at the top of the OECD's PISA rankings of educational systems, had their schools not resolutely shifted from Swedish and French to Finnish and Dutch, respectively, in the twentieth century?
16. A first formulation of the arguments in this and the next section can be found in Van Parijs (2000).
17. See e.g. Stevens *et al.* (2006, p. 175): 'Korean adults, particularly those in the prime child-raising years, are much more likely to take their children along with them when visiting English-dominated countries than when visiting countries dominated by other languages'.
18. As Arthur Schlesinger (1998, p. 127) sums it up in the case of the US: 'We have shifted the basis of admission three times this century – from national origins in 1924 to family reunification in 1965 to needed skills in 1990.'
19. See e.g. Kapur and McHale (2003). To remittances stricto sensu one should add the accumulated assets repatriated at the time of their return by temporary migrant workers and migrants who decide to retire in their home country.
20. See OECD (2002) for various country case studies.
21. In *LJ* 2, I justify this free-riding as a form of compensation (more realistic than direct subsidies to language learning) for the free-riding of English natives on the effort made by all others to produce a lingua franca.
22. On the gradual and very unequal spread of English as the medium of higher education beyond the ground floor, see Ammon (2001) and Maiworm and Wächter (2002).

References

Ammon, U., 2001. *The dominance of English as a language of science: effects on other languages and language communities.* Berlin: Gruyter.

Anderson, B.R.O., 1993. Nationalism. *In:* J. Krieger, ed. *The Oxford companion to the politics of the world.* Oxford: Oxford University Press, 614–619.

Docquier, F. and Marfouk, A., 2005. International migration by educational attainment (1990–2000), Release 1.1. Washington DC: World Bank Publications, 1–8.

Fearon, J.D. and Laitin, D.D, 2000. Sons of the soil: immigrants and the State. Unpublished paper. Stanford University: Department of Political Science.

Gellner, E., 1983. *Nations and nationalism.* Oxford: Blackwell.

Kapur, D. and McHale, J., 2003. Migration's new payoff. *Foreign policy,* 139, 49–57.

Kodelja, Z. and Krivic, M., 2007. Language rights in education in Slovenia. *In: Education, law and language rights.* Antwerp: European Association for Education, Law and Policy, 1–17.

Laitin, D. D., 2004. Language policy and civil war. *In:* P. Van Parijs, ed. *Cultural diversity versus economic solidarity.* Brussels: De Boeck Université, 171–188, at www.etes.ucl.ac.be/Francqui/Livre/Livre.htm.

Laponce, J., 1984. *Langue et territoire.* Québec: Presses uniersitaires de Laval. Translated as: *Languages and their territories.* Toronto: University of Toronto Press, 1987.

Laponce, J., 1993. The case for ethnic federalism in multilingual societies: Canada's regional imperative. *Regional politics and policy,* 3 (1), 23–43.

Laponce, J., 2004. Comments on Laitin and Grin. *In:* P. Van Parijs, ed. *Cultural diversity versus economic solidarity.* Brussels: De Boeck Université, 203–210, at www.etes.ucl.ac.be/Francqui/Livre/Livre.htm

Laponce, J., 2006. *Loi de Babel, et autres régularités des rapports entre langue et politique.* Québec: Presses de l'Université Laval.

Levine, M.V., 1990. *The reconquest of Montreal: language policy and social change in a bilingual city.* Philadelphia, PA: Temple University Press.

Maiworm, F. and Wächter, B., 2002. *English-language-taught degree programmes in European higher education. Trends and success factors.* Bonn: Lemmens.

Mukash, K., 2003. Situation linguistique et dynamique des langues en République Démocratique du Congo contemporaine. Unpublished memo. Kinshasa: Observatoire des langues nationals.

Nelde, P. and Darquennes, J., 2001. Sprachwechsel in der Großstadt – eine Brüsseler Perspektive. *In:* J. Born, ed. *Mehrsprachigkeit in der Romania.* Wien: Praesens, 91–104.

OECD, 2002. *International mobility of the highly skilled.* Paris: Organisation for Economic Co-operation and Development.

Papaux, A., 1997. Droit des langues en Suisse: Etat des lieux. *Revue suisse de science politique,* 3 (2), 131–134.

Patten, A., 2003. What kind of bilingualism? *In:* W. Kymlicka and A. Patten, eds. *Language rights and political theory.* Oxford: Oxford University Press, 296–321.

Rawls, J., 1971. *A theory of justice.* Cambridge, MA: Harvard University Press.

Réaume, D.G., 2003. Beyond personality: the territorial and personal principles of language policy reconsidered. *In:* W. Kymlicka and A. Patten, eds. *Language rights and political theory.* Oxford: Oxford University Press, 271–295.
Renner, K., 1918. Das Selbstbestimmungsrecht der Nationen. *In: besonderer Anwendung auf Oesterreich.* Leipzig and Wien: Franz Deuticke.
Schlesinger, A.M., 1998. *The disuniting of America: reflections on a multicultural society.* Revised and enlarged edition. New York: W.W. Norton.
Stevens, G., Jin, K. and Song H.J., 2006. Short-term migration and the acquisition of a world language. *International migration,* 44 (1), 167–179.
Van Parijs, P., 2000. The ground floor of the world: on the socio-economic consequences of linguistic globalisation. *International political science review,* 21 (2), 217–233.
Van Parijs, P., 2004. Europe's linguistic challenge. *Archives européennes de sociologie,* 45 (1), 111–152.
Van Parijs, P., 2009. Grab a territory! Linguistic dignity and English dominance in the European Union. *In:* J. Poirier *et al.,* eds. *Ties that bind: accommodating diversity in Canada and the European Union.* Bern, Berlin and Brussels: Peter Lang, 155–172.

Climate change and the duties of the advantaged

Simon Caney

Department of Politics and International Relations and Magdalen College, University of Oxford, UK

Climate change poses grave threats to many people, including the most vulnerable. This prompts the question of who should bear the burden of combating 'dangerous' climate change. Many appeal to the Polluter Pays Principle. I argue that it should play an important role in any adequate analysis of the responsibility to combat climate change, but suggest that it suffers from three limitations and that it needs to be revised. I then consider the Ability to Pay Principle and consider four objections to this principle. I suggest that, when suitably modified, it can supplement the Polluter Pays Principle.

It is widely (though not universally) acknowledged that the earth's climate is undergoing profound changes and, moreover, that these changes are, to a large extent, the result of human activity. These changes are predicted to have profound and undesirable effects on people's standard of living, including most notably the standard of living of the most vulnerable and weak. The ill effects will include raised sea-levels which, in turn, destroy habitable land, human settlements and infrastructure. They will, in addition, expose some to greater risks of 'storm-surges'. The increased global warming will induce other malign effects, including higher deaths from drought and malnutrition. In addition to this the increased temperatures will increase the numbers of those exposed to infectious diseases, such as malaria, dengue and cholera. Higher temperatures will also result in death by heat stress. Climate change will, moreover, bring increased rainfall for some areas and this too will issue in harmful effects, causing destructive flooding. Finally, the majority of scientific experts hold that climate change heralds unpredictable weather events and such freak events will threaten human buildings and infrastructure.[1]

This raises the question of who should bear the burdens of dealing with climate change. One can identify at least two principles:

- those who caused the problem should pay (the Polluter Pays Principle – PPP);
- those who have the greatest ability to pay (the Ability to Pay Principle – ATP).[2]

Many discussions focus on the Polluter Pays Principle.[3] In what follows I want to chronicle some of its limitations and argue that a version of the Ability to Pay Principle must play a crucial role.

Before doing so, it is worth clarifying what I mean by 'bearing the burdens of global climate change'. We can distinguish between (at least) two different kinds of duty. First, one might say that there is a duty to cut back on activities which cause climate change. To use the language employed by the Intergovernmental Panel on Climate Change (IPCC), this duty requires people to engage in 'mitigation'. The duties involved would include, for example, a duty to reduce emissions of greenhouse gases (where these include carbon dioxide, methane, nitrous oxide, hydrofluorocarbons (HFCs), perfluorocarbons (PFCs), and sulfur hexafluoride (SF6)). It would, in particular, require cutting back emissions of carbon dioxide. In practice, this would require persons to adopt policies such as reducing air travel, driving less, insulating one's house more efficiently, using less electricity, and so on. The duty to prevent further climate change could also comprise creating and protecting carbon sinks. Let us call this first kind of duty a 'duty of mitigation'. A second kind of duty is the duty to devote resources to protect people from the ill effects of climate change. To employ the usage of the IPCC, this duty is a duty to facilitate and support 'adaptation' to climate change. Let us call this a 'duty of adaptation'. This duty would involve spending money on the following types of activity: building sea-walls which will protect those who live and work near the coast from sea-level rise and from storm surges; subsidizing people to move away from threatened coastal settlements; spending more money inoculating people from infectious diseases; supporting irrigation systems in drought-prone areas; sending overseas aid to victims of malnutrition; and so on.

It is widely recognized that, whatever happens, some adaptation is required. The emission of greenhouse gases has reached such a level and has been taking place for such a long time (since the industrial revolution) that even if emissions levels were dramatically cut there would still inevitably be an increase in temperature and in sea-levels. As a recent statement of the national academies of science of 11 countries (including those of the USA, India, China, Germany and the UK) reports

> Carbon dioxide can remain in the atmosphere for many decades. Even with possible lowered emission rates we will be experiencing the impacts of climate change throughout the twenty-first century and beyond. … Major parts of the climate system respond slowly to changes in greenhouse gas concentrations.

> Even if greenhouse gas emissions were stabilised instantly at today's levels, the climate would still continue to change as it adapts to the increased emission of recent decades.[4]

Furthermore, the distinguished scientist, Michael Mann, has recently stated that 'we're already committed to 50 to 100 years of warming and several centuries of sea-level rise, simply from the amount of greenhouse gases we've already put in the atmosphere' (Appell 2005, p. 23). Indeed recent research has found that '[s]ea level is likely to continue rising for more than 1000 years after greenhouse gas concentrations have been stabilised, so that with even a sizeable mitigation effort adaptation is also likely to be needed' (Lowe *et al.* 2006, p. 35). A policy of mitigation is, therefore, not sufficient.[5] To prevent climate change from jeopardizing the interests of persons some resources will be need to be spent on adaptation.

It is also widely, though not unanimously, accepted that a policy of mitigation is necessary and that one cannot simply rely on adaptation.[6] The need to engage in mitigation has been further underscored by the latest research. For example, recent studies have shown that the West Antarctic Ice Sheet (WAIS) and the Greenland Ice Sheet are both less stable than previously assumed and if these melt they will have severe and dangerous effects on sea-levels.[7] In addition, recent research has found that the Atlantic Thermohaline Circulation is under threat and if this shuts down this will have severe effects on human life.[8] There is, then, an urgent need for a reduction in greenhouse gas emissions to prevent further increases in the earth's temperature and increasing sea-levels. A full account of the duty to bear the burden of climate change must, thus, include both a duty to engage in mitigation and a duty to spend resources enabling persons to adapt to climate change.

Who should bear these burdens?

The 'Polluter Pays' Principle and two concerns

Consider, first, the view that the polluter should pay. This has an immediate intuitive appeal and should play a role in any plausible account of who should pay the price for addressing climate change. It is a strongly held view that if an actor causes pollution (through, say, releasing radioactive waste or emitting dangerous fumes) then that actor is morally responsible for dealing with the ensuing costs to others. The Polluter Pays Principle is, note, a backward-looking or historical principle. Drawing on this principle, it follows that those who contribute to climate change (either by using up excessive amounts of fossil fuels or by deforestation) should make amends for this. If, for example, they have used excessive amounts of greenhouse gases then, ceteris paribus, it is fair to require them to cut back their emissions accordingly (and/or to devote resources enabling the potential victims to adapt to dangerous climate change). This approach has been canvassed by a number of developing countries, most notably Brazil. In a proposal it submitted to the deliberations of the United Nations Framework Convention on Climate Change (UNFCCC) it argued that countries which had emitted more greenhouse gases should bear a greater responsibility in combating climate change.[9] This proposal was subsequently referred to the Subsidiary Body for Scientific and Technological Advice (SBSTA) and it seems unlikely to come into effect.[10] Our question, though, is whether the principle at heart is a valid one.

I shall argue that the Polluter Pays Principle should be supplemented by an additional principle, but before I do so it is important to consider two concerns that might be raised about the Polluter Pays Principle.

Objection 1

One concern that might be raised about the Polluter Pays Principle concerns its practicality. A critic might emphasize the extent of uncertainty in climate science and draw attention to two factors in particular. (1) The first concerns the uncertain nature of the estimated ill effects. The projections of the IPCC, for example, reasonably enough, take the form of projecting that a phenomenon P will increase by between x% and y%. The Third Assessment Report estimates, for example, that between 1990 and 2100 sea-levels will rise by between 0.09 metres and 0.88 metres and the temperature will increase by between 1.4 and 5.8° Celsius (Ahmad *et al.* 2001, p. 3). In addition it regards some of its projections as more confident than others and employs a five-point scale indicating various degrees of confidence (ranging from 95% confidence to 5% confidence) (Schneider and Sarukhan 2001, p. 79). It is hard, then, to specify how much harm will result from this and hence difficult to make people pay in proportion to their causal impact on a problem. For further illustration of this problem consider the category of persons who are suffering from 'water-stress'. On some projections, between 1.1 and 2.8 billion of these people will suffer further reductions in their access to water by 2050 and on other projections the estimate is that between 0.7 and 1.2 billion people will experience a decrease in access to water in this time period (Arnell 2006, p. 167). Estimating the extent of the harm caused by global climate change is therefore immensely difficult. (2) Consider now a second aspect. Take sea-levels again. Sir John Houghton reports that sea-levels are expected to rise by just under two metres by 2100 in Bangladesh, but he adds that without climate change there would be soil erosion anyway and only 70cm of this rise will result from anthropogenic climate change (Houghton 2004, p. 150). If this is so, we then need to ascertain what damage would result from a 70cm rise alone. To gain any non-arbitrary view here would seem to be next to impossible – yet, it is required to implement the Polluter Pays Principle. The key point is that to apply the Polluter Pays Principle we need to be able to specify the harm done and trace it back to the causal actors and where either the nature of the harm is uncertain or unpredictable (point

1) or the link between the climate change and the harm is uncertain (point 2) then this cannot be done.[11]

How serious is this problem? And how damaging is it to the Polluter Pays Principle? Three points can be made in reply. First, one might just reply that the preceding practical problems do not call into question, or undermine in any way, the moral force of the principle. What they reveal is that it is difficult to apply and in seeking to implement it we should be aware of the immense practical problems involved. In themselves, though, they do not establish that the principle is morally implausible. The lessons to be learned from the objection are, then, not that the principle should be rejected but that caution should be exercised when applying it and that we cannot hope for too much exactitude.

Second, it bears noting that climate modellers believe that they are making considerable progress in developing the capacity for the detection and attribution of climate change. Some are increasingly confident that it will be possible to attribute specific events to climate change.[12] For example, Peter Stott, Daithi Stone and Myles Allen have argued that one can attribute the heatwave that occurred in Europe in the summer of 2003 to human forcing (Stott *et al.* 2004).

Third, and finally, it is important to recognize that the problem does not only affect the Polluter Pays Principle. It affects it more acutely but actually all principles which ascribe duties for combating climate change are affected by this problem. To see why this is the case, it is useful to return to the distinction between the 'duty of mitigation' and the 'duty of adaptation'. Consider, first, the duty to fund adaptation. The Polluter Pays Principle is undoubtedly at a disadvantage when compared with alternative principles, such as the Ability to Pay Principle. This can be seen if we consider rising sea-levels again and ask who should finance the process of adaptation needed to ensure that rising sea-levels do not harm people's vital interests. The Polluter Pays Principle, *by its very nature*, must ascertain who caused how much harm and, as such, it must become embroiled in the complex historical problems noted above. It must do this to ascertain who the duty bearers are and the size of their duty. An Ability to Pay approach, by contrast, does not need to enquire into the causes of dangerous climate change in order to determine who should pay for the necessary adaptation. It need not get embroiled in issues surrounding the historical causes for climate change because all it needs to know are, first, what kind of adaptation measures are required and, second, who are the most advantaged. In light of this, a historical approach, like the Polluter Pays Principle, can, therefore, be said to be less practical than competing approaches such as the Ability to Pay Principle.

However, note that the problems of determining cause and effect also affect *all* principles determining who should bear the burdens of climate change. This can be seen if we consider the duty to engage in mitigation. The reason is straightforward: any account of the duty to prevent harms must employ an accurate account of which activities cause those harms and by how much. So even if one adopts an Ability to Pay approach one needs to know the extent of the harms caused by dangerous climate change and what causes those harms. Performance of the duty to mitigate requires this knowledge. It is only once one has this information that one can then specify what the wealthiest must do to perform their duty to prevent dangerous climate change. So *any* theory concerned with preventing further harmful climate change cannot avoid the complex causal issues raised above. The problem is, therefore, not particular to the Polluter Pays approach and, as such, does not give us reason to reject that approach in preference to another one.

Objection 2

Consider now a second challenge to the Polluter Pays Principle. One worry about applying the Polluter Pays Principle to global climate change is that some people were excusably ignorant of the fact that their activities may lead to dangerous climate change. As such it would be unfair to make them pay. They knew not what they were doing and, moreover, their ignorance is excusable.

A number of different counter-arguments might be made in response to this argument. One can identify at least five possibilities. These hold that the 'excusable ignorance' argument does not invalidate or limit the application of the Polluter Pays Principle to climate change because:

Reply (1): ever since the 1990s, it has been widely known that methane, nitrous oxide, hydrofluorocarbons, perfluorocarbons, and sulfur hexafluoride cause climate change.[13]

Reply (2): ever since a pre-1990 date, it has been widely known that carbon emissions *might* cause climate change and agents should have acted according to the 'precautionary principle'.

Reply (3): those responsible for emitting excessive amounts of greenhouse gases have continued to do so even when they have been made aware of the consequences of their actions so the fact that they were excusably ignorant before does not exempt them from being paying for the emissions that they generated when excusably ignorant.[14]

Reply (4): we should adopt a strict liability principle where this holds that if people engage in activities which jeopardize other people's fundamental interests by emitting excessive amounts of greenhouse gases then they should bear the costs of their actions even if they were excusably ignorant of the effects of their actions (see Neumayer 2000, p. 188; Shue 1999, pp. 535–536).

Reply (5): we should adopt a modified strict liability principle where this holds that if people engage in activities which jeopardize other people's fundamental interests by emitting excessive amounts of greenhouse gases, then they should bear the costs of their actions even if they were excusably ignorant of the effects of their actions if *they have benefited from those harmful activities* (see Baer 2006, p. 136; Gosseries 2004, pp. 40–41).[15]

Let us consider each of these responses. Reply (1) clearly has force now and from sometime in the last 15 or so years. However, its obvious limitation is that it cannot cover emissions that precede whatever cut-off date we specify as the date after which one cannot plead excusable ignorance. Given this, let us consider reply (2). This can reach further back into the past than reply (1) but it is hard to say with any specificity the date from which it can be applied. In addition to this, one important question that arises is whether persons who *had reason to think* that greenhouse gases *might* cause climate change should pay the same amount for the consequences of their action as persons who *knew* that greenhouse gases *did* cause climate change. Intuitively this seems wrong but then how much less should those who violate the precautionary principle pay? There is no obvious answer.

Consider now reply (3). Its thesis is that if people would not have cut back on their emissions even if they had not been excusably ignorant then the fact that they were indeed excusably ignorant does not exonerate them. Since they would have emitted just as much anyway, whether or not they were aware of the causes of climate change, their excusable ignorance is not germane: they are required to pay for their emissions. Now reply (3) is hard to dispute on empirical grounds. Those who have known about the effects of their carbon-intensive practices have not engaged in mitigation. Indeed emissions have continued to increase year after year. For example, carbon dioxide emissions stemming from fossil fuel use and industry have grown by more than 3% per annum during the 2000–2004 period (as compared to 1.1% per annum between 1990 and 1999) (Rapauch *et al.* 2007, p. 10288). One might, though, object to reply (3) on procedural grounds. Even if one had overwhelming reason to think that people would not have cut back on their emissions if they had known earlier and so would have acted wrongly, one is not entitled to treat them as if they have in fact acted wrongly. For they have not and it would be a violation of procedural justice to treat them as if they had. They should be given a fair chance to act correctly and reply (3) denies them this.

Given this one might adopt reply (4) and affirm a principle of strict liability. This, however, seems to me to fail to do justice to potential duty-bearers. Any compelling theory of justice must accommodate both the concerns of the rights-bearers (we wish that our rights be upheld) and the concerns of the duty-bearers (the duties entailed by the rights should not be unreasonable). However, an unqualified strict liability approach subordinates the perspectives of the rights-bearers over potential duty-bearers. The latter can plausibly complain ‘why should we pay when we had no idea that our activities were having this effect and, furthermore, when we could not have been expected to know that our activities were harmful?’ Reply (4) is, thus, unfair on the potential duty-bearers.

One might, however, revise reply (4) in light of this objection. Consider, again, the problem with reply (4). Suppose, for example, that by treading on a spot on the ground one causes harm to others on the other side of the globe and suppose that one could not be expected to know that this happens. Pace the argument of the last paragraph, one may conclude here that it is unfair to insist that the person who causes the harm should pay the cost. Now suppose, however, that the person who treads on the spot on the ground derives a benefit from this activity. The behaviour that causes the harm to others also brings them benefits. This considerably changes the situation. In particular, the complaint that it is unfair to make them pay for effects they could not have anticipated loses its force here because, and to the extent that, they have also benefited from this harmful behaviour. This leads us towards reply (5).

However, reply (5) is, as it stands, not quite right because it makes no reference to the size of the benefit. It says simply that where someone has engaged in activities that have a harmful effect that they could not have foreseen then they are liable as long as they have benefited. But it would be implausible to say that they are liable for massive costs even if they only benefited slightly. In line with this, I suggest the following:

Reply (6): we should adopt a modified strict liability principle where this holds that if people engage in activities which jeopardize other people's fundamental interests by emitting excessive amounts of greenhouse gases then (i) they should bear the costs of their actions even if they were excusably ignorant of the effects of their actions if *they have benefited from those harmful activities* and (ii) *their costs should correspond to the benefits they have derived.*[16]

This version of strict liability clearly accommodates the point of view of the duty-bearer for it prevents cases arising where the potential duty-bearer is made to pay large costs even though they have derived only minimal gains. It is, therefore, superior to replies (4) and (5). However, since those who have emitted high levels of greenhouse gases have in fact also benefited considerably from them this principle, in practice, has considerable bite and would impose duties on very many people in industrialised economies. It thus provides considerable protection to the potential victims of dangerous climate change.

Reply (6) thus gives us the resources to meet the argument from 'excusable ignorance'. The Polluter Pays Principle may rightfully apply to those who are excusably ignorant of the consequences of their climate endangering activities if, because, and to the extent that they have benefited from their high emissions.

The 'Polluter Pays' Principle – three limitations

Having addressed two challenges to the application of the Polluter Pays Principle to global climate change we may now consider three more serious problems. One problem with the Polluter Pays Principle is that it cannot cope with the effects on the climate that result from the emissions of earlier generations. On most accounts, carbon dioxide emissions began to rise during the industrial revolution and continued to rise throughout the nineteenth and twentieth century. This means, though, that some of the polluters, and hence some of the duty-bearers, are dead and we therefore need to ascribe the duty to address their emissions to someone else. The principle that the polluter should pay obviously needs supplementation when the polluter no longer exists (Caney 2005, p. 756).

Now when assessing this objection we should bear in mind that the most marked increase in greenhouse gas emissions has taken place over the last 35 years or so. Indeed, it has recently been found that '[s]ince 1751 approximately 329 billion tons of carbon have been released to the atmosphere from the consumption of fossil fuels and cement production. Half of these emissions have occurred since the mid 1970s' (Boden *et al.* 2009). Carbon emissions from fossil fuel burning, cement manufacture and gas flaring rose from 1630 million metric tons of carbon in 1950 (which amounts to 0.64 metric tons of carbon per capita) to 4076 million metric tons of carbon in 1970 (1.10 metric tons per capita). By 1980, 5332 million metric tons of carbon were released (which equates to 1.20 metric tons per capita) and by 2006 the total emissions were a staggering 8230 million metric tons (1.25 metric tons of carbon per capita) (Boden *et al.* 2009). Carbon emissions thus increased more than five-fold between 1950 and 2006. This notwithstanding, most accounts recognise that there was a pronounced and significant increase between 1840 and the mid-twentieth century. For example, emissions rose from a mere eight million metric tons in 1800 to 33 million metric tons in 1840, rising further to 932 million metric tons by 1920 and reaching 1630 million metric tons by 1950 (Boden and Marland 2009). And, of course, many of those causally responsible during the period from 1840 to 1950 (and indeed later) are dead so the Polluter Pays Principle cannot be applied to their emissions. The Polluter Pays Principle is, thus, incomplete.

A second problem with the Polluter Pays Principle arises if and when some climate change occurs which does not stem from human activity. Climate scientists overwhelmingly contend that human activity is the major driver of the current and projected climate change. However, their formulations also often allow that human activity may not be the sole cause of climate change. The 'Summary for Policymakers' in the IPCC's *Climate Change 2001: Synthesis Report* reports, for example, that '*most* of the warming observed over the last 50 years is attributable to human activities' (Watson *et al.* 2001, p. 5, emphasis added). How should we think about any warming that is not anthropogenic? A proponent of the Polluter Pays Principle faces a dilemma here. *Either* she holds that people should be protected against *all* malign climate change (where doing so is not unduly demanding) but then, if this is the case, she needs to go beyond a pure Polluter Pays approach and find some criterion for apportioning the remaining responsibility. She needs, that is, to find some principle to tell us who should bear that portion of the cost of dealing with harmful climate change that stems from non-anthropogenic causes. *Or*, she commits herself to a purist version of the Polluter Pays Principle, which holds that the Polluter Pays Principle is the *only* fair principle for determining duties and hence the only climate change that should be covered is that stemming from human activity. On this view, then, the harm resulting from non-human activities should go unaddressed. But this is implausible. Our concern about climate change (including non-anthropogenic climate change) stems from its impacts on people's lives (their exposure to drought, malnutrition, flooding, disease, heat stress and so forth). Given this, we have reason to be concerned about non-anthropogenic climate change. Someone might claim that climate change that has been imposed by other people is worse in some sense than non-human-induced climate change but it would be odd to think that non-anthropogenic climate change is of no concern at all. From the point of view of the victim, what matters is that dangerous climate change damages one's vital interests. The view that persons are entitled to protection from anthropogenic climate change and not from non-anthropogenic climate change is thus untenable. But if we accept this then an additional principle is required. The proponent of the PPP thus faces a dilemma. Either we ignore non-anthropogenic climate change, but this is morally questionable. Or we call for protection against all malign climate change, but if this is the case an additional principle is required to attribute responsibilities to deal with non-human-induced climate change.[17]

A third, and final, point bears noting. We tend to assume that to make the polluter pay is in practice often to make the affluent pay. That we do so is understandable because industrialised countries like the USA and European countries have traditionally been the highest emitters of greenhouse gases. However, there is not a perfect correlation between high emissions and wealth, and in some instances making people pay in proportion to their emissions would perpetuate the poverty of some and reduce others to poverty. This is true, for example, for many in China and India.

The view that China should not be subject to a strict application of the Polluter Pays Principle is, however, resisted by some. They argue, for example, that China's emissions are now greater than those of the USA so it should bear responsibility for those emissions. In support of this claim they might appeal to a recent report from the Netherlands Environmental Assessment Agency, according to which in 2006 China's total CO_2 emissions were 6,220 million tonnes whereas the USA's CO_2 emissions in that year were 5,801 million tonnes (Nature 2007, p. 1038). China is, moreover, not alone, and India's emissions are considerable. A critic may therefore resist the idea that developing countries should be partially exempted from the Polluter Pays Principle.

This counter-argument is, however, unpersuasive for several reasons. First, the figures cited above refer only to the total amount CO_2 of emitted. China has, however, a much larger population than the USA. China's population in 2006 was 1,323.6 million people as opposed to the USA's 301 million. Thus China's per capita emissions in 2006 were 4.7 tonnes of CO_2 per capita rather than the USA's staggering 19.3 tonnes per capita (Nature 2007, p. 1038). The same point applies if we look further than China. For example, in 2004 the developing countries (including China and India) comprised 80% of the world's population but emitted only 41% of the world's emissions (Rapauch *et al.* 2007, p. 10292). Second, however, the argument under consideration is inappropriate because the standard of living in China is much lower than the USA and it is wrong to impose mitigation duties on some if that jeopardizes their ability to attain a decent standard of living.[18] Third, the second point can be generalised further. And it is worth making the more general point that it would be a mistake to determine who should bear the burden of climate change in isolation from an analysis of their general economic entitlements. So if one holds, as I do, that people should not fall beneath a certain standard of living then the Polluter Pays Principle should be qualified to prevent it being the case that people are made to pay for emissions needed for their fundamental survival.[19]

These points do not – and are not intended to – establish that the Polluter Pays Principle should be abandoned when determining the duties of prevention and adaptation. They point to ways in which the Polluter Pays Principle must be supplemented with an additional principle (or set of principles). They establish that we need a principle of justice to deal with what we might term the Remainder, where I use this term to refer to harmful climate changes that stems from (a) the emissions of earlier generations, (b) non-human-induced climate change, and (c) the (legitimate) emissions of the disadvantaged.

The 'Ability to Pay' Principle

How should we deal with the Remainder? In this section I want to argue that the Remainder should be filled by an 'Ability to Pay' approach. Stated formally, this approach states that the duty to address some problem (in this case, bearing the burdens of climate change) should be borne by the wealthy, and, moreover, that the duty should increase in line with an agent's wealth.[20] In principle, the Ability to Pay approach is indifferent to who caused a harm: its emphasis is on who can rectify that harm. So by contrast with the Polluter Pays Principle it is a forward-looking, rather than a backward-looking, principle. To appraise the plausibility of the Ability to Pay Principle and to help us refine it consider several objections that might be levelled against it.

A: Objection 1 – why should I pay for something that is not my fault?

First, the advantaged might argue that it is unfair to make them cut back on emissions (and/or pay for adaptation) since the climate change in question (the Remainder) is, *ex hypothesi*, not their fault. To adopt an Ability to Pay component, they complain, is to make them bear a burden for something that is no fault of their own.

This objection, however, does not unsettle the use of the Ability to Pay principle. The objection rests on the following assumption: it is wrong that some bear a burden for a problem that is not of their doing. This assumption seems to me highly implausible but the most important point to make in this context is that whatever happens some will be bearing a burden that it is not their fault. To see this consider three options. We might say that the advantaged should pay (option 1) or that the poor should pay (option 2). In both cases, however, some would be bearing a burden that stems from a problem that is not of their doing. We might then hold that nothing should be done (what is termed 'business as usual'): this is option 3. But this too imposes a burden on some because of something that is not of their doing – for in this case victims of climate change (many of whom will be future generations) will have to bear a burden that stems from a problem that they did not cause. So all of the available options violate the assumption. It cannot therefore be used to invalidate an Ability to Pay approach.

We can go further. Reflecting on the three-option scenario just envisaged brings out the intuitive appeal of the Ability to Pay approach. Consider the three options again. In the first place we might hold that the poor should pay. However, to make the least well-off pay in a world where others are able to pay and still live a very affluent life seems perverse. In light of this, we might say that global warming should remain unaddressed. But this too seems unfair – especially on the poor members of some regions (such as Bangladesh, small island states and the Nile Delta) because they are particularly vulnerable to climate change. This leaves one group – the advantaged – and they have less cause for complaint than either of the other two groups.[21] The most advantaged are most able to pay the price without sacrificing any reasonable interests: therefore, they are under a duty to do so.

B: Objection 2 – isn't it counter-intuitive to ignore the historical record?

Consider now a second objection to an Ability to Pay component. A pure Ability to Pay approach holds that the only criterion for apportioning responsibility for bearing a burden is who can best bear that burden. This purist approach is, however, vulnerable to the objection that, by giving no place to the historical genesis of a problem, it ignores a morally relevant consideration. As noted above, an Ability to Pay approach is wholly forward-looking. As such, though, it is in conflict with a deep conviction that who should bear the burdens of climate change cannot be wholly divorced from an understanding of the historical origin of the problem. A wholly forward-looking approach, it might be argued, is out of kilter with some of our deepest moral convictions.

Two responses are available to proponents of the Ability to Pay principle. First, they might dismiss the intuition and bite the (counter-intuitive) bullet. Second, they might seek to accommodate the objection being raised. I shall pursue this second strategy. I propose the following position as an initial step in the right direction:

> **ATP***: The duties to bear the Remainder should be borne by the wealthy but we should distinguish between two groups – (i) those whose wealth came about in ways which endangered the Earth's climate and (ii) those whose wealth came about in ways which did not endanger the Earth's climate – and we should apportion greater responsibility to (i) than to (ii).[22]

To elaborate further: (i) refers to currently alive people whose holdings resulted from a historical process that involved excessively high emissions. So if a person owns £200,000 and if this is the case because their grandparents acquired this wealth in a climate-endangering way then that person would fall into category (i). The key point is that somewhere along the historical chain of events leading them to own their current holdings there have been climate injustices. Those in category (i), then, have received wealth because of the commission of injustices. For convenience's sake I shall term those who belong to category (i) as 'dirty developers' and those in category (ii) as 'clean developers' (even though some of those in category (i) might themselves not have emitted excessive levels of greenhouse gases).

This qualified version of the Ability to Pay has intuitive appeal but can we say more in its favour? I think we can. My suggestion is that those whose wealth did not come about in a climate-endangering way can provide more reasons to justify their wealth (and thereby to resist the claim that they should devote resources to ameliorating climate change) than those whose wealth did come about in a climate-endangering way. They have more reasons at their disposal to justify their view that they should not have to pay for the mitigation and adaptation costs needed to address the ill effects of climate change. The argument can best be illustrated by comparing two people. Suppose that we are apportioning responsibilities for addressing climate change. Imagine that there are two people, A and B, and suppose that they are equally wealthy. The historical process that lead to A's possession of her current wealth is one that involves excessive carbon emissions. (She thus falls into category (i) of the **ATP***.) B's wealth, by contrast, has not come about in climate-endangering ways. Suppose now that someone proposes that A and B should bear part of the burden of dealing with climate change and should do so equally. They will no doubt adduce various reasons to resist this demand. Familiar reasons would include:

(1) taxing the wealthy undermines economic growth because it reduces the incentive to engage in wealth-creation (the economic growth argument).

(2) taxing the wealthy restricts the liberty of the wealthy (the liberty argument).
(3) taxing the wealthy is unfair because they are entitled to their wealth, in virtue of the fact that it came about in a just way (the entitlement argument).

They might also, no doubt, adduce other reasons. Now the relevant point is this: B can invoke all of these reasons in support of her position whereas A can only invoke reasons (1) and (2). *Ex hypothesi*, A cannot invoke an entitlement-based argument in support of her position because her wealth did not come about in a just way. She therefore has less cause for complaint than B. The point can be put in another way: the significance of historic wrongs (like excessive carbon emissions or highly damaging deforestation) is that they discredit historical arguments that take the form 'we're entitled to X because our possession of X came about in a just way'.[23] Now insofar as we are concerned about historic injustices we should ask less of clean developers than dirty developers.

To further determine the plausibility or otherwise of **ATP*** let us consider two additional challenges to it.

C: Objection 3 – why should 'clean developers' pay anything?

Someone might dispute **ATP*** on the grounds that none of the burden should be borne by wealthy persons if their wealth did not come about in a climate-endangering way. The proposal in other words is to delete category (ii) from **ATP***. On this proposal the duty to bear the burden of the Remainder should fall squarely on those privileged members of the world whose wealth came about in a climate-endangering way. This criticism thus posits a challenge: why should the wealthy pay anything if their wealth came about through clean development?

A number of points can be made in reply. First, there are familiar cases where we think that a person is obligated to assist others even when they played no part in the other's poverty or sickness. In such cases we think that a positive duty falls on those able to help. For example, if someone sitting next to you at a table suddenly becomes seriously ill and you're well placed to help, then we tend to think that you should do so. It would be an odd person who refused to aid on the basis that they did not cause this harm. Even if people disagree with Peter Singer's claim that persons are obligated to aid others up and until the point that the cost to them of giving is greater than the benefit received, there is a fixed conviction that there is a duty to aid to some extent (Singer 1972). This leads to a second point: resistance to the idea that those who did not cause a problem can nonetheless be obligated often stems from a concern that they will be subject to unduly demanding duties. But there is, of course, no reason why this need be the case. One can respond to this concern by affirming positive duties on those able to pay so long as it is not too demanding. Third, and finally, as is commonly argued, the best account of what is wrong with causing a harm to befall others appeals to the importance of being able to pursue their interests. But, if it is morally important that persons can pursue their interests, then it entails not just that there is a duty not to harm those interests but also a duty to aid those who are vulnerable.[24] If we hold that there is a duty not to harm someone because such harms leave people unable to advance their fundamental interests then this suggests that we care about people being able to advance their fundamental interests. But if we hold this, it surely entails a positive duty on the behalf of others to advance those interests. The first objection to **ATP*** thus fails.

D: Objection 4 – why focus solely on previous climate injustice?

Let us consider, now, an additional and final objection. This time the concern is with the contention that greater responsibilities should be borne by wealthy persons whose wealth came about in *a climate-endangering way*. Why, a critic might ask, should the Ability to Pay Principle focus solely on 'those whose wealth came about in a climate-endangering way' rather than 'those whose wealth came about in an unjust way'? Imagine, for example, that some have wealth and that they do so because their ancestors participated in the slave trade (and I am assuming that that did not involve high carbon emissions or methane emissions and so on). Or consider those whose current affluence has arisen because they have inherited wealth from ancestors who appropriated land from indigenous peoples (and, again, let us assume that they did not emit high levels of carbon emissions and did not engage in deforestation). Their current holdings are thus based to some extent on a history of injustice: can it not be said of them that they have less claim on their current wealth? Furthermore, the critic might argue, the reasoning adduced in support of the **ATP*** (in particular the argument comparing the clean developer B with the dirty developer A) does not in fact support **ATP***. Let me explain. The argument in question compared A and B and made the point that A could muster less reasons on behalf of their claim to retain their wealth: in particular they could not employ an entitlement-based theory in their defence. But, and this is the key point, the same point could be made about those whose wealth came about because of the slave trade or political corruption or economic imperialism. They too cannot use an entitlement-based theory to defend their current holdings. Thus the normative rationale for **ATP*** actually entails that greater responsibility should be borne by the wealthy whose wealth came about in unjust ways. In light of this line of reasoning, we should revise **ATP*** (and the way in which it defines category (ii)) so that it reads as follows:

> **ATP****: The duties to bear the Remainder should be borne by the wealthy but we should distinguish between two groups – (i) those whose wealth came about

in unjust ways and (ii) those whose wealth came about in ways which were not unjust – and we should apportion greater responsibility to (i) than to (ii).

Given the argument mooted for **ATP*** (i.e. the comparison of A and B above) we should prefer **ATP**** to **ATP***.

Several further comments about **ATP**** are in order. First, someone might argue that it is particularly fitting that those whose holdings stem from a climate injustice make recompense for that particular wrong. Consider, for example, someone whose wealth stems from the fact that their grandparents collaborated with the slave trade: one might think it particularly appropriate that they deal with the contemporary ill effects of slavery. Or consider someone whose wealth came about because their ancestors appropriated wealth from Jews during the Second World War: one might think it appropriate that they address anti-semitism. **ATP**** accommodates such an intuition but it does not make it mandatory. It would allow those whose wealth stems from injustice to discharge their duties in this specific way but it does not require this kind of action. Second, in distinguishing between (i) and (ii) I am not committed to claiming that many or indeed any people fall into category (i). **ATP**** does not assume that there are in fact people in both categories. My point is to establish the morally relevant considerations and categories, not to make an empirical claim. Third, we should record that the **ATP**** needs to be stated more precisely. We need, for example, to say how the duty should be shared among the two groups mentioned. By what formula or rule? In the meantime, however, I hope that the preceding arguments make a persuasive case for **ATP****.

Before considering some implications of the view defended here, it is worth providing a statement of my conclusions. Thus far I have argued for two main positive conclusions. First, I have accepted a qualified version of the Polluter Pays Principle where this holds that

> Principle 1: Persons should bear the burden of climate change that they have caused so long as doing so does not push them beneath a decent standard of living (the *Poverty-Sensitive Polluter Pays Principle*).

Second, however, I have argued that the Polluter Pays Principle cannot cover all aspects of the problem (non-anthropogenic climate change, the emissions of the poor, and the emissions of past generations – what I have termed the Remainder). This leads to my second positive claim. For I have argued that

> Principle 2: The duties to bear the Remainder should be borne by the wealthy but we should distinguish between two groups – (i) those whose wealth came about in unjust ways, and (ii) those whose wealth did not come about in unjust ways – and we should apportion greater responsibility to (i) than to (ii). (*the History-Sensitive Ability to Pay Principle*).

The view defended, then, is a hybrid one that combines two separate principles.

The implications of the hybrid model

This provides the theoretical framework within which I think we should address climate change. I now want to describe it more fully and then explore its practical implications.

Let us begin then by fleshing out these two principles further. Three points are in order. First, nothing has been said so far on who the bearers of these duties are. Many thinkers and commentators treat 'countries' as the bearers of the duties of prevention and adaptation. This, no doubt, is in part a reflection of the fact that much of the focus on combating climate change is on international treaties like the Kyoto Protocol. It is, however, a consequence of the view defended above that the duties outlined above fall not just on states but also on other types of actor. For example, the logic of the *Poverty-Sensitive Polluter Pays Principle* is that all (sufficiently affluent) agents who are causally responsible for high emissions are under an obligation to cut back their emissions according (and/or spend money on adaptation). Now many actors other than national governments play a causal role. These include, for example, (1) individuals for individuals can choose whether to fly or not, what car to drive, how much heating or air-conditioning to use and so on. They also include (2) firms. Firms can frequently choose how much energy they need to consume, how much transportation to employ, the extent of building insulation, the level of heating and so on. They also include (3) sub-state political authorities like cities or the member states of federal systems like the USA. This level of analysis is often neglected, but recent research for the Pew Center on Global Climate Change has revealed how different states in the United States of America pursue quite different policies on climate change. States can exert considerable control over many areas that bear on greenhouse gas emissions (passing regulations on household goods; requiring use of renewable energy sources; restricting carbon emissions of power plants) and some states have pursued more aggressive mitigation policies than others (Pew Center 2006). To give some examples: Connecticut, Maine, Massachusetts, New Hampshire, New York, Rhode Island, and Vermont have pledged themselves to reducing greenhouse gas (GHG) emissions to 10% lower than 1990 levels by 2020. California has committed itself to reducing GHG emissions to 1990 levels by 2020 and New Mexico has pledged to reduce its GHG emissions to 10% lower than its 2000 level by 2020 (Fischer and Constanza 2005, p. 301). Other states have been far less active.[25] A final category of actors who play a causal role in generating climate change is, (4), international financial institutions (who often incentivise environmentally harmful economic growth). The duties generated by the *Poverty-Sensitive Polluter Pays Principle* thus fall to all these kind of actors. The same is true of the **ATP****. The thought underlying the latter is that those able to pay have a duty to do so and hence this duty falls too not simply on affluent 'states' but on any body that can possess wealth, such as individuals, corporations and so on.

Second, it is worth noting that although I have argued that the most advantaged have a leading responsibility to play, my argument also places duties on the least advantaged as well. For if they can develop in ways that do not involve high levels of fossil fuel combustion, and can do so without great cost to themselves, then it would be wrong for them to pursue a high emissions policy.

A third point also bears recording: it might be thought that my position justifies a policy according to which later generations pay for climate change. The thought here is that future generations will be wealthier than current generations and hence more able to pay; as such an 'ability to pay' criterion should allocate duties to them.[26] This, in effect, amounts to a policy of not preventing climate change for now and then trying at some point in the future both to prevent further climate change and also to adapt to the changes that have occurred. Although future people may well be better off than current peoplc, I believe that it does not follow that an Ability to Pay Principle has the implication of postponing action into the future. There are at least two reasons for this. First, although future people may have more wealth, the costs will also be very much greater in the future. It will cost less to prevent the problem from arising than to allow it to arise and then seeking to adapt to it later.[27] Second, unless mitigation takes place now, there will be dangerous climate change to which people are unable to adapt. A failure to mitigate would therefore inevitably result in injury to some future people and it would be wrong knowingly to allow a wrong to occur with a view to seeking to compensate those wronged later. People should not be wronged in the first place. Mitigation now is thus not only cheaper than postponing action but it is also required if we are to respect people's fundamental interests.

Let us, finally, turn to the policy implications of the view defended on pp. 695–708. Different kinds of policy have been proposed to cut back on emissions. These include (among other things): (a) carbon quotas and trading policies, (b) carbon taxes, (c) clean development initiatives, and (d) adaptation programmes. Each of these instruments can be used in line with the view defended above. What is required is a set of measures that prevent people (within reason) from emitting excessive emissions, ensure that those who have emitted more than they should have done cut back their emissions and support adaptation, and that ensure that the most advantaged cover the Remainder. The policy instruments listed above can all serve these objectives.

(a) Consider first a system of carbon quotas and carbon trading. This approach is affirmed in Article 17 of the Kyoto Protocol and a system of carbon-trading (the EU Emissions Trading Scheme) came into effect on 1 January 2005.[28] Advocates of carbon trading often suggest that 'states' have quotas that they can use, or sell, but this is not the only option. Alternatively, one might suggest a scheme where permits are auctioned off to firms who then pass the costs on to the consumer and in which the proceeds are spent to further people's entitlements. Finally, some have proposed a system of individual quotas (what has been Domestic Tradable Quotas).[29] Now a quota-based system can, if effectively enforced, serve the goal of reducing carbon dioxide. Many who favour a system of quotas hold that everyone should have an equal per capita entitlement to emit carbon dioxide.[30] The account developed above would, however, dissent from this in several ways. First, following the Polluter Pays Principle it would hold that those who have in the near past emitted excessive amounts of carbon dioxide should have less now. Second, the arguments above claim that the least advantaged have a stronger claim to emit carbon dioxide than the advantaged. Third, I have argued that the most advantaged should bear the cost of the emissions of both past generations and of the disadvantaged, in which case it follows that the advantaged should not have an equal right to emit carbon dioxide. The key point I wish to make though is that the account developed above can be reflected by a system of emissions quotas and carbon trading.

(b) The view defended above can also, however, employ a system of taxes. In the first place, a system of carbon taxes can be utilised both to discourage people from exceeding their fair share and also to ensure that those who do exceed their fair share pay money in compensation (thereby making the polluter pay). Second, one can ensure that carbon taxes exempt the very poor. In virtue of both of these features, carbon taxes can realize what I termed the *Poverty-Sensitive Polluter Pays Principle* (as defined on p. 708). Third, as proponents of carbon taxes often observe, carbon taxes can produce a 'double dividend'. So as well as discouraging high emissions they can generate funds – funds that can be spent on adaptation.[31] Finally, and moving away from carbon taxes, a system of progressive taxation can be implemented in countries with an extensive history of industrialisation to ensure that the most advantaged pay for those types of climate change not covered by the Polluter Pays Principle (which is what would be required by the *History-Sensitive Ability to Pay Principle* defended above).

The key point to observe then is that the principles I have defended can be implemented via either a 'cap and trade' system of carbon trading or a system of carbon (and other) taxes. Though the principles I defend are rather complex the preceding discussion shows how taxes and trading schemes can be designed to approximate them.

(c) Note, further, that a successful programme of combating climate change must find ways that poor countries can develop and meet their legitimate needs without jeopardizing the earth's atmosphere. However to attain such sustainable development there must be financial schemes which both stimulate research and development of clean technology and which also ensure that such clean technology is transferred from rich to poor countries.[32] This, however, requires funding and this again requires us to turn to the Hybrid View.

(d) Finally, the Hybrid View can determine who should fund adaptation. As was noted earlier, adaptation is necessary. It is widely recognised that the global poor will be highly vulnerable to dangerous climate and therefore their adaptive capacity needs to be developed. Applying the Hybrid View, it is clear that the global poor themselves should not bear the cost. The Poverty-Sensitive Polluter Pays Principle would exempt them (either because of their poverty and/or because their emissions are very low) and since they are disadvantaged they would also be exempted by the Ability to Pay component. There therefore needs to be a global adaptation fund that is funded by those who have emitted excessive amounts of GHGs and by the advantaged of the world.

Conclusion

It is time to conclude. This paper has examined the question of who should bear the burdens of climate change. It would be convenient if we could rely on a simple formula to answer this question. I have argued, however, that no such simple formula is available. The truth is rather more complex than any crude slogan. To answer to the question we need to draw on qualified versions of the Polluter Pays Principle and the Ability to Pay Principle.

Acknowledgements

Earlier versions of this paper were presented at the 'Global Inequalities, Local Injustices' Seminar Series, University of Oxford (November 2005); the Political Theory Seminar, University of Newcastle (November 2005); the Symposium on 'Democracy, Equality and Justice', the British Academy (December 2005); the 11th International Social Justice Conference of the International Society for Justice Research, Humboldt University, Berlin (August 2006); the Conference on 'Global Justice and Climate Change', University of Reading (October 2006); and the Oxford-Princeton 'Global Justice Seminar', at Princeton University (March 2007). I am grateful to members of all the audiences for comments and thank, in particular, Arthur Applbaum, Paul Baer, Brian Barry, Paula Casal, Steve Gardiner, Wilfried Hinsch, Brad Hooker, Andy Hurrell, Vijay Joshi, Peter Jones, Robert Keohane, Melissa Lane, Stephen Macedo, David Miller, Sue Mendus, Lukas Meyer, Helen Milner, Kieran Oberman, Onora O'Neill, Philippe van Parijs, Alan Patten, James Pattison, Jennifer Pitts, Dominic Roser, Henry Shue and Andrew Williams. I am especially grateful to Derek Bell, Matthew Clayton and Edward Page for discussions of the view defended here. This research was conducted as part of an Arts and Humanities Research Council (AHRC) research grant on 'Global Justice and the Environment' and I am grateful to the AHRC for its support. I completed this essay while holding a Leverhulme Research Fellowship and I am grateful to the Leverhulme Trust for its support.

Notes

1. For excellent empirical data on all these see McCarthy *et al.* (2001), Schellnhuber *et al.* (2006), Parry *et al.* (2007).
2. This list is not exhaustive. A third principle holds that those who have benefited from industrialization, and/or from climate change itself, should pay (the Beneficiary Pays Principle – BPP). I have criticised this principle elsewhere and will not

discuss it here. For a defence of the view see Gosseries (2004). For criticism see Caney (2006, pp. 471–476).

3. For defences of this kind of approach see Neumayer (2000) and Shue (1999, pp. 533–537). Shue himself prefers not to describe his position as a polluter pays principle (p. 534) but his position conforms to the PPP as I interpret it.
4. Joint Science Academies' Statement: Global Response to Climate Change (2005).
5. See, further, Hare and Meinshausen (2006).
6. Some, like Bjørn Lomborg, have contested this, arguing that prevention will cost too much and will yield too little. See Lomborg (2001, pp. 305–318, especially p. 318). Lomborg's arguments are, however, unpersuasive. For a good critique see Cole (2003).
7. For discussion of the West Antarctic Ice Sheet see Rapley (2006, pp. 25–27). For discussion of the Greenland Ice sheet see Lowe *et al.* (2006, pp. 29–36).
8. For good discussions of the Atlantic Thermohaline Circulation see Schlesinger *et al.* (2006, pp. 37–47) and Wood *et al.* (2006, pp. 49–54). See also Vellinga and Wood (2002).
9. See 'Paper No. 1 Brazil: Proposed Elements of a Protocol to the United Nations Framework Convention on Climate Change, Presented by Brazil in Response to the Berlin Mandate', Item 3 of the Provisional Agenda of the Seventh Session of the Ad Hoc Group on the Berlin Mandate, FCCC/AGBM/1997/MISC.1/Add.3, 30 May 1997.
10. See the SBSTA's 'Progress Report on the Review of the Scientific and Methodological Aspects of the Proposal by Brazil', Item 4 of the Provisional Agenda of the Fourteenth Session of the SBSTA, Bonn, FCCC/SBSTA/2001/INF.2, 10 July 2001.
11. For further extended analysis on the uncertainties in determining causal responsibility see den Elzen and Schaeffer (2002).
12. See, for example, Allen (2003), Allen and Lord (2004), and Allen *et al.* (2007).
13. This kind of response has been made by a number of different thinkers, though they do not always agree on the date after which the plea of excusable ignorance is inappropriate. See, for example, Singer (2002, p. 34), who proposes 1990 as the cut-off date, and Neumayer (2000, p. 188), who suggests that the cut-off date should be in the mid-1980s. Shue also makes this kind of response but does not specify a key date after which one cannot claim excusable ignorance (Shue 1999, p. 536).
14. I am grateful to Andrew Williams for pressing this response when I presented this paper at the British Academy.
15. This reply is also suggested in passing by Peter Singer (2002, p. 34). Singer, however, does not press the point and in a desire to construct a principle that might enjoy support among industrialised countries he makes no further use of the idea of strict liability in his argument.
16. In his illuminating analysis, Axel Gosseries (2004) also mentions the relevance of the size of the benefit that the excusably ignorant perpetrator receives from their harmful act to the issue of whether (and by how much) that perpetrator owes (2004, pp. 40–41). However, it is not clear from his discussion of liability incurred when excusably ignorant what criteria determine the relationship between the amount of benefit received and the size of the duty owed. On my account, the cost that can be demanded should correspond to the benefit actually enjoyed. It is not clear from Gosseries' account whether he would concur and what he says suggests that he would not (2004, p. 41).
17. This point is made by Edward Page. As he rightly says a PP approach cannot cope where climate change is 'entirely nonanthropogenic in origin' (Page 2006, p. 169.

cf also p. 172). Actually we do not need to imagine a case where it is *wholly* anthropogenic to see the limitations of the Polluter Pays Principle for even if non-anthropogenic causes are *part* of the cause then the Polluter Pays Principle is incomplete.

18. Some make a second kind of argument. They point out that the increase in carbon emissions is most marked in developing countries like China and India. This is true. To take 2004 again, 73% of the increase in emissions came from the 80% of the earth's population that come from developing countries (Raupach *et al.* 2007, p. 10292). However, this does not entail that the Polluter Pays Principle should be applied in full force to China and India. First, as argued in the text above, whether this increase in emissions is justified or not depends in part on the material needs of the Chinese people and the extent to which the increase in emissions is necessary to meet these. Second, even if we ignore this first point, a high rate of increase is not the relevant benchmark anyway. For one needs to know China's absolute level of emissions (per capita), not the rate of increase. So if the increase is great but the level of emissions is still low, then what should inform policy is the fact that the quantity of emissions (per capita) is low.
19. See also Shue's affirmation of a 'guaranteed minimum' principle (1999, pp. 540–544). For an important defence of 'sufficiency' see Frankfurt (1987).
20. See here Shue's affirmation of an 'ability to pay' principle (Shue 1999, pp. 537–540, especially p. 537). (For further discussions where Shue has argued that the wealthy should bear the mitigation and adaptation costs of climate change and that the poor be given less demanding duties see: Shue 1993, pp. 42–43, 56, 58; Shue 1994, pp. 343–366; Shue 1995, pp. 250–257.) Darrel Moellendorf also argues that the Ability to Pay Principle should play a role. In particular, he argues that it is needed to cover the fact that the Polluter Pays Principle cannot deal with the emissions of the dead. See his succinct but perceptive treatment: Moellendorf (2002, pp. 97–100).
21. For an earlier statement of this argument see Caney (2005, pp. 771–772). For a closely related line of reasoning see Moellendorf (2002, p. 100).
22. For a similar, but nonetheless distinct, position see Page's illuminating reflections in *Climate change, justice and future generations* (2006, pp.172–173). Page's suggestion is that there should be 'some "discount" in what is required of the better off when their behaviour is not [the] cause of the problem' (p.172). His view, however, differs from ATP* in several fundamental respects. First, ATP* applies this modified Ability to Pay approach simply to the climate change covered by the Remainder and not to all climate change. Second, Page's claim is that '"ability to pay" arguments gain at least some of their plausibility from the implicit assumption that those who have the ability to solve environmental problems are generally responsible for them' (p. 173). ATP*, by contrast, does not claim this. It contends that those who have the ability to pay have an even greater responsibility if, and because, they have inherited wealth and resources that were produced in a way that involved very high emissions (*even though they themselves were not 'responsible for' those emissions*). Such people are obligated (for ATP*) not because they have emitted high levels themselves (for they might not have) but because they are wealthy and that wealth stems from the excessive emissions of earlier generations.
23. See, further, Caney (2006).
24. This is brought out nicely by Allen Buchanan (2004, pp. 89–92).
25. In addition to this, recent research has shown that the policies pursued by city councils often has a marked impact on climate change. Some cities, for example, belong to the Cities for Climate Protection (CCP) programme and through it adopt

policies that cut emissions. See Betsill and Bulkeley (2004) and Bulkeley and Betsill (2005).
26. I am grateful to Vijay Joshi for raising this issue.
27. This view is strongly confirmed by Sir Nicholas Stern (2007)
28. For Article 17 of The Kyoto Protocol see: http://unfccc.int/resource/docs/convkp/kpeng.html.
29. See Starkey and Anderson (2005); Fleming (2006).
30. See Baer *et al.* (2000); Neumayer (2000, pp. 185–192); Athanasiou and Baer (2002, especially pp. 76–97).
31. One recent study finds, for example, that if a tax of $21 for each metric ton of carbon were universally adopted then it would generate $130 billion per annum. See Sandmo (2005, p. 48).
32. This point should not be confused with support for the 'clean development mechanism' that is articulated in Article 12 of the Kyoto Protocol *(http://unfccc.int/resource/docs/convkp/kpeng.html).* The latter is, I have argued elsewhere, profoundly flawed. For the reasons why see my paper 'Markets, morality and climate change: what, if anything, is wrong with emissions trading?' (Caney forthcoming).

References

Ahmad, Q.K. *et al.,* 2001. Summary for policymakers. *In:* J. McCarthy *et al.,* eds. *Climate change 2001: impacts, adaptation, and vulnerability.* Cambridge: Cambridge University Press.

Allen, M., 2003. Liability for climate change: will it ever be possible to sue anyone for damaging the climate? *Nature,* 421 (6926), 891–892.

Allen, M. and Lord, R., 2004. The blame game: who will pay for the damaging consequences of climate change? *Nature,* 432 (7017), 551–552.

Allen, M. *et al.,* 2007. Scientific challenges in the attribution of harm to human influence on climate. *University of Pennsylvania law review,* 155 (6), 1353–1400.

Appell, D., 2005. Behind the hockey stick. *Scientific American,* 292 (3), 23–24.

Arnell, N., 2006. Climate change and water resources: a global perspective. *In:* H. Schellnhuber *et al.,* eds. *Avoiding dangerous climate change.* Cambridge: Cambridge University Press, 167–175.

Athanasiou, T. and Baer, P., 2002. *Dead heat: global justice and global warming.* New York: Seven Stories Press.

Baer, P., 2006. Adaptation: who pays whom?. *In:* N. Adger, *et al.,* eds. *Fairness in adaptation to climate change.* Cambridge MA: MIT Press, 131–156.

Baer, P., *et al.,* 2000. Equity and greenhouse gas responsibility. *Science* 289 (29), 2287.

Betsill, M. and Bulkeley, H., 2004. Transnational networks and global environmental governance: the cities for climate protection program. *International studies quarterly,* 48 (2), 471–93.
Boden, T. and Marland, G., 2009. Global CO_2 emissions from fossil-fuel burning, cement manufacture, and gas flaring: 1751–2006. Carbon Dioxide Information Analysis Center, Oak Ridge National Laboratory, Oak Ridge, TN. At http://cdiac.ornl.gov/ftp/ndp030/global.1751_2006.ems.
Boden, T.A., Marland, G. and Andres, R.J., 2009. Global, regional, and national fossil-fuel CO_2 emissions. Carbon Dioxide Information Analysis Center, Oak Ridge National Laboratory, US Department of Energy, Oak Ridge, TN. At http://cdiac.ornl.gov/trends/emis/tre_glob.html.
Buchanan, A., 2004. *Justice, legitimacy, and self-determination: moral foundations for international law.* Oxford: Oxford University Press.
Bulkeley, H. and Betsill, M., 2005. Rethinking sustainable cities: multilevel governance and the 'urban' politics of climate change. *Environmental politics,* 14 (1), 42–63.
Caney, S., 2005. Cosmopolitan justice, responsibility and global climate change. *Leiden journal of international law,* 18 (4), 747–775.
Caney, S., 2006. Environmental degradation, reparations and the moral significance of history. *Journal of social philosophy,* 37 (3), 464–482.
Caney, S., forthcoming. Markets, morality and climate change: what, if anything, is wrong with emissions trading?.
Cole, M., 2003. Environmental optimists, environmental pessimists and the real state of the world – an article examining *The skeptical environmentalist: measuring the real state of the world* by Bjorn Lomborg. *Economic journal,* 113 (488), 362–380.
den Elzen, M. and Schaeffer, M., 2002. Responsibility for past and future global warming: uncertainties in attributing anthropogenic climate change. *Climatic change,* 54 (1–2), 29–73.
Fleming, D., 2006. *Energy and the common purpose: descending the energy staircase with tradable energy quotas (TEQs)* at: http://www.teqs.net/book/teqs.pdf.
Fisher, B. and Costanza, R., 2005. Regional commitment to reducing emissions. *Nature,* 438 (7066), 301–302.
Frankfurt, H., 1987. Equality as a moral ideal. *Ethics,* 98 (1), 21–43.
Gosseries, A., 2004. Historical emissions and free-riding. *Ethical perspectives,* 11 (1), 36–60.
Hare, B. and Meinshausen, M., 2006. How much warming are we committed to and how much can be avoided?. *Climatic change* 75 (1–2), 111–149.
Houghton, Sir John, 2004. *Global warming: the complete briefing.* 3rd ed. Cambridge: Cambridge University Press.
Joint Science Academies' Statement: Global Response to Climate Change, 2005. Available from: http://www.royalsoc.ac.uk/displaypagedoc.asp?id=20742.
Lomborg, B., 2001. *The skeptical environmentalist: measuring the real state of the world.* Cambridge: Cambridge University Press.
Lowe, J., *et al.,* 2006. The role of sea-level rise and the Greenland ice sheet in dangerous climate change: implications for the stabilisation of climate. *In:* H. Schellnhuber, *et al.,* eds. *Avoiding dangerous climate change.* Cambridge: Cambridge University Press.
McCarthy, J., *et al.,* eds. 2001. *Climate change 2001: impacts, adaptation, and vulnerability – contribution of working group II to the third assessment report of the Intergovernmental Panel on Climate Change.* Cambridge: Cambridge University Press.
Moellendorf, D., 2002. *Cosmopolitan justice.* Boulder, CO: Westview Press.

Nature, 2007. Gas Exchange: CO_2 emissions 1990–2006. *Nature,* 447 (7148), 1038.
Neumayer, E., 2000. In defence of historical accountability for greenhouse gas emissions. *Ecological economics* 33 (2), 185–192.
Page, E., 2006. *Climate change, justice and future generations.* Cheltenham: Edward Elgar.
Parry, M.L. *et al.,* eds. 2007. *Climate change 2007: impacts, adaptation and vulnerability – contribution of working group II to the fourth assessment report of the Intergovernmental Panel on Climate Change.* Cambridge: Cambridge University Press.
Pew Center on Global Climate Change, 2006. *Climate change 101: state action.* http://www.pewclimate.org/docUploads/101%5FStates%2Epdf
Rapley, C., 2006. The Antarctic ice sheet and sea level rise. *In:* H. Schellnhuber, eds. *Avoiding dangerous climate change.* Cambridge: Cambridge University Press.
Raupach, M. *et al.,* 2007. Global and regional drivers of accelerating CO_2 emissions. *Proceedings of the National Academy of Sciences of the United States of America,* 104 (24), 10288–10293.
Sandmo, A., 2005. Environmental taxation and revenue for development. *In:* A.B. Atkinson, ed. *New sources of development finance.* Oxford: Oxford University Press, 33–57.
Schellnhuber, H. *et al.,* eds. 2006. *Avoiding dangerous climate change.* Cambridge: Cambridge University Press.
Schlesinger, M. *et al.,* 2006. Assessing the risk of a collapse of the Atlantic thermohaline circulation. *In:* H. Schellnhuber *et al.,* eds., 2006. *Avoiding dangerous climate change.* Cambridge: Cambridge University Press.
Schneider, S. and Sarukhan, J., 2001. Overview of impacts, adaptation, and vulnerability to climate change. *In:* J. McCarthy *et al.,* eds. *Climate change 2001: impacts, adaptation, and vulnerability.* Cambridge: Cambridge University Press.
Shue, H., 1993. Subsistence emissions and luxury emissions. *Law and policy* 15 (1), 39–59.
Shue, H., 1994. After you: may action by the rich be contingent upon action by the poor? *Indiana journal of global legal studies,* 1 (2), 343–366.
Shue, H., 1995. Avoidable necessity: global warming, international fairness, and alternative energy. *In: Theory and practice:* NOMOS XXXVII. New York and London: New York University Press.
Shue, H., 1999. Global environment and international inequality. *International affairs,* 75 (3), 531–545.
Singer, P, 1972. Famine, affluence, and morality. *Philosophy & public affairs* 1 (3), 229–243.
Singer, P., 2002. *One world: the ethics of globalization.* New Haven and London: Yale University Press.
Starkey, R. and Anderson, K., 2005. Domestic tradable quotas: a policy instrument for reducing greenhouse gas emissions from energy use. Tyndall Centre for Climate Change Research: Technical Report No. 39. http://www.tyndall.ac. uk/sites/default/files/Domestic%20Tradeable%20Quotas%20%20A%20policy%20instrument%20for%20reducing%20greenhouse%20gas%20emissions%20from%20energy%20use%20(tr39).pdf.
Stern, Sir Nicholas, 2007. *The economics of climate change: the Stern Review.* Cambridge: Cambridge University Press.
Stott, P.A., Stone, D.A. and Allen, M.R., 2004. Human contribution to the European heatwave of 2003. *Nature,* 432 (7017), 610–614.
Vellinga, M. and Wood, R., 2002. Global climatic impacts of a collapse of the Atlantic thermohaline circulation. *Climatic change,* 54 (3), 251–267.

Watson, R., *et al.,* 2001. Summary for policymakers. *In:* R. Watson and the Core Writing Team, eds, *Climate change 2001: synthesis report: contribution of working groups I, II and III to the third assessment report of the Intergovernmental Panel on Climate Change.* Cambridge: Cambridge University Press.

Wood, R., *et al.,* 2006. Towards a risk assessment for shutdown of the Atlantic thermohaline circulation. *In:* H. Schellnhuber *et al.,* eds., *Avoiding dangerous climate change.* Cambridge: Cambridge University Press, 49–54.

Climate justice and historical emissions

Lukas H. Meyer[a] and Dominic Roser[b]

[a]*University of Graz, Austria;* [b]*University of Zürich, Switzerland*

Climate change can be interpreted as a unique case of historical injustice involving issues of both intergenerational and global justice. We split the issue into two separate questions. First, how should emission rights be distributed? Second, who should come up for the costs of coping with climate change? We regard the first question as being an issue of pure distributive justice and argue on prioritarian grounds that the developing world should receive higher per capita emission rights than the developed world. This is justified by the fact that the latter already owns a larger share of benefits associated with emission generating activities because of its past record of industrialisation. The second question appears to be an issue of compensatory justice. After defining what we mean by compensation, we show that different kinds of compensatory principles run into problems when used to justify payments by historical emitters of the North to people suffering from climate change in the South. As an alternative, we propose to view payments from wealthy countries for adaptation to climate change in vulnerable countries rather as a measure based on concerns of global distributive justice.

Introduction

Climate change can be seen as a unique case of historical injustice involving a complex intersection of global and intergenerational justice. It also involves a diversity of goods and bads: first, the benefits of engaging in emission generating activities, such as driving cars, growing rice, or engaging in deforestation;[1,2] second, the climate damages which are a side effect of these activities; and third, payments which allow for adaptation measures to these climate damages. Some of the notable features of the climate change issue are: first, in the past it was predominantly the North which created climate change. Second, due to various factors the South is more vulnerable to climate change. Third, much of the climate change that is caused by emissions materialises with a time lag of several decades after the occurrence of those emissions.

The structure of the problem suggests that the just distribution of emission rights on the one hand and a fair way of dealing with climate damages on the other is a rather complex matter. It differs from the standard problem of how to respond to historical injustices[2] where we often face the problem that earlier generations of one community wronged earlier generations of another community and today's generations of both communities are now looking for an adequate way of responding to this historical fact. In the climate change debate, however, we are faced with the situation that earlier generations of one community (the North) *directly* effect something to the detriment of later generations of the other community (the South).[3] It also differs from some other cases of historical justice in that it is not a problem of exclusively one generation/community being wronged and exclusively another generation/community having committed the wrongs and/or wrongfully benefiting. Rather, victims, wrongdoers, and beneficiaries are dispersed (but unequally so) among different communities and generations. It also differs from other instances of historical injustice in that the activity that constitutes the wrong (that is: emitting) is not something that is wrong *per se* such as genocide or slavery, but rather is only wrongful when done excessively.

We propose to disentangle this combination of questions of intergenerational and global justice posed by climate change by splitting it up:

What level of present emissions can be justified on a global scale? This is a question that we do not answer in this article. We simply presuppose that a justifiable global quota can be determined in some way.[4] While considerations of self-interest, international justice and the significance of the relations between humans and the rest of nature may play a role in determining such a quota, we think that the consideration that yields the most stringent constraint on the size of the justifiable quota is intergenerational justice.

How should this global quota be split up among the present population of the planet? This is the question concerned with the mitigation burden (section 2).

Who should pay for the damages that are caused by emissions, in particular assuming that people have not stayed and will not stay within their fair shares as determined in section 2? This is the question concerned with the adaptation burden (section 3).

We simplify strongly by always referring to the contrast between countries of the South and the North.[5] The distinction between these two regions relies on the fact that there is a correlation – partly based on causal interdependencies – between (1) having emitted more in the past, (2) having more benefits grounded in past emissions, (3) being less vulnerable to climate change, and (4) being wealthier in general. Even though we rely on the simplified perfect correlation for the purpose of our discussion, our argument becomes most relevant where the correlation is not perfect (e.g. a poor country with high past emissions or a wealthy country with high vulnerability). The reason is that any argument that ascribes higher duties to some regions than to others will be based on one of the four features from above. If those features all coincide in the North almost any argument will then ascribe higher duties to the North. In such a case, the sole purpose of the argument consists in the determination of the exact *extent* of the duty of the North. If, however, the four features do not coincide in some countries, analyzing *how exactly* the higher duties of some countries are to be *justified* then becomes more relevant.

Another complication that we bracket is the fact that the size of climate damages is not only determined by emissions. Responsibility for exposing people to climate damages lies also with those who contribute, possibly wrongfully, to vulnerabillity (where vulnerability is understood as the degree to which people are susceptible to suffer from and unable to cope with a given level of climate change). A fuller treatment of compensatory justice in climate change would have to include those who enhance vulnerability as possibly standing under a duty to pay and, where contributing to one's own vulnerability is at stake, as reducing their right to receive payments. Accounting for vulnerability creation, however, is a difficult matter: What level of enhancing vulnerability (or, respectively: what level of failing to engage in measures which decrease vulnerability) are sufficiently high so as to generate a compensatory duty? What kind of activities count as vulnerability creation – does any policy, for example, which limits economic growth qualify? We consider these intricate issues to be problems for another day and focus this text on emissions as the salient cause to climate damages.

Prioritarian distribution of emission rights

In this section we will ask how emission rights should be split up among the present-day global population. We assume that some justifiable global quota has been determined which now must be dealt out to the countries on this planet. We are interested in a fair *initial* allocation of emission rights which may then be changed by subsequent trade.

Determining a fair distribution of emission rights is of high relevance in current climate policy. If the international community decides to cap total emissions then the emissions allowed under this cap *have* to be distributed in some way or other. As the right to emit was unlimited before the cap turned it into a scarce good, there is no pre-existing default distribution of this asset (worth billions of dollars) on which one could fall back in case no distribution was agreed upon. In the Kyoto Protocol a cap was agreed on only for the industrialised countries, with the US ultimately not ratifying the agreement. In general, though, even with Kyoto enacted, the industrialised countries still have higher per capita emissions than the developing countries, which have no limits on emissions. The political philosopher interested in the pattern according to which emissions were dealt out to industrialised nations under the Kyoto Protocol must be disappointed, however. The distribution was not based on the application of any clear-cut and explicit criterion of distributive justice but rather reflects political negotiation[6] in that a strong element of grandfathering[7] is discernible.[8]

The good to be distributed and the standard to be applied

We will judge the initial allocation of tradable emission rights according to prioritarian standards and we must be careful to state clearly what exactly *the good* is to which we apply these standards.[9] We will often use a rough shorthand and simply speak of distributing emissions while obviously what is up for distribution are tradable emission *rights* and not emissions themselves. The goods to which prioritarian standards are applied are, however, the *benefits* that the use of emission rights makes possible and not the emission rights themselves. Emission rights are beneficial because they allow for what we call emission-generating activities such as producing industrial commodities, subsistence farming, or flying to go on vacations.[10] So, what the shorthand of 'distributing emissions' ultimately amounts to is distributing (*by* distributing emission rights) the benefits of engaging in emission-generating activities. Or, *very* roughly but more intuitively, we could say that *by* distributing emission rights we are distributing economic progress – 'very roughly', because, first, economic progress of course does not capture everything that is beneficial about emission-generating activities (sometimes economic progress is not even itself something beneficial), and, second, because there is no one-to-one relationship between emissions and economic progress as some draw much more economic output from the same amount of emissions than others.

We will judge the distribution of goods according to the priority view. This view can be seen as aiming at taking into account the intuitions behind egalitarianism and sufficientarianism in the most plausible way.[11] It is the view that benefiting people matters regardless of how much others have and that we should give greater weight to benefits for people who are badly off than to benefits for people who are well off.

There are two options for applying the priority view to a single good. This can be called a problem of 'local justice',[12] that is, a problem of the just distribution of a certain slice (in our case: emission rights or adaptation costs) of the whole universe of goods. According to the first option the fair distribution of the good is determined as though the distribution of other goods was completely faded out from our view. According to the second option the currently existing unequal background distribution of other goods is taken as given and the fair distribution of the specific good in question is determined in light of it.

Both options are problematic. The largest problem of the first option is that if one is concerned with justice it then seems unnatural to be concerned with the just distribution of some one specific good in abstraction from the highly unequal background distribution of other goods. The problem with the second option is that it would yield a very simple answer: give all the emission rights to the South. However, it seems less than reasonable to aim at bringing the *overall* distribution of goods closer to the ideal by adjusting the distribution of only *one* particular good.

One might want to respond to these problems by denying that we can meaningfully ask how a certain single resource should be distributed; instead, questions of distributive justice can only meaningfully be raised concerning a whole bundle of goods such as, say, natural resources or primary goods (or even: only about the design of institutions affecting the distribution of those goods). However, whether we like it or not, political reality currently hands us such problems of fair distribution of certain specific goods in our non-ideal world. Currently, it is not an issue of much political relevance of how to globally redistribute, say, natural resources or *all* goods in general but the determination of the distribution of the newly created emission rights in contrast is an issue which *cannot* be escaped.

We will rely on the first option when discussing the just distribution of emission rights, i.e. we will in general abstract from the background distribution. The importance of relying on the first option is diminished by the fact that the second option only strengthens, and in no way weakens, the general conclusion we draw, which is that the North should shoulder a larger burden than it does today.

Taking historical emissions into account

We want to argue that, based on prioritarian premises, the historical inequality in emissions gives us reason to tilt the present allocation of emission rights in favour of the South in the sense that its per capita emission rights should be higher than in the North. The difference in historical emissions between the North and the South is far from negligible. Developed countries were responsible for more than three times as many emissions between 1850 and 2002 than developing countries[13] while the latter host a much larger part of humanity. In the policy arena a counterbalance to the historical inequality in emissions was most prominently discussed under the heading of the 'Brazilian Proposal' (1997).[14] The Brazilian Proposal received little support. More generally, there is quite some resistance to counterbalancing past emissions. Frequently heard objections include the following three points:

The first objection states that currently living people should not be made responsible for the acts of their ancestors and should not be put at a disadvantage simply because the people inhabiting their country before them emitted too much.

The second objection states that one can only be blamed for a certain act if one knows – or is liable to know – of the harmful effects of the act, and it is debatable whether knowledge of the harmful effect of emissions was sufficiently widespread until recently.

The third objection points to the relevance of the non-identity problem; no one can claim to be worse off or better off than she would be had another climate policy been pursued in the sufficiently distant past.

Note that each of the objections attacks emissions caused up to different dates of the past. The first concerns emissions by people who are now dead; the second, emissions, say, before the first IPCC report in 1990;[15] and the third emissions (and policies influencing emissions) so early as to be a determining factor of the number and identity of people living today.

There are, however, two ways of taking (part of) past emissions into account that are not susceptible to the three objections. The first way turns on what we consider the relevant units of concern and, in particular, what temporal extension they have. If as prioritarians we do not demand a just distribution of emission benefits at each point in time but rather over the whole lifespan of individuals[16] then one part of past emissions enters very naturally into the fair deal concerning the present distribution of emission rights; namely, the emissions that occurred during the life of the presently living. The simple idea is that people of the North already enjoyed much benefits associated with emissions during their lifetime and therefore a larger part of the remaining benefits should go to people in the South, which gives them the opportunity to 'catch up'.

The first and third objections obviously do not speak against this way of taking past emissions into account. The second objection has no bite either: the above argument does not justify higher emission rights for the South as compensation for past wrongdoing of the North but rather by the idea of realising a just distribution of emission benefits over the lifetime of individuals. If an individual of the North already has used up his share, it does not matter whether he did so knowingly and wrongfully or not.[17]

The second justifiable way of taking past emissions into account for the determination of the presently fair shares relies on the fact that we do not want to achieve a just distribution of *emissions* but rather of *benefits of emissions*. And since the industrialisation of the ancestors of the people currently living in the North yields benefits up to today and much more so for people of the North than the South, this has to be taken into account even if the emissions were caused by people who are now dead.

The first two objections obviously do not speak against this way of taking past emissions into account. The third objection has no bite either: we do not claim that people of the South are worse off than they would have been without emissions in the distant past and neither do we claim that people of the North benefit from industrialisation in the distant past in the sense of being better off than they would have been had there been no industrialisation. They only benefit in the sense that since their conception they have enjoyed being brought up in an industrialised world while others cannot enjoy such circumstances. If there is at present more 'economic progress to be given away' (that is: emission rights to be distributed which allow for the emissions that accompany economic progress), and if we want to hand out shares of economic progress – taken here as the main benefit associated with emissions – according to prioritarian standards then people of the South should get a disproportionate share of emission rights because people of the North have already received a large part of their share by inheritance from their ancestors.

Against this second way of taking the past into account it might also be objected that it is questionable that the receipt of benefits generates any obligations at all, in particular if the benefits were 'imposed' rather than voluntarily accepted, as is the case with being born into an industrialised world. The answer to this worry is that we do *not* rely on the premise that inheriting emission benefits generates obligations to give something to others *in turn*. The argument only presupposes that those who were born with a large 'slice of the pie' have a smaller claim when it comes to splitting up the rest of the pie.

So, our conclusion is that based on the unequal benefits enjoyed by people in the North and the South certain parts of past emissions should be taken into account for the purpose of distributing emissions rights today.[18] Not all inequality in historical emissions should be taken into account, however; those emissions that belonged to people who are now dead and which yield no benefits for the currently living should be written off.

We can now look at the general reason why the three objections do not pose any problem for our two ways of taking past emissions into account. All three objections rely on the idea that lower than equal shares for the North must be grounded in the idea of compensation. The third objection denies that past emissions can be seen as harmful (or beneficial) and, so, if there is no harming (or benefiting), then no compensation is appropriate. The second objection claims that even if past emissions could be seen as harmful, they still cannot be seen as wrongful; as such, no compensation is owed. The first objection goes further in stating that even if past emissions were both harmful and wrongful, still, compensation is not owed, the reason being that compensation is something that the wrongdoer himself must pay and not his descendants.

Even if the objections were based on sound premises when applied to other positions, they have no bite here since our two ways of taking past emissions into account do not rely on the idea of compensation but consider the distribution of emission rights as a problem of pure distributive justice without any reference to harm or wrong.[19] The idea is simply to distribute the benefits associated with emission-generating activities according to the priority view among the presently living – and because people in the North start with a higher level of such benefits people of the South have priority when it comes to deal out the presently available emission rights.[20] This is not to say that the three objections are not important. They are important when it comes to the different question of fairness in adaptation (section 3).

A numerical illustration

To make the points of this chapter more comprehensible we will present the basic idea in a simple numerical illustration. Assume that we have two islands called ‘North’ and ‘South’. Both islands consist of three persons: ‘Old’, ‘Middle’, and ‘Young’. On both islands, Young is born after the death of Old. We have two time-periods: period I and II.

The question is: presupposing the emissions of period I, how should emission rights be distributed in period II among the North and the South? We assume that each island is able and willing to fairly distribute its emission rights internally. An important assumption is that two units of emissions in the North in period I create two units of benefit for the North in period I, and one unit of benefit for the North in period II (assume for example that the two units of emission were used in period I for (i) an airplane flight into vacation and (ii) the building of a school: the airplane flight is beneficial only at the time of the emission while the school building yields a benefit in both periods). The same applies to the South. We assume that the South emitted eight units in period I and the North emitted 12 units in period I.

Assume that there are 10 units of emissions to be distributed in period II. How many should the North get and how many should the South get accord-

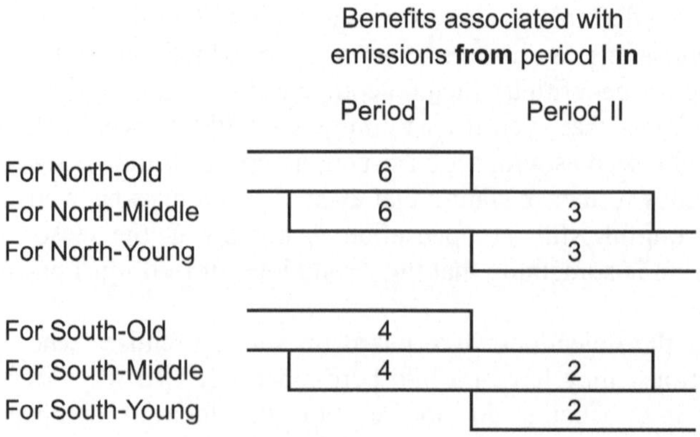

Figure 1.

ing to our reasoning? People in the North alive in period II already own 12 emission benefits. Six of those 12 benefits are those that North-Middle enjoyed in period I (our first way of taking the past into account) and the other six benefits are those that North-Middle and North-Young enjoy in period II as a result of the Northern emissions in period I (our second way of taking the past into account). People in the South alive in period II in contrast only own eight emission benefits (4+2 from South-Middle and 2 from South-Young).

So, our argument says that of the 10 emission benefits to be distributed, the North should get three (together with its 12 benefits this sums up to 15) and the South should get seven (together with its eight benefits this sums up to 15 as well). Given that these emission rights are fairly distributed internally within each island,[21] distributive justice among the people alive in period II is created in such a way. Not all past emissions have been taken into account: The inequality of emissions benefits between North-Old and South-Old in period I will forever remain without relevance.

What would this mean in practice for a post-Kyoto treaty? Enacting the fair solution demands allocating a share of emissions to each country that is either above or below the equal-per-capita share depending on whether the country has a lot or few benefits from past emissions. Countries, then, have to ensure that they internally distribute the mitigation burden fairly, which amounts to disproportionately burdening those citizens who already own many emission benefits. The most accurate way of approximating this is by each citizen's wealth, we submit.

At the country level, however, benefits from past emissions can not only be approximated by the country's wealth but also by a measure which adds up cumulative past emissions of a given country but discounts those emissions according to how far in the past they lie. The idea of such discounting is that emissions closer to the present yield more benefits for the presently living. Relying on such a measure as an approximation for benefits from past emissions instead of relying on wealth as an approximation amounts to either assuming that the current inhabitants of each country should be made responsible for how many benefits are drawn from a given amount of emissions in the past or else to make the simplifying assumption that everyone draws the same amount of benefits from a given amount of emissions. It also leaves open whether wealth is a good specification of what constitutes benefits from emission-generating activities.

Note that these ways of taking past emissions into account for the specification of the distribution of the mitigation burden are similar to but distinct from the Brazilian Proposal. The latter is the most prominent suggestion for taking past emissions into account. However, in its calculations it relied on the cumulative effect of emissions since 1840 on global average surface temperature, that is, it discounted past emissions not according to the benefits they yield today but according to how much damage they do.

Who must pay for climate damages?

The last section discussed a fair deal concerning emissions as the *cause* of climate change and this section discusses a fair deal concerning climate change as the *effect* of these emissions, both with a special eye towards the relevance of the past. The costs of climate change have two aspects: first, the climate damages themselves, and second – since the impact of emissions not only depends on the level of climate change produced by them, but also in the human reaction to this change – the adaptation costs necessary to minimise or at least decrease climate damages. In this section our ultimate concern is justice concerning all costs – i.e. the adaptation costs *plus* the damages that remain even after optimal adaptation. But: since the damages themselves cannot be transferred from one person to another, justice concerning the whole costs of climate change will have to be reached by taking only the *one* aspect of who is responsible for adaptation costs as a variable under control of policy.

The issue of injustice concerning climate damages arises on two levels. First, the South will be hit harder by climate change. This is so independently of how much climate change occurs and who is causally responsible for it. It is likewise so even if only non-anthropogenic climate change occurred or if everybody in the past had stuck to their fair share of emissions. The most important reasons for the higher vulnerability of the South are geographical factors (e.g. the higher temperature independently of climate change), the higher reliance on agriculture and the lower adaptive capacities. Second, and independently of the first point, it is the case that people have exceeded and predictably will exceed their fair shares as determined in the last section. In any realistic scenario the North will have exceeded its share, and will have done so more than the South. In any case, we will presuppose that this is so in this section.

How should climate damages, and in particular the fact that the South will be particularly vulnerable to climate change while at the same time being causally less responsible for it, be dealt with from the point of view of justice? One answer that quickly comes to mind is that the South is owed compensation for its suffering and that the North as the main culprit for climate change should provide sufficient measures of compensation. This section will point out the problems of this view and suggests instead that we should view climate damages primarily as a reason for redistribution due to undeserved benefits and harms rather than compensation.

Distributive and compensatory justice

To argue for this conclusion we will first discuss compensation (in three versions) and then redistribution. One way to make the distinction between the basic idea of redistribution and compensation starts with the premise that there is some *baseline distribution* of goods that is just which is determined on the one hand by a certain criterion (such as the priority view, egalitarianism, or sufficientarianism or possibly simply the status quo distribution) and on the other hand by permissible changes to the distribution (as determined by the criterion) which someone experiences as a result of his own *responsible (and non-wrongful) choices*. Deviations from this baseline then call for two different kinds of reactions. In case the reaction the deviation calls for is *based on the wrongfulness* of what occurred, we are operating in the realm of *compensatory justice*. In case the reaction the deviation calls for is based on the idea of *evening out undeserved* benefits or harms (which are due to for example luck or harmful but non-wrongful actions), we are operating in the realm of *distributive justice*.

The basic idea is to ask: which duties to pay for adaptation to climate change rely for their justification on the wrongfulness of what was done, i.e. which duties can be traced back to the compensatory rationale? Any duties that cannot be so traced back will fall into the category of the redistributive rationale and will be regarded as grounded in the objective of levelling off undeserved benefits and harms. Whether payments for adaptation costs are justified on the basis of the compensatory or redistributive rationale will also help to determine the size of such payments.

Two remarks are appropriate. First, not everybody regards evening out undeserved benefits and harms through redistribution as a moral imperative; and some, namely sufficientarians, regard it as an imperative only up to the point where everybody has ‘enough’. We will assume that undeserved benefits and harms should be evened out according to prioritarian standards, but we believe that the basic point of distinguishing compensatory and redistributive rationales remains interesting also for theorists who do not see undeserved benefits and harms as giving weighty reasons for redistribution.

Second, note that we are operating with such a narrow notion of compensation that it is not completely in line with the way the terminology is used in other contexts where the notion of compensation is also used for payments which are due to non-wrongful harm-doing. All we argue for is that it is an interesting question in the intergenerational context of climate change to separate payments based on wrongfulness from those not based on wrongfulness and, further, that the latter can be seen as based on other (namely, redistributive) concerns than the former.

We will distinguish three versions of compensatory payments depending on who has the duty to come up with them.[22] The most natural duty bearer for compensatory payments is the emitter of wrongful emissions himself: the *Emitter Pays Principle* (EmPP). A second version identifies the beneficiary of wrongful emissions as responsible for providing compensation: the *Beneficiary Pays Principle* (BePP). A third version ascribes the duty to pay compensation to the wrongdoing community: the *Community Pays Principle*

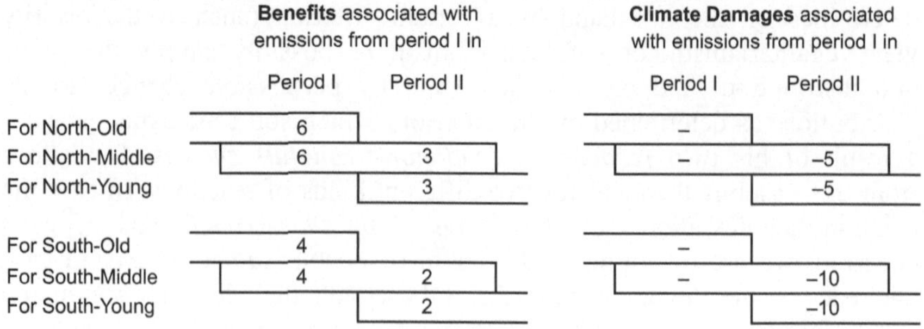

Figure 2.

(CoPP). In discussing these three principles, we will have to answer two questions for each principle: How plausible is it as a principle of compensatory justice in general? And: what kind of compensatory measures can it justify in the climate change context?

In order to illustrate more easily why compensatory measures are difficult to justify we will make use of the numerical example from the last section again. For this section, we add the assumption that the emissions from period I cause climate damages in period II, say five for people in the North and 10 for people in the South (Figure 2).

Compensatory justice and climate damages

There are six basic problems for justifying compensatory payments in the context of climate damages:

Potential payers might be dead.[23]
Potential payers might not have exceeded their fair shares.
Potential payers might have been (blamelessly) ignorant.
Potential recipients might (due to the non-identity problem) only be said to be harmed according to a threshold conception of harm.[24]
Potential payers might (due to the non-identity problem) not be said to have benefited.
Potential recipients might not be wrongfully harmed because climate change may also have non-anthropogenic sources.

First let us look at the principle that demands that the emitter must pay compensation for his wrongful emissions to those who are wronged (EmPP). There is not much doubt that in general (that is, disregarding whether it can usefully be applied to the climate change problem) the idea of such compensation is very well supported by our moral intuitions.[25] This is in contrast to BePP and CoPP where the principle itself is in need of some supporting arguments. The only dispute in the case of EmPP is whether it can justify compensatory payments for the specific case of climate damages or not.

If EmPP is put to the service of justifying compensatory payments one has to identify wrongful emitters and wrongfully harmed persons. Someone emits wrongfully if (1) he exceeded his fair share and (2) he knew or was liable to know about the harmfulness of his emissions. Someone is wrongfully harmed by emissions if he either is worse off due to wrongful emissions than he would otherwise have been or falls below the specified threshold of harm due to the wrongful emissions (or both).[26] Let us use the numerical example to look at what duties to pay compensation and what rights to receive compensation the EmPP can and cannot justify in period II:

North-Old and South-Old cannot have a duty to pay compensation because they are dead.

South-Middle (as well as South-Old) did not exceed its fair share and so must not pay.

North-Middle (as well as the other emitters from period I) might not have been aware, and might neither have been liable to be aware, of the problematic nature of its emissions and thus it can be excused by ignorance of wrongdoing.

North-Young and South-Young can only claim to be wronged – and claim with it a right to compensation – if they fall below the sufficientarian threshold of the threshold understanding of harm. They cannot be said to be harmed simply because climate quality is worse than it would be had there been less emissions in period I.

So, if one could legitimately be excused by ignorance in period I, then EmPP cannot identify *any* wrongful emitter at all to pay compensation payments. If not, it can still only ascribe compensatory duties to North-Middle (even though it is only one of four agents causally responsible for climate change in period II). EmPP also has some trouble in identifying wronged persons: In contrast to South-Middle (and North-Middle), South-Young (and North-Young) can only be said to be wronged – and thus be the rightful recipient of compensatory payments – if they fall below the sufficientarian threshold.

Of course, some assumptions that we made in the numerical model might be loosened and then some duty bearers or right bearers might be identified. First, period I could be defined as being at a point of time when the excuse of ignorance has no more force. Second, damages could be modelled as starting to materialise immediately after the emissions were produced and not only in the next period. Third, the South might also exceed its fair share. Fourth, one might doubt the relevance of the non-identity problem. Our purpose in making these strict assumptions, though, was to highlight all the problems that potentially come up when one makes an attempt at justifying compensatory payments based on EmPP.

Let us turn to the principle that demands that those who have *benefited* from wrongful emissions must pay compensation (BePP). First we have to ask whether it is a legitimate principle in general, that is, apart from the climate change question, to accrue benefits from a wrong imply accepting the duty of compensation. Applied to the issue of climate damages the question is the following: why should people who have committed no wrongful emissions but have only benefited (either from emission-generating activities or from climate change itself) have to pay compensation? Note that the people who received benefits from past emission-generating activities did not ask for these benefits; they were imposed on them, so to speak.

There is no completely obvious answer to the question of whether benefiting from wrongdoing creates a duty of compensation. The difficulty of judging this issue is based on two reasons. First, if one was benefited by a wrong this benefit is most definitely not *deserved*. It is deserved as little as any other benefit one receives by luck (if anything, it is deserved even less).[27] And based on considerations of distributive justice one can see *any* undeserved benefit (and harm) as calling for redistribution regardless of whether one received this benefit due to a wrongful action or brute luck. But what we are asking in discussing the BePP is whether the reception of benefits from a wrong implies a duty which for its justification presupposes the wrongness of the action and not whether it creates a duty of redistribution. The second reason why it is difficult to judge the BePP as a principle of compensatory justice is that in our daily lives we are not used to thinking about cases where the people who commit the wrong are not the ones who benefit from it.[28]

Still, the BePP has to be judged, even if it is difficult. On the one hand, there are clear examples where we do not judge benefiting from an injustice as calling for compensation. Note for example that everybody who uses an x-ray profits from how this technology was refined using data from Hiroshima.[29] On the other hand, there are intuitions to the contrary. Gosseries, for example, interprets benefiting from an action without paying the associated costs in terms of free-riding.[30] Present-day inhabitants of the North can be seen as transgenerational free-riders because they *currently* benefit from *past* emissions that impose costs on people *currently* living in the South. Importantly, Gosseries distinguishes two interpretations of the way in which free-riding can be seen as objectionable. The first interpretation relies on considerations of distributive justice and this is not the relevant case for the BePP. It is the idea sketched a few lines above that, of course, *any* undeserved benefits and harms can be seen as calling for redistribution – and benefits and harms due to injustice committed by others are simply *one* instance of undeserved benefits and harms. But if one relies on this interpretation it is difficult to see what is specific about benefiting from a wrongful action in contrast to benefiting from some other kind of action or event for which one is not responsible. All that one could possibly argue is that, intuitively, there seem to be weightier reasons to even out undeserved deviations from a just baseline that are due to a wrong than to even out undeserved deviations that are due to more general causes. The second interpretation of why free-riding is objectionable relies on what Gosseries calls 'interactive justice', which is similar to our conception of compensatory justice. It is the relevant case for making use of BePP to legitimise compensatory payments. This second way gains some plausibility if one regards benefiting from an action or a scheme or a policy as in some way involving an action, namely the action of willingly *accepting* being benefited by it. Accepting being benefited by wrongful emissions can possibly be seen as transferring (some of) the wrongdoer's duty of compensation to the beneficiary. Another basis for the position that benefiting from wrongdoing calls for compensation is proposed by Butt. He claims that condemnation of injustice implies not being willing to benefit from it while others suffer from it: 'My claim is that taking our nature as moral agents seriously requires not only that we be willing not to commit acts of injustice ourselves, but that we hold a genuine aversion to injustice and its lasting effects. We make a conceptual error if we condemn a given action as unjust, but are not willing to reverse or mitigate its effects on the grounds that it has benefited us.'[31]

Even though we are sceptical of the position that benefiting from wrongful actions not only gives rise to duties of redistribution but also to duties of compensation, we will not commit ourselves to a definite answer. Rather, we will note that *even if* the BePP could be defended as a principle in general, there is still something very questionable about applying it to climate damages. Due to the non-identity problem, North-Young and South-Young (who constitute the people who did not emit in Period I thereby causing climate damages in Period II) cannot be said to have benefited at all. Without past emissions they would not be worse off but rather not exist at all (this is problem e. from the above list). And even if the non-identity problem were irrelevant or could be shown to be of little practical relevance, there still remains an obstacle: if *voluntary acceptance* of benefits should prove to be a condition of their giving rise to compensatory duties, one would have to address the difficult issue of whether abstaining from emigrating from an industrialised country (or rejecting the benefits of living there in some other way) can really count as willingly accepting these benefits. Thus, although BePP seemingly has a larger base of possible duty bearers than the EmPP – not only the emitters themselves but anybody who benefited from the wrongful emissions – it is no more successful in identifying duty bearers than EmPP.

So, both EmPP and the more questionable BePP can only justify a small amount of compensatory measures or none at all. Let us now turn to the principle that demands that present-day members of a community must pay for the wrongs that past members of the community committed (CoPP). We will not commit ourselves to a certain view as to what the adequate specification of the community would be in the context of climate change but we will use countries or other communities with a legal form as the most suggestive examples.

Note that we in no way presuppose the collective *moral* responsibility of today's people living in the North for the emissions of their ancestors in the sense that the currently living would be able to incur blame or guilt for past wrongful emissions. We want to place our arguments firmly on normative individualist grounds. There are sound arguments, however, even on these grounds, to the effect that community membership can, in principle, be a reason to ascribe duties to presently living members of a transgenerational community to provide compensation for the wrongs committed by earlier members.[32]

People can value their membership in certain groups. Accordingly, they will be willing to accept standing under obligations of preserving the group to which they belong. People can have valid reasons for understanding themselves in such a way. First, the group to which they belong might exhibit a general value by being, say, a just or tolerant community. All people have reason to value belonging to such a community insofar as living in, say, a just society is – individually and collectively – of intrinsic value. The groups typically are transgenerational in character. If justice requires, inter alia, providing measures of restitution and compensation for wrongful harm-doing such transgenerational communities will be just, inter alia, by providing compensation to presently living victims of injustices that earlier members of the community committed. Second, people will value their membership in such groups for a further reason: the group might exhibit particular features that are highly relevant for the well-being of its members since they manifest particular ways of communal life. Due to these features of their group's culture people have access to particular options that are highly valuable to them given who they are: the particular culture of their group will often have shaped their social identity in decisive ways.

The two types of reasons for holding membership in one's community or polity to be valuable are interrelated: the intrinsic value of our being a member of a society will depend in part on the ways in which we relate to its particular features, yet we clearly do not attribute intrinsic value to just any society. Rather, for a society to have intrinsic value it will have to fulfil certain minimal requirements concerning its internal and external relations. What these minimal conditions amount to will depend on what universal and particularly weighty reasons for action people can be said to have. It seems plausible to suggest that people ought to value their membership in a society on the condition that their society is just to a reasonable degree. Thus, for them to be able to attribute intrinsic value to their membership, they will have to contribute to the creation and strengthening of the institutions that are necessary for their society fulfilling its obligations of justice. Arguably, among these obligations are those to provide measures of compensation for wrongs that were committed publicly (or even in the name of the community) by its members in the past.

So, given that the intrinsic value of communities is only present under certain conditions, one has reason to see to it that these conditions are fulfilled. And if one of those conditions is that present-day victims of historical injustice are compensated, one has reason based on valuing the community to do so. One's reasons can be partly understood to reflect the idea of a natural duty to justice: we all have the duty to support the realisation of justice and thus, if membership in a community, and the creation of adequate institutions in this community, and the support of the specific goal of compensation payments to victims of historical injustice are necessary prerequisites for justice becoming a reality, then one has a duty to work towards these goals. This is so not as a matter of personal preference of identifying with one's community but reflects categorical reasons: carrying out the natural duty of justice serves a good, the protection of which is thought to be of such importance that people are thought to have categorical reasons for doing so. At the same time, membership in the community is valued in part due to its specific features (its history and unique communal ways of life). When members of such communities fulfil their duties of justice, this will reflect their *wanting* to uphold a particular *self-understanding*, namely, that of being a participating member of their community. For they understand that they can wish to uphold the particular communal way of life of their society (based, in part, on its particular features) only if their society is sufficiently just. This, arguably, requires the provision of restitution and compensation for wrongs that were committed publicly (or even in the name of the community) by its members in the past.

So, the bottom line is that there are ways in which liberals relying on normative individualism can justify why present-day members of countries should accept the duty to make compensatory payments for wrongful emissions of earlier members of the country as demanded by CoPP. Thus, the scope of possible duty-bearers is extended so as to include North-Young and North-Middle paying for the wrong done by the emissions of North-Old. They do this as members of the community of the North.

However, compensatory payments along the lines of CoPP still only cover *wrongful* emissions. And thus, emissions made under ignorance about their harmful nature, and emissions that did not exceed the fair share, as well as non-anthropogenic causes of climate change all remain uncovered. Actually, reliance on CoPP can only complement EmPP and BePP in the sense that it escapes problem a. of the above list of problems (that is, potential polluters might be dead) with the other problems remaining unaffected.

Redistribution as a response to climate damages

Compensation payments for climate damages are difficult to justify for the reasons offered above. And, more importantly, insofar as such arguments (for EmPP, BePP, or CoPP) actually succeed in justifying *some* compensatory measures, they only justify them for *part* of those who cause or suffer from climate change.

Still, the fact that the South has to carry such a large share of climate damages seems to be a situation that cries out for *some* kind of response. And of course, compensation (in the narrow sense of wrongdoers paying something to the wronged persons on the grounds of the injustice committed) is not the only kind of possible response. Rather, given that many effects of climate change can be seen as undeserved harms – and harms which go along with undeserved benefits for other persons – levelling off such effects *on the basis of a concern for distributive justice* is an equally plausible response. In assuming that the priority view is the correct kind of principle for distributing emission rights we assumed that principles of distributive justice do apply at the global level.[33] And consequently, we believe that principles of distributive justice can also be applied (at least to some degree) to the distribution of duties to pay for adaptation measures. Of course, to common moral intuition, demands of compensatory justice seem to have a stronger force than demands based simply on evening out undeserved benefits or harms, particularly at the global level.[34] We do not necessarily want to question that view. However, in the context of climate damages, compensation payments are only justifiable for such a small part of the problem that it is appropriate to direct attention primarily to the redistributive demands. The focus must be turned to sharing undeserved benefits and harms equitably rather than focusing on compensating wronged persons in view of the limited applicability of the latter enterprise.

In practice, a prioritarian redistributive scheme concerned with climate damages amounts to those who are lucky in terms of not being affected much by climate change assisting those who are unlucky in terms of being affected heavily. They owe this assistance *independently* of who caused climate change. Thus according to the redistributive approach to climate damages, even if, contrary to actual fact, it were historically the South that predominantly had created the climate problem, it would still be those vulnerable to a lesser extent who should support adaptive measures in those countries where people were more vulnerable.[35] Another way to install a prioritarian redistributive scheme concerned with climate damages would not only aim at a just pattern concerning this one specific good called 'climate damages' but rather take into account the whole background distribution of other goods.[36] This means making the wealthy assist those who are vulnerable to climate change, which would not make that much of a difference because wealth and low vulnerability are correlated to quite some degree.

In the real world this would mean that countries have to be ranked according to their vulnerability to climate change and those that are highly vulnerable get privileged access to the resources available in a global adaptation fund. The above argument suggests that such a fund would have to be paid for either by those who exhibit low vulnerability or by the wealthy. To some limited extent, it could also be financed by those who, despite all the problems mentioned in section *Compensatory justice and climate damages*, stand under duties to provide measures of compensation. Within countries, raising the money for such a global adaptation fund through progressive taxation could serve as an approximation for making the less vulnerable pay. At the intra-national level, aiming at additional redistribution from the hardly vulnerable to the highly vulnerable might take many different forms, such as government subsidies for adaptation measures in poor communities.

Conclusion

This chapter discussed a fair way of allocating the mitigation and adaptation costs associated with climate change, in particular in the light of the benefits and damages brought forth by past emissions. It presupposed a prioritarian theory of distributive justice and generally proceeded by abstracting from the background inequality existing in the real world. It first discussed mitigation and concluded that the South should get higher per capita emission rights than the North because it has less benefits associated with past emissions to start with. It then discussed who should pay for adaptation costs and argued that it is difficult to frame the duty of the North to those who are highly vulnerable as a duty of compensation; it should primarily be seen as a duty grounded in concerns of distributive justice.

Even though we separated the issues of mitigation and adaptation for analytical purposes, there might be ample reason to link the two issues, in particular when it comes to practical policy-making. In a 'local justice approach' there is no general guideline on which goods to discuss jointly and which goods to discuss separately, and it is of course not at all far-fetched to discuss the two climate change-related goods of emission rights and climate damages in conjunction, particularly given that we have shown that both primarily pose issues of distributive justice.[37] By treating mitigation and adaptation jointly, one could, for example, argue for assisting those with above average vulnerability through the specific 'currency' of emission rights. In linking adaptation and mitigation one could also take note of interdependencies, such as the need for economic progress (and thus the need for emission rights) in poor countries in order to diminish vulnerability (and thus adaptation costs). It is also desirable to link the discussion up more with the background distribution of other goods, which would in general strengthen the duties of the North even more and point to the need for linking development and climate policies, but would in addition also highlight the duties of wealthy individuals within poor countries.

Regardless of which goods are treated jointly both in the policy arena and for purposes of analytical discussion, the message stays the same that almost any argument on climate justice ascribes larger shortcomings to the North than the South in comparison with the ideally just state of affairs. Since there is not much to dispute concerning this general conclusion, the interest of any argument must lie in the *rationale* it gives for this conclusion. It has been the goal of this article to give a plausible justification for this widely accepted claim, in particular by stressing how past emission-generating activities yield unequal benefits and harms for the presently living – an inequality which generally calls for the application of distributive justice rather than compensatory justice.

Acknowledgements

We wish to thank Keith Bustos, Simon Caney, Axel Gosseries, Sarah Kenehan, Pranay Sanklecha and participants at the Manchester Political Theory Workshops for their helpful comments and criticisms.

Notes

1. For simplicity's sake, we refer also to deforestation and other ways of decreasing sinks as emission generating activities. An umbrella term which would more precisely capture both activities which add emissions to the atmosphere and activities which diminish the removal of emissions from the atmosphere would for example be 'emission concentration enhancing activities'.
2. By emissions we always refer to greenhouse gas emissions. In a more complete treatment one would not only cite greenhouse gas emissions as responsible for exposing people to climate damages, but also include the removal of sinks which absorb emissions (in particular deforestation) as well as activities which increase the vulnerability of people to a changed climate.
3. Cf. Gosseries (2004, p. 37). On the topic of historical injustice in general see Meyer (2004, 2005.)
4. One implication of this is that it makes one of the answers to historical injustice more difficult to sustain, namely the answer which argues that one should compensate descendants of wronged persons because those descendants were wronged in that their parents did not receive the appropriate compensation and that as a result of this lack of payments the descendants are worse off than they would be if the compensation to their parents had been paid (after their conception), see Sher (2005) and Meyer (2008, sec. 5.1)
5. For plausible attempts at answering this question, see e.g. Caney (2006b) or Page (2006).
6. When we speak of the North and the South we always implicitly either take those terms as an abbreviation for an individual of the North or the South or else we assume a two-stage process where in a first stage climate justice between the countries of the North and the South is determined after which each country will

then, in a second stage, internally distribute its mitigation and adaptation burdens fairly to individuals.

7. See Depledge (2002, p. 37).
8. Grandfathering refers to the scheme that grants high current emission rights to those with high past emissions. Because this scheme plays an important role in policy debates, it is important to deal with this proposal: see Meyer and Roser (2006, pp. 229ff.) If polluters are actually *entitled* to (a certain proportion of) the emissions level they have historically acquired, then there would be no scope for distributing emissions according to some pattern such as the priority view.
9. See Bartsch and Müller (2000, p. 227).
10. Some people speak of giving everyone a share of the *atmosphere* (Friends of the Earth 2006) or a share of the *climate* (Christian Aid 1999). This is less than precise since the issue is not more or less atmosphere or climate. Others speak of fairly distributing the *absorptive capacity of the atmosphere* (Neumayer 2000). This is not the best description of the good in question either because what is limited is not really the *capacity* of the atmosphere to *absorb greenhouse gases* but rather the willingness of humans to put up with the climate quality that ensues from high concentrations of greenhouse gases in the atmosphere.
11. Besides this, emissions can also be beneficial in a different way, namely through the climate change they cause: selected people (e.g. some farmers in Northern latitudes) profit from a warming world.
12. For a more extensive discussion see e.g. Meyer and Roser (2006), Casal (2007) and Holtug and Lippert-Rasmussen (2007).
13. See Gosseries' remark on this issue in Gosseries (2007) as well as similar remarks in Gosseries (2004). He relies on Elster (1992).
14. See Baumert *et al.* (2005, p.32)
15. For an overview see La Rovere *et al.* (2002)
16. Gosseries (2004) lists some salient dates which might serve as an alternative to 1990.
17. According to Holtug and Lippert-Rasmussen (2007, p. 10) most egalitarians find this latter option more plausible.
18. This approximate conclusion has to be qualified somewhat as a matter of transitory justice (cf. Gosseries 2007): *if* people were legitimately ignorant about the problematic nature of their emissions then *some* legitimate expectations accompany the ownership of their emission benefits.
19. Caney (2006a) argues that evening out inequalities in emissions over time relies on a collectivist framework. Note that by focusing on the *benefits* of past emissions enjoyed by the *presently living*, we can eschew this problem.
20. Note also that there is something peculiar about seeing mitigation as a kind of compensation for not mitigating: it can only be applied in the sense of seeing present mitigation as compensation for past lack of mitigation, but of course not in the synchronic fashion of seeing present mitigation as compensation for a lack of present mitigation. This is in contrast to paying for adaptation costs, which can be seen as compensation for a lack of present mitigation.
21. If the background distribution were taken into account (i.e. the second option) when determining the just distribution of emission rights according to prioritarian standards, we would be faced with a more complex picture but which most plausibly still ascribes much higher emission rights to the South. First, we would additionally have to take into account which countries can draw many benefits from emission rights, based on factors such as geographical circumstances and the current living standards. Second, the interaction between emission rights and the background

distribution would also have to be taken into account in that the allocation scheme can influence economic growth and population growth.

22. North-Young could blame North-Middle for emitting so much in period I as a result of which the whole North gets few emission rights in period II. North-Young might punish North-Middle for this by, for example, cutting its social security.
23. These distinctions and the discussion of problems associated with each principle in the context of climate change justice have been most helpfully introduced and discussed by Simon Caney (2005, 2006a) and Axel Gosseries (2004). In many ways our argument in this section is indebted to their interpretations and analyses.
24. By potential payers we mean people who were either causally responsible for climate change or who grew up in beneficial circumstances that are partly due to emission-generating activities. By potential recipients we mean people who grew up in a place which would exhibit more favourable living conditions if it were not for climate change.
25. The non-identity problem precludes us from saying that future people are harmed (or benefited) by actions that are necessary conditions of their existence (cf. Parfit 1984). This is so if we understand harm in the sense of being made worse off by an action than one would otherwise be. There is however another conception of harm which successfully evades the non-identity problem: by claiming that people can be said to be harmed by actions which make them fall below a certain pre-specified threshold, future people can also be said to be harmed by actions which are a necessary condition of their existence. For a treatment of these issues, see Meyer (2008).
26. Note that we distinguish this principle from 'polluter pays principles' (or also 'strict liability principles') by focusing *only* on wrongful emitters while the polluter pays principle or a strict liability principle or also Moellendorf's (2002, p. 98) causal principle make *any* emitter – whether wrongful or not – pay. Such principles, which make people pay who are causally responsible for emissions irrespective of their culpability, can obviously not serve as principles of compensatory justice in the narrow sense defined above. This is not to say, however, that *in practice* policies relying on such a polluter pays principle could never be justified for certain areas of environmental policy. It can legitimately be put into practice for three reasons:
    (1) In practice, in some areas of environmental policy it might be difficult to hold wrongful and non-wrongful emitters apart; or the two categories might overlap to such a large degree that it would be too cumbersome to hold them apart. Thus, enacting a polluter pays principle might serve as an *approximation* for the policy, which demands compensation from wrongdoers.
    (2) The policy might also serve as an *approximation* for a policy based on the redistributive rationale: because polluters often benefit from their polluting action, making them pay something to the harmed can be seen as evening out undeserved deviations from a just baseline.
    (3) A third and completely unrelated justification is based on instrumental grounds in the following way: According to economists, making people pay for harmful activities sets the right incentives and thus generates efficiency. If emitters (who are assumed to act self-interestedly) have to bear the external costs that appear as side effects of their actions they will only perform an emitting action in case the benefits exceed the costs. Thus, in a society where emitters (whether wrongful or not) are made to pay, all and only those emitting actions will be performed that have a net benefit which brings forth efficiency. However, such an instrumental justification for making emitters pay has no necessary link to the

idea of compensatory or redistributive justice. This can also be seen by noting that such an instrumental justification in fact provides no rationale at all for why the emitters' payments should be handed over to the people harmed by the emissions. The principle's whole idea is to deter people from emitting on a non-optimal level by making them pay, where the optimal level of emissions is set by some pre-specified goals.

27. See note 25.
28. However, in our non-ideal world benefits from wrongdoing can bring an individual closer to the well-being he or she ideally ought to enjoy.
29. See Anwander (2005, p. 40).
30. *Ibid.*
31. See Gosseries (2004).
32. See Butt (2007, p. 143).
33. For an extensive treatment, see Meyer (2005), chapters IV and V.
34. See among others Pogge (1989).
35. See Miller (2004, p. 241, fn. 1) and Gosseries (2004, p. 55).
36. In terms of figure 3, enacting a prioritarian distribution between the North and the South of the specific good of climate damages would amount to a transfer of 5 units of benefits from the North to the South.
37. Cf. the second option from section. The good to be distributed and the standard to be applied.
38. In terms of figure 2, enacting a prioritarian distribution of both benefits and damages jointly would demand giving all the 10 emission rights which are up for distribution in period II to the South and in addition demanding a transfer of two units of benefits from the North to the South. This would leave the people in the South who are alive in period II taken together with zero net benefits and the same is true for the people in the North who are alive in period II taken together.

References

Anwander, N., 2005. Contributing and benefiting: two grounds for duties to the victims of injustice. *Ethics & international affairs,* 19(1), 39–45.

Bartsch, U. and Müller, B., 2000. *Fossil fuels in a changing climate.* Oxford: Oxford University Press.

Baumert, K., Herzog, T. and Pershing, J., 2005. *Navigating the numbers: greenhouse gas data and international climate policy.* Washington, DC: World Resources Institute.

Butt, D., 2007. On benefiting from injustice. *Canadian journal of philosophy,* 37(1), 129–52.

Caney, S., 2005. Cosmopolitan justice, responsibility and global climate change. *Leiden journal of international law,* 18(4), 747–775.

Caney, S., 2006a. Environmental degradation, reparations, and the moral significance of history. *Journal of social philosophy,* 37(3), 464–482.

Caney, S., 2006b. Cosmopolitan justice, rights and global climate change, *The Canadian journal of law & jurisprudence,* 19(2), 255–278.

Casal, P., 2007. Why sufficiency is not enough. *Ethics,* 117(2), 296–326.

Christian Aid, 1999. *Who owes who? Climate change, debt, equity and survival,* http://www.jubileeresearch.org/ecological_debt/Reports/Who_owes_who.htm (accessed 21 February 2008).

Depledge, J., 2002. Continuing Kyoto: extending absolute emission caps to developing countries. *In*: K.A. Baumert, O. Blanchard, S. Llosa and J.F. Perkaus, eds. *Building on the Kyoto protocol: options for protecting the climate.* Washington, DC: World Resources Institute, 31–60.

Elster, J., 1992. *Local justice. How institutions allocate scarce goods and necessary burdens.* Cambridge: Cambridge University Press.

Friends of the Earth, 2006. *Climate justice: a fair share of the atmosphere,* http://www.foe.org.au/resources/publications/climate-justice/A%20fair%20share%20of%20the%20Atmosphere.pdf (accessed 21 February 2008).

Gosseries, A., 2004. Historical emissions and free riding. *Ethical perspectives,* 11(1), 36–60.

Gosseries, A., 2007. Cosmopolitan luck egalitarianism and climate change. *Canadian journal of philosophy supplementary volume,* 31, 279–309.

Holtug, N. and Lippert-Rasmussen, K., 2007. An introduction to contemporary egalitarianism. *In*: Holtug, Nils and Kasper Lippert-Rasmussen, eds. *Egalitarianism. New essays on the nature and value of equality.* Oxford: Oxford University Press, 1–38.

La Rovere, E., de Valente de Macedo, L., and Baumert, K., 2002. The Brazilian proposal on relative responsibility for global warming. *In*: K. Baumert, O. Blanchard, S. Llosa and J. Perkaus, eds. *Building on the Kyoto protocol: options for protecting the climate.* Washington, DC: World Resources Institute, 157–173.

Meyer, L., ed., 2004. *Justice in time. Responding to historical injustice.* Baden-Baden: Nomos.

Meyer, L., 2005. *Historische Gerechtigkeit.* Berlin and New York: de Gruyter.

Meyer, L., 2008. Intergenerational justice. *In*: E.N. Zalta, ed., *The Stanford encyclopedia of philosophy* (2008 edition, forthcoming), http://plato.stanford.edu/archives/sum2003/entries/justice-intergenerational.

Meyer, L. and Roser, D., 2006. Distributive justice and climate change, *Analyse & kritik,* 28(2), 223–249.

Miller, D., 2004. Holding nations responsible. *Ethics,* 114(2), 240–268.

Moellendorf, D. 2002. *Cosmopolitan justice.* Boulder, CO: Westview Press.

Neumayer, E. 2000. In defence of historical accountability for greenhouse gas emissions. *Ecological economics,* 33(2), 185–192.

Page, E.A., 2006. *Climate change, justice and future generations,* Cheltenham: Edward Elgar.

Parfit, D., 1984. *Reasons and persons.* Oxford: Clarendon Press.
Pogge, T., 1989. *Realizing Rawls.* Ithaca, NY: Cornell University Press.
Sher, G., 2005. Transgenerational compensation, *Philosophy & public affairs,* 33(2), 181–201.

Brian Barry: 1936–2009

As mentioned in the Introduction to this volume, many of the papers collected here began life as part of a symposium inspired by Brian Barry's work. Brian attended the meeting, and contributed in his usual robust fashion; mixing humour, commentary, and critique in a series of memorable comments. The intention was to dedicate this collection to Brian and to enjoy its publication with him over a bottle of something. Tragically, Brian died in March, 2009.

Brian's life has been memorably captured in a series of obituaries and remembrances (Kelly 2009; Goodin 2009; Dowding 2009; Weale forthcoming). He was a colossal figure in 20th Century political science and political theory. His contributions often anticipated and shaped the debate to come. His 1965 book, *Political argument* helped revitalise the discipline; *Sociologists, economists and democracy* (1970) was not merely interdisciplinary (as its title suggests), but also introduced to political theory the techniques of rational choice; his contribution (1977) to a collection in honour of his doctoral supervisor H.L.A. Hart explored problems of intergenerational justice; his Tanner Lectures (1980) introduced the problem of global justice; and the two volumes of his *Treatise on social justice* developed a universalist, liberal, theory of justice (whose subject matter systematically includes international and intergenerational relations) just as others were backing away from that possibility (1989; 1995). In between, and sometimes in these volumes, Brian deployed his critical faculties to the full in analysis and critique (for example, in *The liberal theory of justice*), and sometimes in full scale demolition (for example, in the devastating discussion of Kohlberg in the Appendix to *Justice as impartiality*). Finally, and in particular in his last two works, *Culture and equality* and *Why social justice matters* (2001; 2005), Brian addressed those – in the academy and in politics – who would (as he saw it) sacrifice the ideals of liberty and equality to the fashions of multiculturalism and individual responsibility respectively.

Despite a somewhat peripatetic academic existence – he held posts in eleven or so universities – Brian was involved with the discipline of political science on both sides of the Atlantic. He helped organize a coup to resuscitate the British Political Studies Association, was the founding editor of the *British journal of political science*, and transformed (and saved) *Ethics*. Something of the flavour of Brian's personal story, and of his involvement in the discipline can be found in the new Preface that he wrote for the reissue of

Political argument and in a rather self-effacing piece written for a collection on *The British study of politics in the twentieth century* (1990; 1999).

Much of the above will be familiar to readers of this volume, and many will have their own stories of encounters with Brian at conferences and symposia around the world. All will have read his work with admiration and sometimes no doubt with increasing fury. More details can be found, as already mentioned, in pieces already published. What the editors of this volume would like to add is simply a sense of what it was to work with, and under the guidance of, Brian.

For those who knew Brian only through his published works, or who had seen him only at large conferences (where he was seldom at his best), he probably seemed a rather distant and frightening figure. Although his sense of humour was sometimes evident in his writing, it tended to be only the side that dealt in pricking the self-inflated. He could, of course, be just like his public reputation and his relentless critical honesty – which as Keith Dowding notes was a product of his caring so much about the questions being discussed (1999, p. 459) – could be intimidating and, frankly, unnerving. However, that was only a tiny part of the picture. In person, he was generous, loyal, a completely committed teacher and friend, and fiercely protective of the issues and people that mattered to him. Together with, and because of, his wife Anni (whose contribution is beautifully acknowledged in *Culture and equality* and *Why social justice matters*), their apartment in London and then New York became a centre of intellectual exchange for graduate students, visiting academics, and semi-formal regular seminars. These events would often move to the pub, or on other occasions end in a dinner (which Brian and Anni would cook) at which discussion would continue accompanied, and encouraged, by a seemingly endless flow of wine.

Brian taught and encouraged generations of graduate students and young academics. To discuss political theory with him was to "learn on the job" in the best possible way, even if one only realized just how much one should have learned months afterwards when wrestling with some issue that he had clearly foreseen. He often preferred the company of those just starting out to that of more established figures, and he always preferred the company of those who treated him as just a fellow political theorist rather than as a 'great man'. Perhaps the greatest testimony to his personal qualities is that so many of those he taught and nurtured loved him. He will be missed not only by the discipline and the profession, but by countless individuals whose lives and work he touched.

References

Barry, B.M., 1965. *Political argument.* New York: Humanities Press.

Barry, B.M., 1970. *Sociologists, economists, and democracy.* Chicago, IL: Chicago University Press.

Barry, B.M., 1973. *The liberal theory of justice.* Oxford: Oxford University Press.
Barry, B.M., 1977. Justice between generations. In: P.M.S. Hacker and J. Raz, *Law, morality and society. Essays in honour of H.L.A. Hart.* Oxford: Clarendon Press, 268–284.
Barry, B.M., 1980. Do countries have moral obligations? The case of world poverty In: S. McMurrin, *The Tanner lectures on human values ii.* Salt Lake City, UT: University of Utah Press, 2–44.
Barry, B.M., 1989. *Theories of justice: volume 1 of a treatise on social justice.* Hemel Hempstead: Clarendon Press.
Barry, B.M., 1990. *Political argument: a reissue with a new introduction.* Berkeley and Los Angeles, CA: University of California Press.
Barry, B.M., 1995. *Justice as impartiality: volume 2 of a treatise on social justice.* Oxford: Clarendon Press.
Barry, B.M., 1999. The study of politics as a vocation. In: J. Hayward, B. Barry and A. Brown, *The British study of politics in the twentieth century.* Oxford: Oxford University Press on behalf of the British Academy.
Barry, B.M., 2001. *Culture and equality.* Cambridge: Polity.
Barry, B.M., 2005. *Why social justice matters.* Cambridge: Polity.
Dowding, K., 1999. Obituary: Brian Barry. *Political studies,* 57, 459–463.
Goodin, R., 1999. Brian Barry. *Political theory,* 37, 451–454.
Kelly, P., 1999. Brian Barry. *The Guardian,* 31 March, 2009.
Weale, A., forthcoming. Brian Barry. *Proceedings of the British Academy: biographical memoirs of fellows.*

Matt Matravers
Department of Politics, University of York, York, United Kingdom

Lukas Meyer
Department of Philosophy, University of Graz, Austria

Index

Ability to Pay Principle (ATP Principle) 12–14, 203–4, 213–18; history-sensitive 218, 221
adaptation programmes 220
age-differentiated political rights 33
Ahmad, Q.: *et al* 206
Allen, M. 207
American Bill of Rights 49
Anarchy, state and utopia (Nozick) 93
Anderson, B. 194
Andres, R.: Boden, T. and Marland, G. 211
anti-egalitarians 59–60
anti-paternalism 127–9
Appell, D. 205
Appiah, A 177–8
Aristotle 60, 137; *Nicomachean ethics* 60
Arnell, N. 206
autonomy and self-awareness 172–3

Barry, B. 23, 57, 72, 87, 98, 101, 116, 140, 143, 145, 170, 255–7; *Justice as impartiality* 131; *Political argument* (1965) 55
beauty and rarity 171–2
Beetham, D. 40
Beitz, C. 7, 115, 117–19, 121, 123–8, 133
Bell, D. 130–1
Beneficiary Pays Principle (BePP) 239–47
Berlin, I. 168
Berry, A.: and Stewart, F. 152
Beviglia Zampetti, A. 143
biological hybridisation 166
Bobbitt, P. 150
Boden, T.: and Marland, G. 211; Marland, G. and Andres, R. 211
Boli, J.: and Lechner, F. 143, 151
Boris, J. 152
Brazilian Proposal (1997) 233, 237
British Political Studies Association 255
Brugger, W. 49
Buchanan, A. 121, 144
Bush, President G.W. 149
Butt, D. 243

Caney, S. 12–14, 203–28
carbon quotas 220
carbon taxes 220
carbon trading 220
Chadwick, A.: Glasson, J. and Therivel, R. 32
Chambers, C.: and Parvin, P. 6–7, 9, 93–114
Chan, J. 130–1
charity 93–114; disagreement 97–101; ethos 106–11; motivation 103–6; reasons for coercion 95–7, 108–11; unreasonableness 101–2
Charlton, A.: and Stiglitz, J. 143
Charney, E. 131
Chomsky, N. 149
Chwaszcza, C. 144
civil liberty 142
clean development initiatives 220
climate change 203–28; Ability To Pay Principle 12–14, 203–4, 213–18; hybrid view 221–2; Polluter Pays Principle 12–13, 205–13
climate justice and historical emissions 229–53; benefits of emissions 234–7, **236**; climate damages 238–47; emission rights 231–7; redistribution 246–7; South and North 229–31
cloning 174
Cohen, G. 7, 55–6, 74, 77, 84, 93–7, 103–12
Cohen, J. 122

Coleman, J. 139
communal relationships 138
Community Pays Principle (CoPP) 239–47
compensatory justice 238–45, **240**
Confucianism 131
Constanza, R.: and Fischer, B. 219
constitutional conventions 33–4
constitutional rights 47
contingency trust fund 33
contingent brute luck 74–6, 81, 85–7
Convention on Biological Diversity (1992) 10, 162
cooperative community 141
Cornell, T. 30
corrective justice 138–40, 144
Coser, L. 149
cultural and bio-diversity 159–79; heritage and conservation 171–7; levels and degrees 163–5; protection of species and cultures 168–71; synergism 165–8
cultural cosmopolitanism 116
Czempiel, E. 146

Dasgupta, P. 151
Dayton, D. 32
democratic balance sheets 33
democratic participation 142
discursive pluralism 131–3
distributive justice 137–8, 144–6
Dobson, A. 29
Docquier, F.: and Marfouk, A. 194
domestic and global justice 137–58; contingent interdependency patterns 148–50; effects of globalisation 150–5; idea 143–6; interrelations 146–55; social 140–3
domestic tradable quotas 221
Donahue, J.: and Nye, J. 153
Donnelly, J. 142, 152
Dowding, K. 3, 5–6, 71–92, 255–6; and Van Hees, M. 73
Dunn, J. 62
duty of mitigation 204
Dworkin, R. 55–6, 59–60, 62, 74, 170–2

Eberle, E.: and Kommers, P. 50
ecological equilibrium 164
economic equity 142
ecosystems 164
egalitarianism 3–7, 83, 88, 93, 232, 239; liberal 55–70; radical 81–2
Eide, A. 152
Ekeli, K. 30
Emitter Pays Principle (EmPP) 239–47
enlightenment liberalism 98, 111–12, 175–6
environmental sustainability 29
equal opportunity 142
Equality of Opportunity (EoP) 87–8
erosion of democracy 154–5
Essay concerning human understanding (Locke) 62–3
Estlund, D. 84
EU Emissions Trading Scheme 220
European Convention for the Protection of Human Rights 152
evolution 167
ex hypothesi 45
exchange relationships 138–9
expatriate brains 194–5

F-representatives 30
factual pedigree 46
fame after death 31
Fearon, J.: and Laitin, D. 190–1
Federal German Republic 48–9; Federal Constitution Court 50–1; *Grundgesetz* (1949) 48–50
Finegold, L.: and Tzoumis, K. 32
Fischer, B.: and Constanza, R. 219
Flathman, R. 40
Franck, T. 143–4
Frankena, W. 142
Frankfurt, H. 121
freedom of speech 48–51

Galston, W. 94, 98
Gellner, E. 186–7
Glasson, J.: Therivel, R. and Chadwick, A. 32
Goodin, R. 255
Gosseries, A. 242–3
Greenland Ice Sheet 205
Greer, S. 152
Grimm, D. 50
Grubb, M. 154
Gutmann, A. 100

Habermas, J. 41, 47, 52
Hare, R. 142
Hart, H. 255
Hayek, F. 139
Held, D. 143, 151, 154; and McGrew, A. 153
Herder, J. 175–6
Hertz, N. 145, 153

Heyd, D. 8, 10–11, 159–79
Hinsch, W. 39–54
Hobbes, T. 19, 31, 34
Höffe, O. 139, 146
Holy Alliance (1815) 149–50
Homo, L. 30
Honoré, A. 142
Houghton, Sir John 206
human rights 115–35; equality and minimalism 120–33; and justice 133; liberal or full view (LFV) 124–33; meaning 117–19; restricted view (RV) 123–33
Hurley, S. 71
Hustler Magazine vs Falwell 50
hydrofluorocarbons (HFCs) 204

Ingram, D. 170
Intergovernmental Panel on Climate Change (IPCC) 204, 234; Climate Change Synthesis Report (2001) 211
international collaboration 34
International Covenant on Economic, Social and Cultural Rights 125
International Covenants on Civil and Political Rights 125
International Monetary Fund (IMF) 153–4

Jones, C. 7–9, 115–35
justice and community 7–12
justice and democracy 1–3
justice and equality 3–7
justice and the future 12–15
Justice as impartiality (Barry) 131
justifying inequalities principle 142

Kaldor-Hicks compensation 75
Kapstein, E. 143, 150, 154
Kaul, I.: *et al* 144, 154
Kekes, J. 59–60, 66–7
Kelly, P. 3–4, 55–70, 255
Kirchgässner, G. 154
Kitschelt, H. 151
Kleinschmidt, H. 149
Kohler, G.: and Marti, U. 143
Koller, P. 7–9, 137–58
Kommers, P.: and Eberle, E. 50
Krippendorf, E. 149
Krugman, P. 154
Kymlicka, W. 98
Kyoto Protocol 154, 219–20, 231–2, 237

Laitin, D.: and Fearon, J. 190–1
Laponce, J. 185–8, 191; law 185–8
Larmore, C. 94, 99–101
Laslett, P. 62
The law of peoples (Rawls) 61, 68, 124
Lechner, F.: and Boli, J. 143, 151
legal equality 142
legitimacy and constitutional rights 39–54; concepts and conceptions 39–42; contractualism 42–4; justice vs legitimacy 44–6
Legitimitäts-Glaube (Weber) 41
Leibnizian theodicy 162, 171
liberal democracy 8
liberal egalitarianism: basic equality 62–8
Liberal principle of legitimacy (Rawls) 46–7
linguistic justice: dignity and territory 181–202; dominance of English 181–3, 196–8; languages, borders and costs 192–8; pacification argument 190–2; survival without territory 187–90; territoriality regimes 11, 183–8, 190, 192–3, 197
linguistic maps 186
linguistic territorial regimes (LTRs) 11
linguistically free zones 197–8
Locke, J. 26, 55, 61–7; *Essay concerning human understanding* 62–3; *Two treatises* 63
Lowe, J.: *et al* 205
Lucas, J. 139
luck: equality and responsibility 71–92; incentives 84–6; path dependency 79–82; patterns and responsibility 82–4; probabilities 78–9; temperament 80–3
Luhmann, N. 40
Luper-Foy, S. 143

McGrew, A.: and Held, D. 153
MacIntyre, A. 94
Malhotra, A. 32
Mann, M. 205
Mapel, D.: and Nardin, T. 143
Marfouk, A.: and Docquier, F. 194
Marland, G.: Andres, R. and Boden, T. 211; and Boden, T. 211
Marti, U.: and Kohler, G. 143
Matravers, M.: and Meyer, L. 1–15
Merli, F. 152
Meyer, L. 144; and Matravers, M. 1–15; and Roser, D. 229–53
Mill, J.S. 19, 165–8, 173–4
modus vivendi 44

Moellendorf, D. 145
moral cosmopolitanism 115–35
Morgenbesser, S.: and Ullman-Margalit, E. 73
multiculturalism 159–79
Musschenga, A. 170

Nagel, T. 108
Nardin, T.: and Mapel, D. 143
Narveson, J. 84
Nature 212
neo-Kantianism 119–20
Netherlands Environmental Assessment Agency 212
New York Times vs. Sullivan 50
Nickel, J. 142
Nicomachean ethics (Aristotle) 60
Nietzsche, F. 4, 58–9, 67, 173–4
Nolte, G. 50
nonparochial universalism 131
Nordhaus, W. 154
normative authority 40
Norton, B. 165, 174
Nozick, R. 6, 94–6, 108; *Anarchy, state and utopia* 93
Nussbaum, M. 127, 132
Nye, J.: and Donahue, J. 153

O'Neill, O. 144
Opitz, P. 151
ownership community 141
Oxfam International 145–6, 149–50, 153–4

Parekh, B. 173
Parfit, D. 3, 24–5
parochialism 129–31
Parvin, P.: and Chambers, C. 6–7, 9, 93–114
perfluorocarbons (PFCs) 204
personal identity luck 74–8, 86–8
Pitkin, H. 27
pluralism 160, 168–9
plurilingual states 185
Pogge, T. 84, 143, 146, 150, 152, 154
political cosmopolitanism 116
political justice 138–9, 143–4
Political Liberalism (Rawls) 61
political presentism and democratic trusteeship 17–37; conventional theories 22–6; duties and accountability 30–4; future neglect 18–20
political repression 151–2

Polluter Pays Principle (PP Principle) 12–13, 203–13; poverty sensitive 219, 221
posterity impact statements 32–3
power relationships 139
Pritchard, D. 76–7
proto-rights (moral) 46–52
proxy electorate 29
Przeworski, A.: *et al* 151
public justification 43

radical egalitarianism 81
Rapauch, M. *et al* 209, 213
rational argumentation 44–6
Rawls, J. 23–4, 41–2, 51–2, 82–4, 94–107, 128–9, 141–4; *The law of peoples* 61, 68, 124; *Liberal principle of legitimacy* 46–7; *Political Liberalism* 61; *A Theory of Justice* 2, 4, 15, 55–6, 61–8
Raz, J. 56–7, 98, 172–3
Redclift, M.: and Sage, C. 146
Renner, K. 189
Roemer, J. 74, 87–9
Roover, R. 139
Roser, D.: and Meyer, L. 229–53
Ryberg, J.: *et al* 25

Sage, C.: and Redclift, M. 146
Sandel, M. 94
Sarkar, S. 164
Sarukhan, J.: and Schneider, S. 206
Scanlon, T.M. 57, 120–1
Scheffler, S. 107, 116
Schneider, S.: and Sarukhan, J. 206
Sher, G. 174–5
Singer, P. 145–6, 150, 153, 216
Sober, E. 176
solidarity community 141
sons of the soil 190–2
Staveley, E. 30
Steiner, H. 141
Sterba, J. 139
Stewart, F.: and Berry, A. 152
Stiglitz, J. 145, 150, 153–4; and Charlton, A. 143
Stone, C. 32
Stone, D. 207
Stott, P. 207
Strauss, F.J. 50
Subsidiary Body for Scientific and Technological Advice (SBSTA) 206
sufficientarianism 232, 239
sulfur hexafluoride (SF6) 204

suspensive interventions 32
Swiss Confederation 185

Taylor, C. 94, 98–9
Thatcher, Prime Minister M. 149
A Theory of Justice (Rawls) 2, 4, 15, 55–6, 61–2
Therivel, R.: Chadwick, A. and Glasson, J. 32
Thompson, D. 1–3, 12, 17–37, 100
toleration 126–7
tradable emission rights 232
Trade Related Aspects of Intellectual Property Rights (TRIPs) 150
transactional justice 137–9, 143, 145
Tribune of the Plebs (*tribunus plebis*) 30–1
Two treatises (Locke) 63
Tzoumis, K.: and Finegold, L. 32

Ullman-Margalit, E.: and Morgenbesser, S. 73
United Nations (UN) 31–2, 145, 153–4; Framework Convention on Climate Change (UNFCCC) 206; International Bill of Rights 125
United States Constitution 48; First Amendment (1791) 48–9; Supreme Court 49–50
Universal Declaration on Cultural Diversity (2001) 10, 162
Universal Declaration of Human Rights (UDHR) 121, 125–6
utilitarianism 25

Van Hees, M.: and Dowding, K. 73
Van Parijs, P. 10–12

Wade, R. 152
Waldron, J. 4, 55, 61–7
Wall, S. 98
Walzer, M. 94, 123–4
Watson, R.: *et al* 211
Weale, A. 255
Weber, M. 40–1
Weinstock, D. 170
West Antarctic Ice Sheet (WAIS) 205
Williams, A. 84
Wood, P. 161
Woods, N. 145, 152
World Bank 152–4
World Commission on Environment and Development (1988) 167
world poverty 152–4
World Trade Organisation 153–4
wrongness relationships 139–40

Young, M. 100

Zürn, M. 154